# Law of the Sea in South East Asia

The United Nations Convention on the Law of the Sea (LOSC) represents one of the most successful examples of multilateral treaty making in the modern era. The convention has 168 States parties, and most non-signatory States recognise nearly all of its key provisions as binding under customary international law, including the United States. Nevertheless, there remain significant differences in interpretation and implementation of the LOSC among States as well as calls, on occasion, for its amendment.

This book analyses the impact, influence and ongoing role of the LOSC in South East Asia, one of the most dynamic maritime regions in the world. Maritime security is a critical issue within the region, and it is separately assessed in light of the LOSC and contemporary challenges such as environmental security and climate change. Likewise, navigational rights and freedoms are a major issue and they are evaluated through the LOSC and regional state practice, especially in the South China Sea. Special attention is given to the role of navies and non-state actors. Furthermore, the book looks at regional resource disputes which have a long history. These disputes have the potential to increase into the future as economic interests and concerns over food security intensify. Effective LNG and fisheries resource management is therefore a critical issue for the region and unless resolved could become the focal point for significant maritime disputes. These dynamics within the region all require extensive exploration in order to gauge the effectiveness of LOSC dispute resolution mechanisms.

The *Law of the Sea in South East Asia* fills a gap in the existing literature by bringing together a holistic picture of contemporary maritime issues affecting the region in a single volume. It will appeal to academic libraries, government officials, think-tanks and scholars from law, strategic studies and international relations disciplines.

**Donald R. Rothwell** is Professor of International Law at the ANU College of Law, Australia

**David Letts** is Director of the Military Law Program, and Director of the Centre for Military and Security Law at the ANU College of Law, Australia

# Law of the Sea in South East Asia

Environmental, Navigational and Security Challenges

Edited by
Donald R. Rothwell and
David Letts

LONDON AND NEW YORK

First published 2020
by Routledge
2 Park Square, Milton Park, Abingdon, Oxon OX14 4RN

and by Routledge
605 Third Avenue, New York, NY 10017

*Routledge is an imprint of the Taylor & Francis Group, an informa business*

First issued in paperback 2021

© 2020 selection and editorial matter, Donald R. Rothwell and David Letts; individual chapters, the contributors

The right of Donald R. Rothwell and David Letts to be identified as the authors of the editorial material, and of the authors for their individual chapters, has been asserted in accordance with sections 77 and 78 of the Copyright, Designs and Patents Act 1988.

All rights reserved. No part of this book may be reprinted or reproduced or utilised in any form or by any electronic, mechanical, or other means, now known or hereafter invented, including photocopying and recording, or in any information storage or retrieval system, without permission in writing from the publishers.

*Trademark notice*: Product or corporate names may be trademarks or registered trademarks, and are used only for identification and explanation without intent to infringe.

Publisher's Note
The publisher has gone to great lengths to ensure the quality of this reprint but points out that some imperfections in the original copies may be apparent.

*British Library Cataloguing-in-Publication Data*
A catalogue record for this book is available from the British Library

*Library of Congress Cataloging-in-Publication Data*
Names: Letts, David, editor. | Rothwell, Donald, 1959–, editor.
Title: Law of the Sea in South East Asia : environmental, navigational and security challenges / edited by David Letts and Donald R. Rothwell.
Description: New York, NY : Routledge, 2019.
Identifiers: LCCN 2019016905 (print) | LCCN 2019018284 (ebook) | ISBN 9780429021053 (ebk) | ISBN 9780367075026 (hbk)
Subjects: LCSH: Law of the sea—Southeast Asia.
Classification: LCC KZA1146.A785 (ebook) | LCC KZA1146.A785 L39 2019 (print) | DDC 341.4/50959—dc23
LC record available at https://lccn.loc.gov/2019016905

ISBN: 978-0-367-07502-6 (hbk)
ISBN: 978-1-03-224071-8 (pbk)
ISBN: 978-0-429-02105-3 (ebk)

DOI: 10.4324/9780429021053

Typeset in Galliard
by codeMantra

# Contents

| | |
|---|---|
| *List of figures* | vii |
| *List of tables* | ix |
| *List of contributors* | xi |
| *Foreword* | xvii |
| *Preface* | xxi |
| *Table of cases* | xxv |
| *Table of treaties and other international instruments* | xxix |

1 **The law of the sea and South East Asia** 1
DONALD R. ROTHWELL AND DAVID LETTS

2 **Maritime claims in South East Asia** 16
DONALD R. ROTHWELL

3 **An incomplete maritime map: progress and challenges in the delimitation of maritime boundaries in South East Asia** 33
CLIVE SCHOFIELD

4 **Maritime security in South East Asia** 63
DAVID LETTS

5 **Advancing marine environmental security in South East Asia: challenges and opportunities** 80
ROBIN WARNER

6 **Climate change and the law of the sea in the Asia Pacific** 94
KAREN N. SCOTT

7 **The limits of the natural state doctrine: rocks, islands and artificial intervention in a changing world** 118
IMOGEN SAUNDERS

vi *Contents*

8 The Law of the Sea, status and message ambiguity 136
ROB McLAUGHLIN

9 The United Nations Convention on the Law of the Sea
in South East Asia: smooth sailing or stormy seas? 149
TIM STEPHENS

10 'Do As I Do, Not As I Say' – navigational freedom and
the Law of the Sea Convention 163
DALE STEPHENS AND TIMOTHY QUADRIO

11 Regimes of navigation and maritime security in South
East Asia 180
HITOSHI NASU

12 Crossing the Rubicon: Singapore's evolving relations
with China in the context of the 2016 arbitral award 193
SEE SENG TAN

13 Saving the South China Sea fishery 210
MARINA TSIRBAS

14 Dispute resolution and the law of the sea following the
*South China Sea* arbitration 223
NATALIE KLEIN

15 Challenges for the law of the sea in South East Asia:
resolving current controversies and addressing
horizon threats 242
DAVID LETTS AND DONALD R. ROTHWELL

*Index* 259

# List of figures

| | | |
|---|---|---|
| 1.1 | South East Asian Maritime Domain | 3 |
| 3.1 | Maritime Delimitation in the Andaman Sea | 37 |
| 3.2 | Maritime Delimitation in the Bay of Bengal | 39 |
| 3.3 | Maritime Delimitation in the Malacca Strait | 40 |
| 3.4 | Maritime Delimitation in the Singapore Strait | 42 |
| 3.5 | Maritime Claims and Boundaries in the South China Sea | 45 |
| 3.6 | Maritime Delimitation in the Gulf of Thailand | 49 |
| 3.7 | Maritime Claims and Boundaries in the East China Sea | 52 |
| 3.8 | Maritime Delimitation in the Sulu and Celebes Seas | 55 |
| 3.9 | Maritime Delimitation in the Timor Sea | 57 |

# List of tables

| | | |
|---|---|---|
| 2.1 | Maritime Claims in South East Asia | 32 |
| 9.1 | Ratifications by ASEAN Members and Timor-Leste of the LOSC and Its Implementing Agreements | 153 |
| 9.2 | Ratifications by APEC Members of the LOSC and Its Implementing Agreements | 154 |
| 9.3 | Submissions to the Commission on the Limits of the Continental Shelf by ASEAN Members and Timor-Leste | 156 |
| 9.4 | LOSC Declarations by ASEAN Members and Timor-Leste | 157 |

# List of contributors

## Editors

**David Letts** AM, CSM, is an Associate Professor at the ANU College of Law, where he holds appointments as Director of the Military Law Program and Director of the Centre for Military and Security Law. Prior to becoming an academic, David served for more than three decades in the Royal Australian Navy, retiring as a Commodore (1-star). David teaches in the ANU College of Law's military law and international law (especially law of the sea and maritime security law) programmes. His research centres upon the application of legal regimes to military operations, and he has a particular focus on military justice, law of the sea, the law of naval warfare, international humanitarian law and the legal issues that arise on peacekeeping operations. He has been a member of the teaching faculty at the International Institute of Humanitarian Law, Sanremo, Italy since 2001 and is the Course Director for the Institute's annual Naval Operations Law course; he is also an elected Member of the Institute. David has regularly provided expert academic support to the International Committee of the Red Cross, the UN Office on Drugs and Crime and the Centre for Humanitarian Dialogue in their regional maritime programmes.

**Dr Donald R. Rothwell** is Professor of International Law at the ANU College of Law, Australian National University, where he has taught since July 2006. His research has a specific focus on law of the sea, law of the polar regions and implementation of international law within Australia as reflected in 24 authored, co-authored and edited books, and over 200 articles, book chapters and notes. Rothwell is also Co-Editor of the *Australian Year Book of International Law* and Editor-in-Chief of the *Brill Research Perspectives in Law of the Sea*, and was Rapporteur of the International Law Association (ILA) Committee on 'Baselines under the International Law of the Sea' (2012–2018). He has taught a range of courses including Law of the Sea, International Dispute Resolution and Public International Law. Rothwell was previously Challis Professor of International Law and Director of the Sydney Centre for International and Global Law, University of Sydney (2004–2006), where

xii  *List of contributors*

he had taught since 1988. He has acted as a consultant or been a member of expert groups for UNEP, UNDP, IUCN, the Australian Government, and acted as advisor to the International Fund for Animal Welfare (IFAW). In 2015, he was elected as a Fellow to the Australian Academy of Law.

## Authors

**Vice Admiral Tim Barrett,** AO, CSC, RAN, joined the Royal Australian Navy in 1976 as a Seaman Officer and later specialised in aviation. He assumed command of the Royal Australian Navy on 1 July 2014. Vice Admiral Barrett served at sea as both a mariner and aviator in the Australian Fleet and on exchange in the United Kingdom with the Royal Navy. Ashore he held significant staff appointments in the areas of capability development and personnel management. His extensive command experience included Commanding Officer 817 Helicopter Squadron, Commanding Officer HMAS Albatross, Commander Australian Navy Aviation Group, Commander Border Protection Command and Commander Australian Fleet. Vice Admiral Barrett holds a Bachelor of Arts in Politics and History and a Masters of Defence Studies, both from the University of New South Wales, and has completed the Advanced Management Program at Harvard Business School. He recently published '*The Navy and the Nation: Australia's Maritime Power in the 21st Century*' in which he outlined the extensive opportunities for Navy and Australia in implementing the planned investment in naval capability outlined in the Defence White Paper 2016. Vice Admiral Barrett completed his period in command of the RAN on 6 July 2018.

**Dr Natalie Klein** is a Professor at UNSW Sydney's Faculty of Law, Australia. She was previously at Macquarie University where she served as Dean of Macquarie Law School between 2011 and 2017, as well as Acting Head of the Department for Policing, Intelligence and Counter-Terrorism at Macquarie in 2013–2014. Professor Klein teaches and researches in different areas of international law, with a focus on law of the sea and international dispute settlement. She provides advice, undertakes consultancies and interacts with the media on law of the sea issues. Professor Klein has been a Visiting Fellow at the Lauterpacht Centre for International Law at Cambridge University and a MacCormick Fellow at the University of Edinburgh. She is currently a non-resident Fellow at the Lakshman Kadirgamar Institute in Sri Lanka. Prior to joining Macquarie, Professor Klein worked in the international litigation and arbitration practice of Debevoise & Plimpton LLP, served as counsel to the Government of Eritrea (1998–2002) and was a consultant in the Office of Legal Affairs at the United Nations. Her masters and doctorate in law were earned at Yale Law School and she is a Fellow of the Australian Academy of Law.

**Dr Rob McLaughlin** is Professor and Director of the Australian Centre for the Study of Armed Conflict and Society at UNSW Canberra. He researches,

List of contributors  xiii

publishes and teaches in the areas of Law of Armed Conflict, Law of the Sea, Maritime Security Law and Maritime Law Enforcement, and Military Law. He routinely engages in research activities, and course development and delivery, with the ICRC, the Australian Red Cross, the International Institute for Humanitarian Law and the UN Office on Drugs and Crime. Rob came to academia after a career in the Royal Australian Navy as a Seaman officer and a Legal officer. Consequently, his research interests are primarily focussed around issues of practical operational significance. Rob's legal roles in the RAN included Fleet Legal Officer, Strategic Legal Adviser, as a Counsel Assisting the HMAS SYDNEY II Commission of Inquiry, Director Operations and International Law and Director Naval Legal Service.

**Dr Hitoshi Nasu** is Professor of International Law at the University of Exeter and publishes widely in the field of public international law, especially as it relates to various contemporary security issues. He is the author of *International Law on Peacekeeping* (2009), co-author of *The Legal Authority of ASEAN as a Security Institution* (2019) and Co-Editor of *Human Rights in the Asia-Pacific Region: Towards Institution Building* (2011), *Asia-Pacific Disaster Management* (2013), *New Technologies and the Law of Armed Conflict* (2014) and *Legal Perspectives on Security Institutions* (2015).

**Lieutenant Timothy Quadrio** RAN is a Legal Officer in the Royal Australian Navy. In his current role, he is responsible for providing legal advice on military discipline, administration and operations law to RAN units based in Northern Australia. In 2017, Timothy deployed to sea in HMAS *Adelaide* as the joint task group Legal Officer for Indo-Pacific Endeavour, Australia's largest coordinated task group deployment since the early 1980s. Prior to joining the RAN, Timothy was a commercial lawyer in private practice in Sydney. In the five years to 2013, Timothy served as a policy adviser and speechwriter to a minister in the Australian Government. Timothy has honours degrees in law and politics from Macquarie University.

**Dr Imogen Saunders** is a Senior Lecturer at the ANU College of Law, where she teaches international law and international trade law. She completed a Bachelor of Laws and a Bachelor of Science at the University of Western Australia, and competed her PhD at the Australian National University on Article 38(1)(c) of the Statute of the International Court of Justice. Imogen's research interests include the application of international law to newly accessible areas (both physical and virtual) and changing environments. She has examined these concepts in the context of artificial islands, cyberspace and outer space.

**Dr Clive Schofield** is Professor and Head of Research at the Global Ocean Institute, World Maritime University in Malmö, Sweden and is a Visiting Professor with the Australian Centre for Ocean Resources and Security (ANCORS), University of Wollongong (UOW), Australia. He holds a PhD in Geography from the University of Durham, UK and also holds an LLM

xiv *List of contributors*

in international law from the University of British Columbia. His research interests relate to international boundaries and particularly maritime boundary delimitation and marine jurisdictional issues on which he has published over 200 scholarly publications. Clive is an International Hydrographic Office (IHO)-nominated Observer on the Advisory Board on the Law of the Sea (ABLOS) and is a member of the International Law Association's Committee on International Law and Sea Level Rise. He has also been actively involved in the peaceful settlement of boundary and territory disputes by providing advice to governments engaged in boundary negotiations and in dispute settlement cases before the International Court of Justice. Additionally, he recently served as an independent expert witness in the international arbitration case between the Philippines and China.

**Karen N. Scott** is a Professor at the University of Canterbury in New Zealand having previously taught at the University of Nottingham in the UK. She was the Head of the School of Law between 2015 and 2018, Vice-President of the Australian and New Zealand Society of International Law (ANZSIL) from 2011 to 2016 and the General Editor of the *New Zealand Yearbook of International Law* from 2009 to 2012. She researches and teaches in the areas of public international law, law of the sea and international environmental law. Karen has published over 60 journal articles and book chapters in these areas and is the Co-Editor of Rothwell, Oude Elferink, Scott and Stephens (eds), *Oxford Handbook on the Law of the Sea* (2015hb; 2017pb) and of Hemmings, Rothwell, Scott (eds), *Antarctic Security in the Twenty-First Century: Legal and Policy Perspectives* (2012).

**Dr Dale Stephens** CSM, is a Professor at the University of Adelaide Law School. He obtained his Law degree (LL.B (Hons.)) from Adelaide University in 1988. In 1989, he was admitted as a legal practitioner to the Supreme Court of South Australia. That same year, he also joined the Royal Australian Navy. His operational deployments include East Timor and Iraq. He has been awarded the Conspicuous Service Medal, the (US) Bronze Star and the (US) Meritorious Service Medal. He attained the rank of Captain in the Navy. In 2004, Professor Stephens completed an LL.M from Harvard Law School and taught at the US Naval War College during the 2004–2005 academic year. In 2014, he was awarded his Doctor of Juridical Science degree from Harvard Law School. He has published widely in the area of operations law and is a Board member of the *Australian Yearbook of International Law*. Professor Stephens is Director of the Adelaide Research Unit on Military Law and Ethics, Chair of the SA Red Cross IHL Committee and Head of the SA/NT Navy Legal Panel.

**Dr Tim Stephens** is Professor of International Law and Australian Research Council Future Fellow at the University of Sydney. He is President of the Australian and New Zealand Society of International Law. Tim teaches and researches in public international law, with his published work focussing on the international law of the sea, international environmental law and international dispute settlement. He is the co-author with Donald R. Rothwell of *The International Law of the Sea* 2nd (2016).

**Dr See Seng Tan** is Professor of International Relations at the S. Rajaratnam School of International Studies (RSIS), Nanyang Technological University, Singapore. He is the author of *Multilateral Asian Security Architecture: Non-ASEAN Stakeholders* (2015) and *The Making of the Asia Pacific: Knowledge Brokers and the Politics of Representation* (2013).

**Marina Tsirbas** was the Senior Executive Adviser, Policy Engagement at the Australian National University's National Security College (NSC) between 2015 and 2017. Working with the Head of the NSC, Marina established the Policy Engagement role and a futures cell. She convened policy forums and helped develop a new line of policy products, contributing to NSC writing and teaching in the executive and professional development programmes. Marina convened the inaugural high level Women and National Security Conference in April 2017, which has become an annual fixture, examining the nexus between gender and national security and enhancing women's participation in national security. Marina's career has focussed on foreign, trade and security policy and international legal issues. She has worked in the Departments of the Prime Minister and Cabinet and Foreign Affairs and Trade. She served as Australian Deputy Head of Mission in the Netherlands (2000–2003) and as Charge d'Affaires in East Timor for a period. Marina holds an LLM (Cambridge), BA (Jur) and LLB (Hons, 1st) (Adelaide), and has been a Visiting Fellow, Lauterpacht Centre for International Law, Cambridge.

**Dr Robin Warner,** is Professor, Deputy Director and Head of Postgraduate Studies at the Australian National Centre for Ocean Resources and Security (ANCORS), University of Wollongong, Australia. She is a member of the Advisory Board for the Oceans Coasts and Coral Reefs Specialist Group of the IUCN World Commission on Environmental Law. Her research interests include law of the sea, oceans governance, marine environmental law and climate law. She is the author of more than 80 publications on ocean law and policy including *Protecting the Oceans beyond National Jurisdiction: Strengthening the International Law Framework* (2009).

# Foreword

## Law of the Sea Convention in the Asia Pacific region: threats, challenges and opportunities

### *Vice Admiral Tim Barrett, AO, CSC, RAN*[*]

The law of the sea provides the very structure and the legal authority for much of what the Royal Australian Navy does in our region to enhance stability, deter armed confrontations and facilitate maritime trade; therefore, it is of great importance to me as the Chief of the Navy that conferences of this nature are held to debate the issues.

I am not a lawyer – although I do seem to attract them. My past experiences as an operator, particularly as the Commander of Border Protection Command from 2010 to 2011, has taught me the value of keeping my legal team close at hand; they have guided my operational decisions.

Admiral Harry Harris, Commander of the US Pacific Forces said it best from the US perspective at a military law conference I attended recently in Brisbane. He said: 'I'm gonna tell the truth, the whole truth and nothing but the truth'.

And the whole truth is that 70-plus years of security and stability in the Indo-Asia-Pacific didn't just happen on its own. It happened because of a fundamental understanding and commitment among like-minded nations that the law sits above the military and not the other way around.

So my comments today come from the perspective of a mariner, a military practitioner and indeed a nascent author about the importance of a rules-based order for the prosperity of Australia and the region.

Australia has one of the largest maritime domains in the world, and it faces three oceans, with a coastline of more than 32,000 nautical miles – and yet a population of only 25 million.

Ten per cent of the world's sea trade passes through Australian ports. Australia relies on the sea for 98% of our exports – and for a substantial proportion of our domestic freight. About 95% of our data is transmitted through undersea cable.

Our $1.6 trillion economy is dependent on shipping being able to freely navigate the oceans and conduct maritime trade especially through the massive economic trading artery that runs from the Middle East, across the Indian Ocean,

---

[*] Opening Remarks delivered at the conference titled 'The Law of the Sea in the Asia Pacific Region: Opportunities, Threats and Challenges', ANU Centre for Military and Security Law, ANU, Canberra, 22 August 2017.

xviii *Foreword*

through the South China Sea, past Japan and on to North America. And it will only get bigger.

Our reliance on the oceans means that we must constantly have regard to changes that are occurring in our region. Soon, this region will not only be the world's largest producer of goods but also be the largest consumer of them. This will bring greater political and strategic weight to our region.

In a previous role as the Commander of Border Protection Command several years ago, we used to identify eight maritime threats to Australia. There are four worthy of comments here.

First, increasing transnational crime particularly the illegal importation of illicit substances. Two high-profile examples in the last 12 months include a former research vessel being intercepted off the Tasmanian coast by HMAS *Adelaide* and a yacht which was intercepted off the New South Wales coast earlier this year. Both vessels were carrying cocaine with the total estimated value being almost $350 million dollars. This trade is increasing and worryingly we do not know the percentage of the trade that is not being found.

Second, there is growing concern among many nations in our region about environmental changes; be it an increasing trend in severe weather patterns or rising sea levels. Both of these threaten stability by changing the availability of natural resources whether on the seabed, in the subsoil or in the water column, or through the displacement of affected populations. In the future, our issues with migration will not be restricted to those escaping conflict.

Third, maritime terrorism is on the rise. Whether it is from small groups of extremists in South East Asia who board ships and seize sailors for ransom through to attacks launched from the sea on naval and other port facilities, maritime terrorism threatens the ability to safely use the sea in our region. Indeed, my current concerns range from activity in the Sulu Sea to actions off the Yemeni coast where our frigates continue to operate as part of the Combined Maritime Force.

Fourth, with the increasingly aggressive actions taken by some nations to assert their claims over disputed maritime boundaries, there is an increased risk of a regional maritime dispute escalating and the potential for armed confrontations at sea. And given the audience, let's just remind ourselves of the government's position on this.

Australia does not take sides on these territorial disputes and the Navy will continue to exercise our rights under international law to freedom of navigation and overflight. We also encourage countries to resolve disputes peacefully in accordance with international law, including the Law of the Sea Convention.

The Law of the Sea Convention has been fundamental to our region's growth, prosperity and security. We remain committed to advancing this internationally recognised, rules-based order that has been so conducive to ensuring maritime stability and open and reliable maritime trade. But how do we reconcile this with the challenges evident in each nation's interpretation of the Law of the Sea Convention – its ambiguities, its gaps and the inherent tensions that exist because it seeks to balance a number of competing interests, all exacerbated in our region because of its complex maritime geography, long-standing historic

*Foreword* xix

claims, archipelagos and narrow shipping channels. As a result some regional countries appear to exploit these challenges in several key regimes so as to advance their individual interests. Here are three global examples.

First, despite the old adage that 'good fences make good neighbours', there are differences in approach between states as to the use of the straight territorial sea baselines rules. An approach to maximise the use of straight baselines is understandable given the Law of the Sea Convention gives coastal states a powerful incentive to do so. Indeed, it enables them to maximise the extent of their maritime jurisdiction and also limit the activities including the passage of other nation's vessels in the claimed areas. We see this in many parts of our region, particularly in archipelagic waters.

Second, there are differences in approach between states in relation to warships being able to exercise innocent passage. In our region, some take the view that a foreign state must obtain approval in advance from or give prior notification to the coastal state for the passage of its warships through the territorial sea of the coastal state. Many of these states have this requirement because they see it as a significant limitation on their sovereignty and a potential threat to their national security.

Third, differences of view have also emerged in our region over the rights and duties of coastal states in their Exclusive Economic Zone and the rights and duties of user states. This is particularly an issue with regard to the rights of other states to conduct certain activities such as military operations, military surveying, intelligence collection and hydrographic surveying without the permission of the coastal state.

Differences in approach to the interpretation of the Law of the Sea Convention like the ones I have just outlined can cause misunderstanding or disagreement or lead to a stand-off between warships or breaches of the International Regulations for Preventing Collisions at Sea with consequences for safety or possibly even armed conflict at sea.

There are also the emerging challenges which were not of such significance when the Law of the Sea Convention was concluded in 1982. Climate change will likely have significant consequences for global maritime biodiversity, the ability to obtain food and other resources from the sea, the ability to access and utilise the Polar Regions and responsibilities of states for environmental damage caused beyond their national jurisdiction.

Another emerging challenge is the increased ability to explore and exploit the resources of the deep seabed beyond the limits of national jurisdiction. These areas of the world's oceans may contain deposits of key strategic metals and minerals such as copper, cobalt, nickel and manganese. Thanks to technological advances and a stable regulatory regime deep seabed mining is an increasingly attractive option. This will most likely mean that states and other actors come into dispute.

But each of the threats and challenges can also provide the opportunity for the region to work together to build trust and confidence in each other, and the systems which support our prosperity – trust and confidence that is built on sharing xx *Foreword*

the lessons learned, developing collaborative 'rules of the game' to resolve challenges and utilising existing mechanisms under the Law of the Sea Convention or regional forums to avoid confusion. So, it behoves this conference to run the critical debate. The Navy needs you to do this.

And I am not naïve enough to think that debate will produce a binary argument with an easy resolution.

But I'm reminded of what Admiral Harris used to say: 'We can disagree without being disagreeable'.

That's an important distinction to make in these uncertain times.

# Preface

The 1982 United Nations Convention on the Law of the Sea (LOSC) represents one of the most successful examples of multilateral treaty making in the modern era. The convention has 168 States parties and most non-signatory States, including the United States, recognise nearly all of its key provisions as binding under customary international law. Nevertheless, there remain significant differences in interpretation and implementation of the LOSC among States as well as calls, on occasion, for its amendment.

The role of the LOSC in South East Asia was in the spotlight in 2016 following the award of an Annex VII LOSC Arbitral Tribunal in the *South China Sea* arbitration between the Philippines and China. That case raised a number of critical issues with respect to the LOSC and law of the sea more generally, including the status of maritime claims, the characterisation of islands and rocks and protection of the marine environment. More broadly the case, and the legal and political debates which preceded and followed the 2016 award, also highlighted a range of other law of the sea issues across South East Asia including maritime boundaries, navigational rights and freedoms, resource management and maritime security.

Partly in response to these developments, and to also mark the 35th anniversary of the LOSC, on 22–23 August 2017, the Australian National University (ANU) College of Law's Centre for Military and Security Law, in association with the United Services Institute of the Australian Capital Territory, hosted a conference titled 'The Law of the Sea in the Asia Pacific Region: Opportunities, Threats and Challenges' in Canberra. The Conference was attended by approximately 80 delegates from Australia and the Asia Pacific, as well as a small number of delegates from further afield. The Conference explored the legal pressure points that surround the operation of the LOSC by examining a selection of issues through a series of linked discussions over two days. The focus of this discussion was on topics that have particular significance in the Asia Pacific, especially the South China Sea. Subsequently, a number of conference presenters, and some invited academic colleagues, have worked with us to prepare the chapters that comprise this publication.

Building on that 2017 conference, and reflecting on the critical law of the sea issues that were identified, the scope of this book has been redefined to

## xxii *Preface*

concentrate on South East Asia, with reference to the wider Indo-Asia-Pacific included in some chapters where appropriate. In this sense, the chapters do not merely repeat the material presented at the Conference; rather, each chapter has a contemporary focus on maritime issues that have continued relevance for South East Asia. For the purposes of this book, unless otherwise noted, reference to 'the region' encompasses all of the maritime states that comprise the Association of South East Asian Nations (ASEAN) with the focal point being the South China Sea. The maritime area extends from the northern extremity of the South China Sea to the far southern reaches of the Indonesian archipelago, and sweeps from the Pacific edge of the Philippines archipelago to the Andaman Sea. States on the margins on the region, such as Timor-Leste, are also included. Other states and actors who are geographically proximate such as China, Japan, Korea and Taiwan also have interests in the region, whereas others have long-standing historical interests or are contemporary actors in the region such as Australia, India, the United Kingdom and the United States.

The book takes as its foundation the LOSC which all states in South East Asia adhere to and accept. Assessments in the chapters are undertaken of the impact, influence and ongoing role of the LOSC for the region, especially in light of the 2016 *South China Sea* arbitration. Maritime security is a major issue within the region and has been separately assessed in light of the LOSC and contemporary challenges such as environmental security and climate change. Likewise, navigational rights and freedoms are critical issues for the region and they have been assessed through the LOSC and state practice within the region. Special attention in this regard has been given to the role of navies and non-state actors. The region already has a history of resource disputes and these have the potential to increase into the future as economic interests and concerns over food security intensify. Effective oil, gas and fisheries resource management is therefore a critical issue for the region and unless resolved could become the focal point for significant maritime disputes within the region. These dynamics within the region point to the necessity of further assessment of the effectiveness of LOSC dispute resolution mechanisms, and that task has also been undertaken.

Putting together the edited collection of chapters in this book would not have been possible without the commitment of each of the chapter authors and we thank them for their assistance and cheerful response to our editorial prompts. Special mention should also be made of Vice Admiral Tim Barrett RAN, who kindly agreed to revise and update the opening remarks he made at the Conference, thereby providing a substantial and contemporary Foreword for this book. Maps and figures were kindly provided by Professor Clive Schofield and Dr I Made Andi Arsana. Assisting with our editing task, we have had the benefit of working with Mia Stone as our research assistant and we are most grateful for her contribution.

Of course, it would not have been possible to hold the Conference in August 2017, nor would it have been possible to compile this book subsequently, without the generous support of the ANU College of Law for us as researchers. Working in an environment where research is fostered and encouraged provides

*Preface* xxiii

a wonderful incentive to publish scholarly work and we are both most grateful for the encouragement that we routinely receive when undertaking research and writing activities at ANU.

We also extend our thanks to Emma Tyce at Routledge who oversaw the initial phases of the development of this book.

The law in this book is generally stated as at January 2019.

Donald R. Rothwell and David Letts
Canberra, Australia, March 2019

# Table of cases

*Case Concerning Maritime Delimitation and Territorial Questions between Qatar and Bahrain* (Qatar v. Bahrain) [2001] ICJ Rep 40

*Case Concerning Maritime Delimitation in the Black Sea* (Romania v. Ukraine) [2009] ICJ Rep 61

*Case concerning Sovereignty over Pulau Sipadan and Pulau Ligitan* (Indonesia v. Malaysia) [2002] ICJ Rep 625

*Case Concerning the Continental Shelf* (Libyan Arab Jamahiriya v. Malta) [1984] ICJ Rep 3

*Case Concerning the Military and Paramilitary Activities in and against Nicaragua* (Nicaragua v. United States of America) [1986] ICJ Rep 14

*Certain Activities Carried out in the Border Area* (Costa Rica v. Nicaragua) [2017] ICJ Rep 97

*Corfu Channel* (Merits) (United Kingdom v. Albania) [1949] ICJ Rep 4

*Delimitation of the Maritime Boundary between Bangladesh and Myanmar in the Bay of Bengal* (Bangladesh/Myanmar) (2012) 51 ILM 844

*Factory at Chorzów* (Germany v. Poland) [1928] PCIJ (ser A) No 17

*Frontier Dispute* (Burkina Faso v. Mali) [1986] ICJ Rep 554

*Golder v The United Kingdom* [1975] 1 EHRR 524

*Hirsi Jamaa and Others v Italy* (European Court of Human Rights, Grand Chamber, Application No. 27765/09, 23 February 2012)

*In the Matter of an Arbitration before An Arbitral Tribunal Constituted Under Annex VII to the 1982 United Nations Convention on the Law of the Sea between The Republic of the Philippines and the People's Republic of China*, PCA Case no. 2013-19, Award of 12 July 2016

*In the Matter of an Arbitration before An Arbitral Tribunal Constituted under Annex VII to the 1982 United Nations Convention on the Law of the Sea between*

xxvi   *Table of cases*

*The Republic of the Philippines and the People's Republic of China*, PCA Case no. 2013-19, Award on Jurisdiction and Admissibility of 29 October 2015

*In the Matter of an Arbitration before An Arbitral Tribunal Constituted under Annex VII to the 1982 United Nations Convention on the Law of the Sea between Guyana and Suriname*, PCA Case no. 2004-04, Award of 17 September 2007

*In the Matter of an Arbitration before an Arbitral Tribunal Constituted under Annex VII of the 1982 United Nations Convention on the Law of the Sea between the Italian Republic and the Republic of India concerning the 'Enrica Lexie' Incident*, PCA Case no. 2015–28, Order of 29 April 2016

*In the Matter of the Bay of Bengal Maritime Boundary Arbitration between the People's Republic of Bangladesh and the Republic of India*, PCA Case no. 2010–16, Award of 7 July 2014

*In the Matter of the Chagos Marine Protected Area Arbitration before an Arbitral Tribunal Constituted under Annex VII of the United Nations Convention on the Law of the Sea between the Republic of Mauritius and the United Kingdom of Great Britain and Northern Ireland*, PCA Case no. 2011-03, Award of 18 March 2015

*In the Matter of the Maritime Boundary between Timor-Leste and Australia before a Conciliation Commission Constituted under Annex V of the 1982 United Nations Convention on the Law of the Sea between the Democratic Republic of Timor-Leste and the Commonwealth of Australia*, PCA Case no. 2016-10, Report and Recommendations of the Compulsory Conciliation Commission between Timor-Leste and Australia on the Timor Sea of 9 May 2018

*Island of Palmas* (Netherlands v. US) (1928) 2 RIAA 829

*Land and Maritime Boundary between Cameroon and Nigeria* (Cameroon v. Nigeria; Equatorial Guinea intervening) [2002] ICJ Rep 303

*Land Reclamation by Singapore in and around the Straits of Johor* (Malaysia v Singapore) (Provisional Measures) (2003) 126 ILR 487

*Legal Status of Eastern Greenland* (Denmark v. Norway) [1933] PCIJ (Ser A/B) No 53

*Legality of the Threat or Use of Nuclear Weapons* (Advisory Opinion) [1996] ICJ Rep 226

*Magallona et al. v Ermita et al. (July 16, 2011) Supreme Court of the Philippines*

*Medvedyev and Others v France* (European Court of Human Rights, Grand Chamber, Application No. 3394/03, 29 March 2010)

*MV Saiga No. 2* (Saint Vincent and The Grenadines v Guinea) (1999) ITLOS case no. 2

*Nevada v. Hall (1970) 440 US 410*

*North Sea Continental Shelf* (Germany v. Denmark; Germany v. Netherlands) [1969] ICJ Rep 3

*Request for Interpretation of the Judgement of 15 June 1962 in the Case Concerning the Temple of Preah Vihear* (Cambodia v Thailand) (Provisional Measures) [2011] ICJ Rep 537

*Request for Interpretation of the Judgment of 15 June 1962 in the Case concerning the Temple of Preah Vihear* (Cambodia v. Thailand) [2013] ICJ Rep 281

*Sovereignty over Pedra Branca/Pulau Batu Puteh, Middle Rocks and South Ledge* (Malaysia v. Singapore) [2008] ICJ Rep 12

*Sovereignty over Pulau Ligitan and Pulau Sipadan* (Indonesia/Malaysia) [2002] ICJ Rep 625

*The 'ARA Libertad' Case* (Argentina v. Ghana) (Provisional Measures) (ITLOS, Case no. 20, 15 December 2012) (2014) 156 ILR 186

*The I'm Alone* (Canada/United States of America) 3 RIAA 1609

*The Paquete Habana* (1900) 175 US 677

*The Red Crusader* (1962) 35 ILR 485

*The Schooner Exchange v. McFaddon* (1812) 11 US 116

*Whaling in the Antarctic* (Australia v Japan; New Zealand intervening) [2014] ICJ Rep 226

# Table of treaties and other international instruments

## Abbreviations used in this table

| | |
|---|---|
| A | Adopted |
| ATNIF | Australian Treaties Not In Force |
| ATS | Australian Treaty Series |
| C&AI | J.I. Charney and L.M. Alexander (eds), *International Maritime Boundaries* I, Dordrecht: Martinus Nijhoff, 1993 |
| C&AII | J.I. Charney and L.M. Alexander (eds), *International Maritime Boundaries* II, Dordrecht: Martinus Nijhoff, 1993 |
| C&AIII | J.I. Charney and L.M. Alexander (eds), *International Maritime Boundaries* III, The Hague: Martinus Nijhoff, 1998 |
| C&SIV | J.I. Charney and R.W. Smith (eds), *International Maritime Boundaries* IV, The Hague: Martinus Nijhoff, 2002 |
| C&SV | D.A. Colson and R.W. Smith (eds), *International Maritime Boundaries* V, Leiden: Martinus Nijhoff, 2005 |
| C&SVI | D.A. Colson and R.W. Smith (eds), *International Maritime Boundaries* VI, Leiden: Martinus Nijhoff, 2011 |
| LVII | C. Lathrop (ed), *International Maritime Boundaries* VII, Dordrecht: Martinus Nijhoff, 2016 |
| CTS | Consolidated Treaty Series |
| EIF | Entry into Force |
| ILM | International Legal Materials |
| LIS | Limits in the Seas |
| OS | Open for Signature |
| UNTS | United Nations Treaty Series |

****************

| | |
|---|---|
| 1898 | Treaty of Paris between Spain and the United States, OS – 10 December 1898, EIF – 11 April 1899, 187 CTS 100 |
| 1900 | Treaty between Spain and the United States for the Cession of Outlying Islands of the Philippines, OS – 7 November 1900, EIF – 23 March 1901, 189 CTS 108 |
| 1945 | Charter of the United Nations, OS – 26 June 1945, EIF – 24 October 1945, 1 UNTS XVI |

xxx    *Table of treaties and other international instruments*

| | |
|---|---|
| 1958 | Convention on the Territorial Sea and Contiguous Zone, OS – 29 April 1958, EIF – 10 September 1964, 516 UNTS 206 |
| 1958 | Convention on the Continental Shelf, OS – 29 April 1958, EIF – 10 June 1964, 499 UNTS 311 |
| 1966 | International Convention for the Conservation of Atlantic Tunas, OS – 14 May 1966, EIF – 21 March 1969, 673 UNTS 63 |
| 1966 | International Covenant on Civil and Political Rights, OS – 19 December 1966, EIF – 23 March 1976, 999 UNTS 171 |
| 1968 | Treaty on the Non-proliferation of Nuclear Weapons, OS – 1 July 1968, EIF – 5 March 1970, 729 UNTS 161 |
| 1969 | Convention on the Law of Treaties, OS – 23 May 1969, EIF – 27 January 1980, 1155 UNTS 331 |
| 1969 | Agreement between the Government of Malaysia and the Government of the Republic of Indonesia on the Delimitation of the Continental Shelf between the Two Countries, OS – 27 October 1969, EIF – 7 November 1969, (1970) LIS 1 |
| 1970 | Treaty between the Republic of Indonesia and Malaysia on Determination of Boundary Lines of Territorial Waters of the Two Nations at the Strait of Malacca, OS – 17 March 1970, EIF – 8 October 1971, (1973) LIS 50 |
| 1971 | Agreement between the Government of the Republic of Indonesia and the Government of the Kingdom of Thailand Relating to the Delimitation of a Continental Shelf Boundary Between the Two Countries in the Northern Part of the Strait of Malacca and in the Andaman Sea, OS – 17 December 1971, EIF – 16 July 1973, (1978) 81 LIS |
| 1971 | Agreement between the Government of the Commonwealth of Australia and the Government of the Republic of Indonesia Establishing Certain Seabed Boundaries, OS – 18 May 1971, EIF – 8 November 1973, 974 UNTS 307 |
| 1971 | Agreement between the Government of the Republic of Indonesia, the Government of Malaysia and the Government of the Kingdom of Thailand Relating to the Delimitation of the Continental Shelf Boundaries in the Northern Part of the Strait of Malacca, OS – 21 December 1971, EIF – 16 July 1973, (1978) LIS 81 |
| 1972 | Agreement between the Government of the Commonwealth of Australia and the Government of the Republic of Indonesia Establishing Certain Seabed Boundaries in the Area of the Timor and Arafura Seas, Supplementary to the Agreement of 18 May 1971, OS – 9 October 1972, EIF – 8 November 1973, 974 UNTS 319 |
| 1972 | Convention on the International Regulations for Preventing Collisions at Sea, OS – 20 October 1972, EIF – 15 July 1977, 1050 UNTS 16 |

*Table of treaties and other international instruments* xxxi

| | |
|---|---|
| 1972 | Convention on the Prevention of Marine Pollution by Dumping of Wastes and Other Matter, OS – 29 December 1972, EIF – 30 August 1975, 1046 UNTS 120<br>1996: Protocol to the London Convention on the Prevention of Marine Pollution by Dumping of Wastes and Other Matter, OS – 8 November 1996, EIF – 24 March 2006, (1997) 36 ILM 1 |
| 1973 | International Convention for the Prevention of Pollution from Ships, OS – 2 November 1973, as Modified by the Protocol of 1978 Relating Thereto, OS – 17 February 1978, EIF – 2 October 1983, 1340 UNTS 62 |
| 1973 | Agreement Stipulating the Territorial Sea Boundary Lines between Indonesia and the Republic of Singapore in the Strait of Singapore, OS – 25 March 1973, EIF – 29 August 1974, (1974) LIS 60 |
| 1974 | Agreement between the Government of the Republic of India and the Government of the Republic of Indonesia Relating to the Delimitation of the Continental Shelf Boundary between the Two Countries, OS – 8 August 1974, EIF – 17 December 1974, (1975) LIS 62 |
| 1974 | Agreement Between Japan and the Republic of Korea Concerning Joint Development of the Southern Part of the Continental Shelf Adjacent to the Two Countries, OS – 30 January 1974, C&A I: 1073 |
| 1974 | Agreement between Japan and the Republic of Korea Concerning the Establishment of Boundary in the Northern Part of the Continental Shelf Adjacent to the Two Countries, OS – 30 January 1974, EIF – 22 June 1978, (1979) LIS 75 |
| 1976 | Treaty of amity and co-operation in Southeast Asia, OS – 24 February 1976, EIF – 15 July 1976, 1025 UNTS 316 |
| 1977 | Agreement between the Government of the Republic of India and the Government of the Republic of Indonesia on the Extension of the 1974 Continental Shelf Boundary between the Two Countries in the Andaman Sea and the Indian Ocean, OS – 14 January 1977, EIF – 15 August 1977, (1981) LIS 93 |
| 1978 | Agreement between the Government of the Republic of India and the Government of the Kingdom of Thailand on the Delimitation of Seabed Boundary between the Two Countries in the Andaman Sea, OS – 22 June 1978, EIF – 15 December 1978, (1981) LIS 93 |
| 1978 | Agreement between the Government of the Republic of India, the Government of the Republic of Indonesia and the Government of the Kingdom of Thailand Concerning the Determination of the Trijunction Point and the Delimitation of the Related Boundaries of the Three Countries in the Andaman Sea, OS – 22 June 1978, EIF – 2 March 1979, (1981) LIS 93 |
| 1978 | Agreement between the Government of the Kingdom of Thailand and the Government of India on the Maritime Boundary between |

xxxii  *Table of treaties and other international instruments*

|      | |
|------|---|
|      | the Two Countries in the Andaman Sea from Point 7 to the Trijunction Point (Point T) between Thailand, India and Myanmar, OS – 22 June 1978, EIF – 15 December 1978 |
| 1979 | Treaty between the Kingdom of Thailand and Malaysia Relating to the Delimitation of the Territorial Seas of the Two Countries, OS – 24 October 1979, EIF – 15 July 1982, C&A I: 1096 |
| 1979 | Memorandum of Understanding between Malaysia and the Kingdom of Thailand on the Delimitation of the Continental Shelf Boundary between the Two Countries in the Gulf of Thailand, OS – 24 October 1979, EIF – 15 July 1982, C&A I: 1105 |
| 1979 | Memorandum of Understanding between the Kingdom of Thailand and Malaysia on the Establishment of a Joint Authority for the Exploitation of the Resources of the Sea-Bed in a Defined Area of the Continental Shelf of the Two Countries in the Gulf of Thailand, OS – 21 February 1979, C&A I: 1107 |
| 1980 | Convention on the Conservation of Antarctic Marine Living Resources, OS – 20 May 1980, EIF – 7 April 1982, 1329 UNTS 47 |
| 1980 | Agreement between the Government of the Socialist Republic of the Union of Burma and the Government of the Kingdom of Thailand on the Delimitation of the Maritime Boundary between the Two Countries in the Andaman Sea, OS – 25 July 1980, EIF – 12 April 1982, 1276 UNTS 447 |
| 1981 | Memorandum of Understanding between the Government of the Republic of Indonesia and the Government of Australia Concerning the Implementation of a Provisional Fisheries Surveillance and Enforcement Agreement, OS – 29 October 1981, EIF – 1 February 1982, C&AII: 1229 |
| 1982 | Agreement on Historic Waters of Vietnam and Kampuchea, OS – 7 July 1982, EIF – 7 July 1982, C&AIII: 2357 |
| 1982 | Nauru Agreement Concerning Cooperation in the Management of Fisheries of Common Interest, OS – 11 February 1982, EIF – 4 December 1982, available online at www.pnatuna.com/sites/default/files/Nauru%20Agreement_0.pdf |
| 1982 | United Nations Convention on the Law of the Sea, OS – 10 December 1982, EIF – 16 November 1994, 1833 UNTS 397<br>1994: Agreement Relating to the Implementation of Part XI of the United Nations Convention on the Law of the Sea of 10 December 1982, OS – 28 July 1994, EIF – 28 July 1996, 1836 UNTS 42<br>1995: Agreement for the Implementation of the Provisions of the United Nations Convention on the Law of the Sea of 10 December 1982 Relating to the Conservation and Management of Straddling Fish Stocks and Highly Migratory Fish Stocks, OS – 4 August 1995, EIF – 11 December 2001, 2167 UNTS 88 |

*Table of treaties and other international instruments*  xxxiii

| | |
|---|---|
| 1986 | Agreement between the Socialist Republic of the Union of Burma and the Republic of India on the Delimitation of the Maritime Boundary in the Andaman Sea, in the Coco Channel and the Bay of Bengal, OS – 23 December 1986, EIF – 14 September 1987, (1988) 27 ILM 1144 |
| 1988 | Convention for the Suppression of Unlawful Acts against the Safety of Maritime Navigation, OS – 10 March 1988, EIF – 1 March 1992, 1678 UNTS 221 |
| 1989 | Treaty between Australia and the Republic of Indonesia on the Zone of Cooperation in an Area between the Indonesian Province of east Timor and Northern Australia, OS – 11 December 1989, EIF – 9 February 1991, [1991] ATS 9 |
| 1990 | Agreement between the Government of Malaysia and the Government of the Kingdom of Thailand on the Constitution and Other Matters Relating to the Establishment of the Malaysia-Thailand Joint Authority, OS – 30 May 1990, C&AI: 1111 |
| 1992 | United Nations Framework Convention on Climate Change, OS – 9 May 1992, EIF – 21 March 1994, 1771 UNTS 107<br>1997: Kyoto Protocol to the United Nations Framework Convention on Climate Change, OS – 11 December 1997, EIF – 16 February 2005, 2303 UNTS 214<br>2015: Paris Agreement, OS – 12 December 2015, EIF – 4 November 2016, (2016) 55 ILM 743 |
| 1992 | Convention on Biological Diversity, OS – 5 June 1992, EIF – 29 December 1993, 1760 UNTS 79 |
| 1992 | Memorandum of Understanding between Malaysia and the Socialist Republic of Vietnam for the Exploration and Exploitation of Petroleum in a Defined Area of the Continental Shelf Involving the Two Countries, OS – 5 June 1992, EIF – 5 June 1992, C&AIII: 2335 |
| 1993 | Agreement between the Government of the Union of Myanmar, the Government of the Republic of India and the Government of the Kingdom of Thailand on the determination of the trijunction point between the three countries in the Andaman Sea, OS – 27 October 1993, EIF – 24 May 1995, C&AIII: 2369, C&SV: 3781 |
| 1993 | Agreement to Promote Compliance with International Conservation and Management Measures by Fishing Vessels on the High Seas, OS – 24 November 1993, EIF – 24 April 2003, 2221 UNTS 91 |
| 1994 | Marrakesh Agreement Establishing the World Trade Organization, OS – 15 April 1994, EIF – 1 January 1996, 1867 UNTS 3 |
| 1995 | Agreement Between the Government of Malaysia and the Government of the Republic of Singapore to Delimit Precisely the Territorial Waters Boundary in Accordance with the Straits |

| | |
|---|---|
| | Settlement and Johore Territorial Waters Agreement 1927, OS – 7 August 1995, EIF – 7 August 1995, C&AIII: 2351 |
| 1997 | Agreement between the Government of the Kingdom of Thailand and the Government of the Socialist Republic of Vietnam on the Delimitation of the Maritime Boundary Between the Two Countries in the Gulf of Thailand, OS – 9 August 1997; EIF – 27 December 1997, C&SIV: 2683 |
| 1997 | Treaty Between the Government of Australia and the Government of the Republic of Indonesia Establishing an Exclusive Economic Zone Boundary and Certain Seabed Boundaries, OS – 14 March 1997, [1997] ATNIF 4 |
| 2000 | Agreement between China and Viet Nam on the Delimitation of the Territorial Sea, the Exclusive Economic Zones and Continental Shelves in Beibu Bay/Bac Bo Gulf, OS – 25 December 2000, EIF – 30 June 2004, 2336 UNTS 179 |
| 2000 | Convention on the Conservation and Management of Highly Migratory Fish Stocks in the Western and Central Pacific Ocean, OS – 5 September 2000, EIF – 19 June 2004, 2275 UNTS 43 |
| 2000 | Agreement on the Delimitation of the Territorial Sea, Exclusive Economic Zones and Continental Shelves in the Beibu Gulf [Gulf of Tonkin] between the People's Republic of China and the Socialist Republic of Vietnam, OS – 25 December 2000, EIF – 30 June 2004, 2336 UNTS 179 |
| 2001 | Memorandum of Understanding between the Royal Government of Cambodia and the Royal Thai Government regarding the Area of their Overlapping Maritime Claims to the Continental Shelf, OS – 18 June 2001, EIF – 18 June 2001, C&SV: 3743 |
| 2002 | Declaration on the Conduct of Parties in the South China Sea, A – 4 November 2002, available online at https://asean.org/?static_post=declaration-on-the-conduct-of-parties-in-the-south-china-sea-2 |
| 2002 | Timor Sea Treaty between the Government of East Timor and the Government of Australia, OS – 20 May 2002, EIF – 2 April 2003, [2003] ATS 13 |
| 2003 | Agreement between the Government of the Socialist Republic of Vietnam and the Government of the Republic of Indonesia concerning the delimitation of the Continental Shelf Boundary, OS – 26 June 2003, EIF – 29 May 2007, C&SVI: 4301 |
| 2004 | Treaty on Mutual Legal Assistance in Criminal Matters, OS – 29 November 2004, EIF – 1 November 2005, 2336 UNTS 271 |
| 2005 | Agreement between the Democratic People's Republic of Korea and the People's Republic of China on the Joint Development of Offshore Petroleum, OS – 12 December 2005 |
| 2006 | Treaty between Australia and the Republic of Timor-Leste on Certain Maritime Arrangements in the Timor Sea, OS – 12 January 2006, EIF – 23 February 2007, [2007] ATS 12 |

*Table of treaties and other international instruments*  xxxv

| | |
|---|---|
| 2007 | Charter of the Association of Southeast Asian Nations, OS – 20 November 2007, EIF – 15 December 2008, 2624 UNTS 223 |
| 2009 | Agreement on Port State Measures to Prevent, Deter and Eliminate Illegal, Unreported and Unregulated Fishing, OS – 22 November 2009, EIF – 5 June 2016, [2016] ATS 21 |
| 2009 | Treaty between the Republic of Indonesia and the Republic of Singapore relating to the Delimitation of the Territorial Seas of the Two Countries in the Western Part of the Strait of Singapore, OS – 10 March 2009, EIF – 10 March 2009, LVII: 4823 |
| 2012 | Agreement on Strengthening Implementation of the Niue Treaty on Cooperation Fisheries Surveillance and Law Enforcement in the South Pacific Region, OS – 2 November 2012, EIF – 30 July 2015, [2017] ATS 11 |
| 2013 | Arms Trade Treaty, OS – 2 April 2013, EIF – 24 December 2014, [2014] ATS 42 |
| 2014 | Treaty between the Republic of Singapore and the Republic of Indonesia relating to the Delimitation of the Territorial Seas of the Two Countries in the Eastern Part of the Strait of Singapore, OS – 3 September 2014, EIF – 10 January 2017, LVII: 4835 |
| 2014 | Agreement between the Government of the Republic of the Philippines and the Government of the Republic Indonesia Concerning the Delimitation of the Exclusive Economic Zone Boundary, OS – 23 May 2014, available online at www.officialgazette.gov.ph/2014/05/23/agreement-between-the-government-of-the-republic-of-the-philippines-and-the-government-of-the-republic-indonesia-concerning-the-delimitation-of-the-exclusive-economic-zone-boundary/ |
| 2015 | ASEAN Convention against Trafficking in Persons, Especially Women and Children, 0S-21 November 2015, not yet in force, available online at https://asean.org/asean-convention-against-trafficking-in-persons-especially-women-and-children/ |
| 2018 | Treaty Between Australia and The Democratic Republic of Timor-Leste Establishing their Maritime Boundaries in the Timor Sea, OS – 6 March 2018, [2018] ATNIF 4 |
| 2018 | Memorandum of Understanding between the Association of Southeast Asian Nations and the Government of Australia to Counter International Terrorism, OS – 17 March 2018, EIF – 17 March 2018, available online at http://setnas-asean.id/vendor/webarq/admin-lte/plugins/elfinder/files/KS%20Eksternal/ASEAN-Australia%20MoU%20on%20International%20Terrorism.pdf |

# 1 The law of the sea and South East Asia

*Donald R. Rothwell and David Letts*

## 1.1 Introduction

South East Asia is a unique maritime space which combines States and archipelagic States that cluster around the South China Sea and its related waters. It also includes very large coastal States, such as China, and much smaller island States, such as Singapore and Timor-Leste, a landlocked State in the case of Laos and a political entity that is not universally recognised as a State in the case of Taiwan. The region properly includes waters on either side of the Malay Peninsula and therefore encompasses the Andaman Sea, which encompasses Indian territories and maritime claims. Major powers have territories, and assert maritime claims, on the periphery of South East Asia, including Australia to the south, which shares a maritime domain with Indonesia and Timor-Leste, and Japan and South Korea to the north, who both share a maritime domain with China. The region is also one that has been heavily influenced by the events of the Second World War and the Vietnam War, the emergence of newly independent States and significant population growth and economic development. Partly due to the geography of the region where States share both land and maritime boundaries with the South China Sea at its centre, South East Asia has a very strong maritime focus. As a result, the law of the sea has historically and certainly in the twenty-first century been of great significance to the region. Notwithstanding the importance for South East Asian States of the Association of South East Asian Nations (ASEAN),[1] which other than China, India, Taiwan and Timor-Leste includes all regional States as members, and which provides a strong sense of regional purpose and unity, the States within the region all have their own distinctive national interests, which are also reflected in their maritime interests.

Partly as a result of these variable circumstances, the region has seen a variety of maritime claims asserted that are based upon the 1982 United Nations Convention on the Law of the Sea (LOSC),[2] but which interpret the LOSC

---

1 The ten members of ASEAN comprise Brunei, Cambodia, Indonesia, Laos, Malaysia, Myanmar, Philippines, Singapore, Thailand and Vietnam. Timor-Leste applied to become a member of ASEAN in 2011 and the application remains pending.
2 United Nations Convention on the Law of the Sea, 10 December 1982, 1833 UNTS 397 [hereafter LOSC].

## 2 Donald R. Rothwell and David Letts

differently. Extending from claims to straight baselines and historic bays that are the subject of protest, maritime claims throughout South East Asia encompass all those that are permissible under the LOSC to those which remain subject to recommendation by the Commission on the Limits of the Continental Shelf (CLCS). Claims have also been made that sit outside of the LOSC, such as China's 'Nine-Dash Line' claim in the South China Sea that was the subject of consideration in the *South China Sea* arbitration.[3]

This chapter seeks to set the scene for an understanding of the law of the sea in South East Asia. It does so by first defining the maritime domain of the region and considers the States that make up South East Asia. Consideration is also given to the international organisations and institutions which have been active in, and influential throughout, the region. An introductory assessment is then undertaken of some of the critical law of the sea issues confronting the region, ranging from disputes over the South China Sea to navigational rights and freedoms, maritime security, resource management and dispute resolution.

## 1.2 The South East Asian maritime domain

There has been long-standing academic debate and discourse over what comprises 'South East Asia'[4] and differing views exist amongst scholars which are partly influenced by their academic discipline. From a law of the sea perspective, there is no clearly defined region known as 'South East Asia' as referenced in the LOSC or related treaties. Legally, a starting point for defining the region is certainly ASEAN. While the ASEAN Charter does not identify any geographic limits, the ASEAN States are certainly at the core of what comprises South East Asia. The South China Sea and its related waters and gulfs are central to the South East Asian maritime domain, and accordingly all States which have territorial claims in and adjoining the South China Sea, whether they be recognised or contested, are States which make up the region. The maritime domain also includes the archipelagic waters of Indonesia and the Philippines. While these waters, consistently with the LOSC, fall within the national maritime domain of those archipelagic States, they are also waters that are within the remit of the LOSC with respect to navigational rights and freedoms and overflight for foreign flagged vessels and aircraft.

The South East Asian maritime domain then, for the purposes of this chapter and the book, encompasses all of the waters of the South China Sea extending as far north as the Gulf of Tonkin and Luzon Strait to as far south as the Strait of Singapore. The waters of the Indonesian and Philippine archipelago are

---

3 *In the Matter of an Arbitration before An Arbitral Tribunal Constituted under Annex VII to the 1982 United Nations Convention on the Law of the Sea between The Republic of the Philippines and the People's Republic of China*, PCA Case no. 2013-19, Award of 12 July 2016 [*South China Sea* arbitration].

4 D.K. Emmerson, '"Southeast Asia": What's in a Name?' (1984) 15 *Journal of Southeast Asian Studies* pp. 1–21.

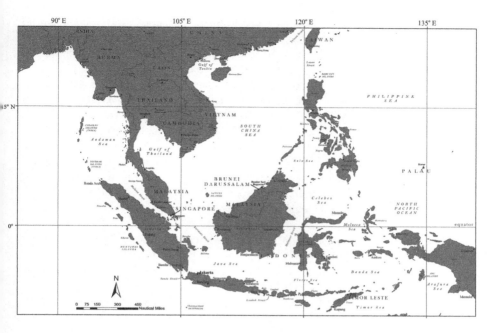

*Figure 1.1* South East Asian Maritime Domain.

included, as are those of Timor-Leste. In the west, the Andaman Sea is included, encompassing the maritime domain generated from the Andaman and Nicobar Islands, the western Malay Peninsula and Myanmar. In the east, the Indonesian and Philippine archipelagos facing the Pacific are the outer limits of South East Asia in that sector and as such the Federated States of Micronesia, Palau and Papua New Guinea are beyond the region. This area is illustrated in Figure 1.1.

## 1.3 South East Asia and the LOSC

South East Asian States had much to gain from the conclusion of the LOSC and played an active role in negotiations at the Third United Nations Conference on the Law of the Sea from 1973 to 1982. This was perhaps best illustrated by the role played by Ambassador Tommy T.B. Koh (Singapore) as the President of the Conference (1981–1982), who had, in turn, succeeded another Asian diplomat, Hamilton Shirley Amersinghe (Sri Lanka) who was elected President from the opening session. All then-existing States participated in the conference deliberations, and all signed the LOSC in 1982 other than Brunei (1984) and Cambodia (1983). Except Cambodia, all then subsequently ratified the Convention, whereas Timor-Leste which gained independence in 2002 acceded to the LOSC in 2013. This level of enthusiasm for the LOSC amongst regional States is understandable given the significant benefits to be gained from being a party to the Convention, especially with respect to maritime claims and entitlements. This is perhaps no better illustrated than the situation of both Indonesia and the Philippines, who

## 4 Donald R. Rothwell and David Letts

gained recognition as archipelagic States under Part IV of the Convention but also for the so-called 'Strait States' of Indonesia, Malaysia,[5] and Singapore who benefitted from the clarity Part III of the LOSC gave to the navigational regime through the Straits of Malacca and Singapore and in particular the recognition of their specific entitlements as the adjoining coastal States.

Consistent with Article 310 of the LOSC, seven States from within the region have made declarations other than with respect to Part XV elections (which deal with dispute resolution).[6] A number of these declarations relate to maritime claims and should be noted. India's 1995 declaration stated that it

> ... understands that the provisions of the Convention do not authorize other States to carry out in the exclusive economic zone and on the continental shelf military exercises or manoeuvres, in particular those involving the use of weapons or explosives without the consent of the coastal State.[7]

China's 1996 declaration upon ratification referred to its entitlement to claim a 200 nautical mile exclusive economic zone (EEZ) and continental shelf and its sovereignty over certain archipelagos and islands as identified under Chinese law. It also made clear its position with respect to requiring prior notification or advance approval before foreign warships could seek to exercise the right of innocent passage.[8] Malaysia's 1996 declaration had a particular focus on navigation rights under Articles 22 and 23 with respect to the requirement of ships carrying nuclear and other dangerous cargoes to obtain prior authorization until such time as other measures were adopted, and reiterated certain safeguard mechanisms under Article 233.[9] Thailand's 2011 declaration stated with respect to navigation in the EEZ that

> ... enjoyment of the freedom of navigation in accordance with relevant provisions of the Convention excludes any non-peaceful use without the consent of the coastal State, in particular, military exercises or other

---

5  For a general discussion of Malaysia's position with respect to the law of the sea, see M.J. Valencia, *Malaysia and the Law of the Sea*, Kuala Lumpur: Institute of Strategic and International Studies, 1991.

6  Those States are China, India, Malaysia, the Philippines, Thailand, Timor-Leste and Vietnam.

7  India (29 June 1995), 'United Nations Convention on the Law of the Sea: Declarations Made upon Signature, Ratification, Accession or Succession or Anytime Thereafter', available online at www.un.org/Depts/los/convention_agreements/convention_declarations.htm#India upon ratification.

8  China (7 June 1996), 'United Nations Convention on the Law of the Sea: Declarations Made upon Signature, Ratification, Accession or Succession or Anytime Thereafter', available online at www.un.org/Depts/los/convention_agreements/convention_declarations.htm#China upon ratification.

9  Malaysia (14 October 1996), 'United Nations Convention on the Law of the Sea: Declarations Made upon Signature, Ratification, Accession or Succession or Anytime Thereafter', available online at www.un.org/Depts/los/convention_agreements/convention_declarations.htm#Malaysia upon ratification.

*The law of the sea and South East Asia* 5

activities which may affect the rights or interests of the coastal State; and it also excludes the threat or use of force against the territorial integrity, political independence, peace or security of the coastal State.[10]

The Philippines declaration upon signature, confirmed on ratification, with respect to its interpretation of archipelagic status in a manner consistent with the Philippines Constitution and previous treaties ceding sovereign rights over the islands that comprise the Philippines, has been particularly contentious. The declaration provided

> 7. The concept of archipelagic waters is similar to the concept of internal waters under the Constitution of the Philippines and removes straits connecting these waters with the economic zone or the high seas from the rights of foreign vessels to transit passage for international navigation.[11]

A number of States responded to aspects of the Philippine's declaration, including Australia, Bulgaria, the Soviet Union, Ukraine and the United States.[12]

## 1.4 States in South East Asia

When assessing maritime claims in South East Asia, there are two types of States that need to be considered from a LOSC perspective: coastal States and flag States.[13] The coastal States within the region are simply those which have a coastal front. In this respect, it needs to be recalled that States such as Indonesia (54,716 km) and the Philippines (36,289 km) have some of the longest coastal fronts amongst coastal States due in large part to the thousands of islands that comprise their archipelagos, whereas Brunei (161 km) and Singapore (193 km) have comparatively small coastal fronts.[14] The existence of coastal States within the region may be subject to change, and historically this has occurred in South East Asia, especially in the decolonisation period following the Second World

---

10 Thailand (15 May 2011), 'United Nations Convention on the Law of the Sea: Declarations Made upon Signature, Ratification, Accession or Succession or Anytime Thereafter', available online at www.un.org/Depts/los/convention_agreements/convention_declarations.htm#Thailand upon ratification.

11 Philippines (10 December 1982 and 8 May 1984), 'United Nations Convention on the Law of the Sea: Declarations Made upon Signature, Ratification, Accession or Succession or Anytime Thereafter', available online at www.un.org/Depts/los/convention_agreements/convention_declarations.htm#Philippines

12 The US protest of January 1986 is reproduced at J.A. Roach and R.W. Smith, *Excessive Maritime Claims*, 3rd ed., Leiden: Martinus Nijhoff, 2012, p. 214; the Australian protest of 3 August 1988 is reproduced in (1992) 12 *Australian Year Book of International Law*, p. 383.

13 While port States are also recognised in the LOSC and have an important role in law enforcement, particularly in collaboration with coastal States, they are not of direct relevance for this analysis.

14 For details, see Central Intelligence Agency (USA), 'Coastline' *CIA World Factbook*, available online at www.cia.gov/LIBRARY/publications/the-world-factbook/fields/print_2060.html

## 6 *Donald R. Rothwell and David Letts*

War which saw the majority of the region's coastal States gain independence by the time of the LOSC negotiations. However, the transition of Timor-Leste to independence in 2002 was a reminder that new States are capable of emerging and that this may have an impact upon the maritime order, in particular with respect to the delimitation of maritime boundaries.[15] Another feature of the region is that two very large coastal States, China and India, assert regional maritime claims from their claimed territories which in the case of China includes its south eastern mainland. For these States, their South East Asian law of the sea interests also need to be seen against their wider interests in the law of the sea, which in the case of India encompasses a very distinctive maritime domain in the Indian Ocean.

There are two particular issues that arise in South East Asia with respect to coastal States. The first is whether an entity that claims to be a State is recognised as such for the purposes of international law and this applies to the situation of Taiwan (Republic of China). Taiwan has many of the attributes of a State but is not widely recognised as such.[16] Its ambiguous status in international law can partly be explained by its history, the position of China (People's Republic of China (PRC)) towards Taiwan which it views as an integral part of its territory, and its economic significance with a 2017 GDP of US$567 billion making it a global top 25 economy. While Taiwan is not a party to the LOSC, it occupies territory within the South China Sea and asserts maritime claims and its law of the sea practice is founded upon the LOSC.[17] The status of Taiwan arose in the context of the *South China Sea* arbitration because of the attention given in that case to the characterisation of Itu Aba, a maritime feature that is occupied by Taiwan but was determined to be a rock by the tribunal,[18] and from which maritime claims have been asserted.[19] However, Taiwan, while recognised by 17 States,[20] is not generally recognised as a State in international law because of the 'one China' policy adopted by the great majority of States. While Taiwan

---

15 See the general discussion in D.R. Rothwell and M. Tsamenyi (eds), *The Maritime Dimensions of Independent East Timor*, Wollongong: Centre for Maritime Policy, University of Wollongong, 2000.

16 See the discussion in P.L. Hsieh, 'An Unrecognized State in Foreign and International Courts: The Case of the Republic of China on Taiwan' (2006–2007) 28 *Michigan Journal of International Law* p. 765.

17 For an assessment of Taiwan's maritime claims and their conformity with the LOSC, see Department of State (USA), 'Taiwan's Maritime Claims' (2005) no. 127 *Limits in the Seas*; and more generally C. Schofield, 'Trouble over the Starting Line: State Practice Concerning Baselines in the South China Sea', in S. Wu, M. Valencia, and N. Hong (eds), *UN Convention on the Law of the Sea and the South China Sea*, Farnham: Ashgate, 2015, pp. 123, 136–137.

18 *South China Sea* arbitration, note 3, [401]; in recognition of the sensitivity associated with the status of Taiwan, the tribunal referred to the 'Taiwan Authority of China' throughout the proceedings.

19 Ibid., [433].

20 C. Horton, 'El Salvador Recognizes China in Blow to Taiwan', *The New York Times*, 21 August 2018, available online at www.nytimes.com/2018/08/21/world/asia/taiwan-el-salvador-diplomatic-ties.html

The law of the sea and South East Asia   7

has been separately accommodated in certain treaties as a 'fishing entity', its marginal status is such that it does not have a significant impact upon maritime claims in the region.[21]

The second issue that is particularly relevant in parts of the South China Sea is whether a coastal State is the recognised sovereign with respect to territory that generates maritime claims. Not only does this exist with respect to the claims made by China in relation to territory currently occupied by Taiwan,[22] and not only is it as such a part of the dispute over the existence of Taiwan as a State in international law – it also relates to the legitimacy of the territorial claims made by South East Asian States to islands, rocks, reefs and other maritime features throughout the region. This raises issues as to the legitimacy of the claims made by coastal States based on their status as the territorial sovereign of the land that they claim, occupy and from which they seek to assert a LOSC maritime claim. In some instances, efforts have been made to resolve these disputes, such as the referral by Malaysia and Singapore of their disputes over Pedra Branca/Pulau Batu Puteh and associated maritime features to the International Court of Justice.[23] In other instances, these disputes remain unresolved, such as in the multiple overlapping and contested claims to various features in the South China Sea made by Brunei, China, Malaysia, Philippines, Taiwan and Vietnam.[24]

Finally, flag States are also present in South East Asia. They may take two forms. They may be South East Asian flag States whose vessels navigate through the waters of the region, or they may be flag States from beyond the region. Navigation by South East Asian flagged vessels will encompass the complete ranging of shipping including various forms of government vessels, including warships, to a range of commercial and private vessels. The number of fishing vessels operating in the region was in 2014 estimated as being 1.27 million vessels.[25] Another characteristic of local shipping is the number of inter-island and intra-State ferries that operate within the region, in particularly within Indonesia and the Philippines, with maritime incidents involving ferries resulting in loss of

---

21 See *Convention on the Conservation of Highly Migratory Fish Stocks in the Western and Central Pacific Ocean*, 5 September 2000, 2275 UNTS 43, Annex I.

22 China's declarations with respect to a territorial sea have historically encompassed 'Taiwan and its surrounding islands'; see People's Republic of China, 'Declaration of the Government of the People's Republic of China on China's Territorial Sea' (4 September 1958), in Office of Policy, Law and Administration, State Oceanic Administration (PRC), *Collection of the Sea Laws and Regulations of the People's Republic of China*, 3rd ed., Beijing: State Oceanic Administration, 2001, and People's Republic of China, Law on the Territorial Sea and the Contiguous Zone (25 February 1992); both discussed in *South China Sea* arbitration, note 3 [174–175].

23 *Sovereignty over Pedra Branca/Pulau Batu Puteh, Middle Rocks and South Ledge* (Malaysia v. Singapore) [2008] ICJ Rep 12.

24 R. Beckman, 'The UN Convention on the Law of the Sea and the Maritime Disputes in the South China Sea', (2013) 107 *American Journal of International Law* pp. 142, 144.

25 Statista, 'Number of Fishing Vessels in Southeast Asia from 2008 to 2014 (in Million Vessels)', April 2017, available online at www.statista.com/statistics/781937/number-of-fishing-vessels-asean/

## 8  Donald R. Rothwell and David Letts

life.[26] The region historically has also been a place where European powers have exercised influence through their navies,[27] and more recently over the past century where the United States has been dominant. Other adjacent States with flag State interests within the region include Australia, India, Japan and South Korea.

### 1.5  International and regional institutions and the law of the sea in South East Asia

In considering the role of international and regional institutions in the law of the sea in South East Asia, the United Nations (UN) is the starting point. The UN played a pivotal role in the development of the modern law of the sea as the international organisation that promoted and supported the debates and discussions that resulted in the four 1958 Geneva Conventions on the Law of the Sea, and then eventually the LOSC in 1982. These five treaties have all had an enormous impact on South East Asia's maritime domain; particularly those of Indonesia and the Philippines as archipelagic States. Since the entry into force of the LOSC, the State Parties to the Law of the Sea (SPLOS) has also played an important role for South East Asian States in providing an ongoing global forum for the discussion of law of the sea issues at the UN. LOSC institutions established following entry into force of that Convention have also been significant for the region through their decisions, determinations and oversight of various law of the sea issues including the International Seabed Authority, International Tribunal for the Law of the Sea and the CLCS. An ad hoc body, the Annex VII Arbitral Tribunal established under the LOSC and which handed down the award in the *South China Sea* arbitration, has probably had the most significant impact upon how aspects of the LOSC are now viewed within the region. The International Court of Justice has also been influential both through its law of the sea jurisprudence in matters such as maritime boundary delimitation which has established a benchmark for South East Asian States in determining some of their maritime boundaries but also through its decisions which have directly addressed regional maritime disputes such as the *Pedra Branca* case and territorial disputes such as the 2002 *Case concerning Sovereignty over Pulau Ligitan and Pulau Sipadan* between Indonesia and Malaysia.[28] Other international institutions such as the International Maritime Organization (IMO) have had a significant impact upon ensuring the safety of navigation within the region and have also played important roles in assisting regional States in managing shipping in the Straits of Malacca and Singapore, and in the designation of Indonesian archipelagic sea lanes.

---

26  See, for example, 'Hundreds of Philippines Ferry Disaster Survivors Pulled from the Sea', *The Guardian*, 21 December 2017, available online at www.theguardian.com/world/2017/dec/21/philippines-ferry-carrying-238-passengers-and-crew-sinks

27  For an historical perspective on the history of shipping in the region and the law of the sea, see R.P. Anand, 'Maritime Practice in South-East Asia until 1600 A.D. and the Modern Law of the Sea', (1981) 30 *International and Comparative Law Quarterly* pp. 440–454.

28  *Sovereignty over Pulau Ligitan and Pulau Sipadan* (Indonesia/Malaysia) [2002] ICJ Rep 625.

The law of the sea and South East Asia   9

A characteristic of South East Asia is that it does not have strong regional institutions; however, it needs to be acknowledged that ASEAN has been in existence since 1967 and during that time it has grown from the original five member States to the current ten. During that time, and especially more recently, ASEAN has begun to demonstrate greater interest in maritime affairs especially with respect to maritime security. An ASEAN initiative of particular relevance for the law of the sea in South East Asia has been efforts to develop in collaboration with China settled policies with respect to the South China Sea by way of written instruments. As discussed below, the success of these initiatives to date has been much debated. Another feature of ASEAN has been the development of additional forums with non-ASEAN members who have significant trade and other interests in South East Asia. The ASEAN Regional Forum[29] has been particularly important in allowing for a wider dialogue between ASEAN members and other States with maritime interests in South East Asia. Finally, it can be noted that the Asia Pacific Economic Cooperation (APEC) Forum also includes many States with interests in South East Asia, and provides an additional forum for the discussion of matters of a wider Asia Pacific interest of which South East Asia is a key component.

## 1.6 Critical law of the sea issues in South East Asia

Nowhere else in the world is presently subject to the number of law of the sea issues that are prevalent throughout South East Asia. The unique geographic characteristics of the region, where littoral and archipelagic States lie in such close proximity to each other, as well as the dominance of maritime trade that is destined for ports within the region and further afield, creates an environment where the importance of the law of the sea is without global precedent. The law of the sea issues that affect the region include sovereignty disputes over a variety of maritime features in the South China Sea, different understandings of navigational rights and freedoms, a range of maritime security concerns, disputes over marine living and non-living resources, pressures that are placed on the marine environment as well as the consequences that arise from attempts to settle maritime disputes through a variety of mechanisms. Brief consideration of each of these issues will be provided as a prelude to more detailed discussion contained in later chapters of this book.

### 1.6.1 The South China Sea

The existence of inter-state disputes over a selection of maritime features in the South China Sea has been the dominant South East Asian maritime issue during recent years. The importance of the South China Sea can be gleaned

---

29 Members comprise Australia, Bangladesh, Brunei Darussalam, Cambodia, Canada, China, Democratic People's Republic of Korea, European Union, India, Indonesia, Japan, Lao PDR, Malaysia, Mongolia, Myanmar, New Zealand, Pakistan, Papua New Guinea, Philippines, Republic of Korea, Russia, Singapore, Sri Lanka, Thailand, Timor-Leste, United States and Vietnam; see details available online at http://aseanregionalforum.asean.org/

## 10  Donald R. Rothwell and David Letts

from looking at the geography of the area it covers, whereupon it becomes immediately obvious that the South China Sea occupies a central strategic position in the region. The Tribunal in the *South China Sea* arbitration described the area as

> ... a semi-enclosed sea in the western Pacific Ocean, spanning an area of almost 3.5 million square kilometres ... [which] ... lies to the south of China; to the west of the Philippines; to the east of Viet Nam; and to the north of Malaysia, Brunei, Singapore, and Indonesia.[30]

The South China Sea contains valuable fishing grounds as well as a diverse maritime environment among its atolls, reefs and shoals and is thought to have substantial oil and gas reserves beneath its waters.[31]

Vast amounts of maritime trade pass through the South China Sea, with one estimate of the value of the trade varying between a range of USD 5.3 trillion to USD 3.4 trillion[32] and the lower end of this range still representing more than 20% of global trade. In terms of volume, in its 2017 catalogue of statistics the United Nations Conference on Trade and Development (UNCTAD) has assessed that more than 61% of seaborne trade is delivered through Asian ports with over 10 billion tons of goods being loaded and unloaded in Asian ports.[33] Much of this trade passes through the South China Sea.

The major claimants to the maritime features located in the South China Sea are China,[34] the Philippines, Vietnam, Malaysia, Indonesia and Brunei. The claims made by each are complicated and involve differing interpretations of historical events[35] as well as differing understanding of the impact of the LOSC. The main areas that are in dispute are waters to the north-east of the Natuna Islands,[36] the area around the Scarborough Shoal,[37] maritime features and water

---

30  *South China Sea* arbitration, note 3, [3].

31  Lowy Institute, 'South China Sea', (n.d.), available online at www.lowyinstitute.org/issues/south-china-sea; see also 'Why is the South China Sea Contentious?', *BBC News*, 12 July 2016, available online at www.bbc.com/news/world-asia-pacific-13748349

32  Centre for Strategic and International Studies, 'How Much Trade Transits the South China Sea?' (n.d.), available online at https://chinapower.csis.org/much-trade-transits-south-china-sea/

33  Development Statistics and Information Branch (UNCTAD), 'World Seaborne Trade' (n.d.), available online at http://stats.unctad.org/handbook/MaritimeTransport/WorldSeaborneTrade.html

34  The claims over maritime feature in the South China Sea that have been made by the People's Republic of China (PRC) are mirrored by those made by the Republic of China (Taiwan). A succinct summary of the history and nature of these claims can be found on the website of the Peace Palace Library, 'South China Sea Territorial Disputes' (n.d.), www.peacepalacelibrary.nl/library-special/south-china-sea-territorial-disputes/

35  For an overview of the history of the South China Sea disputes, see T.L.A. Nguyen, 'Origins of the South China Sea Dispute' in J. Huang and A. Billo (eds). *Territorial Disputes in the South China Sea: Navigating Rough Waters*, Basingstoke: Palgrave Macmillan, 2015, pp. 15–35.

36  Indonesia and PRC/ROC.

37  Philippines and PRC/ROC.

in the vicinity of the Spratly Islands,[38] and the Paracel Islands.[39] There are also some disputed areas in the Gulf of Thailand.[40] Prospects for any quick resolution of most of the claims to the disputed areas seem remote in the immediate future, with limited prospect for the main claimants seeking external assistance or recourse to a body such as the International Court of Justice to resolve the matter.

These inter-state disputes provide a complicated geo-political environment in which maritime security issues are situated. In an attempt to limit the potential for escalation of tension over these disputed areas, ASEAN and the People's Republic of China signed a Declaration on the Conduct of Parties in the South China Sea (DOC)[41] in 2002 which adopts 'self-restraint' as the key principle governing inter-action in the region. However, agreement on the 'code of conduct in the South China Sea' (COC) that is envisaged under clause 10 of the DOC has not progressed with any speed. The latest development with the COC at the time of writing was the reported agreement on a single negotiating text in August 2018, but with 'significant hurdles' remaining to be overcome before any document is produced for finalisation.[42]

### 1.6.2 Navigational rights and freedoms

One key law of the sea issue that regularly arises in South East Asia is the difference in interpretation that States apply to the navigational (and overflight) rights and freedoms that exist under the LOSC and customary international law. These interpretative differences mainly affect military vessels and aircraft but there is also scope for interference with commercial navigation, especially in areas that coastal States may consider are proximate to sensitive security installations. Freedom of navigation in the territorial sea by warships and other government vessels is perhaps the most contentious issue, given that the territorial sea by definition is '… an adjacent belt of sea …'[43] in and over which the coastal State has sovereignty subject only to the right of innocent passage.[44] Notwithstanding that the LOSC stipulates that '… ships of all States … enjoy the right of innocent passage through the territorial sea'[45] there are a number of South East Asian States that interpret this right in a restrictive manner. Similarly, there are some States that

---

38 Vietnam, PRC/ROC, Brunei, Malaysia and the Philippines.
39 Vietnam and PRC/ROC.
40 Malaysia, Cambodia, Thailand and Vietnam.
41 '2002 Declaration on the Conduct of Parties in the South China Sea', 4 November 2002, available online at https://asean.org/?static_post=declaration-on-the-conduct-of-parties-in-the-south-china-sea-2
42 See CSIS Expert Working Group, 'A Blueprint for a South China Sea Code of Conduct', *Asia Maritime Transparency Initiative*, 11 October 2018, available online at https://amti.csis.org/blueprint-for-south-china-sea-code-of-conduct/
43 LOSC, Article 2(2).
44 LOSC, Article 17.
45 Ibid.

## 12 Donald R. Rothwell and David Letts

purport to restrict the manner in which military vessels and aircraft can operate in the EEZ by seeking to impose prior notification or prior permission requirements. Reactions from South East Asian States towards vessels and aircraft that are navigating or flying in a manner that the coastal State finds objectionable have varied considerably, but this is complimented by an equally varied range of responses taken by the States of the vessels or aircraft involved.

### 1.6.3 Maritime security

The term 'maritime security' has not yet acquired a definition that resonates with wide acceptance.[46] Some of the individual components that make up the elements of maritime security include such diverse, but inter-related issues as the law of the sea; maritime regulation and enforcement activities; dealing with piracy and armed robbery at sea; maritime terrorism; illegal fishing and harvesting of marine living resources; trafficking in drugs and other illegal products; irregular movement of people at sea; and using the sea to distribute arms and weapons of mass destruction. This list seems formidable, and perhaps explains why such a focus on maritime security has emerged in South East Asian waters where most, if not all, of the maritime security concerns identified above have emerged. Methods of dealing with maritime security issues in South East Asia have varied widely. One conspicuous absentee from forthright action in South East Asia has been the United Nations Security Council which has been noticeably quiet in terms of issuing any Resolution that addresses a South East Asian maritime security concern. The Security Council has, however, used its powers under Chapter VII of the Charter of the United Nations[47] to deal with maritime security issues in other regions of the world.[48] Within South East Asia, the role played by ASEAN to address maritime security concerns has also varied and each of the States that comprise the region have adopted similarly diverse practices.[49]

### 1.6.4 Living resource management

The waters of South East Asia have throughout history been a focal point for fishing and its marine living resources play a significant role in the region's

---

46 J. Kraska and R. Pedrozo, *International Maritime Security Law*, Leiden: Martinus Nijhoff, 2013, p. 1.

47 *Charter of the United Nations*, 26 June 1945, 1 UNTS XVI [hereafter *UN Charter*].

48 For example, the Security Council has passed numerous Resolutions dealing with piracy and armed robbery off the coast of Somalia from 2008 to 2018, including UNSCR 2442 (2018) of 6 November 2018. Also, notwithstanding the security concerns posed by the movement of Rohingya refugees from Myanmar, the Security Council has failed to pass any resolution dealing with this issue as at 1 January 2019. This provides a contrast to action authorized by the Security Council to deal with the situation off the coast of Libya in 'Resolution 2437 (2018)', 3 October 2018, UN Doc. S/RES/2437 (2018).

49 See generally on the role of ASEAN and maritime security in the region: H. Nasu et al., *The Legal Authority of ASEAN as a Security Institution*, Cambridge: Cambridge University Press, 2019.

culture, economy and society. However, as noted in 2018 by the Asia Foundation, while the region 'has one of the most diverse marine ecosystems in the world ... overfishing and destructive fishing threaten its sustained existence' and currently 64% of the region's fisheries resource base is at a medium to high risk of overfishing.[50] The latest United Nations Secretary-General's annual Report on *Oceans and the law of the sea* devotes a substantial part to steps that have been, and might yet be, taken to achieve an equitable balance between achieving economic growth and protecting the marine environment.[51] Although the Secretary-General's Report is not directly targeted at South East Asia, many of the principles addressed in the Report have direct relevance for the region. For example, the Report notes that '... urgent action is needed to improve the management of global fish stocks ...'.[52] The sustainable harvesting of marine living resources from South East Asian waters not only has food security but also regional security implications.[53] However, commercial pressures for increasing supplies of fish and other marine products have the potential to irreversibly deplete the stock to levels from which recovery might be quite impossible. The impact of a substantial decline in fish stocks on local populations would also be profound.

### 1.6.5 Oil and gas development

South East Asia does not play a prominent role in world oil and gas production in terms of total amounts produced; nor does the region hold significant oil and gas reserves when compared with world totals.[54] For example, the International Energy Agency (IEA) reports that China is one of the largest producers of crude oil in the world (2017 provisional data), but China is also the largest net importer of crude oil (2016 data).[55] No South East Asian State appears in the IEA's list of the largest net exporters of crude oil.[56] The picture is a little different in the case of natural gas where China and Australia both appear in the IEA's list of the largest producers (2017 provisional data) of natural gas.[57] Australia, Indonesia and Malaysia are all in the IEA's list of the world's largest net exporters of natural gas (2017 provisional data), while Japan, China and Korea all appear in the list

---

50 K.J. DeRidder and S. Nindang, 'Southeast Asia's Fisheries Near Collapse from Overfishing', *The Asia Foundation*, 28 March, 2018, available online at https://asiafoundation org/2018/03/28/southeast-asias-fisheries-near-collapse-overfishing/

51 United Nations General Assembly, 'Oceans and the Law of the Sea: Report of the Secretary-General', 5 September 2018, UN Doc. A/73/, pp. 8–12 [hereafter 'Report of the Secretary-General'].

52 Ibid., p. 10.

53 See generally Nasu, note 49, especially Chapter 7 'Food Security'.

54 World Energy Council, Energy Resources, South East Asia & Pacific, see details available online at www.worldenergy.org/data/resources/region/southeast-asia-pacific/oil/

55 International Energy Agency, 'Key World Energy Statistics', (n.d.) see details available online at www.iea.org/statistics/kwes/supply/

56 Ibid.

57 Ibid.

14 *Donald R. Rothwell and David Letts*

for largest net importers of natural gas (2017 provisional data).[58] Nevertheless, a number of countries in South East Asia and the Pacific[59] do have substantial oil and gas reserves, with most of these reserves located in the wider region's maritime environs. However, the World Energy Council notes that these reserves are declining and further oil and gas exploration and development will be required if oil and gas production is to be maintained at meaningful levels. The prospect of such development easily occurring in South East Asia is one of the issues that will be explored later in this book.

### 1.6.6 *Marine environmental protection/security*

Protection of the marine environment is a key issue throughout the world. In this respect, the United Nations Secretary-General has noted that

> the state of the oceans has never been more perilous. Despite the efforts of the international community to protect and preserve the maritime environment and its living marine resources, the health of the oceans continues to be adversely affected by major pressures simultaneously, such as pollution, including marine debris, especially plastics, physical degradation, increased overfishing, alien invasive species and underwater noise and the impacts of climate change and ocean acidification.[60]

Each of these issues identified by the Secretary-General has relevance to the maritime regions of South East Asia, where the semi-enclosed nature of the South China Sea, coupled with the deleterious effects of high-density shipping activity, magnifies the impact of damage to the marine environment.[61] Threats to fish stocks, as well as the ecosystems that support these stocks, have the potential to raise tension at local, national and regional levels with consequent impact on the overall security situation in South East Asia. Some steps have been taken by States in the region, and ASEAN, to deal with the damage caused to the marine environment, and aspects of environmental damage received careful consideration in the *South China Sea* arbitration.[62] Some of these steps will be analysed later in this book, but at this stage it is sufficient to recognise that the marine environment in South East Asia is in a delicate state and concerted effort will be needed to protect and preserve the resources that are contained within the region's maritime spaces.

---

58 Ibid.
59 World Energy Council, note 54; Vietnam, Indonesia, Malaysia, Australia, Brunei Darussalam, Timor-Leste and Thailand have the largest known oil reserves in South East Asia and the Pacific region.
60 Report of the Secretary-General, note 51, p. 2.
61 Ibid., p. 12.
62 See generally the discussion in T. Stephens, 'The Collateral Damage from China's 'Great Wall of Sand': The Environmental Dimensions of the *South China Sea Case*', (2016) 34 *Australian Year Book of International Law* pp. 41–52.

### 1.6.7 Dispute settlement

Settlement of disputes among States by peaceful means has been an essential aspect of international law since the adoption of the UN Charter in 1945. States are required to '... refrain in their international relations from the threat or use of force against the territorial integrity or political independence of any state, or in any other manner inconsistent with the Purposes of the United Nations'.[63] The LOSC reflects this prohibition, in slightly different terms, by requiring States Parties to 'settle disputes by peaceful means'[64] and adhere to 'peaceful uses of the seas'.[65] However, the LOSC goes further by providing a mechanism whereby States can deal with disputes pursuant to Part XV of the Convention. One of the significant aspects of the LOSC dispute settlement regime is that it entails a wide variety of choice available to States when looking for a mechanism to settle a dispute arising under the Convention. States may choose any peaceful means of settling a dispute that they wish to adopt[66] or conciliation,[67] or they may seek the assistance of the ICJ, ITLOS, an arbitral tribunal or a special arbitral tribunal.[68] This variety of choice is one of the unique features of the LOSC and States in the region have made use of a majority of these dispute settlement options, although with varying levels of satisfaction and compliance with the outcomes.

## 1.7 Conclusion

This brief introductory chapter has identified a number of the issues that will be addressed in further detail in the chapters that follow. It can be seen from the initial assessment that the South East Asian maritime domain is a complex environment that contains many diverse influences that underscore the law of the sea challenges faced by the region.

---

63 *UN Charter*, Article 2(4).
64 LOSC, Article 279.
65 LOSC, Article 301.
66 LOSC, Article 280.
67 LOSC, Article 284.
68 LOSC, Article 287. Procedures for establishing an arbitral tribunal, and special arbitral tribunal, are contained, respectively, in LOSC Annex VII and VIII.

# 2 Maritime claims in South East Asia

*Donald R. Rothwell*

## 2.1 Introduction

Partly due to the geography of South East Asia where, excepting India and Timor-Leste, all States share both land and maritime boundaries with the South China Sea at its centre, the region has a very strong maritime focus. As a result, the law of the sea has historically and certainly in the twenty-first century been of great significance to the region. Notwithstanding the importance for South East Asian states of the Association of South East Asian Nations (ASEAN), which other than China, India, Taiwan and Timor-Leste includes all regional States as members, and which provides a strong sense of regional purpose and unity, the States within the region all have their own distinctive national interests, which are also reflected in their maritime interests.

Partly as a result of these variable circumstances, the region has seen a variety of maritime claims asserted that are based upon the 1982 United Nations Convention on the Law of the Sea (LOSC),[1] but which interpret the LOSC differently. Extending from claims to straight baselines and historic waters, maritime claims throughout South East Asia encompass all those that are permissible under the LOSC. In some instances, claims to a continental shelf beyond 200 nm remain subject to final recommendation by the Commission on the Limits of the Continental Shelf (CLCS). Claims have also been made that sit outside of the LOSC, such as China's 'Nine-Dash Line' claim in the South China Sea that was the subject of consideration in the *South China Sea* arbitration.[2] This chapter considers these issues by commencing with an assessment of one of the most significant aspects of the maritime claims of the region; the claims to archipelagic State status by Indonesia and the Philippines. State practice with respect to historic claims and baselines are assessed, before moving to a consideration of maritime claims.

---

1 United Nations Convention on the Law of the Sea, 10 December 1982, 1833 UNTS 397 [hereafter LOSC].

2 *In the Matter of an Arbitration before An Arbitral Tribunal Constituted Under Annex VII to the 1982 United Nations Convention on the Law of the Sea between The Republic of the Philippines and the People's Republic of China*, PCA Case no 2013–19, Award of 12 July 2016 [hereafter *South China Sea* arbitration].

## 2.2 Archipelagic states

Reflective of the eventual significance that came to be associated with the question of archipelagos during the Third United Nations Conference on the Law of the Sea,[3] the LOSC devotes Part IV to archipelagic States. Part IV contains key definitional provisions concerning the characterisation and identification of archipelagic States, the drawing of archipelagic baselines, the rights and entitlements of archipelagic States, and navigation and overflight within archipelagos. Article 46 of the LOSC defines both an 'archipelagic State' and 'archipelago'. The two definitions are linked, and to understand the former it is first important to comprehend the juridical definition accorded to the term archipelago.[4] This definition, while focussing on the geographic features of an island group, also incorporates additional dimensions. Article 46 (b) provides that an archipelago

> means a group of islands, including parts of islands, interconnecting waters and other natural features which are so closely interrelated that such islands, waters and other natural features form an intrinsic geographical, economic and political entity, or which have historically been regarded as such.

This definition clearly reflects some of the essential elements that emerged in the Indonesian and Philippines' campaign during the 1950s and 1960s for recognition of archipelagic status,[5] with its focus not only upon the land but also the waters of the archipelago, and the notion that the two are 'closely interrelated'. A number of the elements require further elaboration.

The first is that the archipelago include a 'group of islands'. The second is that the definition encompasses 'parts of islands' and as such includes islands that have two or more sovereign States located on their land mass. Examples include Borneo (Brunei/Malaysia/Indonesia), New Guinea (Indonesia/Papua New Guinea) and Timor (Indonesia/Timor-Leste). The third component to note is the inclusion of 'inter-connecting waters and other natural features' within the archipelago. Given the maritime focus, this includes all waters that are between the islands, irrespective of the designation they may have previously had under international law, and other features including atolls, cays, reefs, rocks, shoals and low-tide elevations. Artificial or man-made features are not included. The fourth component is that these features – land in the form of islands, smaller associated maritime features and the waters between them – must be so 'closely interrelated' that together they 'form an intrinsic geographical, economic and political entity, or which have historically been regarded as such'. The connection between the islands comprising the archipelago can therefore be on multiple levels.

---

3 See the discussion in D.R. Rothwell and T. Stephens, *The International Law of the Sea*, 2nd ed., Oxford: Bloomsbury, 2016, pp. 189–191.
4 L.L. Herman, 'The Modern Concept of the Off-Lying Archipelago in International Law', (1985) 23 *Canadian Yearbook of International Law* pp. 172, 179–185.
5 See the discussion in J.G. Butcher and R.E. Elson, *Sovereignty and the Sea: How Indonesia became an Archipelagic State*, Singapore: NUS Press, 2017; D.P. O'Connell, 'Mid-Ocean Archipelagos in International Law', (1971) 45 *British Yearbook of International Law* pp. 1, 26–27, 33–36, 40.

18    *Donald R. Rothwell*

Article 46 (a) defines an 'archipelagic State' as a State 'constituted wholly by one or more archipelagos and may include other islands'.[6] There are important geographical limitations associated with this definition. The first self-evidently is that the State must consist of at least one archipelago. The definition is also wide enough to encompass a State comprised of more than one geographic archipelago. The second is that the State can only be comprised of islands, and as such no part of the archipelagic State can include parts of a continental land mass. This is significant in South East Asia as it means that Malaysia cannot assert an archipelagic State claim even though a significant part of the State is comprised of islands, as that part of Malaysia located on the Malay Peninsula is part of continental Asia. A similar constraint exists with respect to India's Andaman and Nicobar Islands in the Andaman Sea. The third element is that the archipelago is comprised of features that are islands. To that end, the LOSC Article 121 definition of an island, including that it is naturally formed, is important. An archipelagic State cannot therefore be formed by the creation of artificial islands clustered around a naturally formed island.

At the time that the LOSC was concluded in 1982, Indonesia, the Philippines and a number of additional States such as Antigua and Barbuda, Cape Verde, Fiji and the Solomon Islands had taken steps towards achieving archipelagic status, either by way of enacting new laws providing a framework for archipelagic claims including the recognition of archipelagic waters, or by actually having declared baselines and proclaimed archipelagic waters.[7] A total of 22 States have sought to proclaim themselves as archipelagic States, with Indonesia and the Philippines the two largest and most significant archipelagic States. Beyond South East Asia, there are seven other archipelagic States in the Asia Pacific.[8]

Indonesia and the Philippines enjoy certain entitlements as archipelagic States under the LOSC, the most significant of which is the ability to draw straight archipelagic baselines so as to effectively enclose the islands of the archipelago, and the ability to exercise sovereignty over the waters of the archipelago known as 'archipelagic waters'. While it is commonly accepted that both Indonesia and the Philippines have drawn their archipelagic baselines consistently with Article 47 of the LOSC, there has been a need to make adjustments over time. Indonesia was faced with the need to adjust its archipelagic baselines following the independence of East Timor/Timor-Leste in 2002, which had the effect of limiting Indonesia's ability to continue previously drawn archipelagic baselines which extended to and from that territory, and also following the 2002 decision of the

---

6  LOSC, Article 46 (a).

7  For a review of that practice, see B. Kwiatkowska, 'The Archipelagic Regime in Practice—Making or Breaking International Law?', (1991) 6 *International Journal of Estuarine and Coastal Law* p. 1.

8  Those archipelagic States include Fiji, Kiribati, Marshall Islands, Papua New Guinea, Solomon Islands, Tuvalu and Vanuatu; the remaining archipelagic States are Antigua and Barbuda, The Bahamas, Cape Verde, Comoros, Dominican Republic, Grenada, Jamaica, Maldives, Mauritius, Saint Vincent and the Grenadines, Sao Tome and Principe, Seychelles and Trinidad and Tobago.

*Maritime claims in South East Asia* 19

ICJ in the *Sovereignty over Pulau Ligitan and Pulau Sipadan* case between Indonesia and Malaysia which clarified sovereignty over certain disputed islands.[9] These adjustments to Indonesia's Article 47 straight archipelagic baselines, while locally significant, did not impair Indonesia's capacity to retain its status as an archipelagic State consistent with the LOSC. Other notable elements within Article 47 include that straight archipelagic baselines are not to cut off high seas or EEZ access from the territorial sea of another State,[10] which is relevant for Indonesia where some of the islands that are part of its archipelagic claim share land boundaries with Brunei, Malaysia, Papua New Guinea and Timor-Leste.

Given the significance associated with their claims, and the size of their archipelagos, the state practice of Indonesia and the Philippines is closely observed. In 2009, Indonesia deposited with the United Nations a revised set of geographical coordinates of points consistent with Article 47 (9) of the LOSC. These coordinates are based on Government Regulation No 38 (2002) as amended by Government Regulation No 27 (2008).[11] A total of 192 baselines are identified in the Indonesian coordinates, which include a mix of normal and archipelagic baselines. The baselines range in length from as little as 0.51–122.75 nm with a total length of 6,920 nm enclosing an area of 4,986,325 square kilometres of which the water area is 3,081,756 square kilometres making for a water to land ratio of 1.61 to 1.[12] In 2009, the Philippines also deposited with the United Nations a set of geographical coordinates of points, which for the first time proclaimed archipelagic baselines consistent with the LOSC.[13] These baselines were based upon Republic Act No 9522 which had, in turn, amended earlier Philippine legislation.[14] The Philippines identified a total of 101 basepoints and baselines which range in length from 0.08 nm to 122.83 nm with a total length of 2,808 nm enclosing 887,909 square kilometres of which the water area is 589,739 square kilometres making for a water to land ratio of 1.98 to 1.[15] Republic Act No 9522 also reaffirms in section 3 that the Philippines 'has dominion, sovereignty and jurisdiction over all portions of the national territory as defined in the Constitution'. A separate declaration is also made in Republic Act No 9522 with respect to the islands that form the Kalayaan Island Group and Scarborough Shoal, which are determined as a 'Regime of Islands' for the

---

9  *Sovereignty over Pulau Ligitan and Pulau Sipadan (Indonesia/Malaysia)* [2002] ICJ Rep 625.

10  LOSC, Article 47 (5).

11  MZN67.2009 (Maritime Zones Notification) United Nations (25 March 2009), available online at www.un.org/depts/los/LEGISLATIONANDTREATIES/PDFFILES/mzn_s/mzn67.pdf

12  See the analysis in Department of State (USA), *Indonesia: Archipelagic and Other Maritime Claims and Boundaries* (Limits in the Sea No 141), Washington: Department of State, 2014, pp. 2–3.

13  Mary Ann Palma, 'The Philippines as an Archipelagic and Maritime Nation: Interests, Challenges and Perspectives', (2009) *RSIS Working Paper* No 182, pp. 4–5. Under the previous baselines, for example, a baseline across Moro Gulf was 140.05 nm in length.

14  MZN 69.2009 (Maritime Zones Notification) United Nations (21 April 2009), available online at www.un.org/depts/los/LEGISLATIONANDTREATIES/PDFFILES/mzn_s/mzn69.pdf

15  Department of State (USA), *Philippines: Archipelagic and Other Maritime Claims and Boundaries* (Limits in the Sea No 142), Washington: Department of State, 2014, p. 3.

20   *Donald R. Rothwell*

purposes of Article 121 of the LOSC.[16] The Philippines baselines and provisions of Republic Act No 9522 have been protested by China with respect to their contested sovereignty over Huangyan Island, and the islands of the reefs of the Nansha Islands (which the Philippines refer to as the Kalayaan Island Group),[17] which are reflective of ongoing sovereignty tensions over islands within the South China Sea.

In addition to giving Indonesia and the Philippines significant entitlements as archipelagic States to the archipelagic waters that fall on the landward side of the archipelagic baselines, consistent with Article 48 the breadth of the territorial sea, contiguous zone, EEZ and continental shelf claims of these States is measured from the archipelagic baselines. For both States, this is significant as the more generous straight archipelagic baseline system in Article 47 provides a capacity to assert maritime claims from comparatively long baselines drawn to and from the outer islands of the archipelago that would not be permissible under the straight baseline regime that otherwise applies to coastal States. In the case of the Philippines, this is highlighted by its drawing of straight archipelagic baselines from Luzon to the Batan Islands in Luzon Strait, and from Mindanao to and between the islands of the Sulu Archipelago across the Sulu Sea to Palawan which fronts the South China Sea.

## 2.3 Historic claims

Before assessing maritime claims within the context of the LOSC, some comment must be made on the status of historic claims within the region. The LOSC does not expressly address historic claims, other than noting that some coastal States may claim historic bays,[18] and that States may exempt consideration of historic bays and titles from the compulsory dispute settlement procedures under Part XV of the LOSC.[19] This apparent gap in the LOSC, with respect to historic claims, has resulted in much debate as to their status, including whether some historic claims have any ongoing status following conclusion of the Convention. In this respect, it needs to be noted that the LOSC's Preamble makes clear that 'matters not regulated by this Convention continue to be governed by rules and principles of general international law'. There has been a history of a number of historic claims, or equivalent, having been made in South East Asia, and in 2007 Symmons listed claims to historic bays by South East Asian States as including

---

16  Republic Act No 9522 (2009) (Philippines) s. 3.
17  Communication from the Government of China received by the Secretary-General of the United Nations, CML/12/2009 (13 April 2009); which, in turn, promoted a response from Vietnam with respect to China's assertions of sovereignty: Communication from the Government of Vietnam received by the Secretary-General of the United Nations, No 86/HC-2009 (8 May 2009); available online at www.un.org/Depts/los/LEGISLATIONANDTREATIES/STATEFILES/PHL.htm
18  LOSC, Article 10 (6).
19  LOSC, Article 298 (1) (a).

those made by Cambodia ('certain Cambodian waters'), Philippines (the 'treaty limits'), Thailand (Gulf of Thailand, Bight of Bangkok) and Vietnam (Gulf of Tonkin).[20]

The most significant and extensive of the historic claims to waters in South East Asia has been China's 'nine-dash line'. The line appeared in numerous Chinese maps throughout the twentieth century[21] and was referred to in Chinese diplomatic communications with respect to the South China Sea, the most significant of which was a 7 May 2009 Chinese *Note Verbale* to the Secretary-General of the United Nations in response to a joint submission to the CLCS by Malaysia and Vietnam.[22] This *Note Verbale* resulted in objections from Indonesia, Malaysia, the Philippines and Vietnam.[23] The 'nine-dash line' comprises nine dashed lines that run south of the Gulf of Tonkin along the Vietnamese coast, before turning off the coast of Malaysia and Brunei to proceed off the west coast of the Philippines to just south of Taiwan.[24] The legal status of the line was considered by the tribunal in the *South China Sea* arbitration where it was observed that to the tribunal's knowledge 'China has never expressly clarified the nature or scope of its claimed historic rights'.[25] It was noted that the 'nine-dash line' first appeared in official Chinese maps in 1948 as an 11 dash line, and that two dashes drawn in the Gulf of Tonkin were removed in 1953 after which 'the line has appeared consistently in that nine-dash form in official Chinese cartography since that date'.[26]

The tribunal determined that a review of China's position with respect to the 'nine-dash line' indicated China claimed rights to the living and non-living resources within the line, and that apart from any area of territorial sea generated from land features within the area, did not claim any of the waters within the limits of the line to be either territorial sea or internal waters.[27] Upon a review of the LOSC and its relevant provisions, and the characterisation of China's position as one of a claim to historic rights with respect to the living and non-living

---

20 C.R. Symmons, *Historic Waters in the Law of the Sea: A Modern Re-Appraisal*, Leiden: Martinus Nijhoff Publishers, 2007, Appendix.

21 See the historical background outlined in Z. Gao and B.B. Jia, 'The Nine-Dash Line in the South China Sea: History, Status, and Implications', (2013) 107 *American Journal of International Law* pp. 98–124.

22 *Note Verbale* from the Permanent Mission of the People's Republic of China to the United Nations to the Secretary-General of the United Nations, No CML/17/2009 (7 May 2009), available online at http://www.un.org/Depts/los/clcs_new/submissions_files/mysvnm33_09/chn_2009re_mys_vnm_e.pdf

23 See Vietnam (8 May 2009), Malaysia (20 May 2009), Philippines (4 August 2009) and Indonesia (8 July 2010), available online at www.un.org/Depts/los/clcs_new/submissions_files/submission_mysvnm_33_2009.htm

24 L. Fisler Damrosch and B.H. Oxman, 'Agora: The South China Sea Editor's Introduction', (2013) 107 *American Journal of International Law* pp. 95, 96 where a map appears depicting the 'nine-dash line'.

25 *South China Sea* arbitration, note 2, [180].

26 Ibid., [181].

27 Ibid., [214].

## 22    *Donald R. Rothwell*

resources of the South China Sea, the tribunal was of the view that the LOSC did not preserve or protect historic rights and agreements to 'the extent of any incompatibility' and that China's claims were 'not compatible' with the EEZ and continental shelf.[28] The view taken by the tribunal was therefore that

> China's claims to historic rights, or other sovereign rights or jurisdiction, with respect to the maritime areas of the South China Sea encompassed by the relevant part of the 'nine-dash line' are contrary to the Convention and without lawful effect to the extent that they exceed the geographic and substantive limits of China's maritime entitlements under the Convention.[29]

Accordingly, given this unanimous finding by the tribunal, it is clear that the 'nine-dash line' has no basis in the law of the sea and does not confer any historic maritime rights in favour of China. This is to be distinguished from any historic rights to islands in the South China Sea, which is a matter over which the tribunal did not possess jurisdiction.[30]

This view of the status of the 'nine-dash line' is not one that is shared by Chinese scholars. Gao and Jia writing in 2013 observed that

> The reasonable proposition ... is that the nine-dash line, after sixty years of evolution, has become synonymous with a claim of sovereignty over the island groups that always belonged to China and with an additional Chinese claim of historical rights of fishing, navigation, and other marine activities (including the exploration and exploitation of resources, mineral or otherwise) on the islands and in the adjacent waters.[31]

The Chinese Society of International Law in a major study published in 2018 have also concluded that the tribunal erred in its findings that China enjoyed no historic rights in the South China Sea,[32] and have observed that

> The Tribunal acted *ultra vires* and mishandled China's historic rights in the South China Sea. These errors deprive its decisions of any binding force. China's historic rights in the South China Sea are well established in general international law and naturally will continue to exist.[33]

In a 2014 analysis of the Chinese claim, the US Department of State observed

---

28  Ibid., [246].
29  Ibid., [278].
30  Ibid., [266–267].
31  Goa and Jia, note 21, p. 108.
32  Chinese Society of International Law, 'The South China Sea Arbitration Awards: A Critical Study', (2018) 17 *Chinese Journal of International Law* pp. 207, 449–472.
33  Ibid., p. 472.

*Maritime claims in South East Asia* 23

unless China clarifies that the dashed-line claim reflects only a claim to islands within that line and any maritime zones that are generated from those land features in accordance with the international law of the sea, as reflected in the LOS Convention, its dashed-line claim does not accord with the international law of the sea.[34]

Following the *South China Sea* arbitration China has not abandoned its 'nine-dash line' claim, and other than rejecting the tribunal's decision has not sought to officially give any greater clarity to the actual extent of the claim that it asserts in the South China Sea. Finally, while Taiwan sought to make submissions to the Arbitral tribunal,[35] since the *South China Sea* award it has remained silent on the status of the 'nine-dash line' and whether it seeks to make any historic claim to the South China Sea.[36]

With respect to the other historic claims in South East Asia, in 1982 Cambodia and Vietnam made a joint claim to parts of the Gulf of Thailand as historic waters,[37] which was subject to protest by the governments of Singapore, Thailand and the United States.[38] Also in 1982, Vietnam made an historic waters claim to parts of the Gulf of Tonkin, which was subject to protest from France, Thailand and the United States.[39] However, in 2000, Vietnam and China reached agreement on a maritime boundary in the Gulf of Tonkin which delimited the territorial sea, continental shelf and the EEZ,[40] and in reaching this agreement Vietnam appears to have discarded its historic waters claim in the Gulf of Tonkin.[41] The subsequent publication in 2004 of a map depicting the China/Vietnam Gulf of Tonkin maritime boundary would appear to remove any doubt that in reaching agreement with respect to the maritime boundary

34 Department of State (USA), *China: Maritime Claims in the South China Sea* (Limits in the Sea No 143), Washington: Department of State, 2014, p. 24.

35 *South China Sea* arbitration, note 2, [142].

36 C. Hurng-Yu, 'The Phantom of the U-shaped Line: A Challenge for Southeast Asia's Security', 9 May 2018, *Asia Maritime Transparency Initiative*, available online at amti.csis.org/phantom-u-shaped-line/; who notes that in the early 1990s notwithstanding some support from scholars for Taiwan to assert an historic waters claim within the 'U-shaped (nine-dash) line', Taiwan's Legislative Yuan rejected such an enlarged concept … because it was inconsistent with the UNCLOS [LOSC] definition of historic waters'.

37 *Agreement on Historic Waters of Vietnam and Kampuchea*, 7 July 1982, reproduced in J.I. Charney and L.M. Alexander, *International Maritime Boundaries*, 3rd vol., Dordrecht: Martinus Nijhoff, 1998, p. 2357; as discussed in J.A. Roach and R.W. Smith, *Excessive Maritime Claims*, 3rd ed., Leiden: Martinus Nijhoff, 2012, p. 42.

38 Roach and Smith, note 37, p. 42, n.17.

39 Ibid., pp. 53–54, n.36.

40 *Agreement on the Delimitation of the Territorial Sea, Exclusive Economic Zones and Continental Shelves in the Beibu Gulf [Gulf of Tonkin] between the People's Republic of China and the Socialist Republic of Vietnam*, 25 December 2000, 2336 UNTS 179.

41 Z. Keyuan, 'The Sino-Vietnamese Agreement on Maritime Boundary Delimitation in the Gulf of Tonkin', (2005) 36 *Ocean Development and International Law* pp. 13, 15.

24   *Donald R. Rothwell*

Vietnam did not insist upon recognition of its previous historic waters claim.[42] The other historic maritime claims in South East Asia are made by the Philippines and encompass waters that would otherwise be considered part of the territorial sea and are assessed in more detail below.

## 2.4  Baselines

The territorial sea baseline is the point from which all maritime claims are asserted as all maritime claims are measured from that point. The normal baseline, as provided for by LOSC Article 5, is the 'low-water line' along the coast, and while there is some margin of appreciation for coastal States when determining that limit, it is rare that the interpretation of Article 5 has a significant impact on the normal baseline with consequences flowing to the outer limits of maritime claims.[43] Coastal States have much greater flexibility when the territorial sea baseline is a straight baseline (Article 7), a bay closing/straight baseline (Article 10) or an archipelagic baseline (Article 47).[44] The effect of these types of baselines is that the coastal State is able to rely upon an artificially drawn line that may be some distance from the natural coastline as the starting point from which not only the territorial sea is delimited but from which all the other maritime zones are also measured. The end result is that the maritime claims of the coastal State may extend much further from the coastline than may otherwise be the case, thereby creating significant benefits with respect to sovereignty within the territorial sea and sovereign rights and jurisdiction in the EEZ and continental shelf. It needs to also be recalled that the coastal State enjoys absolute sovereignty over the internal waters that are on the landward side of the baseline, subject to the right of innocent passage in only very limited circumstances,[45] or in the case of an archipelagic State complete sovereignty over archipelagic waters subject to certain rights of navigation.[46]

In South East Asia, the most significant issues regarding baselines have involved the interpretation of Article 7, especially with respect to matters relating to whether a coastline is deeply indented or cut into, whether there exists a

---

42  'List of Geographical Coordinates of Points, as Specified in the Agreement between the People's Republic of China and the Socialist Republic of Viet Nam on the Delimitation of the Territorial Sea, the Exclusive Economic Zone and Continental Shelf in Beibu Bay/Gulf of Tonkin, which was signed by the Two Countries on 25 December 2000' (2005) 56 *Law of the Sea Bulletin* p. 138.

43  For a particular discussion regarding the significance of the normal baseline in the context of the South China Sea, see C. Schofield, 'Trouble over the Starting Line: State Practice Concerning Baselines in the South China Sea' in S. Wu, M. Valencia, and N. Hong (eds), *UN Convention on the Law of the Sea and the South China Sea*, Farnham (UK): Ashgate, 2015, pp. 123, 126–131.

44  For general observations regarding these baselines, see C. Schofield, 'Departures from the Coast: Trends in the Application of Territorial Sea Baselines under the Law of the Sea Convention' in D. Freestone (ed), *The 1982 Law of the Sea Convention at 30: Successes, Challenges and New Agendas*, Leiden: Martinus Nijoff, 2013, p. 49.

45  LOSC, Article 8 (2).

46  Those being the right of innocent passage, and archipelagic sea lanes passage: LOSC, Articles 52 and 53.

Maritime claims in South East Asia   25

fringe of islands along the coast and the length of straight baselines.[47] Straight baselines drawn by Myanmar, China, Thailand and Vietnam have been subject to protest from both neighbouring States and from States outside of the region including by France, Germany, the United States and the European Union (EU) on behalf of its members.[48] Thailand, for example, has drawn a series of 16 straight baselines across the Gulf of Thailand which connect small maritime features including islands and an offshore archipelago in a manner which does not follow the general direction of the coast.[49] Setting aside the drawing of straight baselines to and from maritime features whose sovereignty is contested, one of the major grounds for these diplomatic protests has been concerns over the excessive length of certain straight baselines. In this respect, it needs to be observed that Article 7, unlike Article 47 with respect to straight archipe-lagic baselines, does not identify any length constraints on straight baselines. Nevertheless, there are constraints on how Article 7 straight baselines can be drawn and the International Court of Justice in *Qatar v Bahrain* observed that the provision was to be 'applied restrictively'.[50] China, Malaysia, Myanmar and Vietnam have all drawn straight baselines in excess of 100 nm, with Vietnam's straight baselines system comprising five lines in excess of 100 nm of which two are as long as 161 nm. The effect of this claim is to enclose Vietnam's mainland south of the Gulf of Tonkin by way of a number of small islands that are distant from the coast.[51] Schofield has noted that 'Vietnam claims an area of approx-imately 27,000 nm$^2$ (93,000 km$^2$) as internal waters, landward of its straight baselines'.[52] The United States, which along with China, France, Germany and Thailand lodged diplomatic protests over this straight baseline system, observed that 'there is no basis in international law for the system of straight baselines [declared by Vietnam]'.[53]

Other than Indonesia and the Philippines, no other State in the region has asserted archipelagic claims, however in the *South China Sea* arbitration the tri-bunal commented on whether archipelagic baselines could be draw in the vicin-ity of the Spratly Islands. Responding to a potential claim by China to be able to draw straight archipelagic baselines around the Spratly Islands, the tribunal made clear that China 'is constituted principally by territory on the mainland

---

47 These matters have most recently been considered by the International Law Association, see C.G. Lathrop, J.A. Roach, and D.R. Rothwell (eds), 'Baselines under the International Law of the Sea: Reports of the International Law Association Committee on Baselines under the Inter-national Law of the Sea', (2018) 2.1–2 *The Law of the Sea* pp. 1–173.
48 See the data attached in Table 2.1.
49 S. Kopela, *Dependent Archipelagos in the Law of the Sea*, Leiden: Martinus Nijhoff, 2013, pp. 82–83, Figure 7 – p. 269.
50 *Case Concerning Maritime Delimitation and Territorial Questions Between Qatar and Bahrain* (Qatar v. Bahrain) [2001] ICJ Rep 40 [212].
51 Department of State (USA), *Straight Baselines: Vietnam* (Limits in the Sea No. 99), Washington: Department of State, 1983, p. 5.
52 Schofield, note 44, pp. 137–138.
53 Roach and Smith, note 37, p. 99; see also D. Thanh Hai, 'Vietnam's evolving claims' in L. Buszynski and C.B. Roberts (eds), *The South China Sea Dispute: Political, Legal and Regional Perspectives*, New York: Routledge, 2015, pp. 83, 85.

## 26 Donald R. Rothwell

of Asia and cannot meet the definition of an archipelagic State'.[54] The tribunal then went on to observe that even the Philippines could not draw straight archipelagic baselines around the Spratly Islands due to the requirement of Article 47 that the baselines enclose the main islands and meet the area of water to area of land ratio, observing that the 'ratio of water to land in the Spratly Islands would greatly exceed 9:1 under any conceivable system of baselines'.[55] Based on these assessments, at least for the *South China Sea* arbitration tribunal, only archipelagic States are able to draw straight archipelagic baselines, and there is limited scope in Article 7 to draw straight baselines around groups or clusters of islands located within the South China Sea.

In this respect, the practice of Taiwan is notable. Taiwan is not a party to the LOSC; however, its practice in the law of the sea generally seeks to adhere to the Convention. In 1999, a Taiwan Executive Yuan established a series of straight baselines around the coast of its main island, and its offshore islands.[56] A total of 18 straight baselines have been drawn around the main island, out of a total of 22 segments, of which the most complex include segments T8–T13 that encloses the Pescadores in Taiwan Strait,[57] which given the location of those islands raises issues as to whether these islands could be considered to be an Article 7 (1) fringe of islands. In this respect, the straight baselines around the main island have the appearance of archipelagic baselines, and while Taiwan has not formally declared itself to be an archipelagic State, it certainly has many of the characteristics of such a State including that it is a territory formed by islands and archipelagos. Taiwan has also declared straight baselines around Pratas Reef, which lies 230 miles to the southwest of the main island, and a normal baseline around Macclesfield Bank which lies a further 280 miles to the southwest.[58] The United States is of the view that 'Taiwan uses straight baselines in many areas where the normal baseline ... should be used'.[59] However, given the distinctive status of Taiwan and the unusual diplomatic relations it has with its South East Asian neighbours and other States, Taiwan's baselines have not been the subject of protest in the same manner as may be the case if it was a recognised State.

## 2.5 LOSC maritime claims

The practice of South East Asian States with respect to maritime claims is framed against the LOSC, and the additional entitlements enjoyed by the two archipelagic States of being able to assert their maritime claims from the outer limits

---

54 *South China Sea* arbitration, note 2, [573].

55 Ibid., [574].

56 Decree No. Tai 88 Nei Tze #06161, Executive Yuan Gazette, vol 5. No. 6, Feb. 10, 1999 at pp. 36–37.

57 Department of State (USA), *Taiwan's Maritime Claims* (Limits in the Seas No. 127), Washington: Department of State, 2005, p. 12.

58 Ibid., p. 14.

59 Ibid.

*Maritime claims in South East Asia* 27

of their straight archipelagic baselines. In that regard, the region is distinctive as waters that would otherwise be within the Indonesian or Philippines EEZ and continental shelf are archipelagic waters over which extensive sovereign entitlements are enjoyed. Another dynamic of the region's maritime claims is the somewhat unique situation of Singapore, given its proximity to Malaysia across the narrow Strait of Johor and Indonesia across the Straits of Malacca and Singapore, such that its maritime domain is significantly constrained by these neighbouring States. The maritime claims of all States within the region will now be reviewed. Given its unique status, Taiwan will be considered separately.

All States, other the Philippines, claim a 12 nautical mile territorial sea and consistent with respective national laws these territorial sea claims are asserted from baselines, which include the normal baseline, straight baselines or archipelagic baselines. The significant exception is the Philippines which through a combination of its colonial history and treaties, and its practice since independence in 1946 has to date not properly articulated the extent of its territorial sea claims. Whilst under Spanish colonial occupation, a three nautical mile territorial sea extended from the low-water line around the islands comprising the archipelago.[60] Following the Philippines being ceded to the United States in 1898 under the Treaty of Peace, an irregular rectangle line was declared which encompassed all of the main islands of the archipelago, other than the most southern islands of Mindanao.[61] The 1900 Treaty of Washington supplemented the 1898 Treaty of Paris, and gave further clarity to the islands ceded to the United States,[62] however during the American colonial period the national territory, effectively the territorial sea, was only considered to extend for three nautical miles.[63] Following independence, and in tandem with the Philippines' claims for recognition as an archipelago, Republic Act No. 3046 (1961) was adopted which declared the baselines which surrounded the Philippines and provided that the waters between the baselines and the Treaty of Paris limits were to be territorial waters.[64] The reach of Republic Act No. 3046 was subsequently extended in 1978 by Presidential Decree No. 1596 and 1599 which encompassed the Kalayaan Island Group and a Philippines Exclusive Economic Zone, and the nominal reach of the territorial sea was also extended to encompass the modified sovereign limits of the Philippines.[65] During the LOSC negotiations, the Philippines appreciated that its position with respect to the territorial sea extending from its baselines to the 1898 Treaty of Paris limits created some issues with

---

60 J.L. Batongbacal, 'The Maritime Territories and Jurisdictions of The Philippines and the United Nations Convention on the Law of the Sea', (2001) 76 *Philippine Law Journal* pp. 123, 125.

61 *Treaty of Peace between the United States of America and the Kingdom of Spain*, 10 December 1898, 187 CTS 100, Article III.

62 *Treaty Between the Kingdom of Spain and the United States of America for Cession of Outlying Islands of the Philippines*, 7 November 1900, 189 CTS 108.

63 Batongbacal, note 60, p. 126.

64 Ibid., p. 136.

65 Ibid., pp. 139–143.

## 28   *Donald R. Rothwell*

respect to the conformity of the Philippines maritime claims and the 12 nautical mile territorial sea as provided for under the LOSC.[66] The Philippines nevertheless proceeded to sign and ratify the Convention, albeit with a declaration that generated objections from a number of other States.[67]

The Philippine position remains as outlined above and has been subject to protest[68]; however, efforts have been made to bring clarity to the law and in 2014 'An Act to Define the Maritime Zones of the Republic of the Philippines' passed through the House of Representatives, and made its way before the Senate in 2016. The Act would provide that

> The territorial sea of the Philippines shall refer to the belt of sea measured twelve (12) nautical miles from the baselines or from the low-water line, as the case may be. The Philippines shall exercise sovereignty over its territorial sea and the airspace over it as well as its seabed and subsoil in accordance with the UNCLOS and other existing laws and treaties.[69]

Characterising the Philippines claim to the waters on the seaward side of its baselines to the Treaty of Paris outer limits is challenging as the Philippines historically has not used the term 'territorial sea' to describe these waters, which Filipino scholars refer to as more akin to 'historic waters'[70] and one that is 'unique in international law'.[71] Notwithstanding the Philippines position regarding the status of these waters, as navigational rights and freedoms within the waters of the archipelago, including to the Treaty of Paris limits, have continued to be enjoyed by the international community disputes over the status of this claim have been neutralised.

With respect to the contiguous zone, six States make such a claim.[72] The fact that not all South East Asian States assert a contiguous zone is broadly consistent with global state practice where not all eligible coastal States assert such a claim.[73] All coastal States within the region claim an EEZ, other than Singapore, which to date has not asserted such a claim partly due to its distinctive

---

66  See 'Statement of the Head of the Philippine Delegation', reproduced in ibid., pp. 150–152.

67  Objections to the Philippines Declaration were made by Australia (3 August 1988); Belarus (24 June 1985); Bulgaria (17 September 1985); Russian Federation (25 February 1985); Ukraine (8 July 1985); see United Nations Treaty Collection: Chapter XXI Law of the Sea 6. United Nations Convention on the Law of the Sea, available online at http://treaties.un.org/

68  Roach and Smith, note 37, pp. 146–147 noting protests lodged by the United States in 1985 and 1986.

69  An Act to Define the Maritime Zones of the Republic of the Philippines, Seventeenth Congress of the Republic of the Philippines, Senate S. No. 93 (June 30, 2016).

70  L. Bautista, 'Philippine Territorial Boundaries: Internal Tensions, Colonial Baggage, Ambivalent Conformity', (2011) 16 *JATI – Journal of Southeast Asian Studies* pp. 35, 36.

71  J.W. Dellapenna, 'The Philippines Territorial Water Claim in International Law', (1970) 5 *Journal of Law and Economic Development* pp. 45, 48.

72  Cambodia, China, Myanmar, Thailand, Timor-Leste and Vietnam.

73  Rothwell and Stephens, note 3, pp. 82–83.

geographical circumstances and the immediate need to determine maritime boundaries with its neighbours if it were to do so. Singapore, does, nevertheless reserve to itself the right to make such a claim and it may be possible to do so if in the future its circumstances were to change.[74] Continental Shelf claims have been made by all South East Asian States other than Singapore and Thailand, and of these claims all are asserted to a minimum of 200 miles or the edge of the continental margin other than in the case of Cambodia whose claim extends to 200 miles. Submissions have been made to the CLCS by China (East China Sea), India (including the Western Andaman sector), Indonesia, Malaysia (jointly with Vietnam), Myanmar, the Philippines and Vietnam (singly and jointly with Malaysia). Of these submissions, the Indonesian and Philippines submissions have been the subject of CLCS recommendations consistent with Article 76 (8), and the Philippines has progressed to formally proclaim a continental shelf beyond 200 miles in the Benham Rise region.[75] Preliminary information with respect to a CLCS submission has also been made by Brunei. Following objections and determinations as to the existence of a dispute in the case of the submissions made by Myanmar (dispute with Bangladesh),[76] Malaysia/Vietnam (disputes with China and the Philippines)[77] and Vietnam (disputes with China and the Philippines),[78] deliberation by the CLCS of those Article 76 submissions have been deferred.

With respect to Taiwan, in 1998, it enacted two laws providing for the territorial sea and contiguous zone, and the EEZ and continental shelf, respectively.[79] The view of the United States and scholars is that Taiwan's maritime claims are consistent with the LOSC and customary international law.[80] However, Taiwan's continental shelf does not have a precise outer limit

---

74 The United Nations Division for Ocean Affairs and the Law of the Sea in 'Table of claims to maritime jurisdiction (as at 15 July 2011)', available online at www.un.org/depts/los/LEGISLATIONANDTREATIES/PDFFILES/table_summary_of_claims.pdf notes that Singapore has stated that 'Should the limits of its territorial sea or Exclusive Economic Zone overlap with claims of neighbouring countries, Singapore will negotiate with those countries with a view to arriving at agreed delimitations in accordance with international law'.

75 See M.Z.N.88.2012.LOS (Maritime Zone Notification) (17 July 2012), available online at www. un.org/depts/los/LEGISLATIONANDTREATIES/PDFFILES/mzn_s/mzn88ef.pdf; and M.Z.N.88.2012.LOS Add.1 of 20 March 2018 (Maritime Zone Notification), available online at http://www.un.org/depts/los/LEGISLATIONANDTREATIES/PDFFILES/mzn_s/mzn 88LOS_ef.pdf

76 CLCS, 'Statement by the Chairman of the Commission on the Limits of the Continental Shelf on the progress of work in the Commission' CLCS 64, 1 October 2009, [40], available online at documents-dds-ny.un.org/doc/UNDOC/GEN/N09/536/21/PDF/N0953621.pdf? OpenElement

77 Ibid., [92].

78 Ibid., [106].

79 Law of the Territorial Sea and Contiguous Zone of the Republic of China of 1998, as reproduced in Department of State (USA), *Taiwan's Maritime Claim*, note 57, pp. 20–24; and Law on the Exclusive Economic Zone and the Continental Shelf of the Republic of China of 1998; as reproduced in ibid., pp. 26–33.

80 Department of State (USA), *Taiwan's Maritime Claims*, note 57, p. 2; Hurng-Yu, note 36.

30 *Donald R. Rothwell*

with the Law on the Exclusive Economic Zone and the Continental Shelf 1998 stating that the continental shelf 'is the submarine area that extends beyond its territorial sea through the natural prolongation of its land territory to the outer edges of the continental margin',[81] which uses part of the text of Article 76 of the LOSC without specifying the minimum extent of 200 miles or the potential outer limits of the continental shelf consistent with Article 76 (4). Given that Taiwan is precluded from making a submission to the CLCS, its outer continental shelf entitlements are reliant upon an acceptance that the Article 76 definition of the continental shelf will gain acceptance as reflecting customary international law.

## 2.6 Concluding remarks

In many respects, the maritime claims of South East Asian states are not exceptional. While the region could be characterised as being representative of the whole gamut of maritime claims and entitlements that are permitted under the LOSC, the presence of the two largest archipelagic States in the international community, and the impact they have upon maritime claims and entitlements within the region, does make South East Asia exceptional. In another sense, the region is also atypical because some of the maritime claims and entitlements that have been made by coastal States are the subject of significant protest by neighbouring States and also more generally the international community. In this respect, the *South China Sea* arbitration looms large, including the response by some members of the international community to asserted maritime claims in the South China Sea.

South East Asian maritime claims are dominated by the archipelagic claims of Indonesia and the Philippines because of the sheer size of their archipelagos and associated straight archipelagic baselines. While both States have sought to ensure that their straight archipelagic baselines are in compliance with the LOSC, issues have arisen with respect to other aspects of Part IV of the LOSC, especially regarding compliance with the navigational regime of archipelagic sea lanes passage. However, over time, contentious issues have gradually been resolved through state practice and with the assistance of the International Maritime Organization (IMO).[82] While Indonesia and the Philippines are *de jure* archipelagic States, issues have arisen with respect to *de facto* archipelagic claims. In the *South China Sea* arbitration, a question arose as to whether China was an archipelagic State as the Philippines had raised issues with respect to China's use of straight baselines that could have been assimilated with LOSC Article

---

81 Exclusive Economic Zone and the Continental Shelf 1998 (Republic of China), Article 2.

82 See the discussion in Rothwell and Stephens, note 3, pp. 268–276 especially with respect to the role of the IMO in the designation of archipelagic sea lanes; see also Robin Warner, 'Implementing the Archipelagic Regime in the International Maritime Organization' in D.R. Rothwell and S. Bateman (eds), *Navigational Rights and Freedoms and the New Law of the Sea*, The Hague: Martinus Nijhoff, 2000, pp. 170–187.

47 archipelagic baselines. The tribunal observed that the use of archipelagic baselines is 'strictly controlled by the Convention' and that their use is limited to archipelagic States,[83] and that as China was principally a mainland Asian State it did not meet the definition of an archipelagic State and accordingly had no entitlement to draw straight archipelagic baselines. This aspect of the *South China Sea* arbitration puts coastal States on notice that the provisions of Part IV of the LOSC with respect to archipelagic claims will be strictly interpreted by international courts and tribunals. However, as Taiwan's practice has also highlighted, some island States have sought to draw Article 7 straight baselines in a manner that approximates an archipelagic claim. In this regard, a distinction needs to be made between the potential baseline claims of island States in the region and those of continental States.

The historic maritime claims of China and the Philippines have also been contentious. While the tribunal in the *South China Sea* arbitration comprehensively addressed the status of China's 'nine-dash line', given China's official position as to the status of the award and its subsequent actions in which it has not taken any steps respecting that the award is final and binding and modifying its maritime claims in conformity with the award,[84] the status quo remains. Indeed, since 2016, it would appear that as a result of its ongoing South China Sea land reclamation and artificial island building activities that China has sought to further advance its territorial presence within the region. Ambiguity remains, however, as to China's asserted maritime claims and entitlements in the South China Sea. A similar position exists regarding the Philippines' reliance upon the Treaty of Paris limits and whilst this distinctive historical position is well known, there is ambiguity as to the precise level of maritime sovereignty and jurisdiction that the Philippines seeks to assert. Nevertheless, what on paper would appear to be an excessive maritime claim in the context of the LOSC has not proven to be particularly contentious with neighbouring and other maritime States, and there is some prospect that the Philippines will soon move to clarify the extent of its claim to a territorial sea in conformity with the LOSC.

Finally, it can be observed that more traditional LOSC maritime claims within the region are not yet finally settled. Either jointly or individually, India, Malaysia, Vietnam, Myanmar, the Philippines and Indonesia have all made CLCS submissions. Brunei and China have likewise indicated an intention to make a future claim. If, and when, these submissions are reviewed, and recommendations are made, these States will all have an entitlement to assert an

---

83 *South China Sea* arbitration, note 2, [573].

84 See 'Statement of the Ministry of Foreign Affairs of the People's Republic of China on the Award of 12 July 2016 of the Arbitral Tribunal in the South China Sea Arbitration Established at the Request of the Republic of the Philippines' (2016/07/12) reproduced as Annex III in Chinese Society of International Law, note 32, where it is stated: 'the Ministry of Foreign Affairs of the People's Republic of China solemnly declares that the award is null and void and has no binding force. China neither accepts nor recognizes it'.

## 32   *Donald R. Rothwell*

adjusted continental shelf claim which will further impact upon the region's maritime relations. This highlights that maritime claims in South East Asia are dynamic and will continue to evolve for some time (Table 2.1).

*Table 2.1* Maritime Claims in South East Asia

| State | Territorial Sea | Contiguous Zone | EEZ | Continental Shelf | CLCS Submission |
|---|---|---|---|---|---|
| Brunei | 12 | | 200 | CM/200 | PI |
| Cambodia | 12 | 24 | 200 | 200 | |
| China | 12 | 24 | 200 | CM/200 | PI; S #63 – East China Sea |
| India | 12 | 24 | 200 | CM/200 | S #48 |
| Indonesia (AS) | 12 | | 200 | CM/200 | S + Rec #12 |
| Malaysia | 12 | | 200 | CM/200 | S #33 (Joint) |
| Myanmar | 12 | 24 | 200 | CM/200 | S #16 |
| Philippines (AS) | Undefined | | 200 | CM/200 | S + Rec #22 |
| Singapore | 12 | | | | |
| Thailand | 12 | 24 | 200 | | |
| Timor-Leste | 12 | 24 | 200 | CM/200 | |
| Vietnam | 12 | 24 | 200 | CM/200 | S #33 (Joint); S #37 |

**Legend**: AS – Archipelagic State; CM – Continental Margin; PI – Preliminary Information; S # – Submission Number; Rec – Recommendation.

# 3   An incomplete maritime map

## Progress and challenges in the delimitation of maritime boundaries in South East Asia

*Clive Schofield*

## 3.1 Introduction

While the land boundaries of South East Asia are largely well established and stable in character, as reflected by familiar lines on political maps of the region,[1] the equivalent maritime map of South East Asia is profoundly incomplete. The objective of this chapter is to provide a survey of progress as well as challenges in the delimitation of boundaries in maritime South East Asia.

Maritime South East Asia encompasses a series of semi-enclosed seas located between the East Asian continental mainland and islands offshore. This arc of regional and sub-regional seas includes, from west to east, the Andaman Sea, located between India's Andaman and Nicobar Islands and the mainland coasts of Myanmar and Thailand to the east and Indonesia's island of Sumatra to the south. These waters are connected via the Malacca and Singapore Straits to the South China Sea and Gulf of Thailand, framed by the mainland littoral of Indochina to the west and China to the north, and Borneo and the archipelagos of the Philippines and Indonesia to the east and south. To the north lies the East China Sea, with mainland China to the west; the Korean peninsula and Taiwan to the north and south, respectively; and Japan's Ryukyu Island chain to the east. Ocean spaces beyond the East and South East Asian island chains, including the Philippines Sea, Celebes Sea and the Timor and Arafura Seas, are also considered in this survey.

The relatively constrained scope of these semi-enclosed seas and thus the proximity of States to one another, coupled with the broad maritime claims that South East Asian States have advanced, has resulted in numerous potential maritime boundaries, overlapping claims and maritime delimitation disputes. These disputes are caused or compounded by complex coastal geography, including the presence of numerous islands, sovereignty over many of which is subject to dispute. The above-mentioned survey of South East Asian practice in the delimitation of maritime boundaries follows a brief contextual section relating

---

1 The major exceptions to this rule relate to the status of Taiwan and the long-standing but largely dormant claim of the Philippines to what Malaysia regards as its Province of Sabah in northern Borneo.

34  *Clive Schofield*

to the evolution of ocean boundary-making. The chapter seeks to highlight the complexity and diversity of delimitation scenarios and concludes with some considerations on remaining challenges that need to be overcome before the maritime map of South East Asia is completed.

## 3.2 The evolution of ocean boundary-making and South East Asia

The vast majority of South East Asian States are parties to the United Nations Convention on the Law of the Sea (LOSC),[2] which therefore represents the international law applicable to maritime delimitation between South East Asian States. The coastal States involved have been enthusiastic claimants of the full suite of maritime zones provided for under the Convention, notably territorial seas out to 12 nautical miles (nm), exclusive economic zones (EEZs) out to 200 nm and continental shelf rights. These maritime claims are predominantly measured from baselines along the coast, a number of which in the South East Asian context can be considered to be excessive in character.[3] As a result of these maritime claims, coupled with the proximity of South East Asian coastal States to one another, multiple overlapping maritime claims, and thus potential maritime boundaries, have resulted in the region.

Where the maritime claims of neighbouring States overlap, a potential maritime boundary situation exists. Thus, if there is less than 24 nm of opposing coastlines, a potential territorial sea boundary will exist, while if coastal States coastlines are within 400 nm of one another a potential EEZ boundary will arise. In relation to the delimitation of the territorial sea, LOSC Article 15 applies and offers a clear preference for the use of an equidistance or median line. This does not apply, however, if the States concerned agree to the contrary or there exists an 'historic title or other special circumstances' in the area to be delimited which justify a departure from the equidistance line.

Under the 1958 Convention on the Continental Shelf, delimitation was also to be effected by the use of median lines unless, similarly, an agreement to the contrary or 'special circumstances' existed that justified an alternative approach.[4] However, the relevant provisions of LOSC Articles 74 and 83 dealing with delimitation of the continental shelf and EEZ, respectively, merely provide, in identical general terms, that agreements should be reached on the basis of international law in order to achieve 'an equitable solution' with no preferred method of delimitation indicated.

Despite this lack of clear guidance for the delimitation of, particularly, continental shelf and EEZ boundaries under LOSC, it is notable that equidistance

---

2 United Nations Convention on the Law of the Sea, 10 December 1982, 1833 UNTS 397 [hereafter LOSC]. Cambodia is the only South East Asian State which remains a non-party to LOSC; see also discussion in Chapter 1 by Rothwell and Letts and Chapter 9 by Stephens.

3 See discussion by Rothwell in Chapter 2.

4 *Convention on the Continental Shelf,* 29 April 1958, 499 UNTS 311, Article 6.

An incomplete maritime map    35

has found enduring popularity as a method of delimitation in State practice.[5] Furthermore, there has been a distinct shift in recent jurisprudence towards the application of a three-stage approach. This was arguably most clearly articulated in the 2009 Judgement in the *Black Sea Case*[6] between Romania and Ukraine as being, at the first stage, that a provisional delimitation line should be established using geometrically objective methods *unless there are compelling reasons that make this unfeasible* in the particular case'[7]; at the second stage, assessment is to be made as to 'whether there are factors calling for the adjustment or shifting of the provisional equidistance line in order to achieve an equitable result'[8]; and at the third stage, verification of the resulting potential delimitation line is undertaken through what the Court termed a 'disproportionality test'.[9] Subsequent cases involving maritime boundary delimitation have similarly applied this three-stage approach to maritime delimitation. These have included cases before the International Court of Justice (ICJ), the International Tribunal for the Law of the Sea (ITLOS) and before international arbitral tribunals.[10] Efforts towards the delimitation of maritime boundaries in maritime South East Asia should be viewed against the context of this notable evolution in the law of the sea regarding ocean boundary-making.

## 3.3 Progress in maritime boundary delimitation in South East Asia

### 3.3.1 *The Andaman Sea and the Bay of Bengal*

Despite the presence of complex coastal geography characterised by major archipelagos, most notably that of Indonesia, but also the Andaman and Nicobar Islands groups, as well as highly questionable straight baseline claims, the maritime map of the Andaman Sea is largely complete. In the Andaman Sea area, maritime boundary agreements have been reached between Burma

---

5 J.R.V. Prescott and C.H. Schofield, *Maritime Political boundaries of the World*, Leiden: Martinus Nijhoff, 2005, pp. 238–239. See also, L. Legault and B. Hankey, 'Method, Oppositeness and Adjacency, and Proportionality in Maritime Boundary Delimitation' in J.I. Charney and L.M. Alexander (eds), *International Maritime Boundaries*, Vol. I, Dordrecht: Martinus Nijhoff, 1993, pp. 203, 214.

6 *Case Concerning Maritime Delimitation in the Black Sea* (Romania v. Ukraine) [2009] ICJ Rep 61 [hereafter *Black Sea Case*].

7 Ibid., [116] (emphasis added).

8 Ibid., [120]. At this point, the Court cited its earlier Judgement in the *Cameroon/Nigeria Case* in support of its ruling; see *Land and Maritime Boundary between Cameroon and Nigeria* (Cameroon v. Nigeria; Equatorial Guinea intervening) [2002] ICJ Rep 303 [288].

9 Ibid., [122], [210]–[216].

10 See, for example, M.D. Evans, 'Maritime Boundary Delimitation' in D.R. Rothwell et al. (eds), *Oxford Handbook of the Law of the Sea*, Oxford: Oxford University Press, 2015, pp. 254, 259–261.

## 36  Clive Schofield

(Myanmar) and India concerning all maritime zones[11]; between Burma and Thailand relating to the territorial sea, continental shelf and subsequently the EEZ[12]; between India and Indonesia for the continental shelf and more recently the EEZ[13]; between Thailand and both India and Indonesia with regard to delimitation of the continental shelf[14]; and between Malaysia and both Thailand and Indonesia for territorial sea and continental shelf boundaries.[15] Additionally, a number of trilateral agreements have been achieved to finalise the location of the tripoint where the above-mentioned bilateral maritime boundaries converge and meet. These include agreements for the Indonesia-Malaysia-Thailand,[16] India-Indonesia-Thailand[17] and the India-Myanmar-Thailand[18] tripoints (see Figure 3.1).

This near comprehensive network of maritime boundary agreements has been achieved through negotiations and predominantly on the basis of equidistance

---

11  *Agreement between the Socialist Republic of the Union of Burma and the Republic of India on the Delimitation of the Maritime Boundary in the Andaman Sea, in the Coco Channel and the Bay of Bengal*, 23 December 1986, (1988) 27 ILM 1144.

12  *Agreement between the Government of the Socialist Republic of the Union of Burma and the Government of the Kingdom of Thailand on the Delimitation of the Maritime Boundary between the Two Countries in the Andaman Sea*, 25 July 1980, 1276 UNTS 447.

13  *Agreement between the Government of the Republic of India and the Government of the Republic of Indonesia Relating to the Delimitation of the Continental Shelf Boundary between the Two Countries*, 8 August 1974, (1975) LIS 62; *Agreement between the Government of the Republic of India and the Government of the Republic of Indonesia on the Extension of the 1974 Continental Shelf Boundary between the Two Countries in the Andaman Sea and the Indian Ocean*, 14 January 1977, (1981) LIS 93.

14  *Agreement between the Government of the Republic of India and the Government of the Kingdom of Thailand on the Delimitation of Seabed Boundary between the Two Countries in the Andaman Sea*, 22 June 1978, (1981) LIS 93; *Agreement between the Government of the Republic of Indonesia and the Government of the Kingdom of Thailand Relating to the Delimitation of a Continental Shelf Boundary Between the Two Countries in the Northern Part of the Strait of Malacca and in the Andaman Sea*, 17 December 1971, (1978) 81 LIS.

15  *Agreement between the Government of the Republic of Indonesia, the Government of Malaysia and the Government of the Kingdom of Thailand Relating to the Delimitation of the Continental Shelf Boundaries in the Northern Part of the Strait of Malacca*, 21 December 1971, (1978) LIS 81; *Treaty between the Republic of Indonesia and Malaysia on Determination of Boundary Lines of Territorial Waters of the Two Nations at the Strait of Malacca*, 17 March 1970, (1973) LIS 50.

16  *Agreement between the Government of the Republic of Indonesia, the Government of Malaysia and the Government of the Kingdom of Thailand Relating to the Delimitation of the Continental Shelf Boundaries in the Northern Part of the Strait of Malacca*, 21 December 1971, (1978) LIS 81 (hereafter *Indonesia-Malaysia-Thailand Continental Shelf Agreement*).

17  *Agreement between the Government of the Republic of India, the Government of the Republic of Indonesia and the Government of the Kingdom of Thailand Concerning the Determination of the Trijunction Point and the Delimitation of the Related Boundaries of the Three Countries in the Andaman Sea*, 22 June 1978, (1981) LIS 93.

18  *Agreement between the Government of the Union of Myanmar, the Government of the Republic of India and the Government of the Kingdom of Thailand on the Determination of the Trijunction Point between the Three Countries in the Andaman Sea*, 27 October 1993, reprinted in D.A. Colson and R.W. Smith (eds), *International Maritime Boundaries*, Vol. V, Leiden: Martinus Nijhoff, 2005, p. 3782.

An incomplete maritime map  37

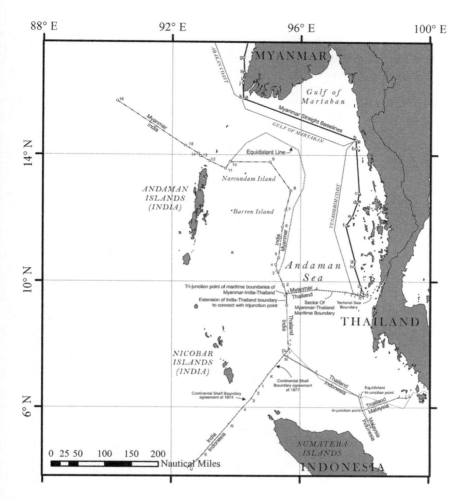

*Figure 3.1* Maritime Delimitation in the Andaman Sea.

lines. In view of the complexity of the coastal geography and apparently excessive baseline claims involved, this progress in maritime delimitation appears at first glance to be surprising. Closer examination suggests that the presence of islands that might otherwise be expected to present a major obstacle to the reaching of a maritime delimitation agreement have tended to be balanced or offset by questionable baseline claims along mainland shorelines. Thus, for example, Myanmar's highly questionable straight baseline in the Gulf of Martoban which is fully 222 nm in length[19] was set against India's small, volcanic Barren and

19 United States Bureau of Intelligence and Research, 'Straight Baselines: Burma', (1970) 14 *International Boundary Study Series A: Limits in the Seas* p. 1.

## 38  Clive Schofield

Narcondam Islands in the agreement between Burma and India.[20] This seems to have offered the opportunity for flexibility and trade-offs in negotiations.[21] Alternatively, the presence of islands on both sides of the area to be delimited allowed for insular features to be accorded weight in the construction of the final maritime boundary line, as was the case in delimitation scenarios between Thailand and both Burma and India.

In order to complete the maritime delimitation picture in this sub-region, a number of agreements relating to continental shelf jurisdiction, notably India-Thailand, Indonesia-Malaysia, Indonesia-Thailand and Malaysia-Thailand, need 'upgrading' to EEZ delimitations. Achieving these EEZ delimitation agreements is, however, complicated by Indonesia's view that seabed and water column boundaries need not be coincident (see below).

The maritime boundary delimitation picture further north in the Bay of Bengal has been clarified considerably in recent years through two international judicial decisions. First, the 14 March 2012 ITLOS ruling on the *Dispute Concerning Delimitation of the Maritime Boundary between Bangladesh and Myanmar in the Bay of Bengal*,[22] and the 7 July 2014 Award of the LOSC Annex VII Arbitral Tribunal *In the Matter of the Bay of Bengal Maritime Boundary Arbitration* between Bangladesh and India.[23] The Tribunals in both of these cases employed the above-mentioned three-stage approach to maritime boundary delimitation. In so doing, they both found reason at the second stage of the process to adjust the provisional delimitation line based on equidistance on the basis of the concavity of Bangladesh's coast relative to that of its immediate neighbours, Myanmar to the east and India to the west.[24] The effect of these rulings is that Bangladesh's maritime entitlements form an elongated 'V' shape in the Bay of Bengal (Figure 3.2).[25]

An additional consequence is the creation of two partially overlapping 'grey areas' of Bangladeshi extended continental shelf areas, overlain by yet to be delimited water column within 200 nm.[26]

---

20  The Gulf of Martoban closing line was given no weight whilst the Barren and Narcondam islands were awarded partial effect; see J.I. Charney and L.M. Alexander (eds), *International Maritime Boundaries*, Vol. II, Dordrecht: Martinus Nijhoff, 1993, p. 1332.

21  It has been noted that the small, isolated and largely uninhabited nature of Barren and Narcondam islands may well have been a factor in the delimitation negotiations and that while Burma's controversial straight baselines may have been set aside, Burma could nonetheless argue that its coastline on the Bay of Martoban is distinctly concave and, moreover, that Burma had a significant advantage in terms of the ratio of relative coastal lengths; see ibid., pp. 1333–1335.

22  *Delimitation of the Maritime Boundary between Bangladesh and Myanmar in the Bay of Bengal* (Bangladesh/Myanmar) (2012) 51 ILM 844 [hereafter *Bangladesh-Myanmar Case*]; see also, C.H. Schofield, A. Telesetsky and S. Lee, 'A Tribunal Navigating Complex Waters: Implications of the *Bay of Bengal Case*', (2013) 44 *Ocean Development and International Law* p. 363.

23  *In the Matter of the Bay of Bengal Maritime Boundary Arbitration between the People's Republic of Bangladesh and the Republic of India*, PCA Case no. 2010-16, Award of 7 July 2014 [hereafter *Bangladesh-India Case*].

24  See *Bangladesh-Myanmar Case*, note 22, [293]–[297], [329]–[331].

25  *Bangladesh-India Case*, note 23, [400]–[421], [478].

26  *Bangladesh-Myanmar Case*, note 22, [463]–[476]; *Bangladesh-India Case*, note 23, [503]–[508].

*An incomplete maritime map* 39

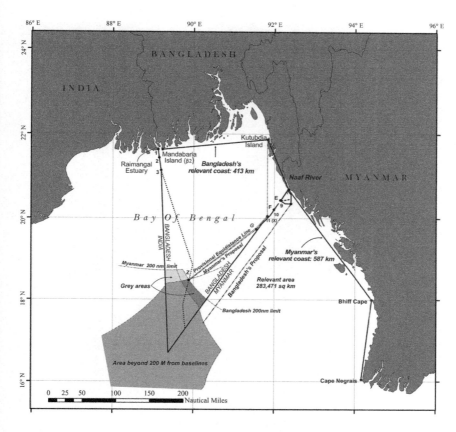

*Figure 3.2* Maritime Delimitation in the Bay of Bengal.

### 3.3.2 *Malacca and Singapore Straits*

Indonesia and Malaysia concluded a territorial sea agreement in 1970[27] and a continental shelf boundary agreement on 21 December 1971.[28] The latter agreement defines a boundary line through much of the Malacca Strait (see Figure 3.3).

---

27 *Treaty between the Republic of Indonesia and Malaysia on Determination of Boundary Lines of Territorial Waters of the Two Nations at the Strait of Malacca*, 17 March 1970, (1973) LIS 50 [hereafter *Indonesia-Malaysia Territorial Sea Agreement*].
28 *Indonesia-Malaysia-Thailand Continental Shelf Agreement*, note 16; see also *Agreement between the Government of Malaysia and the Government of the Republic of Indonesia on the Delimitation of the Continental Shelf between the Two Countries*, 27 October 1969, (1970) LIS 1 [hereafter *Indonesia-Malaysia Continental Shelf Agreement*]; see also, United States Bureau of Intelligence and Research, 'Territorial Sea Boundary Indonesia-Malaysia', (1970) 50 *International Boundary Study Series A: Limits in the Seas* p. 1.

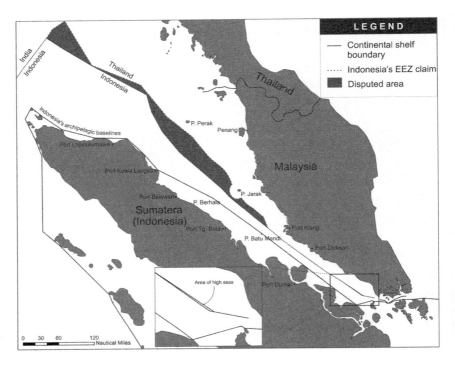

*Figure 3.3* Maritime Delimitation in the Malacca Strait.

Although the agreement referred to equidistance as a basis for delimitation,[29] in practice the boundary line is closer to the Indonesian than to the Malaysian coast. This favourable outcome for Malaysia may be linked to Indonesia's desire at the time of the negotiation for support for the then controversial concept of archipelagic status and archipelagic baselines to enclose mid-ocean archipelagos.[30] In the context of Indonesia-Malaysia delimitation negotiations, Malaysia countered Indonesia's use of archipelagic baselines by applying the straight baselines system to enclose all its islands off the coast of the western Malay Peninsula.[31] If Malaysia's straight baselines were discounted, Indonesia would have gained substantially more continental shelf than under the terms of their

---

29 Ibid., United States Bureau of Intelligence and Research, p. 7.
30 The then controversial nature of Indonesia's initial 1960 archipelagic baselines designation is illustrated by the fact that they were subject to protest by the United States on the grounds that it had not 'recognized the so-called 'archipelagic principle' as an accepted principle of international law', See, United States Bureau of Intelligence and Research, 'Straight Baselines: Indonesia', (1971) 35 *International Boundary Study Series A: Limits in the Seas* p. 9.
31 The Malaysian Directorate of National Mapping issued an official map, *Peta Menunjukkan Sempadan Perairan dan Pelantar Benua Malaysia* or 'Map Showing the Territorial Waters and Continental Shelf Boundaries of Malaysia', often referred to as the *Peta Baru* [new map] on 21 December 1979. Although no baselines are shown on these maps, the fact that in certain areas

*An incomplete maritime map*  41

continental shelf agreement.[32] More recently, on 1 May 2007, Malaysia enacted the Baselines of Maritime Zones Act 2006.[33] This legislation is, however, enabling in character and it does not include any geographical coordinates relating to a system of straight baselines.[34]

In 1996, Malaysia unilaterally declared that it considered the continental shelf boundaries in the north Malacca Strait concluded between Indonesia and Malaysia to represent the boundary for the EEZ as well.[35] While Indonesia apparently accepted Malaysia's use of straight baselines as a basis for the delimitation of the continental shelf in 1969, Indonesia has refused to recognise the use of these straight baselines to delimit the water column in the area, resulting in an area of overlapping claims to water column jurisdiction in the central Malacca Strait.[36]

As noted above, in the southern part of the Malacca Strait where the opposite coasts of Indonesia and Malaysia are within 24 nm of one another, these two States have delimited a boundary agreement for their territorial sea.[37] This territorial sea boundary coincides with the southern part of the continental shelf delimitation line for most of its length. The exception is in the extreme southern part of the Malacca Strait where the two States' territorial sea boundaries diverge from one another, creating a small triangular area of high seas between them.[38]

---

the outer limit of the Malaysian territorial sea claim is marked with straight lines indicates that Malaysia has constructed a system of straight baselines.

32 See *Indonesia-Malaysia Continental Shelf Agreement*. Prescott observed that if a strict line of equidistance was drawn in this sector, Indonesia would gain about 1,000 nm$^2$ of continental shelf; see J.R.V. Prescott, 'Indonesia's Maritime Claims and Outstanding Delimitation Problems', (1995–1996) *Boundary and Security Bulletin*, p. 94.

33 V.L. Forbes, 'The Territorial Sea Datum of Malaysia', (2007) 14 *MIMA Bulletin* pp. 3, 7–8.

34 Some of Malaysia's straight baselines, those relating to Sarawak and Sabah Provinces on the island of Borneo are, however, illustrated on a map included in Malaysia's joint submission to the UN Commission on the Limits of the Continental Shelf (CLCS) with Vietnam for extended continental shelf rights in the South China Sea. See Malaysia and Socialist Republic of Viet Nam, Joint Submission to the Commission on the Limits of the Continental Shelf, Executive Summary, 6 May 2009, available online at www.un.org/Depts/los/clcs_new/submissions_files/submission_mysvnm_33_2009.htm, [hereafter 'Malaysia-Vietnam Joint Submission'].

35 Upon its ratification of the LOSC, Malaysia declared that if the maritime area is less than 200 nm from baselines, the boundary for the EEZ shall be the same line with the boundary of continental shelf; see *Malaysian Declaration Upon Ratification of the Convention of the Law of the Sea 1982*, 14 October 1996, available online at www.un.org/depts/los/convention_agreements/convention_declarations.htm#Malaysia%20Upon%20ratification

36 Indonesia's unilateral maritime claims or 'forward position' regarding its unresolved maritime boundaries are illustrated on its official maps; see for example, 'Peta Negara Kesatuan Republik Indonesia [Map of the Unitary State of the Republic of Indonesia]', Badan Informasi Geospasial [Agency for Geospatial Information], Cibinong, 2017 [hereafter Map of Indonesia, 2017]. See also, L. Bernard and C.H. Schofield, 'Separate Lines: Challenges and Opportunities of Differentiated Seabed and Water Column Boundaries' in M.H. Nordquist and J.N. Moore (eds), *International Marine Economy: Law and Policy*, Leiden: Martinus Nijhoff, 2017, pp. 282, 313–315.

37 *Indonesia-Malaysia Territorial Sea Agreement*.

38 Ibid.

42  Clive Schofield

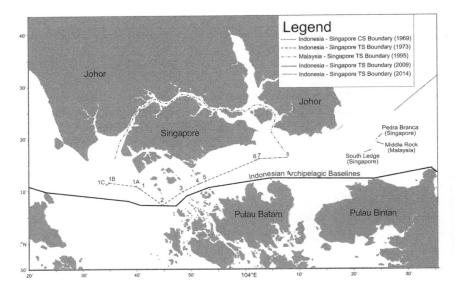

*Figure 3.4* Maritime Delimitation in the Singapore Strait.

In the Johor Strait, lying between Malaysia and Singapore, a dividing line has been in place since as early as 1927 and more recently a boundary agreement between these neighbours in 1995.[39] Meanwhile, in the Singapore Strait, Indonesia and Singapore have concluded a series of territorial sea boundary agreements, first in 1973 in respect of the central portion of the two States area to be delimited,[40] then a western extension signed in 2009[41] and a further agreement on an eastern extension reached in 2014 (see Figure 3.4).[42]

This piecemeal progress in territorial sea delimitation between Indonesia and Singapore provides an interesting example of how a maritime boundary issue

39 *Agreement between the Government of Malaysia and the Government of the Republic of Singapore to Delimit Precisely the Territorial Waters Boundary in Accordance with the Straits Settlement and Johore Territorial Waters Agreement 1927*, 7 August 1995, reprinted in J.J. Charney and L.M. Alexander (eds), *International Maritime Boundaries*, Vol. III, The Hague: Martinus Nijhoff, 1988, p. 2351.
40 *Agreement Stipulating the Territorial Sea Boundary Lines between Indonesia and the Republic of Singapore in the Strait of Singapore*, 25 March 1973, (1974) LIS 60; see also, United States Bureau of Intelligence and Research, 'Territorial Sea Boundary: Indonesia-Singapore', (1974) 60 *International Boundary Study Series A: Limits in the Seas* p. 1.
41 *Treaty between the Republic of Indonesia and the Republic of Singapore relating to the Delimitation of the Territorial Seas of the Two Countries in the Western Part of the Strait of Singapore*, 10 March 2009, reprinted in C. Lathrop, *International Maritime Boundaries*, Vol. VII, Dordrecht: Brill, 2016, p. 4823.
42 *Treaty between the Republic of Singapore and the Republic of Indonesia relating to the Delimitation of the Territorial Seas of the Two Countries in the Eastern Part of the Strait of Singapore*, 3 September 2014, reprinted in ibid., p. 4835.

*An incomplete maritime map*  43

may be divided or sliced up and solved one sector at a time rather than considered as a whole. This approach may have been rendered more palatable to these States due to close proximity of the coastlines concerned and thus the restricted maritime spaces to be divided between them, thus limiting the stakes.

One notable aspect of these agreements relates to Singapore's normal baselines, coincident with the low-water line along the coast. Since the first Indonesia-Singapore territorial sea boundary agreement was concluded in 1973, Singapore's coastline and thus normal baseline has changed considerably and advanced seaward as a consequence of extensive land reclamation projects. With respect to the 2009 and 2014 agreements, the parties agreed that the alterations to Singapore's baselines as a result of its reclamation along its coasts would have no impact on the position of the maritime delimitation line.[43]

Further east in the Strait of Singapore, Indonesia and Malaysia are yet to delimit their territorial seas. A complex trilateral maritime delimitation scenario also exists between Indonesia, Malaysia and Singapore at the eastern end of the Singapore Straits and into the extreme south west of the South China Sea. Malaysia and Singapore's case before the ICJ[44] removed a major obstacle to maritime delimitation in that the Court resolved the parties' sovereignty dispute over insular features located at the eastern end of the Singapore Strait. In particular, the ICJ ruled that sovereignty over Pedra Branca/Pulau Batu Puteh rests with Singapore and sovereignty over Middle Rocks rests with Malaysia.[45] Sovereignty over South Ledge, a low-tide elevation (LTE) located to the south of Middle Rocks, was not specifically determined by the Court.[46] However, this creates a unique maritime delimitation scenario where a very small and uninhabited (save for government personnel) island belonging to one State (Singapore) is located between the mainland (Malaysia) and a larger island (Indonesia) all in close proximity to one another and well within their overlapping 12 nm territorial sea

---

43 Ibid., pp. 4817–4818, 4830–4831.

44 *Sovereignty over Pedra Branca/Pulau Batu Puteh, Middle Rocks and South Ledge* (Malaysia v. Singapore) [2008] ICJ Rep 12. As the nearest above high-tide feature to South Ledge is Middle Rocks, Malaysia is likely to argue that South Ledge falls within its territorial sea. See, R. Beckman and C.H. Schofield, 'Moving Beyond Disputes over Island Sovereignty: ICJ Decision Sets Stage for Maritime Boundary Delimitation in the Singapore Strait', (2009) 40 *Ocean Development and International Law* pp. 1, 22.

45 *Sovereignty over Pedra Branca/Pulau Batu Puteh, Middle Rocks and South Ledge* (Malaysia v. Singapore) [2008] ICJ Rep 12, [300]. The island was referred to as 'Pedra Branca' by Singapore and 'Pulau Batu Puteh' by Malaysia. As the Court determined that sovereignty rested with Singapore the feature will hereafter be referred to as 'Pedra Branca'.

46 *Sovereignty over Pedra Branca/Pulau Batu Puteh, Middle Rocks and South Ledge* (Malaysia v. Singapore) [2008] ICJ Rep 12 [295]–[297], [300]; the court instead found that sovereignty over South Ledge 'belongs to the State in the territorial waters of which it is located', The Court pointed out that international law is not clear on whether low-tide elevations can be considered territory from the viewpoint of acquisition of sovereignty and referred back to its ruling in the Qatar/Bahrain Case; see *Case concerning Maritime Delimitation and Territorial Questions between Qatar and Bahrain* (Qatar v. Bahrain) [2001] ICJ Rep 40, [205]–[206].

## 44   Clive Schofield

claims.[47] It can be anticipated that Indonesia and Malaysia are likely to argue that the role of Pedra Branca constitutes a 'special circumstance' under Article 15, justifying a departure from the median line.[48] In this context, restricted 3 or 6 nm enclaving or semi-enclaving may offer a solution.[49]

### 3.3.3 South China Sea

The South China Sea is arguably best known as an arena of potential maritime conflicts and an area hosting intractable maritime and sovereignty disputes, especially relating to islands. Nonetheless, some incremental progress has been achieved in terms of maritime boundary delimitation towards the margins of this large semi-enclosed sea. For example, the above-mentioned Indonesia and Malaysia boundary agreement of 1969, delimited not only the two States' continental shelf rights in the Malacca Strait but also provided for two lateral delimitation lines in the south-western part of the South China Sea.[50] While the western segment between peninsular Malaysia and, principally, Indonesia's Natuna Islands group, is an equidistance boundary line, the eastern segment between Malaysia's Sarawak Province on the island of Borneo and the Natuna Islands is an adjusted equidistance boundary line favouring Malaysia.[51] Again, it is understood that Indonesia accepted an outcome to Malaysia's advantage in return for its support of Indonesia's archipelagic State concept.[52] Negotiations between Indonesia and Vietnam to, essentially, bridge the gap between these two lateral Indonesia-Malaysia continental shelf boundaries were initiated in 1972. However, agreement was not forthcoming until 2003.[53]

Although continental shelf boundaries have been agreed between Indonesia, Malaysia and Vietnam in the south-western part of the South China Sea, agreement on water column boundaries has yet to be reached. In an analogous fashion to the situation in the Malacca Straits, Indonesia has claimed water column jurisdiction beyond the agreed continental shelf boundary lines, that is, to the north of its continental shelf boundary with Vietnam, and to the east of its continental shelf boundary with Malaysia (see Figure 3.5).[54]

---

47  Pedra Branca is located 7.7 nm from the Malaysian coast, 7.6 nm from the Indonesia island of Bintan and 0.6 nm from Middle Rocks. See, Beckman and Schofield, note 44, p. 19.

48  Ibid., p. 21.

49  Ibid., p. 23.

50  *Indonesia-Malaysia Continental Shelf Agreement.*

51  'Indonesia – Malaysia (Continental Shelf)' in Charney and Alexander, note 5, p. 1021; Bernard and Schofield, note 36, p. 315.

52  Bernard and Schofield, note 36, p. 316.

53  *Agreement between the Government of the Socialist Republic of Vietnam and the Government of the Republic of Indonesia concerning the delimitation of the Continental Shelf Boundary,* 26 June 2003, reprinted in D.A. Colson and R.W. Smith (eds), *International Maritime Boundaries,* Vol. VI, Leiden: Martinus Nijhoff, 2011, p. 4301. See also, Bernard and Schofield, note 36, p. 3156.

54  See, for example, Map of Indonesia, 2017, note 36.

*An incomplete maritime map* 45

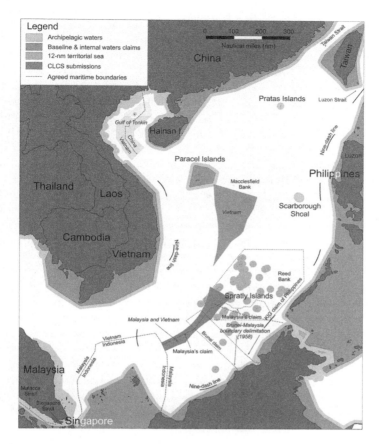

*Figure 3.5* Maritime Claims and Boundaries in the South China Sea.

Indonesia appears to be of the view that seabed and water column boundaries need not coincide, something which reflects Indonesia's experience with Australia in the Timor Sea (see below), but which runs counter to the general preference in State practice and jurisprudence towards the use of 'single', all-purpose maritime boundaries coincident for both the continental shelf and EEZ.[55]

Additionally, China and Vietnam reached agreement in 2000 on maritime boundary delimitation through the Gulf of Tonkin (Vietnam)/Beibu Gulf (China) in conjunction with the creation of multiple zones straddling the boundary line relating to joint fishing activities.[56] Furthermore, Brunei and Malaysia

---

55 Bernard and Schofield, note 36, p. 283.
56 *Agreement on the Delimitation of the Territorial Sea, Exclusive Economic Zones and Continental Shelves in the Beibu Gulf [Gulf of Tonkin] between the People's Republic of China and the Socialist Republic of Vietnam*, 25 December 2000, 2336 UNTS 179; see also N.H. Thao, 'Maritime Delimitation and Fishery Cooperation in the Tonkin Gulf', (2005) 36 *Ocean Development and International Law*, p. 25.

## 46 Clive Schofield

inherited territorial sea boundaries from the United Kingdom[57] and also appear to have clarified their maritime boundary issues through a 16 March 2009 Exchange of Letters (see Figure 3.5).[58]

The fundamental dispute, or disputes, between the South China Sea littoral States that prevent maritime delimitation from progressing in the South China Sea relates to sovereignty over islands and island groups. In particular, these include the Paracel Islands in the north-west, Pratas Island in the north, Scarborough Reef (or Shoal) in the north-east and the Spratly Islands in the southern part of the South China Sea (see Figure 3.5).[59] Without resolution on the core question of sovereignty over the disputed insular features of the South China Sea, progress towards maritime boundary delimitation remains profoundly compromised. A further dimension to the South China Sea disputes relates to the status of insular features. That is, whether they should be classified as islands capable of generating EEZ and continental shelf rights, 'rocks' within the meaning of LOSC Article 121(3) incapable of doing so, LTEs, or wholly and permanently submerged components of the sea floor. The status of insular features is important from a maritime delimitation perspective because this impacts on their capacity to generate maritime entitlements and therefore whether overlapping maritime zones exist that require the delimitation of a maritime boundary. The potential role of insular features as basepoints influencing the course of a maritime delimitation line will likewise be directly impacted by their status.

The Award of the Arbitral Tribunal in the *South China Sea* case between the Philippines and China, delivered on 12 July 2016,[60] was not directly concerned with either questions of sovereignty over islands or maritime delimitation in the South China Sea. However, the tribunal sought to assess some of the maritime claims of the parties, especially those of China, as well as clarify ambiguities in the law of the sea. Consequently, its findings are potentially relevant to the

---

57 The territorial sea boundaries between Brunei and Malaysia were defined in 1958 out to the 100 fathom isobath through two British Orders in Council See Charney and Alexander, note 5, p. 924.

58 See I. Storey, 'Brunei's Contested Sea Border with China', in B. Elleman, S. Kotkin and C.H. Schofield (eds), *Beijing's Power and China's Borders*, Armonk: M.E. Sharpe, 2013, pp. 36, 39–41. It is also notable that Brunei's submission of preliminary information to the CLCS further states that maritime boundaries between Brunei and Malaysia have been delimited by virtue of the 1958 Orders in Council and 'an Exchange of Letters dated 16 March 2009' which served to delimit territorial sea, EEZ and continental shelf rights 'to a distance of 200 nautical miles'; see 'Brunei-Darussalam's Preliminary Submission concerning the Outer Limits of Its Continental Shelf', 12 May 2009, available online at www.un.org/Depts/los/clcs_new/commission_preliminary.htm

59 See C.H. Schofield, 'Adrift on Complex Waters: Geographical, Geopolitical and Legal Dimensions to the South China Sea Disputes' in L. Buszynski and C. Roberts (eds), *The South China Sea and Australia's Regional Security Environment*, London: Routledge, 2014, pp. 24, 25–26.

60 *In the Matter of an Arbitration before an Arbitral Tribunal Constituted under Annex VII to the 1982 United Nations Convention on the Law of the Sea between The Republic of the Philippines and the People's Republic of China*, PCA Case no. 2013-19, Award of 12 July 2016 (hereafter *South China Sea* arbitration).

## An incomplete maritime map   47

delimitation of maritime boundaries both within and beyond the South China Sea. The word 'potentially' is used here since, strictly speaking, the Award of the tribunal is only binding on the two parties to the case, and because China has consistently rejected both the jurisdiction of the tribunal to hear the case and its subsequent Award.[61]

The Arbitral Tribunal determined that any historic rights to resources in the waters within China's apparent claim to areas within the so-called Nine-Dash line were superseded where such claims are incompatible with the maritime zones set out under LOSC.[62] Further, the tribunal found all of the Spratly Islands to be 'rocks' within the meaning of LOSC, Article 121(3) which are therefore not able to generate maritime claims beyond a 12 nm territorial sea.[63] Should they be implemented, these aspects of the Award would serve to significantly reduce the scope of the maritime areas of the South China Sea. Under this scenario, instead of encompassing the entirety of the waters within the Nine-Dash line,[64] overlapping maritime claims would be essentially restricted to 12 nm pockets of water around the disputed islands.[65]

Moreover, implementation of the Award would mean that the Philippines, and by extension, Malaysia, Brunei and Indonesia, are able to claim EEZ rights out to 200 nm from their coasts. This would lead to the need for a series of predominantly lateral maritime boundaries between the adjacent mainland or main island territories of the South China Sea littoral States coupled with territorial sea boundaries between proximate islands in the Spratly Islands archipelago should sovereignty over these features ultimately be determined to belong to more than one of the claimant States and the islands concerned be proximate enough to one another. Additionally, the ruling creates, or confirms the existence of, a pocket of high seas in the central part of the South China Sea.[66] The Award also has potential implications for maritime delimitation scenarios beyond the South

---

61  China has stated that both of the Tribunal's awards are 'null and void' and lack 'no binding force'; see Ministry of Foreign Affairs of the People's Republic of China. 'Statement of the Ministry of Foreign Affairs on the Award on Jurisdiction and Admissibility of the South China Sea Arbitration by the Arbitral Tribunal Established at the Request of the Republic of the Philippines', 30 October 2015, available online at www.fmprc.gov.cn/mfa_eng/zxxx_662805/t1310474.shtml;'Statement of the Ministry of Foreign Affairs on the Award of 12 July 2016 of the Arbitral Tribunal Established at the Request of the Republic of the Philippines, The South China Sea Issue', 12 July 2016, available online at www.fmprc.gov.cn/nanhai/eng/snhwtl-cwj_1/t1379492.htm

62  *South China Sea* arbitration, note 60, [246].

63  Ibid., [646].

64  An area understood to cover approximately 80% of the South China Sea.

65  Additionally, where lateral boundaries have not been agreed, overlapping maritime claims may exist between adjacent States bordering the South China Sea.

66  Certain South China Sea coastal States appear to be already convinced that such a pocket exists, as witnessed by their submissions to the CLCS relating to continental shelf rights seawards of 200 nm from their mainland baselines; see Malaysia-Vietnam Joint Submission, note 34;China, 'Submission to the Commission on the Limits of the Continental Shelf in Respect of Vietnam's Extended Continental Shelf: North Area (VNM-N), Executive Summary', 7 May 2009,

## 48   Clive Schofield

China Sea involving either historic maritime claims or islands, or both. It is, as yet, unclear, however, whether the *South China Sea* arbitration will be followed in future cases involving these factors or in analogous State practice.

Ultimately, as far as maritime boundary delimitation in the South China Sea is concerned, in light of the persistence of competing claims to sovereignty over islands, coupled with China's ongoing rejection of the Arbitral Tribunal's findings, prospects looks bleak. There is perhaps some scope for progress in delimitation efforts where the overlapping claims involved are bilateral rather than multilateral in character. For example, China and Vietnam could extend their existing boundary agreement beyond the confines of the Gulf of Tonkin. However, this potential continuation of their boundary would be of limited extent before the potential role of disputed islands, in this instance the Paracel Islands, would come into play.

### 3.3.4 Gulf of Thailand

The Gulf of Thailand is a semi-enclosed arm of the South China Sea bounded by Malaysia, Thailand, Cambodia and Vietnam. The Gulf's restricted size means that no coastal State can claim a full 200 nm EEZ entitlement. The presence of numerous islands, islets and rocks, some of which have been subject to sovereignty disputes, coupled with excessive straight baselines claims, dubious treaty interpretations, and differing, self-serving applications of equidistance as a method of constructing unilateral claim lines have complicated the jurisdictional picture.[67] As a result, the delimitation of maritime boundaries in the Gulf of Thailand has proved to be particularly problematic. Instead the Gulf of Thailand has proved to be a fertile area for practically oriented alternatives to the delimitation of maritime boundary lines – maritime joint development zones (JDZs; see Figure 3.6).

With respect to maritime boundary agreements, these are limited to the territorial sea[68] and a relatively short, partial, section of continental shelf boundary[69] between Malaysia and Thailand concluded in 1979. Additionally, an agreement on continental shelf and EEZ rights in the central Gulf was reached between Thailand and Vietnam in 1997.[70] The latter agreement was achieved despite

---

available online at www.un.org/Depts/los/clcs_new/submissions_files/mysvnm33_09/chn_2009re_mys_vnm_e.pdf

67  See C.H. Schofield and M. Tan-Mullins, 'Claims, Conflicts and Cooperation in the Gulf of Thailand', (2008) 22 *Ocean Yearbook* p. 75.

68  *Treaty between the Kingdom of Thailand and Malaysia Relating to the Delimitation of the Territorial Seas of the Two Countries*, 24 October 1979, reprinted in Charney and Alexander, note 5, p. 1096.

69  *Memorandum of Understanding between Malaysia and the Kingdom of Thailand on the Delimitation of the Continental Shelf Boundary between the Two Countries in the Gulf of Thailand*, 24 October 1979, reprinted in Charney and Alexander, note 5, p. 1105.

70  *Agreement between the Government of the Kingdom of Thailand and the Government of the Socialist Republic of Vietnam on the Delimitation of the Maritime Boundary Between the Two*

*An incomplete maritime map* 49

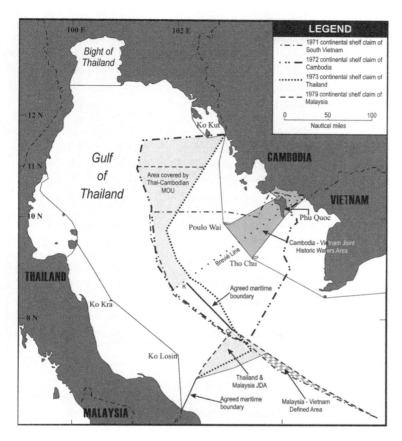

*Figure 3.6* Maritime Delimitation in the Gulf of Thailand.

each sides' mutually problematic claims to straight baselines which appear to have effectively cancelled each other out.[71] The agreement has, however, been subject to protest on the part of Cambodia.[72] In particular, Cambodia objects to the Thai-Vietnamese agreement's characterisation of its western terminal point, Point K, as being 'situated on the maritime boundary between the Socialist

---

*Countries in the Gulf of Thailand*, 9 August 1997, reprinted in J.I. Charney and R.W. Smith (eds), *International Maritime Boundaries*, Vol. IV, The Hague: Martinus Nijhoff, 2002, p. 2683 [hereafter *Thailand-Vietnam Boundary*].

71 Notably, Vietnam's baselines dating from 1982 and Area 4 of Thailand's baseline system declared in 1992; see Vietnam, *Declaration on Baseline of Territorial Waters*, 12 November 1982, available online at www.un.org/Depts/los/LEGISLATIONANDTREATIES/PDF-FILES/VNM_1982_Statement.pdf; *UN Law of the Sea Bulletin*, 25 June 1994, pp. 82–84, available online at www.un.org/Depts/los/LEGISLATIONANDTREATIES/PDFFILES/THA_1992_Announcement.pdf

72 See *Thailand-Vietnam Boundary*, Article 3.

## 50   Clive Schofield

Republic of Vietnam and the Kingdom of Cambodia'. As Prescott dryly noted, this fixing of the Cambodia-Thailand-Vietnam tripoint by the latter two States 'might come as a surprise to the Cambodian authorities'.[73]

The joint zones defined in the Gulf of Thailand are consistent with Articles 74(3) and 83(3) of LOSC which provide identical terms that pending agreement being reached on the delimitation of the continental shelf or EEZ, respectively, 'the States concerned, in a spirit of understanding and cooperation, shall make every effort to enter into provisional arrangements of a practical nature'.[74] These include the *Agreement on Historic Waters of Vietnam and Kampuchea* of 7 July 1982,[75] the Thai-Malaysian Memorandum of Understanding and subsequent agreement on a joint development area (JDA) of 1969 and 1990, respectively,[76] and the Malaysia-Vietnam MoU relating to the exploration for, and exploitation of, petroleum in a 'Defined Area' on the continental shelf of 5 June 1992.[77] Additionally, on 18 June 2001, Cambodia and Thailand signed a *Memorandum of Understanding regarding the Area of their Overlapping Claims to the Continental Shelf* in the Gulf of Thailand of 18 June 2001.[78] The area covered by the MoU appears to coincide with the parties' overlapping claims area, the largest such disputed maritime zone remaining in the Gulf of Thailand. Within this area, the parties agreed to seek maritime delimitation north of 11°N and a joint maritime development agreement to the south of that line.[79] Despite the time that has elapsed since the Cambodia-Thailand MoU was concluded and periodically intensive negotiations, agreement between the parties on either maritime delimitation or joint development has yet to eventuate.

---

73  See, J.R.V. Prescott, *The Gulf of Thailand*, Kuala Lumpur: Maritime Institute of Malaysia, 1998, p. 41.

74  LOSC, Articles 74(3), 83(3).

75  *Agreement on Historic Waters of Vietnam and Kampuchea*, 7 July 1982, reprinted in Charney and Alexander, note 39, p. 2364 [*Cambodia-Vietnam (1982)*]; K. Kittichaisaree, *The Law of the Sea and the Maritime Boundary Delimitation in South-East Asia*, Oxford: Oxford University Press, 1987, pp. 180–181.

76  *Memorandum of Understanding between the Kingdom of Thailand and Malaysia on the Establishment of a Joint Authority for the Exploitation of the Resources of the Sea-Bed in a Defined Area of the Continental Shelf of the Two Countries in the Gulf of Thailand*, 21 February 1979, reprinted in Charney and Alexander, note 5, p. 1107; *Agreement between the Government of Malaysia and the Government of the Kingdom of Thailand on the Constitution and Other Matters Relating to the Establishment of the Malaysia-Thailand Joint Authority*, 30 May 1990, reprinted in Charney and Alexander, note 5, p. 1111.

77  *Memorandum of Understanding between Malaysia and the Socialist Republic of Vietnam for the Exploration and Exploitation of Petroleum in a Defined Area of the Continental Shelf Involving the Two Countries*, 5 June 1992, reprinted in Charney and Alexander, note 39, p. 2335.

78  *Memorandum of Understanding between the Royal Government of Cambodia and the Royal Thai Government Regarding the Area of their Overlapping Maritime Claims to the Continental Shelf*, 18 June 2001, reprinted in Colson and Smith, note 18, p. 3743.

79  Ibid., Article 2.

## 3.3.5 East China Sea

Maritime delimitation in the East China Sea has to a large extent been prevented by a combination of two factors: sovereignty disputes over islands and opposing claims to entitlement among the littoral States.[80] Aside from longstanding concerns over the status of Taiwan, island sovereignty disputes in the East China Sea relate to a group of small and uninhabited islands in the southern part of the East China Sea. These features are known as the Senkaku Islands to the State presently administering them (Japan) and the Diaoyu and Tiao Yu T'ai to the other claimant States (China and Taiwan, respectively).

These territorial disputes over islands give rise to associated overlapping maritime claims in the southern part of the East China Sea. These overlaps are, however, set within the context of fundamentally differing approaches to maritime entitlements in the East China Sea as a whole between China and Korea on the one hand and Japan on the other hand. Japan is understood to claim an equidistance or median line between opposing coastlines.[81] In contrast, China not only suggests that the disputed islands are under its own sovereignty but that the majority of the continental shelf of the East China Sea, including areas of seabed within 200 nm of Japan are rightfully China's on 'natural prolongation' principles.[82] China's assertions with respect to 'extended' continental shelf rights, that is, continental shelf seawards of the 200 nm limit from China, yet simultaneously within 200 nm of Japan, indicates as much. China's claims are consistent with the axis of the Okinawa Trough which lies in close proximity to Japan's Ryukyu Island chain (see Figure 3.7).[83]

Korea similarly asserts continental shelf jurisdiction beyond the median line with Japan.[84]

While disputes over island sovereignty, as well as opposing views on the applicable principles of entitlement and thus the basis for maritime delimitation have prevented agreement on maritime boundaries in the East China Sea, a number of provisional arrangements of a practical nature in the form of JDZs have been

---

80 See, C.H. Schofield and I. Townsend-Gault, 'Choppy Waters Ahead in a 'sea of peace, cooperation and friendship'?: Slow Progress Towards the Application of Maritime Joint Development to the East China Sea', (2011) 35 *Marine Policy* p. 25.

81 That Japan utilises basepoints on the above-mentioned islands, sovereignty over which is disputed, is a further problematic aspect of Japan's claims from China/Taiwan's perspective.

82 See *North Sea Continental Shelf* (Germany v. Denmark; Germany v. Netherlands) [1969] ICJ Rep 3 [hereafter *North Sea Continental Shelf Cases*].

83 See China, 'Submission by the People's Republic of China Concerning the Outer Limits of the Continental Shelf beyond 200 Nautical Miles in Part of the East China Sea, Executive Summary', 14 December 2012, available online at www.un.org/depts/los/clcs_new/submissions_files/chn63_12/executive%20summary_EN.pdf

84 See Republic of Korea, 'Partial Submission to the Commission on the Limits of the Continental Shelf, Executive Summary', December 2012, available online at www.un.org/Depts/los/clcs_new/submissions_files/kor65_12/executive_summary.pdf

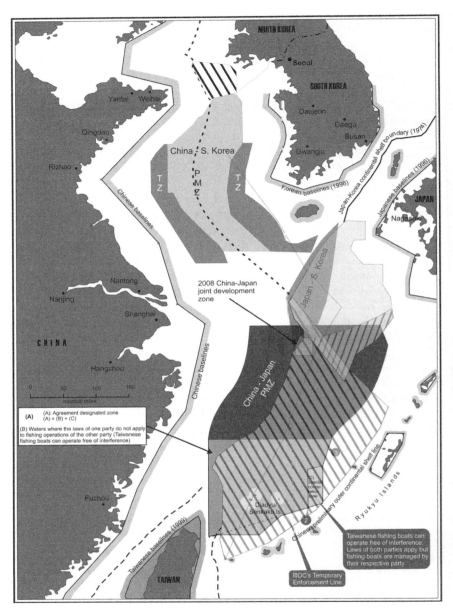

*Figure 3.7* Maritime Claims and Boundaries in the East China Sea.

*An incomplete maritime map* 53

concluded in the region. These include the 1974 Japan-Korea JDZ agreement,[85] a reported 2005 North Korea-China JDZ[86] and a 2008 agreement in principle on a China-Japan joint zone.[87]

To the north of the Japan-Korea JDZ, agreement was reached on a continental shelf delimitation line which extends from the northern East China Sea, through the Korea Strait and into the southern part of the Sea of Japan (East Sea to Korea).[88] Additionally, the East China Sea States have entered into a number of joint fishing arrangements among themselves, notably those between China and Japan, China and Korea, and Japan and Korea.[89] While these joint fisheries zones, as cooperative efforts to address shared fisheries management issues, represent a positive step forward, they do have drawbacks; notably that they provide for enforcement on a flag State basis with minimal joint enforcement envisaged and include no provisions for enforcement against third parties.[90] Further, they encompass only part of the areas of overlapping maritime claims and, indeed, these zones partially overlap with one another, creating a complex patchwork of joint zones.[91] These joint fisheries zones have also not prevented ongoing fisheries disputes, especially between China and Korea.[92] Additionally, on 10 April 2013, Japan and Taiwan reached a fisheries agreement which included the maritime area around the above-mentioned disputed islands, but innovatively

---

85 See *Agreement between Japan and the Republic of Korea Concerning Joint Development of the Southern Part of the Continental Shelf Adjacent to the Two Countries*, 30 January 1974, reprinted in Charney and Alexander, note 5, p. 1073.

86 *Agreement between the Democratic People's Republic of Korea and the People's Republic of China on the Joint Development of Offshore Petroleum*, 12 December 2005; see also K. Lee, 'Recent Developments of Maritime Delimitation in Northeast Asia from an International Law Perspective' in M.H. Nordquist and J.N. Moore (eds), *Maritime Border Diplomacy*, Dordrecht: Martinus Nijhoff, 2012, pp. 135, 138.

87 See 2008 *Principled Consensus on the East China Sea Issues*, available online at www.fmprc. gov.cn/eng/xwfw/s2510/t466632.htm; and reproduced in G. Jianjun, 'A Note on the 2008 Cooperation Consensus between China and Japan in the East China Sea', (2009) 40 *Ocean Development and International Law* p. 291, pp. 302–303.

88 *Agreement between Japan and the Republic of Korea Concerning the Establishment of Boundary in the Northern Part of the Continental Shelf Adjacent to the Two Countries*, 30 January 1974, (1979) LIS 75.

89 The agreements area as follows: The China-Japan agreement of 11 November 1997 relating to part of the East China Sea; The Japan-Korea agreement of January 2000 in respect of parts of both the East China Sea and Sea of Japan (East Sea to Korea) and the China-Korea agreement of 30 June 2001 dealing with parts of the Yellow Sea; see S.P. Kim, 'The UN Convention on the Law of the Sea and New Fisheries Agreements in North East Asia', (2003) 27 *Marine Policy*, pp. 97–109.

90 C.H. Schofield, 'Blurring the Lines: Maritime Joint Development and the Cooperative Management of Ocean Resources', (2009) 8 *Issues in Legal Scholarship* p. 22.

91 S. Lee, Y.K. Park and H. Park, 'The Complex Legal Status of the Current Fishing Pattern Zone in the East China Sea', (2017) 81 *Marine Policy* pp. 219–228.

92 See, for example, S.K. Kim, 'Illegal Chinese Fishing in the Yellow Sea: A Korean Officer's Perspective', (2012) 2 *Journal of East Asia and International Law* p. 455.

## 54  *Clive Schofield*

side-stepped the issue by excluding the islands and their territorial seas from the joint fishing arrangement zone (see Figure 3.7).[93]

### 3.3.6 Philippine Sea

East of the East China Sea lies the Philippine Sea. A potential maritime boundary exists here between Japan and Palau relating to their 'extended' or 'outer' continental shelf areas. Both States have made submissions to the Commission on the Limits of the Continental Shelf (CLCS) relating to the Southern Kyushu-Palau Ridge Region. Japan's submission in this area appears to be reliant on the maritime entitlements of its southernmost land territory, Okinotorishima. This feature consists of a pair of extremely small coral rocks protruding only a few centimetres above sea level. Japan has gone to extreme lengths to protect these features from erosion, including the construction of sea defences that are vertically higher than the rocks and entirely encircle them.[94] The main purpose of these engineering works appears to be to preserve their 'naturally formed' and 'above high-tide' status and therefore Japan's maritime claims from them.[95]

While sovereignty over Okinotorishima is uncontested, China and Korea nonetheless protested Japan's claims to extensive zones of maritime jurisdiction based on Okinotorishima. For example, in 2004, China asserted that in its view Okinotorishima is no more than a 'rock' within the meaning of LOSC Article 121(3) and thus incapable of generating either EEZ or continental shelf rights.[96] In light of these protests, the CLCS deferred consideration of the relevant part of Japan's submission.[97] Against this backdrop, any delimitation of continental shelf rights beyond 200 nm from baselines along the coast for the Southern Kyushu-Palau Ridge Region appears unlikely.

---

93 D.K. Wang, 'Taiwan-Japan Fisheries Agreement: Light at the End of a Dark Tunnel', (2016) 1 *Asia-Pacific Journal of Ocean Law and Policy* pp. 127, 129.

94 The costs associated with these major engineering works in such a remote location reportedly exceeded US$200 million; see C.H. Schofield and I.M.A. Arsana, 'Beyond the Limits?: Outer Continental Shelf Opportunities and Challenges in East and Southeast Asia', (2009) 31 *Contemporary Southeast Asia* pp. 28, 46–47.

95 Schofield and Arsana, note 94 pp. 46–47.

96 Article 121(3) of the LOSC states that: 'Rocks which cannot sustain human habitation or an economic life of their own shall have no exclusive economic zone or continental shelf'. Regarding China's assertion that Okinotorishima is a mere 'rock'; see, M. Fackler, 'Japan's Ultranationalists: Stuck between a Rock and a Hard Sell', *The Wall Street Journal*, 20 February 2005; see also, China, '*Note verbale* from the Permanent Mission of the People's Republic of China to H.E. Mr Ban Ki-Moon, Secretary-General of the United Nations', 6 February 2009, UN Doc. CML/2/2009 (translation), available online at www.un.org/Depts/los/clcs_new/submissions_files/jpn08/chn_6feb09_e.pdf

97 See Japan, 'Submission to the Commission on the Limits of the Continental Shelf, Executive Summary', 12 November 2008, available online at www.un.org/Depts/los/clcs_new/submissions_files/submission_jpn.htm

*An incomplete maritime map* 55

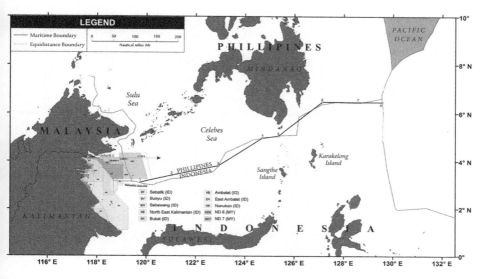

*Figure 3.8* Maritime Delimitation in the Sulu and Celebes Seas.

Further south, Palau has potential maritime boundaries with both the Philippines and Indonesia. These maritime boundaries remain undelimited. Here it can be observed that the large archipelagic States of the Philippines and Indonesia are likely to press their smaller neighbour in delimitation negotiations. This is evidenced by Indonesia's official maps. which depict not only Indonesia's agreed maritime boundaries with neighbouring States but also its 'forward position', that is, its unilateral maritime claims, with respect to neighbouring States. With respect to Palau, Indonesia's 2017 map shows Palau's southernmost islands, Tobi and Helen Islands, as fully enclaved in pockets of territorial sea surrounded by Indonesian EEZ, and the southernmost islands of Palau's main group of islands, Ana and Merir Islands, located further north, as semi-enclaved, only accorded 12 nm territorial seas in the direction of Indonesia.

### 3.3.7 *Celebes Sea*

Maritime delimitation between Malaysia and the Philippines through the Balabac Strait linking the South China Sea and Celebes (or Sulawesi) Sea is essentially forestalled by the Philippines historical and ongoing claims to sovereignty over the Sabah region of northern Borneo. Delimitation has, however, been possible further east and on 23 May 2014, Indonesia and the Philippines concluded a maritime boundary in the Celebes Sea (see Figure 3.8).[98] The initial negotia-

---

98 *Agreement between the Government of the Republic of the Philippines and the Government of the Republic Indonesia Concerning the Delimitation of the Exclusive Economic Zone Boundary*, 23

## 56  *Clive Schofield*

tion began in 1994, but remained dormant for almost a decade before talks were reactivated again in 2003.[99] Intriguingly, although the text of the agreement refers to the boundary as an EEZ boundary, it expressly excludes the continental shelf.[100] Specifically, Article I(3) of the agreement states '[t]his Agreement shall not prejudice any rights or positions of the Contracting Parties with regard to the delimitation of the Continental Shelf boundary'. In October 2014, both countries' Foreign Ministers released a joint statement declaring their intentions to convene a joint technical team to discuss the delimitation of the seabed boundary in the Celebes Sea.[101] The exclusion of continental shelf rights from the agreement may relate to incomplete knowledge of the parties concerning seabed resources at stake in the region. It is also consistent with the pattern of Indonesian practice in maritime delimitation of not necessarily having a single all-purpose boundary.[102]

Further south, maritime delimitation is complicated by the presence of islands, notably Pulau Sipadan and Pulau Ligitan, located offshore the terminus of the Indonesia-Malaysia land boundary on the coast (see Figure 3.8). On 17 December 2002, the ICJ delivered its Judgement in the *Case concerning Sovereignty over Pulau Sipadan and Pulau Ligitan (Indonesia/Malaysia)*.[103] This ruling removed a notable obstacle to maritime delimitation in the Celebes Sea in that the ICJ determined that sovereignty over these islands rests with Malaysia rather than Indonesia. However, the two States have overlapping maritime claims which appear to reflect their opposing views as to the status of these islands and thus their role in maritime boundary delimitation. This dispute over the so-called 'Ambalat offshore area' is also linked to access to seabed energy resources understood to be located in the area to be delimitated.[104]

### 3.3.8 Timor and Arafura Seas

In the early 1970s, prior to Timor-Leste's independence, Australia and Indonesia entered into negotiations towards the delimitation of their continental shelf

---

    May 2014, available online at www.gov.ph/2014/05/23/agreement-between-the-government-of-the-republic-of-the-philippines-and-the-government-of-the-republic-indonesia-concerning-the-delimitation-of-the-exclusive-economic-zone-boundary/ [hereafter *Philippines-Indonesia EEZ Boundary Agreement*].

  99  A.H. Oegroseno, 'How Indonesia and the Philippines Solved their Maritime Dispute', *The Diplomat*, 14 June 2014, available online at http://thediplomat.com/2014/06/how-indonesia-and-the-philippines-solved-their-maritime-dispute/

100  *Philippines-Indonesia EEZ Boundary Agreement*, Article I (3).

101  P. Esmaqual II, 'Philippines, Indonesia Eye Undersea Boundary', *Rappler*, 16 October 2014, available online at www.rappler.com/nation/72199-philippines-indonesia-continental-shelf-boundary

102  Bernard and Schofield, note 36, pp. 316–317.

103  *Case concerning Sovereignty over Pulau Sipadan and Pulau Ligitan* (Indonesia v. Malaysia) [2002] ICJ Rep 625.

104  See, C.H. Schofield and I. Storey, 'Energy Security and Southeast Asia: The Impact of Maritime Boundary and Territorial Disputes', (2005) 4 *Harvard Asia Quarterly* p. 36.

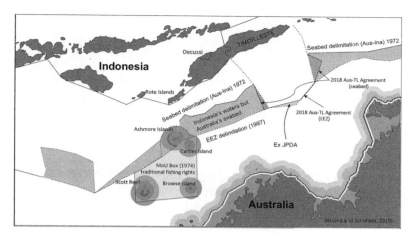

*Figure 3.9* Maritime Delimitation in the Timor Sea.

boundaries in the Timor Sea.[105] The timing of the negotiations leading to the conclusion of the Australia-Indonesia continental shelf agreement was a critical factor. This was because the negotiations between Australia and Indonesia occurred in the immediate aftermath of the ICJ issuing its 1969 Judgement in the *North Sea Continental Shelf* cases where the court found that 'natural prolongation' should be a key consideration in delimiting the continental shelf.[106] The presence of the Timor Trough, which reaches depths in excess of 3,000 m, running parallel to and much closer to Timor than to Australia, had a significant influence on these negotiations, resulting in continental shelf delimitation lines significantly nearer to Indonesia than Australia.

Due to the presence of then Portuguese Timor (the future Timor-Leste), the Australian-Indonesian continental shelf delimitation lines were divided into two sections, resulting in what became popularly known as the 'Timor Gap' (see Figure 3.9).

In 1975, Indonesia occupied and subsequently annexed East Timor and, despite international criticism, Australia subsequently acknowledged Indonesia's *de facto* sovereignty over Timor-Leste in January 1978 and gave its *de jure*

---

105 *Agreement between the Government of the Commonwealth of Australia and the Government of the Republic of Indonesia Establishing Certain Seabed Boundaries*, 18 May 1971, 974 UNTS 307; *Agreement between the Government of the Commonwealth of Australia and the Government of the Republic of Indonesia Establishing Certain Seabed Boundaries in the Area of the Timor and Arafura Seas, Supplementary to the Agreement of 18 May 1971*, 9 October 1972, 974 UNTS 319.
106 The ICJ ruled that 'delimitation is to be effected … in such a way as to leave as much as possible to each party all those parts of the continental shelf that constitute a natural prolongation of its land territory into and under the sea, without encroachment on the natural prolongation of the land territory of another state': *North Sea Continental Shelf Cases* [101].

## 58   Clive Schofield

recognition to the Indonesian position in March 1979.[107] However, by the time that Australia and Indonesia came to negotiate delimitation in the Timor Gap, the international legal circumstances had evolved considerably. In particular, in its judgement in the 1985 *Libya/Malta* case the ICJ, on the basis of developments in the international law of the sea including the conclusion of LOSC and the introduction of the EEZ concept, effectively dismissed any role for geophysical factors in determining the course of boundary delimitation within 200 nm of the coast.[108] Consequently, Indonesia steadfastly refused to simply, as it were, 'join up' the existing, discontinuous Australia-Indonesia continental shelf boundaries. This impasse was side-stepped through the creation of a joint zone solution – the Timor Gap Zone of Cooperation.[109] Subsequent agreements between Australia and Indonesia relating to the water column of the Timor Sea have been broadly based on equidistance, creating the unconventional but not unique scenario that water column boundary lines lie well to the south of previously agreed seabed boundaries.[110]

Following the independence of Timor-Leste on 20 May 2002, a succession of joint zone arrangements have been instituted for the Timor Gap, notably the Joint Petroleum Development Area (JPDA) established through the Timor Sea Treaty of 2002[111] and under the *Treaty on Certain Maritime Arrangements in*

---

107 *In the Matter of the Maritime Boundary between Timor-Leste and Australia before a Conciliation Commission constituted under Annex V of the 1982 United Nations Convention on the Law of the Sea between the Democratic Republic of Timor-Leste and the Commonwealth of Australia,* PCA Case no. 2016-10, Report and Recommendations of the Compulsory Conciliation Commission between Timor-Leste and Australia on the Timor Sea of 9 May 2018, p. 8.

108 *Case Concerning the Continental Shelf* (Libyan Arab Jamahiriya v. Malta) [1984] ICJ Rep 3 [39].

109 *Treaty between Australia and the Republic of Indonesia on the Zone of Cooperation in an Area between the Indonesian Province of east Timor and Northern Australia,* 11 December 1989, [1991] ATS 9. The Timor Gap Zone of Cooperation covered an area of 60,500 km² and effectively plugged the Timor Gap. It was divided into three sub-zones – a central Zone A where revenues were to be shared on a 50:50 basis, a smaller Zone B to the south where sharing was on the ratio 90:10 in favour of Australia and a narrow Zone C, where the ratio was 90:10 in favour of Indonesia.

110 See *Memorandum of Understanding between the Government of the Republic of Indonesia and the Government of Australia Concerning the Implementation of a Provisional Fisheries Surveillance and Enforcement Agreement,* 29 October 1981, reprinted in Charney and Alexander, note 20, p. 1238; *Treaty Between the Government of Australia and the Government of the Republic of Indonesia Establishing an Exclusive Economic Zone Boundary and Certain Seabed Boundaries,* 14 March 1997, [1997] ATNIF 4 [hereafter *Australia-Indonesia (1997)*]; see also, Bernard and Schofield, note 36, pp. 304–310; M. Herriman and M. Tsamenyi, 'The 1997 Australia-Indonesia Maritime Boundary Treaty: A Secure Legal Regime for Offshore Resource Development?', (1998) 29 *Ocean Development and International Law,* p. 373; S.B. Kaye, 'The Use of Multiple Boundaries in Maritime Boundary Delimitation law and Practice', (1998) 19 *Australian Yearbook of International Law,* p. 49.

111 *Timor Sea Treaty between the Government of East Timor and the Government of Australia,* 20 May 2002, [2003] ATS 13; signed on the day Timor-Leste became independent.

*the Timor Sea* (CMATS) of 2006.[112] A significant breakthrough occurred on 6 March 2018 with the signing of a maritime boundary agreement between Australia and Timor-Leste.[113] This historic accord was achieved through the first application of compulsory conciliation pursuant to Article 298 and Section 2 of Annex V of LOSC. Through this innovative means of dispute resolution which essentially provided for a facilitated negotiation process, Australia and Timor-Leste were able to agree on the delimitation of an EEZ boundary in the central part of the Timor Sea predominantly on the basis of equidistance as well as lateral continental shelf boundary lines which are considerably more favourable to Timor-Leste (see Figure 3.9).[114]

Although the agreement provides for the establishment of a 'Special Regime' for the Greater Sunrise complex of natural gas fields[115] that represent the main resource at stake in the dispute, the decision on the development of these reserves has yet to occur. The treaty links the revenue sharing relating to Greater Sunrise to the issue of the destination for the pipeline from the fields onshore in order to reflect the economic benefits associated with downstream processing activities. Thus, should the pipeline go to Australia, Timor-Leste would receive 80% of the government revenues arising from the development. However, if the pipeline is constructed to Timor-Leste, 70% of such revenues would go to Timor-Leste.[116] The decision on the development of Greater Sunrise also involves the consortium of oil and gas companies that hold commercial rights over the fields. While the oil companies are understood to favour piping the resources of Greater Sunrise onshore to Australia, Timor-Leste is strongly in favour of bringing the pipeline and associated downstream industrial development and employment opportunities to Timor-Leste. At the time of writing agreement had yet to be reached between this consortium and the States concerned over the destination of the pipeline and thus the development of Greater Sunrise.

## 3.4 Challenges and prospects

This chapter has sought to provide a 'grand tour' of the present state of progress in the delimitation of maritime boundaries in the series of semi-enclosed seas that collectively make up maritime South East Asia. It is certainly the case that considerable progress has been achieved with some maritime areas, such as the

---

112 *Treaty between Australia and the Republic of Timor-Leste on Certain Maritime Arrangements in the Timor Sea*, 12 January 2006, [2007] ATS 12.
113 *Treaty between Australia and The Democratic Republic of Timor-Leste Establishing their Maritime Boundaries in the Timor Sea*, 6 March 2018, [2018] ATNIF 4.
114 Ibid., Articles 2, 4. It is notable that Article 3 innovatively allows for the adjustment of the continental shelf delimitation lines in anticipation of future Indonesia-Timor-Leste maritime delimitation negotiations. These continental shelf boundaries presently terminate at points coincident with the terminal points of the Australia-Indonesia continental shelf boundaries referred to above and therefore do not prejudice Indonesia's existing continental shelf rights.
115 Ibid., Annex B.
116 Ibid., Annex B, Article 2.

60 *Clive Schofield*

Andaman Sea and Bay of Bengal, hosting a near complete array of maritime boundaries between the coastal States concerned. It is also abundantly clear that progress has been uneven and that many maritime boundaries remain to be delimited. Indeed, the delimitation of maritime boundaries for some parts of maritime South East Asia, such as the East and South China Seas, has been limited to peripheral areas.

This systematic appraisal of South East Asian seas demonstrates that these waters are undoubtedly characterised by geographical as well as legal complexity. A number of persistent impediments to completing the maritime map of South East Asia exist. Sovereignty disputes over islands remain the key obstacles to progress as such disputes need to be resolved before efforts towards maritime boundary delimitation can be engaged in. The long-standing disputes over islands in, for example, the South China Sea and the southern part of the East China Sea thus go a long way to explaining the lack of progress towards the completion of the maritime political map of South East Asia. Moreover, even where sovereignty disputes over islands in the region have been resolved, for instance concerning Pulau Sipadan and Pulau Ligitan in the Celebes Sea and over Pedra Branca, Middle Rocks and South Ledge at the eastern end of the Singapore Strait, the status of the insular features in question and thus their role in the delimitation of maritime boundaries has proved to be a focus for dispute instead.

Conflicting interpretations and approaches to issues of maritime entitlement as well as historic claims also represent major obstacles preventing further boundary agreements being reached in maritime South East Asia. China and Korea's position that their continental shelf rights should be determined on the basis of their natural prolongation, and thus into areas which Japan considers to be part of its EEZ as they are on the Japanese side of a median line between opposite coasts, severely complicates maritime delimitation negotiations in the East China Sea. Similarly, China's apparent claims to historic rights encompassing much of the South China Sea, as well as sovereignty claims over the disputed islands groups therein, would seem to eliminate the possibility of meaningful progress in relation to maritime boundary delimitation there.

The *South China Sea* arbitration, especially the interpretation of the regime of islands and conclusions in respect of historic rights and the law of the sea, might be expected to be of significant assistance in terms of clarifying these heretofore unresolved and ambiguous aspects of the law of the sea. Should it be respected, these findings would serve to dramatically reduce the scope of overlapping maritime claims in the South China Sea, thereby simplifying maritime boundary delimitation issues there. However, China's rejection of the Award and the reluctance of certain States to prejudice their own national interests and maritime claims may well serve to undermine its influence.

While States have advanced what can be regarded as excessive straight baseline claims, in the context of maritime delimitation negotiations, they have often proved to be adept at addressing such problems. Either opposing systems of straight baselines have, in effect, cancelled each other out, as appears to have been the case in the Gulf of Thailand or excessive straight baselines have been counter-balanced by the opposing coastal State's use of questionable insular basepoints as was the case in the Andaman Sea.

This illustrates that, even in the face of coastal geographical complexities, where enough political will exists, the necessary compromises can be made to reach an accord. As ever, this represents the essential ingredient to achieving any maritime boundary agreement. Deep-seated historical tensions, such as those between Japan and both China and Korea, undermine this essential need to compromise. Competition over valuable marine resources, both living and non-living, engage directly with national interests and are thus often intimately linked to these historical and geopolitical considerations.

The unresolved maritime boundaries, overlapping maritime claims and maritime boundary disputes that exist in maritime South East Asia are problematic in a number of ways. In particular, the existence of disputed waters tends to undermine law and order at sea as well as impair or compromise good oceans governance including the sustainable management of valuable but also vulnerable marine living resources. Additionally, from a resource perspective, overlapping claims usually prevent access to seabed energy resources. Moreover, conflicting maritime claims can provide a source of friction and flashpoints for potential conflict between neighbouring States, with the consequent potential to endanger international peace and security.

The counterpoint to this is that progress in the delimitation of maritime boundaries has the potential to confirm jurisdiction over marine spaces for the purpose of maritime surveillance and enforcement activities with a view to maintaining maritime security. Moreover, maritime delimitation serves to clarify rights over, and thus facilitate access to and management of, valuable marine resources therefore touching on core national interests. Delimitation also has the potential to remove a troublesome source, or excuse, for bilateral and multilateral disputes.

While it is difficult to envisage the resolution of the primary impediments to completing the maritime political map of South East Asia, especially sovereignty disputes over islands and the fundamentally differing viewpoints on the basis for entitlements to maritime zones that are evident in the region, nonetheless, there are grounds for some optimism. First, there remain a number of bilateral, rather than more complex multilateral, maritime boundary situations in the region that have yet to be addressed and these are likely to be more readily resolved. Second, the evolution in ocean boundary-making has provided a clearer three-stage approach to maritime boundary delimitation than existed previously. Third, South East Asian States have increasingly sought to resolve their maritime boundary issues through international law and law of the sea mechanisms including the resolution of sovereignty disputes over islands through the ICJ, the delimitation of maritime boundaries and related law of the sea issues via ITLOS and LOSC Annex VII arbitrations as well as, most recently, through the first use of conciliation under LOSC.

Finally, maritime South East Asia features substantial and innovative practice in terms of alternatives to the delimitation of maritime boundaries in the form of maritime JDZs and joint resource management mechanisms. These cooperative instruments provide for the joint development of seabed energy resources in the Gulf of Thailand and joint fisheries resources in the East China Sea. While the success of these initiatives has been variable, their adoption must be welcomed as a positive step, even if disputed waters need to be dealt with through shared zones and on an interim basis. This is particularly the case because achieving a more complete maritime map of the region delivers enhanced jurisdictional clarity and certainty, which, in turn, enables both access to, and the management of, valuable marine resources while also promoting good oceans governance.

# 4 Maritime security in South East Asia

*David Letts*

## 4.1 Introduction

The use of the term 'security', and its numerous subordinate offspring, including 'national security', 'human security'[1] and 'maritime security', to describe a wide variety of geo-strategic situations that are linked to various types of threat has been an increasing feature of political and academic discourse since the risk of global conflict between 'Western' powers and the former Soviet bloc reduced at the conclusion of the Cold War.[2] The reduction in one kind of threat did not, however, represent any lessening of overall security challenges as new pressures emerged through the presence of regional conflicts and tension as well as the activities of a variety of non-state actors.

In the maritime domain, 'maritime security' can be used to describe an ever-expanding number of issues that affect the manner in which ocean spaces are used by a wide variety of interested parties. At a macro level, some of these issues relate to activities that are undertaken by military vessels and aircraft in, over and under the sea; other issues have a stronger focus on law enforcement operations which may (or may not) involve military vessels. At a micro level, maritime security may be viewed from the perspective of local inhabitants residing along coastlines who rely on obtaining resources from the ocean for their daily existence, or who use the ocean for local trade and to visit family and friends.

---

1 National security is commonly used in reference to those issues which affect the security of the state itself while human security is more focussed on the individual welfare of citizens.

2 In relation to the emergence of the term 'national security', Hugh White notes

> It is no coincidence that this idea emerged in the years after the Cold War. For forty years until 1989, one specific security issue – major war – was seen to have dominated threat perceptions, and one specific policy instrument – conventional armed forces and the intelligence apparatus that supported them – was seen to have dominated national policy priorities.

H. White, 'The Idea of National Security: What Use is it to Policymakers?', (2012) *National Security College Occasional Paper No. 3*, p. 55, available online at https://nsc.crawford.anu.edu.au/files/uploads/nsc_crawford_anu_edu_au/2017-05/occasional-3-white.pdf

## 64 David Letts

Although there are many regions throughout the world where maritime security concerns exist, those that affect South East Asia demand particular attention for a number of reasons. The strategic location of South East Asia, at the intersection of the Pacific and Indian Oceans and as a key element of the busy trade route between Asia and Europe, necessarily amplifies the effect that any deterioration in maritime security would have. Additionally, the major maritime trade routes are characterised by a number of unique geographical features including the 'choke points' of the Singapore and Malacca Straits as well as the porous boundaries provided by the two largest archipelagic states (Indonesia and the Philippines). Further, the semi-enclosed status of the South China Sea provides a confining dimension to the region. Finally, all of the states that constitute South East Asia (except Laos) have a coastline and therefore maritime trade plays a dominant role among the region's economies.

This chapter will initially examine the concept of security to understand how it can be applied in practice before exploring a broad range of maritime security issues that exist in South East Asia. In this way, the chapter will provide the context in which the remaining chapters of the collection are situated. Consideration of the role that states and the Association of Southeast Asian Nations (ASEAN)[3] have played in addressing maritime security issues, as well as other institutional involvement in the region, will also be provided.

## 4.2 The concept of 'security'

Security can take many forms, but at its most basic level it can be considered that security relates to freedom from danger or risk. This concept can be applied at an international level to explain and examine inter-state behaviour, at a national level to assess the way in which states adopt security policies and practices and it can also be used to examine the way in which individuals respond to the environment in which they exist. Issues such as economic progress, physical survival and care of the natural environment can all form part of the concept of 'security' at each of these levels.

One way of analysing the components that make up the concept of security is to adopt a starting position that assesses whether a situation of peace or war exists in any particular region. In this manner, security can be equated with the absence of threats from one state towards another state which then contemplates a peaceful and 'secure' coexistence between, and among, states under the umbrella of a range of international laws and structural alliances among states.[4] Components that make up 'security' from this perspective could be

---

3 The Association of Southeast Asian Nations (ASEAN) was established in 1967 with five initial members and lists among its aims '...the promotion of regional peace and stability through abiding respect for justice and the rule of law and adherence to the principles of the United Nations Charter': see details available online at https://asean.org/asean/about-asean/history/.

4 N.D. White, *Advanced Introduction to International Conflict and Security Law*, Cheltenham: Edward Elgar, 2014, p. 1.

*Maritime security in South East Asia* 65

characterised as comprising the conventions and other international agreements that are designed to ensure and or enhance mutual survival, safety, economic and human security.

Another way of looking at security is to consider how it has been developed and refined during the course of the twentieth century. At one stage, prominence was given to individual states and their national security concerns, which inevitably led to the right of a state to project its power and protect itself through the use of force (if necessary) being the dominant factor in international relations, and such use of force was permitted under international law.

However, the development of security concepts that involve collective action by states through the creation of lasting international organisations such as the United Nations, where the principle of 'collective security' takes precedence over a narrower concept of 'national security',[5] has challenged this notion and fundamentally altered the legal landscape insofar as relations between states is concerned. The most striking outcome of this shift can be found in the prohibition on the 'threat or use of force against the territorial integrity or political independence of any state' that is contained in the United Nations Charter.[6]

Of course, this assessment does not preclude states from understandably having a focus on issues that directly affect them and their citizens, with an expectation that states will be heavily involved in dealing with the most pressing security issues that exist at any given time. Rather, it is the manner in which states can lawfully address those concerns that has now altered.

There are other ways in which the concept of security can be viewed. For example, from an individual perspective, security could have a very personal and localised focus whereby the only factor that the individual is really concerned about is whether their own safety, and that of those who are closest, is at risk. Contextualising this idea in the maritime environment, this type of security concern might include the ability of an individual to adequately support a family through the provision of the basic needs for human survival by harvesting fish and other products from the sea.

Finally, from an international law perspective, security is fundamentally concerned with ensuring that those threats which could be described as being directly related to the very existence of a state or its population are regulated.[7]

---

5 See generally *Charter of the United Nations*, 26 June 1945, 1 UNTS XVI [hereafter *UN Charter*]. Note in particular Chapter I which stipulates the purposes and principles of the United Nations, and Chapters VI and VII which, respectively, deal with 'Pacific Settlement of Disputes' and 'Action with Respect to Threats to the Peace, Breaches of the Peace and Acts of Aggression'.

6 *UN Charter*, Article 2 (4).

7 In the context of considering whether the use of nuclear weapons by a state was lawful, the International Court of Justice considered the scope and nature of threats to the very existence of a state in *Legality of the Threat or Use of Nuclear Weapons* (Advisory Opinion) [1996] ICJ Rep 226 [97], concluding that 'it cannot reach a definitive conclusion as to the legality or illegality of the use of nuclear weapons by a State in an extreme circumstance of self-defence, in which its very survival would be at stake'.

## 66   *David Letts*

This leads to the conclusion that a key purpose of international law is to assist with the reduction of violence in situations of international armed conflict (IAC) and non-international armed conflict (NIAC) by adequately dealing with these threats.[8] However, the role of international law in addressing security issues is not limited to conflict situations as there are many facets of international law that deal with issues and events that have a security focus but fall short of being part of a situation where armed conflict is present.[9]

## 4.3 Maritime security

Turning now to consideration of how these security concepts apply in the maritime environment, it is first necessary to address what is meant by 'maritime security' from a definitional perspective. Lowe has described the term 'maritime security' as being 'amorphous'[10] which reflects both the expansive notion of the concept of maritime security as well as highlighting the complexities involved in understanding its boundaries. Similarly, the opening sentence in Kraska and Pedrozo's comprehensive volume *International Maritime Security Law* notes '[T]here is no uniform or universally accepted definition of 'maritime security' but we regard it as a stable order of the oceans subject to the rule of law at sea'.[11] Others have noted that the meaning of the term 'maritime security' will differ depending on the perspective of the user or the context in which the term is being used[12] and it has also been suggested that use of the term has occurred '…in a carefree and underdeveloped way'.[13]

So, with a starting position that reflects a lack of agreement and clarity regarding any precise definition of the term 'maritime security', the application of the term to the situation that exists in South East Asia could be problematic. However, despite the absence of an agreed definition, there are some common elements in terms of describing what components might influence, affect and comprise maritime security that exist. For example, there is support for the view that maritime security is simply the maritime element of the wider security landscape that now dominates the international arena.[14] Issues such as safety of the

---

8  White, note 4, p. 1.

9  Ibid., pp. 10–11 where, *inter alia*, arms control, limiting private violence, post-conflict transition from war to peace and protecting peace and justice are all noted as being part of the '…underlying purposes of international conflict and security law'.

10  N. Klein, *Maritime Security and the Law of the Sea*, Oxford: Oxford University Press, 2011, General Editors' Preface, p. vi.

11  J. Kraska and R. Pedrozo, *International Maritime Security Law*, Leiden: Martinus Nijhoff, 2013, p. 1.

12  N. Klein, J. Mossop and D.R. Rothwell, 'Australia, New Zealand and Maritime Security' in N. Klein, J. Mossop and D.R. Rothwell (eds), *Maritime Security: International Law and Policy Perspectives from Australia and New Zealand*, London: Routledge, 2010, pp. 1, 5–8.

13  C. Rahman, 'Concepts in Maritime Security: A Strategic Perspective on Alternative Visions for Good Order and Security at Sea, with Policy Implications for New Zealand', (2009) *Centre for Strategic Studies: New Zealand* Discussion Paper No. 07/09 p. 29.

14  Ibid.

*Maritime security in South East Asia* 67

maritime shipping industry, protection of the marine environment, regulation of fishing activity, prevention of illegal dumping and pollution, protection of borders and regulation of the movement of people at sea have all been identified as forming part of maritime security. Dealing with the threats posed by pirates and armed robbery at sea, as well as those occasioned by trafficking of narcotics and illicit goods, arms proliferation, terrorist activity, and the use of private maritime security companies to address these threats can also be considered as forming part of the overall maritime security picture. Further, and this issue is particularly relevant in South East Asia, responding to natural disaster through the provision of humanitarian assistance and disaster relief can also be considered as an aspect of maritime security.

In terms of addressing maritime security threats, the responsibility rests primarily upon states, and in particular those states that possess sufficient military or law enforcement assets to successfully undertake the task. Often, the immediate response to a maritime security issue will be initiated by the coastal state(s) most directly affected, but in some cases there might be a lack of capacity or lack of willingness to do so. Increasingly, there have also been occasions when the United Nations Security Council might seek to address an issue through the adoption of a Resolution that calls upon all states to cooperate in dealing with a particular issue.[15] Additionally, the United Nations Secretary-General provides an annual report on oceans and law of the sea to the United Nations General Assembly which contains, *inter alia*, a section that deals with maritime security. In the report for the period 1 September 2017 to 31 August 2018, the Secretary-General noted a number of maritime security issues affecting South East Asia, including the threat from piracy and armed robbery against ships, illicit traffic in narcotic drugs and psychotropic substances by sea, port security and efforts to build capacity to deal with these threats.[16]

## 4.4 Maritime security issues in South East Asia

Having set the broad parameters in which this chapter will sit, focus will now turn to some of the key maritime security issues that exist in South East Asia. Some of these issues will benefit from much more detailed consideration in later chapters of this book while others will only be mentioned in this chapter. In dealing with the issues in this way, it is not intended to create a hierarchy of importance for any particular maritime security issue as each separate issue has

---

15 For example, United Nations Security Council, 'Resolution 2240 (2015)', 9 October 2015, UN Doc. S/RES/2240 (2015), which was renewed for a further 12 months by United Nations Security Council, 'Resolution 2437 (2018)', 3 October 2018, UN Doc. S/RES/2437 (2018), which seeks to address the flow of people across the Mediterranean Sea from Libya through a series of vessel inspection and seizure measures. These Resolutions have been authorized by the Security Council under the powers provided by Chapter VII of the *UN Charter*.

16 United Nations General Assembly, 'Oceans and the law of the sea: Report of the Secretary-General', 5 September 2018, UN Doc. A/73/, p. 5 [hereafter 'Report of the Secretary-General'].

## 68  David Letts

the potential to create uncertainty and security risk on its own. Rather, the sheer number of issues that could be addressed as falling within the scope of maritime security is vast, so it is necessary to limit the number of topics that are assessed so that only the more significant issues are dealt with in this chapter.

### 4.4.1 Maritime terrorism

South East Asia has not been immune from instances of maritime terrorism in the past, and it should not be thought that terrorist organisations have ignored the possibility of striking targets in the region in the future. While many terrorist incidents in the region have occurred on land, there were also a significant number that occurred at sea or which used the maritime domain to launch the attack. Terrorist organisations are active throughout South East Asia, with Indonesia, Malaysia, the Philippines and Thailand all being the subject of terrorist attacks in recent years.[17] Perhaps the most difficult terrorist threat to deal with has been that posed by the Abu Sayaff Group (ASG) in the Philippines, which resulted in a concerted military campaign that culminated in the five-month siege of Marawi from May to October 2017.[18]

By way of example, and while not occurring in South East Asia, terrorist incidents such as the attack on *MV Limburg* off the port of Aden in 2002[19] can have a direct effect on corporations that are based in the region, and in that sense have a consequential impact on maritime security. It has been reported that the attack on *MV Limburg*

> ...directly contributed to a short-term collapse of international shipping business in the Gulf; led to a $0.48-per-barrel hike in the price of Brent crude oil; and, as a result of the tripling of war-risk premiums levied on ships calling at Aden, caused the Yemeni economy to lose an estimated $3.8 million a month in port revenues.[20]

If such an attack was successfully carried out in the busy waterways of the South China Sea, especially in the heavily congested chokepoints around Singapore, the economic impact would be equally devastating.

---

17 Since 2004, the United States Department of State has published 'Country Reports on Terrorism' which are intended to provide a '...complete report on terrorism with regard to those countries and groups meeting criteria set forth in the legislation': see details at www.state.gov/j/ct/rls/crt/.

18 M. Hart, 'Is Abu Sayyaf Really Defeated?', *The Diplomat*, 23 November 2017, available online at https://thediplomat.com/2017/11/is-abu-sayyaf-really-defeated/

19 *MV Limburg* was attacked off the coast of Yemen by a small vessel packed with explosives on 6 October 2002 while under charter to the Malaysian oil firm Petronas. One crew member from the *Limburg* was killed in the attack (as well as two terrorists) and 12 crew members were injured.

20 P. Chalk, 'Maritime Terrorism in the Contemporary Era: Threat and Potential Future Contingencies', in National Memorial Institute for the Prevention of Terrorism, *The MIPT Terrorism Annual 2006*, Oklahoma City: MIPT, 2006, p. 26.

## Maritime security in South East Asia   69

Attacks against shipping that is involved in maritime trade is not the only tactic available to maritime terrorist groups.[21] In 2004, the ASG was assessed as being responsible for the sinking of *Superferry 14* in the Philippines. The vessel was sailing on a scheduled voyage from Manila to northern Mindanao when an explosion occurred onboard which sparked a fire that quickly spread throughout the vessel. There were 116 reported fatalities among the passengers and crew, the vessel was abandoned and subsequently sank, and the attack has been described as the most deadly terrorist attack at sea.[22] ASG has carried out other attacks at sea in the region, including taking vessels and hostages for ransom at regular intervals.[23] The results of these attacks have varied widely with some ransoms being paid, some hostages reportedly escaping from their captors, other hostages being released without a ransom, while other hostages have been killed.[24]

Attacks against shipping and crews are not the only instances of maritime terrorism that have occurred in recent years. There have also been attacks from the sea against shore targets by ASG, such as that which occurred in April 2000 at a resort on Sipadan Island in Malaysia when 21 tourists were kidnapped and held for ransom until the '…ASG reportedly received a fifteen-million-dollar ransom from the Philippine government' in 2001.[25] Of course, the potential for further attacks from the sea, such as those that occurred in Mumbai in 2008 when the Taj Hotel and other facilities were seized by terrorists, remains a distinct possibility.[26]

---

21  A number of groups have been reported to have the intention and capability to conduct maritime terrorist activity in South East Asia: Abu Sayyaf Group (ASG) which is predominately located in the Mindanao province of the Philippines; the Gerakan Aceh Merdeka (GAM) which operated in Indonesia's Aceh province from 1976 until a peace agreement with the Indonesian government was signed in 2005; and Jemaah Islamiyah (JI) which continues to operate in Indonesia, Malaysia, the Philippines, Thailand and Cambodia. The Australian Government has listed ASG and JI as terrorist organisations under Division 102 of the *Criminal Code Act 1995* (Cth) see details at www.nationalsecurity.gov.au/Listedterroristorganisations/Pages/default.aspx.

22  Chalk, note 20, p. 32.

23  Details of some of the early maritime attacks carried out by ASG have been listed by Chalk, note 20, pp. 36–37 and R. Banlaoi, 'Maritime Terrorism in Southeast Asia – The Abu Sayyaf Threat', (2005) 58 *Naval War College Review* pp. 9–12.

24  For a selection of the news reports covering the maritime terrorist activities of ASG, see '4 Malaysians released by Abu Sayyaf: Philippine Military', *Channel NewsAsia*, 8 June 2016, available online at www.channelnewsasia.com/news/asia/4-malaysians-released-by-abu-sayyaf-philippine-military-7961232; S. Karun, Escaped Biju Kolara Veetil Recounts Philippines Horror', *The Times of India*, 12 August 2012, available online at https://timesofindia.indiatimes.com/city/kochi/Escaped-Biju-Kolara-Veetil-recounts-Philippines-horror/articleshow/15453267.cms; 'ASG Claims Abducting German off Sabah', *GMA News Online*, 7 November 2016, available online at www.gmanetwork.com/news/news/regions/587769/asg-claims-abducting-german-off-sabah/story/

25  Banlaoi, note 23, pp. 8, 11.

26  The attacks in Mumbai occurred over the period 26–28 November 2008 when a group of Pakistani terrorists travelled from Karachi to Mumbai by boat, capturing a fishing trawler along the way and killing its crew before landing in Mumbai where multiple locations were attacked with 164 people being killed. CNN has produced a sheet of 'Fast Facts' describing

## 70    David Letts

### 4.4.2 Piracy, robbery and violence at sea

Closely aligned to maritime terrorism, but distinct from it, are the threats posed by piracy, robbery and violence at sea.[27] It has been noted by one author more than a decade ago that '...acts of piracy and armed robbery against ships have a long history in Asian waters, particularly in Southeast Asia...'[28] and this history was underscored by '...a steady rise in the number of reported incidents of piracy and sea robbery throughout the 1990s and then a dramatic jump towards the end of the decade and into the early 2000s'.[29] However, the nature of the threat in South East Asia has been overshadowed by that which emerged off the north east coast of Africa in the mid-late 2000s when threats to maritime security from pirates and other maritime crimes emanating from Somalia required significant international action to bring these threats under control.[30]

While considerable international effort was put in place to deal with the threat of piracy and armed robbery at sea in African waters,[31] at the same time there

---

the Mumbai attacks see CNN Library, 'Mumbai Terror Attacks Fast Facts', 13 November 2018, available online at https://edition.cnn.com/2013/09/18/world/asia/mumbai-terror-attacks/index.html and a film (*Hotel Mumbai*) depicting the events was released in September 2018, see details at 'Terrorism at the Taj: 'Hotel Mumbai' pulls no punches at TIFF', *The Conversation*, 14 September 2018, available online at https://theconversation.com/terrorism-at-the-taj-hotel-mumbai-pulls-no-punches-at-tiff-102971

27 United Nations Convention on the Law of the Sea, 10 December 1982, 1833 UNTS 397, Article 101 [hereafter LOSC], provides a definition of 'piracy' which is widely adopted and in simple terms requires an illegal act of violence or detention, or any act of depredation, done for private ends by the crew or passengers of one ship against another vessel outside of a state's territorial sea; any such acts that occur within a state's territorial sea are not piracy and are often described as 'armed robbery' or 'sea robbery' and are subject to the jurisdiction of the coastal state within whose waters the incident occurs. For example, the International Chamber of Commerce's International Maritime Bureau Piracy Reporting Centre (IMB PRC), established in 1992 and based in Kuala Lumpur, states on its website that it: '...follows the definition of Piracy as laid down in Article 101 of the 1982 United Nations Convention on the Law of the Sea ... and Armed Robbery as laid down in Resolution A.1025 (26) adopted on 2 December 2009 at the 26th Assembly Session of the International Maritime Organisation (IMO)', see details available online at www.icc-ccs.org/piracy-reporting-centre. An explanation of the distinction between the terms 'piracy', 'robbery' and 'violence at sea' is provided in D. Letts, 'Piracy: Some Questions of Definition and Jurisdiction', (1999) 104 *Maritime Studies*, pp. 26–27.

28 S. Bateman, 'Assessing the Threat of Maritime Terrorism: Issues for the Asia-Pacific Region', (2006) 2 *Security Challenges* p. 80.

29 I. Storey, 'Addressing the Persistent Problem of Piracy and Sea Robbery in Southeast Asia', (2016) 30 *ISEAS Yusof Ishak Institute Perspective* p. 2.

30 United Nations Security Council Resolution 1816 (2008) '*condemns and deplores* all acts of piracy and armed robbery against vessels in territorial waters and the high seas off the coast of Somalia' and authorizes the use of '*all necessary means*' to repress acts of piracy and armed robbery': United Nations Security Council, Resolution 1816 (2008), 2 June 2008, S/RES/1816 (2008). This Resolution has been renewed by the Security Council each subsequent year with the latest Resolution at the time of writing being United Nations Security Council, Resolution 2442 (2018), 6 November 2018, S/RES/2442 (2018).

31 Although the major emphasis has been dealing with piracy and robbery at sea off the coast of Somalia, there is also a considerable amount of piracy and robbery at sea occurring in the waters off the coast of West Africa that represents a threat to maritime trade in that region.

Maritime security in South East Asia  71

remained a constant threat of piratical and criminal activity against shipping in South East Asian waters. Over this period, the two major piracy and sea robbery reporting bodies both recorded an increase in attacks in South East Asia from 2009 to 2015[32] but the latest figures available at the time of writing show a marked decrease from the peak reached in 2015.[33] Nevertheless, the threat to maritime security from acts of piracy and sea robbery remains an issue in the region and comment regarding steps that have been taken to deal with the threat will be provided later in this chapter.

### 4.4.3 Trafficking of narcotics, people and illicit goods

Regional maritime security is clearly affected by incidents of illegal trafficking of narcotics, people and illicit goods. The issue is not confined to South East Asia, and in terms of narcotics the seizures made off the Horn of Africa and in the Caribbean Sea have generally attracted a lot more attention than those that have occurred at sea in South East Asia. Nevertheless, trafficking of narcotics poses a significant threat – not least because of the close links that exist between such activity, organised crime and terrorist groups.

Similarly, the unregulated movement of people by sea poses a large number of maritime security threats, especially where such movement is undertaken on a mass scale, typically using vessels that are ill-suited for the purpose, and orchestrated by persons or organisations that seek to profit from maximising the number of people transported with little or no regard for the safety of those onboard. This issue has been highlighted in the section of the United Nations Secretary-General's Report dealing with 'migration by sea' where it is noted that

> [T]ens of thousands of people continue to migrate by sea, often in perilous conditions, resulting in large numbers of deaths that are often unreported. There is an urgent need to improve search and rescue operations, including the provision of a place of safety, as well as to increase international cooperation.[34]

Regional responses to the movement of people by sea have typically adopted a hard-line approach, whereby the focus has been on trying to prevent such travel ostensibly due to the safety as well as the security risks that accompany unauthorized flows of people. For instance, the stance adopted by successive Australian governments since the arrival of *MV Tampa* in Australian waters in August

---

32 Storey, note 29, p. 5 notes that both the IMB PRC and the Regional Cooperation Agreement on Combating Piracy and Armed Robbery against Ships in Asia (ReCAAP) Information Sharing Centre (ISC) reported an increase in incidents across this period.

33 ReCAAP reporting for the period January – September 2018 identifies the figures were 'among the lowest during the 10-year period of January-September of 2009–2018', see details available online www.recaap.org/resources/ck/files/reports/quarterly/Single-sheet%20Summary%20 for%20ReCAAP%20ISC%203rd%20Quarter%202018%20Report(1).pdf

34 Report of the Secretary-General, note 16, p. 7.

## 72 David Letts

2001 culminated in the introduction of 'Operation Sovereign Borders' in 2013. The purpose of Operation Sovereign Borders is to demonstrate that '[T]he Australian Government is committed to protecting Australia's borders, combating people smuggling in our region, and preventing people from risking their lives at sea'.[35] The policy adopted by Australia includes turning back boats when safe to do so as well as preventing settlement in Australia of anyone who attempts to travel illegally to Australia by boat.[36]

The responses to movement of people at sea adopted by governments in South East Asia can be illustrated by the actions of states following the fleeing of Rohingya from Myanmar. Reports vary, but somewhere between 600,000 and 1 million Rohingya have been displaced since violence erupted in Myanmar's Rakhine State in 2012 and intensified in 2017.[37] Many of the Rohingya population left Myanmar by boat and it has been reported that there were 200 deaths at sea since August 2017.[38] While Bangladesh has been the place of refuge for most of those fleeing from Myanmar, there have also been a significant number of arrivals in Thailand, Malaysia and Indonesia.[39] There has been some criticism levelled at the response of these governments but at least one of them has taken a public stance on the issue by declaring that the '...conflict [is] no longer Myanmar's internal affair, as it had fuelled an exodus of refugees that could destabilise the region...'.[40] These words underscore the key issue from a maritime security perspective as such movement of people at sea must inevitably impact on the security and stability of the region.[41]

---

35 See details at Australian Government, Department of Home Affairs, 'Operation Sovereign Borders (OSB)', (n.d.), available online at https://osb.homeaffairs.gov.au/

36 See details at Australian Government, Department of Home Affairs, 'Outside Australia?', (n.d.), available online at https://osb.homeaffairs.gov.au/en/Outside-Australia#

37 Allegations have been made that the ruling regime in Myanmar has been involved in 'ethnic cleansing' of Rohingya by carrying out security operations in the Myanmar state territory of Rakhine; these claims have been consistently denied by Myanmar, see 'UN chief says plight of Rohingya a "human rights nightmare", *RTE*', 2 July 2018, available online at www.rte.ie/news/world/2018/0702/974683-un-rohingya/; Human Rights Watch, 'Rohingya Crisis', (n.d.), available online at www.hrw.org/tag/rohingya-crisis; A. Abdullah, 'Rohingya crisis: a year since it shocked the world, what's changed?', *The Conversation*, 13 August 2018, available online at https://theconversation.com/rohingya-crisis-a-year-since-it-shocked-the-world-whats-changed-101209

38 Report of the Secretary-General, note 16, p. 7.

39 E. Albert and A. Chatzky, 'The Rohingya Crisis' *Council on Foreign Relations*, 5 December 2018, available online at www.cfr.org/backgrounder/rohingya-crisis

40 Ibid; see also J. Funston, 'Malaysia and the Rohingya – Humanitarianism and Domestic Imperatives', (2018) 3 *paradigm_Shift — People Movement*, p. 46 available online at https://asiapacific.anu.edu.au/sites/default/files/News/paradigm_shift_issue_03_-_people_movement_-_digital.pdf

41 The US State Department provides an annual global assessment of human trafficking, which includes comprehensive analysis of steps taken by individual countries to deal with the issue. See Department of State (US), *Trafficking in Persons Report 2018*, (n.d.) available online at www.state.gov/j/tip/rls/tiprpt/2018/

### 4.4.4 Arms proliferation

The legitimate sale of weapons between and among states is a divisive issue. On the one hand, it can be considered that continuing such trade is a contributing factor in perpetuating unrest throughout the world while a contrary view would see such trade as an important right that states are free to exercise.[42] Various attempts have been made to limit the freedom of states to engage in the arms trade through United Nations actions[43] as well as through the adoption of a number of treaties dealing with the topic such as the Arms Trade Treaty[44] and the nuclear weapon non-proliferation Treaty.[45] Civil society has also played a role in seeking to limit the arms trade.[46]

However, from a maritime security perspective, it is the use of the sea to illicitly distribute weapons and other items of military equipment that poses a substantial threat to stability in the region. The geography of South East Asia naturally lends itself to the movement of these items by sea, and the existence of this threat has been recognised by the establishment of the United Nations Regional Centre for Peace and Disarmament in Asia and the Pacific (UNRCPD).[47] The focus of UNRCPD has been to assist states address the threats that accompany the illicit trade of small arms and light weapons (SALW), deal with the threats posed by proliferation of weapons of mass destruction (WMD) as well as helping in '...improving disarmament outreach and advocacy'.[48]

---

42  On its website, the United Nations Office for Disarmament Affairs has noted:

> Governments remain central providers of security. This is their sovereign right and responsibility, to be performed in conformity with the rule of law. To effectively execute these tasks, their armed and security forces legitimately employ a range of weaponry, which they acquire through national production or through import. Exporters and importers need to ensure those weapons are transferred and stored safely, and not end up in the wrong hands. Governments also have a responsibility to ensure public safety and have a vested interest in providing human security and development to their citizens. Therefore, ensuring that arms in private ownership do not enter illicit circuits must be part of the equation for every country.

See details available online at www.un.org/disarmament/convarms/att/

43  For example, UN Security Council Resolution 2117 (2013) dealing with small arms and light weapons and UN Security Council Resolution 1718 (2006) which set up an 'arms and related material embargo' in relation to the Democratic People's Republic of Korea.

44  *Arms Trade Treaty*, 2 April 2013, [2014] ATS 42; for an early assessment of the importance of the treaty for South East Asia see P.K.K. Hangzo, 'The Arms Trade Treaty: Implications for Southeast Asia', (2013) 106 *RSIS Commentaries*, p. 1, available online at www.rsis.edu.sg/wp-content/uploads/2014/07/CO13106.pdf

45  *Treaty on the Non-proliferation of Nuclear Weapons*, 1 July 1968, 729 UNTS 161.

46  For example, the work undertaken by Arms Control Association; see details available online at www.armscontrol.org/.

47  The UNRCPD website contains information regarding its purpose and activities, as well as country-specific information of arms control measures undertaken by countries in the region. See details available online at http://unrcpd.org/.

48  Ibid.

74  *David Letts*

A link clearly exists between illicit trade in SALW, proliferation of WMD, disarmament endeavours and the overall security situation in South East Asia's maritime environs. The use of weapons to attack and disrupt shipping, undertake piracy and armed robbery at sea, threaten those using the sea for trade or business purposes, as well as carrying out acts of terror are all salient reasons why there is a continuing and urgent need for states to put in place effective measures to disrupt and eliminate this trade.

### 4.4.5 *Other maritime security concerns*

There are a range of other maritime security issues that exist in the South East Asia region. For example, the prevalence of illegal, unreported and unregulated (IUU) fishing and the exploitation of marine living and non-living natural resources in an unsustainable manner are both issues that affect the region's stability and security.[49] Environmental damage and marine pollution caused by vessels operating in the region can also have an effect on maritime security and so can maritime accidents.

Additionally, the region is prone to severe weather events as a result of volcanic eruptions, earthquakes and landslides, floods, typhoons and cyclones and other natural disasters. Coastal communities are especially vulnerable as was demonstrated in December 2004 when a devastating tsunami struck South East Asia.[50] In 2015, the United Nations Economic and Social Commission for Asia and the Pacific reported that the Asia Pacific '...continued to be the world's most disaster prone region. One hundred and sixty disasters were reported in the region, accounting for 47% of the world's 344 disasters'.[51] The response to these disasters has involved extensive humanitarian assistance and disaster relief operations, involving military and other resources from affected states as well as the provision of assistance from within South East Asia and further afield.

This, in turn, raises the question of whether the presence of naval vessels, coast guard vessels and other law enforcement vessels that are responding to disasters as potential forces of 'good' could also potentially be viewed as a source of friction and tension between states even though these vessels are ostensibly undertaking benign activity in the form of humanitarian operations.

---

49  The United Nations Food and Agriculture Organisation notes the links between IUU fishing, corrupt local administrations and (potentially) organised crime, as well as the impact of IUU fishing on coastal communities; see details available online at www.fao.org/iuu-fishing/en/.

50  It has been reported that 'the Boxing Day tsunami in 2004 is believed to be the deadliest tsunami in history, killing more than 230,000 people across 14 countries': 'Boxing Day tsunami: How the disaster unfolded 10 years ago', *ABC News*, 24 December 2014, available online at www.abc.net.au/news/2014-12-24/boxing-day-tsunami-how-the-disaster-unfolded/5977568

51  United Nations Economic and Social Commission for Asia and the Pacific, 'Disasters in Asia and the Pacific: 2015 Year in Review', 10 March 2016, available online at www.unescap.org/sites/default/files/2015_Year%20in%20Review_final_PDF_0.pdf

## 4.5 A selection of responses to maritime security issues in South East Asia

So far in this chapter, the focus has been on illustrating a number of the more significant maritime security threats that exist in South East Asia. The final section of the chapter will briefly examine some of the measures that have been put in place to deal with these threats by looking at the action of states, regional organisations, as well as some non-governmental organisations.

### 4.5.1 State action

The recognition by states that maritime security in South East Asia needs to be addressed has been operationalised in a number of different ways. The LOSC[52] provides a basis for states to deal with maritime security threats that occur in their maritime zones while also recognising that freedom of navigation must exist in those same zones. The introduction of maritime (and air) patrols in areas of high risk is one way that states have responded to the threats, and some of these patrols have been undertaken in a coordinated manner. For example, in April 2016, the navies of Singapore, Malaysia, Thailand and Indonesia celebrated ten years of conducting the Malacca Straits Patrols which were instituted at a time when the Malacca Strait was under threat as a 'war-risk area'.[53] These patrols have now resulted in a vast improvement in the maritime security of the Singapore and Malacca Straits although as noted earlier these locations remain susceptible to ongoing piracy and sea robbery incidents.

Singapore also hosts the Information Fusion Centre at the Changi naval base[54] which was established in 2009 as a coordinating centre that '...plays a key role in securing the region's waters against maritime security threats such as piracy, sea robbery, weapons proliferation and maritime terrorism, as well as contraband and drug smuggling'.[55] Since 2017, coordinated patrols have also been instituted in the Sulu Sea between the Philippines, Indonesia and Malaysia[56] to

---

52 For example, LOSC, Article 25, provides that a '...coastal State may take the necessary steps in its territorial sea to prevent passage which is not innocent'. See also LOSC, Articles 56, 58 in relation to the exercise of rights, duties and jurisdiction in the EEZ.

53 This assessment was made by the Lloyds insurance group and was down-graded after the introduction of air and sea patrols in 2004: see details at MINDEF Singapore, 'Fact Sheet: The Malacca Straits Patrol', 21 April 2015, available online at www.mindef.gov.sg/web/portal/mindef/news-and-events/latest-releases/article-detail/2016/april/2016apr21-news-releases-00134/

54 See details at MINDEF Singapore, 'Fact Sheet: Information Fusion Centre', 27 September 2016, available online at www.mindef.gov.sg/web/portal/mindef/news-and-events/latest-releases/article-detail/2016/september/2016sep27-news-releases-02341/

55 N. Low, 'Navy's Information Fusion Centre Helps Keep Region's Waters Safe', *The Straits Times*, 17 May 2018, available online at www.straitstimes.com/singapore/navy-intel-centre-helps-keep-regions-waters-safe

56 The introduction of the Sulu Sea patrols was widely reported at the time; see for example, F. Chan and W. Soeriaatmadja, 'Joint Sulu Sea patrols launched; info-sharing from S'pore

## 76 David Letts

deal with the threats that have emerged in that area as a result of terrorist activity in the southern part of the Philippines.

Finally, states have enthusiastically embraced attendance at the annual Shangri-La dialogue which is organised by the International Institute for Strategic Studies and has been held in Singapore since 2002. This meeting brings together senior government and military leaders for two days of discussion where regional defence and security issues are canvassed in high-level plenary sessions, break-out groups and bilateral meetings.[57] Not surprisingly, the topic of regional maritime security has featured prominently in these meetings for many years and this provides another example of action taken by states to deal with the issue.

### 4.5.2 Regional organisations: ASEAN

The primary regional organisation that has a role to play in addressing maritime security issues in South East Asia is ASEAN. From an initial membership of five nations, ASEAN now comprises ten members covering the entire South East Asia region as well as having formal 'external relations' with a large number of states and organisations.[58]

There are numerous examples of action taken by ASEAN to address the broader security concerns that affect the region, and while the focus is not always directly on the maritime domain, clear linkages exist in many of these endeavours. For example, in relation to efforts to address the illegal trafficking of people through the region, ASEAN has produced a hierarchy of documents, commencing with the ASEAN Declaration Against Trafficking in Persons, Particularly Women and Children (2004), which was followed by the ASEAN Convention Against Trafficking in Persons, Especially Women and Children (2015)[59] and complemented by the ASEAN Plan of Action Against Trafficking in Persons, Especially Women and Children (2015).[60] The plan contemplates the need for '...strong international cooperation and a comprehensive regional approach to prevent, suppress, and punish trafficking in persons, especially women and children, in

---

next', *The Straits Times*, 20 June 2017, available online at www.straitstimes.com/asia/joint-sulu-sea-patrols-launched-info-sharing-from-spore-next

57 See details at International Institute for Strategic Studies, 'IISS Shangri-La Dialogue 2018' (n.d.), available online at www.iiss.org/events/shangri-la-dialogue/shangri-la-dialogue-2018

58 See ASEAN 'External Relations' (n.d.), available online at https://asean.org/asean/external-relations/ stating that 'ASEAN Foreign Ministers Meeting may confer on an external party the formal status of Dialogue Partner, Sectoral Dialogue Partner, Development Partner, Special Observer, Guest, or other status'.

59 ASEAN Convention Against Trafficking in Persons, Especially Women and Children, 21 November 2015, not yet in force, available online at https://asean.org/asean-convention-against-trafficking-in-persons-especially-women-and-children/

60 ASEAN Plan of Action Against Trafficking in Persons, Especially Women and Children, 22 November 2015, available online at www.asean.org/wp-content/uploads/2015/12/APA-FINAL.pdf

*Maritime security in South East Asia* 77

all forms of sexual, labour, and organ trafficking'.[61] Clearly, any attempt to implement the plan without taking into account the need to include measures that confront the use of ASEAN maritime regions would be grossly ineffective as it would ignore a significant avenue for trafficking activity.

A similar approach can be seen following the Twelfth ASEAN Ministerial Meeting on Transnational Crime which was held in Myanmar on 31 October 2018 where the Ministers '...reaffirmed our commitment in strengthening cooperation in the fight against transnational crime to enhance regional unity and strength'.[62] Again, the inclusion of a maritime component as part of the cooperative effort will be a critical factor in successfully achieving ASEAN's objectives in fighting against transnational crime. Complementing these efforts was the statement released following the ASEAN Defence Ministers' Meeting-Plus in relation to steps to be taken to deal with the threat of terrorism in the region.[63] Although no specific mention of measures that will be taken to deal with maritime terrorism threats was included in the statement, it is readily apparent that '...effective counter-narrative strategies and initiatives...'[64] must include those that are effective in the maritime domain.[65]

All of these actions by ASEAN point to a willingness to put words on paper that appear to be squarely aimed at dealing with the most important security issues that are confronting the region, including those that are most urgent in terms of maritime security. Less certain, however, is how much concrete action ASEAN is willing to undertake to address 'head-on' the maritime security issues that affect the region although conducting joint naval exercises with China, as occurred in October 2018, is a welcome start.[66]

Nevertheless, criticisms of ASEAN's role persist. One criticism is that ASEAN has not adopted '...a more pro-active role in the fight against piracy and sea-robbery in Southeast Asia'[67] while another suggestion is that ASEAN's focus on 'consensus' leads to inactivity – especially in areas where contested maritime

---

61  Ibid.
62  ASEAN, 'Joint Statement: Twelfth ASEAN Ministerial Meeting on Transnational Crime', 31 October 2018, available online at https://asean.org/storage/2018/10/Adopted-Joint-Statement-of-12th-AMMTC.pdf
63  ASEAN, 'Joint Statement by the ADMM-Plus Defence Ministers on Preventing and Countering the Threat of Terrorism', 20 October 2018, available online at https://asean.org/storage/2018/10/Final-ADMM-Plus-Joint-Statement-on-Preventing-and-Countering-Terrorism.pdf
64  Ibid.
65  For a detailed overview of action taken by ASEAN in dealing with maritime security issues, see H. Nasu et al., *The Legal Authority of ASEAN as a Security Institution*, Cambridge: Cambridge University Press, 2019, pp. 112–138.
66  R. Beckman, 'Why ASEAN Should Hold More Maritime Drills with China and US', *Straits Times*, 31 October 2018, available online at https://cil.nus.edu.sg/publication/why-asean-should-hold-more-maritime-drills-with-china-and-us/
67  Storey, note 29, p. 11.

## 78  David Letts

claims exist.[68] These are valid concerns and reflect the overly cautious approach that is a hallmark of 'the ASEAN way'.

### 4.5.3 Other maritime security initiatives

It is not possible to provide a comprehensive review of all the confidence building and security enhancement activities that are currently underway in South East Asia; instead, some information will be provided regarding a small selection of these activities.

Since 2014, the International Committee of the Red Cross through its series of 'LOAC at Sea' workshops in South East Asia[69] has adopted the approach of bringing together selected groups of naval officers from the region to discuss law of the sea, naval warfare and maritime security concerns. These workshops have been attended by delegates from South East Asian nations as well as the wider region and are intended to be confidence building measures and information exchange among participants.

Additionally, the Centre for Humanitarian Dialogue has initiated a number of activities which focus on the role played by coast guards and law enforcement vessels in the South China Sea,[70] and there has also recently been an increased emphasis and presence from the United Nations Office on Drugs and Crime's (UNODC) Global Maritime Crime Program.[71] Further, the United States Pacific Command[72] has convened an annual International Military Operations and Law Conference for three decades which provides a forum for military officers, departmental and regional officials and academics to canvass some of the region's pressing legal issues – including those that involve maritime security.

---

68  See R. Emmers, 'ASEAN Minus X: Should This Formula Be Extended?', (2017) 199 *RSIS Commentary*, available online at www.rsis.edu.sg/wp-content/uploads/2017/10/CO17199.pdf

69  V. Bernard, 'War and Security at Sea: Warning Shots', (2016) 98 *International Review of the Red Cross* p. 392; an ICRC press release regarding the 2018 'LOAC at Sea' workshop that was held in Shanghai is available online at International Committee of the Red Cross, 'China: Senior Military Officers Seek Greater Respect for Law of Armed Conflict at Sea', 8 May 2018, available online at www.icrc.org/en/document/china-law-armed-conflict-sea-shanghai

70  Details of the Centre for Humanitarian Dialogue's South China Sea activities can be found online at www.hdcentre.org/stage/activities/south-china-sea/ and a similar press release regarding the 2017 workshop held in Kuala Lumpur is available online at www.icrc.org/en/document/malaysia-experts-discuss-humanitarian-law-application-maritime-context

71  Details of a range of initiatives being undertaken by UNODC in the region can be found on the UNODC Regional Office for Southeast Asia and the Pacific website; see details at www.unodc.org/southeastasiaandpacific/. In October 2018 a 'table-top' maritime security workshop was held in Manila in cooperation with the International Maritime Organisation; see S.A. Lakshmi, 'IMO Focus on Maritime Security', *Marine Link*, 18 October 2018, available online at www.marinelink.com/news/imo-focus-maritime-security-442813

72  Now designated US Indo-Pacific Command. The name was changed on 31 May 2018. See details at C.H.M. Smith, U.S. Indo-Pacific Command, 'U.S. Indo-Pacific Command Holds Change of Command Ceremony', 30 May 2018, available online at www.pacom.mil/Media/News/News-Article-View/Article/1535776/us-indo-pacific-command-holds-change-of-command-ceremony/

All of these measures are part of the response to dealing with maritime security threats that exist in South East Asia and play a role in improving and enhancing maritime security throughout the region. No single measure provides a complete solution to the region's maritime security concerns, but each has a part to play in ensuring that steps are taken to control the threats that confront the region.

## 4.6 Conclusion

The purpose of this chapter has been to provide an overview of some of the more significant maritime security issues that are confronting South East Asia. These issues include inter-state sovereignty disputes, maritime terrorism, piracy, robbery and violence at sea; a range of illegal trafficking activities; arms proliferation; IUU fishing; and responses to natural disasters. States have taken the lead in some areas, especially where the consequences of the problem are directly affecting the state concerned. ASEAN is also playing a role, although the nature of the way in which ASEAN conducts its business leaves a concern regarding how effective it can be in dealing with the threats that exist in the maritime domain. Finally, a range of United Nations bodies, and other organisations, are also active in the region, and their efforts are also part of the solution that is needed to comprehensively deal with maritime security in South East Asia.

# 5 Advancing marine environmental security in South East Asia

## Challenges and opportunities

*Robin Warner*

### 5.1 Introduction

As a multiplier of global and regional insecurity drivers, including overfishing, poverty, social fragility and transnational crime, marine environmental degradation has the potential to exacerbate insecurity in South East Asia. This chapter examines a range of marine environmental challenges, with a particular emphasis on climate-related factors, contributing to destabilisation and insecurity in the marine and coastal environments of South East Asia, including ocean warming, sea level rise and severe weather events.[1] To avert and mitigate the worst impacts of climate change on maritime security in South East Asia, multilateral collaboration is needed at many levels. Accordingly, the chapter will also examine a variety of global and regional initiatives in South East Asia with the potential to mitigate the maritime security implications of marine environmental degradation and climate change impacts. These initiatives include: transboundary marine environmental protection projects, fisheries conservation and sustainable use agreements, cooperative arrangements to combat transnational crime and creative solutions to maritime disputes. Finally, the chapter also considers how these collaborative ocean governance structures can be further developed to cope with the ongoing effects of marine environmental degradation and climate change on maritime security in South East Asia.

### 5.2 Climate change imspacts on fisheries and marine biodiversity in South East Asia

The adverse effects of climate change impose an extra burden on the already stressed fisheries and marine biodiversity of South East Asia. The expected consequences of global ocean warming include increased thermal stress on tropical species and communities, with the probability of substantial change and significant species loss.[2] An increase in $0.6°C–0.7°C$ in water temperature

---

1 Although this chapter is focussed on South East Asia, there are also some places where comments regarding the wider Asia Pacific have been incorporated.

2 W.W.L. Cheung et al., 'Projections of Global Marine Biodiversity Impacts under Climate Change Scenarios', (2009) 10 *Fish and Fisheries* pp. 235–251.

*Advancing marine environmental security*  81

is predicted for the tropical regions of South East Asia leading to increased stratification reducing ventilation in the oceans, reduced primary productivity and reduced food supplies for fish species.[3] Higher water temperatures are also forecast to affect the timing and success of fish migrations, spawning, sex ratios and peak abundance for some species.[4] Warmer oceans will also result in more frequent algal blooms, less dissolved oxygen and an increased incidence of disease and parasites leading to less abundant species and composition.[5]

Typically, the distribution of tropical marine species reflects a range close to the upper level of their thermal tolerance. Under increasing temperatures, they are likely to show local extinction in their original habitats and where possible, shift through movement or larval transport to their preferred thermal range in higher latitudes.[6] Cheung et al. have modelled likely patterns of such changes and predicted species extinction in the equatorial South Asian/Indian Ocean and West Pacific Ocean with the highest levels being in the enclosed Java Sea. They have also modelled changes in maximum fishery catch potential to 2055. Their projections show widespread reductions of 30%–50% in most of the equatorial Asia Pacific through reductions in current tropical fisheries.[7] Some species may survive by gradual relocation to suitable habitats in higher latitude areas that have warmed. This is likely to cause a cascade effect, with such relocation causing competition with, and displacement of, species for which the temperature range of the invaded location has become too high.[8]

In addition to the changes expected to flow from gradually rising mean sea-surface temperatures, relatively short periods of extreme temperature rise can also have major impacts on marine biodiversity. In 1998–1999, substantial areas of the Indo-Pacific experienced a prolonged period of severe high water temperatures which caused widespread coral bleaching.[9] Many days of water temperatures, $2°C$ or more above normal summer maximum temperatures, stressed corals which responded by rejecting their symbiotic algae, zooxanthellae. The stress continued for so long that there was widespread coral death, with large areas experiencing more than 95% coral mortality.[10] In many of these areas, there has been short-term recovery of coral cover; however, recovery of

---

3 WorldFish Centre, *The Threat to Fisheries and Aquaculture from Climate Change*, Penang: World Fish Center, 2007, pp. 2–4.

4 Ibid.

5 Ibid.

6 O. Hoegh-Guldberg, 'Implications of Climate Change for Asian-Pacific Coastal and Oceanic Environments', in R. Warner and C. Schofield (eds), *Climate Change and the Oceans. Gauging the Legal and Policy Currents in the Asia Pacific and Beyond*, Cheltenham: Edward Elgar, 2012, p. 40.

7 Cheung et al., note 2, p. 245.

8 Ibid.

9 Medcalf defines the Indo-Pacific region as follows: 'The Indo-Pacific is best understood as a super-region with hard-to-define outer limits and distinct subregions yet an unquestionably Asian core': R. Medcalf, 'In Defence of the Indo-Pacific: Australia's New Strategic Map', (2014) 68 *Australian Journal of International Affairs* pp. 470, 473.

10 Hoegh-Guldberg, note 6, p. 36.

## 82   *Robin Warner*

the structural complexity and necessary habitat for the broad range of species associated with healthy coral reefs is a much longer-term prospect. Of particular note has been the similar widespread coral bleaching events in recent years on the Great Barrier Reef and in the Pacific with causes similarly attributed to rising sea-surface temperatures as well as ocean acidification.[11]

Sea level rise, leading to inundation of land territory, is already affecting South East Asia and the Pacific Island states with similarly deleterious effects to fisheries and aquaculture productivity. Vietnam is especially vulnerable and has already experienced a 2.5–3 cm increase in sea level over the past 50 years. In the Lower Mekong basin, the sea level has already risen by as much as 3 cm with further increases predicted, possibly as much as 1 m by the end of the century.[12] The loss of land and salt water intrusion induced by sea level rise has resulted in damage to, and loss of, freshwater fisheries and a reduced area available for land-based aquaculture.[13]

The increased likelihood of severe weather events associated with climate change such as large waves and storm surges poses higher direct risks to fishers including loss of gear and aquaculture stock and damage to aquaculture facilities.[14] Responses to salinity changes have prompted the building of more dykes and water gates along coastlines in South East Asia, fragmenting fisheries habitats and disturbing fish migration and spawning.[15] The changed location and timing of ocean currents and upwelling linked to climate change are expected to alter nutrient supply to fish in surface waters leading to changes in distribution and productivity of open sea fisheries.[16]

There are substantial socio-economic implications of the physical impacts of climate change on marine ecosystems for the fisheries and aquaculture-dependent populations of South East Asia. Small fishing communities in many areas will face greater uncertainty in their livelihoods as availability, access, stability and use of aquatic food and supplies lessen and work opportunities diminish.[17] The poor inhabitants of rural communities in low-lying coastal and delta areas of Vietnam, Thailand, Cambodia and China and the islands of

---

11 Ibid.

12 Mekong River Commission, 'Reducing the Impact of Climate Change on the Mekong Basin: the MRC's Climate Change and Adaptation Initiative', (n.d.), available online at http://archive. iwlearn.net/mrcmekong.org/ccai/Climate-change-n-adaptation-initiative.htm

13 World Fish Center, note 3, p. 3.

14 Ibid., p. 4.

15 Ibid., pp. 6–7; National Intelligence Council (NIC), 'Southeast Asia: The Impact of Climate Change to 2030: Geopolitical Implications', Conference Report 2010-02, (January 2010), p. 20, available online at www.dni.gov/files/documents/2010%20Conference%20Report_ Southeast%20Asia_The%20Impact%20of%20Climate%20Change%20to%202030.pdf

16 World Fish Center, above note 3, p. 3.

17 E.H. Allison et al., 'Vulnerability of National Economies to the Impacts of Climate Change on Fisheries', (2009) 10 *Fish and Fisheries* p. 188; NIC, note 15, pp. 16–17; FAO, 'Report of the FAO Expert Workshop on Climate Change Implications for Fisheries and Aquaculture', FAO Fisheries Report no. 870, 7–9 April 2008, pp. 22–23, available online at www.fao.org/ docrep/011/i0203e/i0203e00.htm

*Advancing marine environmental security* 83

Indonesia and the Philippines have limited adaptive capacity to the direct ravages of climate change on their aquatic food sources and fisheries and aquaculture infrastructure.[18] Climate change impacts will also affect alternative food supplies, decreasing crop yields on land and reducing fresh water supplies resulting in the imposition of additional costs to manage water resources, coastal erosion, disease and other health risks. Some analysts have predicted that the reduction in basic food supplies derived from fisheries and aquaculture operations as a consequence of climate change could be a contributing factor in destabilising some South East Asian societies and could fuel social tension in the region.[19] A 2010 report from the US National Intelligence Council (NIC) on 'The Geopolitical Implications of Climate Change to 2030 for Southeast Asia' noted the critical dependence of Indonesia on coastal and marine development, including fisheries production and shrimp farming which together were estimated as employing 20 million people and accounting for 25%–30% of Indonesia's GDP.[20] This report forecasts that at a minimum, climate change will alter the movement of fish stocks but at some point could also have a gross disruptive impact on the marine food chain leading to the serious depletion or collapse of crucial regional fisheries and aquaculture supplies such as those of the South China Sea.[21] The prospect of dwindling fish and aquaculture supplies in the offshore maritime zones of South East Asia heightens the potential for fisheries disputes and illegal fishing both within and beyond the region. An increased incidence of marine resource conflicts and illegal fishing will inevitably lead to tension between states in South East Asia with the accompanying negative consequences for regional security.

The depletion or even collapse of major fisheries as a result of climate change impacts and other factors such as overfishing will result in declining food and economic security in South East Asia which is already heavily dependent on fish as a key source of protein for its populations and for export commodities. This highlights the need for coastal States and regional fisheries management organisations (RFMOs) to adjust their conservation and management regimes in response to a changing and dwindling pool of fisheries resources. As coral reefs and other marine ecosystems degrade, processes such as environmental impact assessment (EIA) and marine spatial planning (MSP) including the designation and good management of marine-protected areas in coastal zones and beyond will become increasingly important in conserving marine living resources and biodiversity. Declining food resources may also provide a catalyst for inter-State and intra-State disputes in South East Asia leading to a less predictable and secure maritime environment for trading and military access.

---

18 Allison, above note 17, p. 191.
19 NIC, above note 15, p. 17; C. Jasparro and J. Taylor, 'Climate Change and Regional Vulnerability to Transnational Security Threats in Southeast Asia', (2008) 13(2) *Geopolitics* p. 240.
20 NIC, above note 15, p. 16.
21 Ibid., p. 17.

84  *Robin Warner*

## 5.3 Potential impacts of climate change on population movements in South East Asia

As the oceans absorb more of the heat generated by global warming, seawater expands and causes a rise in sea levels. Taking into account the effects of glacial and ice sheet melting, the Intergovernmental Panel on Climate Change (IPCC) has made a variety of projections based on different scenarios of global average sea level rise ranging from 0.26 to 0.98 m by the end of the century.[22] The IPCC has also forecasted changing precipitation patterns likely to produce more intense tropical storms and storm surges which together with sea level rise will cause more severe flooding.[23] Sea level rise and the more severe weather events associated with climate change may threaten the territory of coastal States leading to small island States becoming uninhabitable. These impacts will have varying effects in South East Asia depending primarily on coastal topography. Over the long term, most of the deltas in the region will be permanently submerged or eroded away with Vietnam expected to lose over 14,000 square miles of delta and significant delta areas disappearing in Thailand, Myanmar and Indonesia.[24] The combined effects of sea level rise, storm activity, changes in sea temperature and salinity will threaten the mangrove forests of the region leading to substantial erosion of coastal deltas in South East Asia. These effects will also lead to the inundation of multiple small islands, especially in the Indonesian and Philippines archipelagos with Indonesia projected to lose 2,000 small islands by 2030.[25] Coastal cities, towns and villages in South East Asia will also confront the risk of inundation from sea level rise and wild weather resulting in the destruction of housing and infrastructure. As well as socio-economic disruption and civil unrest within States of the region, the aftermath of sea level rise and the severe weather events associated with climate change could lead to mass displacements of persons seeking shelter and economic viability beyond their own States.[26]

The trend towards greater volumes of environmental refugees transiting ocean areas in South East Asia and beyond has a range of security implications for those governments and international organisations responsible for developing policy and practical responses. The likely higher numbers of vulnerable displaced persons will provide additional opportunities for people smuggling networks

---

22 IPCC, 'Summary for Policymakers' in T.F. Stocker et al. (eds), *Climate Change 2013: The Physical Science Basis. Contribution of Working Group I to the Fifth Assessment Report of the Intergovernmental Panel on Climate Change*, Cambridge: Cambridge University Press, Cambridge, 2013, p. 25, available online at www.climatechange2013.org/images/report/WG1AR5_SPM_FINAL.pdf

23 Ibid., p. 23

24 NIC, note 15, p. 17; Jasparro and Taylor, note 19, p. 239.

25 NIC, note 15, p. 17.

26 P.J. Smith, 'Climate Change, Mass Migration and the Military Response', (2007) 51(4) *Orbis* pp. 618–619; J. Barnett and W.N. Adger, 'Climate Change, Human Security and Violent Conflict' (2007) 26 *Political Geography* p. 643.

Advancing marine environmental security   85

to flourish. As a result, there will be greater public pressure on governments of transit and destination States such as Malaysia, Indonesia and Australia to tighten border security and devote more law enforcement and immigration resources to the detection and processing of boat people.[27] The hazardous nature of people smuggling operations which entail movement by sea in overcrowded and unseaworthy vessels will also impose extra responsibilities on already overstretched regional navies and coastguards to respond to distress calls and escort people smuggling vessels to processing centres.

The increased frequency and severity of weather-related disasters associated with climate change is likely to lead to loss of dwellings and the spread of disease in South East Asia and the need for augmented disaster relief services.[28] Confronted with such severe weather events, the high volumes of shipping transiting the region may become more vulnerable to accidents at sea. Similarly, offshore energy installations could be more prone to damage and less able to provide reliable sources of energy.[29]

## 5.4 Potential impacts of climate change on maritime disputes in South East Asia

It has long been recognised that the physical alterations of coastlines and inundation of small islands expected to occur as the effects of climate change intensify will have significant implications for the resolution of maritime disputes. As coastlines recede due to erosion and flooding, there may be demands to alter the boundaries between coastal States traditionally measured from the territorial sea baselines and the positions taken by States in maritime delimitation negotiations with opposite or adjacent States may fluctuate.[30] The inundation of islands is also likely to affect the sovereignty claims of the islands' inhabitants as well as their sovereign rights to offshore maritime resources.[31] There are many unresolved disputes over maritime boundaries and island territories in South East Asia particularly in the South China Sea.[32]

---

27  Barnett and Adger, note 26, p. 649.
28  Jasparro and Taylor, note 19, pp. 248–50; NIC, above note 15, p. 21.
29  NIC, note 15, p. 23.
30  D. Caron, 'When Law Makes Climate Change Worse: Rethinking the Law of Baselines in Light of a Rising Sea Level' (1990) 17 *Ecology Law Quarterly* pp. 621–653; C. Paskal, 'How Climate Change is Pushing the Boundaries of Security and Foreign Policy', *Chatham House Briefing Paper*, June 2007, p. 3.
31  C. Schofield, 'Shifting Limits? Sea Level Rise and Options to Secure Maritime Jurisdictional Claims' (2009) 3(4) *Carbon and Climate Law Review* pp. 405–416, 409–410; D. Freestone, 'International Law and Sea Level Rise' in R. Churchill and D. Freestone (eds), *International Law and Global Climate Change*, London: Graham and Trotman, 1990, p. 113.
32  For more information on these disputes, see Schofield in Chapter 3; see also the discussion in NIC, note 15, pp. 49–51; P.F. Herman and G.F. Treverton, 'The Political Consequences of Climate Change', (2009) 51(2) *Survival* pp. 137, 143.

## 86  *Robin Warner*

The impacts of climate change on coastlines and islands will further complicate the settlement of the multiparty dispute over the Spratly Islands in the South China Sea. The South China Sea is the world's largest sea at over a million square miles and contains some of the world's most important maritime trade routes. It has abundant fisheries and hydrocarbon reserves and forms the maritime boundary between China and South East Asia.[33] China, Taiwan, Vietnam, Malaysia, Indonesia, Brunei and the Philippines have all been longstanding claimants to the Spratly Islands, groups of small islets and coral atolls in the centre of the South China Sea, some of which have the capacity to generate extensive offshore zones with the accompanying sovereign rights to the associated resources. China's historic claims in the South China Sea are the most substantial extending as far south as Indonesia's Anambas Islands including the Natuna Islands.[34] With the onset of sea level rise, many of the Spratly Islands are likely to be permanently submerged, depleting the basis for territorial sovereignty claims dependent on these insular features. As the adverse impacts of climate change deepen for many of the claimant States to the Spratly Islands, heightened competition for dwindling resources will increase the potential for escalation of tensions between these States. If claimant States choose to enforce their claims through the use of military power, this could lead to more confrontations at sea.[35]

## 5.5  Mitigating the adverse impacts of climate change on maritime security

To mitigate the security implications of climate change and avert some of its detrimental effects on the socio-economic stability and environmental integrity of the Asia Pacific, ongoing cooperation among regional States, extra regional partners and international organisations is needed at many levels. Some of this cooperation is already occurring but will require extension and innovative development to address the adverse impacts of climate change on the security of the region. This section of the chapter will examine some of the relevant global and regional initiatives and ways in which they can be further developed.

### 5.5.1  Transboundary marine environmental protection initiatives

The most direct and cohesive efforts to mitigate and adapt to the adverse impacts of climate change on the coastlines and marine biodiversity of South East Asia are taking place in multilateral marine environmental protection fora. Two

---

33  NIC, note 15, p. 50.

34  L. Buszynski and I. Sazlan, 'Maritime Claims and Energy Cooperation in the South China Sea' (2007) 29 *Contemporary Southeast Asia* pp. 143–151.

35  J.F. Bradford, 'The Growing Prospects for Maritime Security Cooperation in Southeast Asia' (2005) 58(3) *Naval War College Review* p. 70.

regional initiatives which have been taken in East Asia and the Asia Pacific to protect the shared marine environment have strong climate change components. Partnerships in Environmental Management in East Asian Seas (PEMSEA) and the Coral Triangle Initiative (CTI) reflect a common concern among East Asian States and some adjacent Pacific States for their shared marine environment in both the semi-enclosed seas of East Asia and the Pacific Ocean areas to the east of Japan and the Philippines. A group of 11 States and 22 non-State entities are partners in PEMSEA, which was established as a regional project of the Global Environment Facility (GEF) in 1994 with the initial aim of preventing and managing marine pollution in the East Asian seas.[36] PEMSEA's principal objective has developed into building interagency and inter-sectoral and intergovernmental partnerships for achieving the sustainable development of East Asian seas.[37] PEMSEA is the regional coordinating mechanism for the Sustainable Development Strategy for the Seas of East Asia (SDS-SEA), a shared marine strategy among 14 countries in the region. Updated in 2015, the SDS-SEA contains seven strategies and related objectives and action programs for the sustainable development of coasts and oceans.[38] The ADAPT strategy focusses on climate change adaptation and disaster risk reduction and management by strengthening capacities and measures for preparing, adapting and responding to natural and man-made hazards.[39] One of the key action programmes in the SDS-SEA, Integrated Coastal Management (ICM), has adopted an integrated approach to protecting, restoring and managing natural habitats for biodiversity conservation, including climate change adaptation.[40] A range of protection and restoration activities have been implemented under this programme, including mangrove reforestation in Manila Bay, coral reef rehabilitation in Bali and protection and conservation of reef marshes in the Bohai Sea.[41]

The CTI is another example of non-treaty-based maritime cooperation in the Asia Pacific with a strong focus on climate change adaptation. The Coral Triangle is a region located along the equator at the confluence of the Western Pacific and Indian Oceans which covers all or part of the exclusive economic zones (EEZs) of six countries: Indonesia, Malaysia, the Philippines, Papua New Guinea, the Solomon Islands and Timor-Leste. The CTI is regarded by scientists as one of the richest repositories of marine biodiversity on earth containing 76% of all known coral species, 37% of coral reef fish and 33% of the world's coral reefs. It is also the most prolific location for mangrove forests and spawning and

---

36 PEMSEA, 'About PEMSEA', (n.d.), available online at www.pemsea.org/about-pemsea
37 Ibid.
38 PEMSEA, 'Regional Marine Strategy', (n.d.), available online at http://pemsea.org/our-work/regional-marine-strategy
39 Ibid.
40 PEMSEA, 'Habitat Protection', (n.d.) available online at http://pemsea.org/our-work/habitat-protection
41 Ibid.

88    *Robin Warner*

juvenile growth areas for the world's largest tuna fishery.[42] Threats to the CTI region include overfishing, destructive fisheries practices, land-based sources of marine pollution and the ravages of climate change.[43] The CTI was proposed by Indonesia in 2007 as a multilateral partnership to protect the region's coastal and marine resources. The member States of Indonesia, the Philippines, Malaysia, Timor-Leste, Papua New Guinea and the Solomon Islands have committed to five overall goals over ten years:

- The designation of priority seascapes;
- Implementing an ecosystem approach to managing fisheries and other marine resources;
- The establishment of marine-protected areas;
- Developing strategies to adapt to climate change and
- The protection of threatened species.[44]

Member States implement activities specified under the CTI Coral Reefs, Fisheries and Food Security Regional Plan of Action and corresponding CTI National Plans of Action. Many of the regional and national actions under the CTI are contributing directly to climate change adaptation along the coasts and in the offshore maritime zones of South East Asia.[45]

### 5.5.2 Fisheries conservation and sustainable use arrangements

Whereas Pacific Island nations have developed comprehensive regional fisheries management agreements for tuna and non-tuna species, implemented through the Western Central Pacific Fisheries Commission and the South Pacific Regional Fisheries Commission, South East Asia is not as well equipped for long-term conservation and sustainable use of fish stocks. The South East Asian Fisheries Development Centre (SEAFDEC) provides a forum for ASEAN member States to discuss issues of common interest around fisheries and build consensus but it has a purely advisory rather than an ongoing management role for regional fisheries.[46] Some more general multilateral research bodies such as the Asia Pacific Fisheries Commission (APFIC) established through FAO and the Asian Fisheries Society provide information exchange mechanisms but have no power to take concrete conservation measures to address the adverse impacts of climate change and other destructive fisheries practices on regional fisheries.[47] Some

42  CTI, 'Frequently Asked Questions', (n.d.), available online at www.coraltriangleinitiative.org/frequently-asked-questions-0
43  Ibid.
44  Ibid.
45  Ibid.
46  SEAFDEC, 'About SEAFDEC', (n.d.), available online at www.seafdec.org/about/
47  FAO, 'Asia Pacific Fisheries Commission' (n.d.), available online at www.fao.org/apfic/en/; see also Asian Fisheries Society, (n.d.), available online at www.asianfisheriessociety.org/#

*Advancing marine environmental security* 89

project-based activities such as the GEF-funded project on reversing environmental degradation trends in the South China Sea and the Gulf of Thailand and the PEMSEA SDS-SEA described in the previous section have included fisheries in their mandate but they are not long-term regional management bodies for fisheries.[48] As the effects of climate change on fish stocks and marine ecosystems become more severe, the need to implement effective adaptation strategies through regional fisheries management arrangements with binding powers to adopt conservation measures will become more pressing.[49]

## 5.6 Cooperative arrangements to combat transnational crime in the Asia Pacific

Cooperative maritime surveillance and enforcement arrangements coupled with criminal justice links between regional partners are critical in combating the transnational criminal activities, such as people smuggling and illegal fishing, which are likely to escalate as climate change impacts adversely affect coastal habitats and marine resources in the Asia Pacific. In the case of people smuggling, cooperation between source, transit and destination countries is essential. Connections need to be forged at all levels of the criminal justice system including intelligence exchange between source, transit and destination countries, cooperative arrangements for 'at sea' enforcement between neighbouring States and links between investigation and prosecution authorities of regional States. In the Asia Pacific, the Bali Process on People Smuggling, Trafficking in Persons and Related Transnational Crime (Bali Process) co-chaired by Indonesia and Australia, is a multilateral initiative which began in 2002 primarily to combat people smuggling. It involves over 48 States including most South East Asian and Pacific States.[50] Early multilateral initiatives under the Bali Process focussed on people smuggling throughout the Asia Pacific and involved operational and policy officials from law enforcement, immigration, justice and development agencies. Practical measures that have been taken include:

- The development of model legislation by Australia and China to criminalise people smuggling and trafficking in persons to enable police investigation, prosecution and extraditions. This model legislation has subsequently been used by many regional countries in the development of their own legislation;

---

48 GEF, 'Reversing Environmental Degradation Trends in the South China Sea and the Gulf of Thailand – Project Summary', (n.d.), available online at www.thegef.org/project/reversing-environmental-degradation-trends-south-china-sea-and-gulf-thailand; PEMSEA, 'Sustainable Development Strategies for the Seas of East Asia', 20 November 2015, available online at http://pemsea.org/publications/reports/sustainable-development-strategy-seas-east-asia-sds-sea-2015

49 C. Wilkinson et al., 'Strategies to Reverse the Decline in Valuable and Diverse Coral Reefs, Mangroves and Fisheries: The Bottom of the J-Curve in Southeast Asia' (2006) 49 *Ocean and Coastal Management* pp. 764, 775.

50 Bali Process, 'About the Bali Process', (n.d.), available online at www.baliprocess.net/

## 90  Robin Warner

- The convening of a law enforcement and document fraud workshop in China;
- Two workshops convened by the UN High Commissioner for Refugees (UNHCR) in Thailand and Fiji on best practice procedures for determining the status of asylum seekers and on balancing a country's right to determine who enters its territory with the right of victims of persecution or violence to seek and receive protection in other countries and
- A workshop among law enforcement agencies developed by the Australian Federal Police (AFP) focussing on cooperation in identifying and targeting key people smugglers and traffickers in the region.[51]

At the Sixth Regional Ministerial Conference of the Bali Process in March 2016, Ministers reinforced the region's commitment to tackling irregular maritime migration, by agreeing to establish a Consultation Mechanism and gave the Co-Chairs authority to convene discussions on urgent irregular migration issues. The Co-Chairs convened the first meeting under the Consultation Mechanism on 13 October 2017 in Jakarta to discuss irregular migration in the region. This initiative has established an important dialogue among members on ways in which the Bali Process and individual member States can strengthen cooperation to address irregular migration.[52]

A wide reaching and functional criminal justice cooperation network has been identified by the Bali Process as essential to combating transnational criminal activity including people smuggling in the Asia Pacific. Although some progress has been made with establishing mutual legal assistance and extradition relationships between the member States of the Bali Process at both bilateral and multilateral levels, the criminal justice cooperation framework in the region is far from comprehensive.[53] The 2004 ASEAN Mutual Legal Assistance Treaty is a positive step, but to fully implement criminal justice cooperation in the region, further bilateral mutual legal assistance and extradition arrangements tailored to the specific needs of regional partners need to be negotiated.[54]

A noticeable gap in the maritime law enforcement apparatus of South East Asia is the lack of cooperative maritime surveillance and enforcement arrangements between States to combat transnational criminal activities such as people smuggling and illegal fishing. While there have been some successful examples

---

51 Ibid.

52 Bali Process, 'Bali Process Strategy for Cooperation. October 2017 Update – 12th Ad Hoc Senior Officials' Meeting', October 2017, available online at www.baliprocess.net/UserFiles/baliprocess/File/BP%20Strategy%20-%20Update%20for%2012th%20AHG%20SOM%20-%20final%202%20November%202017.pdf

53 Anti-corruption Initiative for Asia and the Pacific (ADB/CECD), *Mutual Legal Assistance, Extradition and Recovery of Proceeds of Corruption in Asia and the Pacific. Frameworks and Practices in 27 Asian and Pacific Jurisdictions*, Manila: Asian Development Bank, 2007, available online at www.oecd.org/site/adboecdanti-corruptioninitiative/mutuallegalassistanceextradi-tionandrecoveryofproceedsofcorruptioninasiaandthepacific.htm

54 *Treaty on Mutual Legal Assistance in Criminal Matters*, 29 November 2004, 2336 UNTS 271.

of coordinated maritime surveillance and enforcement against piracy and armed robbery at sea with the trilateral patrols of Singapore, Indonesia and Malaysia in the Strait of Malacca,[55] and more recently the coordinated trilateral patrols launched by Indonesia, Malaysia and the Philippines against terrorist activities in the Sulu-Sulawesi Seas,[56] these cooperative arrangements have not been extended to a broader range of transnational criminal activities including people smuggling and illegal fishing. With climate change as one of the drivers increasing this type of transnational criminal activity, States in South East Asia could consider following the example of Pacific States with their 2012 Agreement on Strengthening Implementation of the Niue Treaty on Cooperation Fisheries Surveillance and Law Enforcement in the South Pacific Region and their subsidiary agreements at a bilateral level.[57] With greater flows of displaced persons travelling through the region, cooperative resettlement agreements on a bilateral or multilateral basis may also be required.

## 5.7 Finding solutions to maritime resource disputes

The negative impacts of climate change, combined with the other regional insecurity drivers in South East Asia, will provoke more competition for declining marine living resources and untapped non-living resources such as offshore hydrocarbons. There is already ample evidence of tension and active confrontation among some South East Asian States over access to the living and non-living resources in the South China Sea and the Ambalat block, a fossil-fuel-rich area of seabed in the Celebes Sea off East Borneo.[58] These simmering disputes highlight the urgency of negotiating creative solutions to maritime disputes which will enable equitable access to, and distribution of, available marine resources. Many analysts have suggested that joint development arrangements be negotiated to facilitate exploitation of the hydrocarbon resources of the South China Sea with the resolution of territorial sovereignty claims deferred to accommodate such exploitation.[59] There are some models for this type of arrangement such as the 2002 Timor Sea Treaty between Australia and Timor-Leste although the

---

55 J.F. Bradford, 'Shifting the Tides against Piracy in Southeast Asian Waters', (2008) 48(3) *Asian Survey* p. 473.

56 P. Parameswaran, 'New Sulu Sea Trilateral Patrols Officially Launched in Indonesia' *The Diplomat*, 4 August 2016, available online at https://thediplomat.com/2016/08/new-sulu-sea-trilateral-patrols-officially-launched/

57 *Agreement on Strengthening Implementation of the Niue Treaty on Cooperation Fisheries Surveillance and Law Enforcement in the South Pacific Region*, 2 November 2012, [2017] ATS 11.

58 Buszynski and Sazlan, note 34, pp. 144–151; NIC, note 15, 49–50.

59 Buszynski and Sazlan, note 34, pp. 166–168; Z. Gao, 'The South China Sea: From Conflict to Cooperation', (1994) 25 *Ocean Development and International Law* pp. 345, 358–359; M.J. Valencia and M. Miyoshi, 'Southeast Asian Seas: Joint Development of Hydrocarbons in Overlapping Claim Areas', (1986) 16 *Ocean Development and International Law* pp. 211, 253–254.

## 92 *Robin Warner*

number of claimants to the Spratly Islands in the South China Sea amplifies the challenges involved in achieving an agreement acceptable to all parties.[60]

In the fisheries sphere, there are limited conservation and management arrangements in South East Asia. Negotiating more of these agreements may assist in preventing potential disputes between regional States over declining fish stocks and in adapting to the changes which could occur as a result of climate change. China and Vietnam negotiated two agreements in 2000 and 2004 to conserve, manage and exploit the fisheries resources of the Beibu Gulf (Gulf of Tonkin): the 2000 Agreement between the Government of the Peoples Republic of China and the Socialist Republic of Vietnam on Fishery Cooperation in Beibu Gulf, and a 2004 Protocol to the earlier agreement.[61] These agreements are administered by a Joint Fishery Committee with members from both parties.[62] Three zones are designated, the Common Fisheries Zone, the waters in transitional arrangements and the buffer zone for small size fishing boats. The Common Fisheries Zone covers 33,500 square kilometres which is 27.9% of the Gulf's total area. The parties committed to long-term fisheries cooperation in this area over the initial 12-year term of the agreement and further extensions to the agreement have been negotiated. The number of vessels with access to the Common Fisheries Zone is determined annually taking into account allowable catches established on the basis of joint regular surveys of fisheries resources, the impact on respective fisheries activities of both parties and the need for sustainable development of the resources while respecting the principle of equality and mutual benefit. The waters under transitional arrangements were established as an interim measure to limit the number of fishing vessels of each party which could access certain areas of their respective EEZs for four years after the 2000 agreement entered into force. The buffer zone for small-sized fishing boats (no more than 60 HP or 15 m in length) was established to avoid disputes caused by the inadvertent illegal entry of small-sized fishing boats of one party into the territorial sea of another. Under the agreement, if either party finds small-sized fishing boats of the other party in its waters or the buffer zone, it may give the boats a warning to leave or take necessary measures to repel them from the area without the use of force or detention and arrest.[63] Some Chinese analysts have argued that overall, the Agreement's implementation has produced numerous positive results for China and Vietnam including strengthened

---

60  *Timor Sea Treaty between the Government of East Timor and the Government of Australia*, 20 May 2002, [2003] ATS 13.

61  *Agreement on the Delimitation of the Territorial Sea, Exclusive Economic Zones and Continental Shelves in the Beibu Gulf [Gulf of Tonkin] between the People's Republic of China and the Socialist Republic of Vietnam*, 25 December 2000, 2336 UNTS 179; see details in Y. Yu and Y. Mu, 'The New Institutional Arrangements for Fisheries Management in Beibu Gulf', (2006) 30(3) *Marine Policy* pp. 249, 250; and H.T. Nguyen, 'Maritime Delimitation and Fishery Cooperation in the Tonkin Gulf', (2005) 36 *Ocean Development and International Law* pp. 25–45.

62  Yu and Mu, note 61.

63  Ibid., pp. 254–255.

cooperation on fisheries management, a reduction in fisheries conflicts and the more equitable sharing of fisheries resources.[64]

## 5.8 Conclusion

While marine environmental degradation and climate change impacts may not be the most direct catalysts for regional insecurity in South East Asia, they have a compounding effect on other causes of regional insecurity. As multipliers of other insecurity drivers, such as overfishing, destructive fisheries practices, environmental degradation, poverty, fragile social circumstances and transnational crime, marine environmental degradation and climate change impacts represent a potent non-traditional security threat in South East Asia. If climate change adaptation measures are not rigorously implemented, the adverse impacts of warming temperatures and ocean acidity on fisheries combined with overfishing and destructive fisheries practices could lead to the collapse of some regional fish stocks, precipitating a food security crisis. Strengthening the regional measures already in place to reverse environmental degradation and combat transnational crimes such as people smuggling and illegal fishing will also be important in reducing the vulnerability of coastal populations displaced by the sea level rise and severe weather events associated with climate change. Re-examining the maritime boundary and resource-related disputes which exist in South East Asia to determine whether creative solutions can be found to maximise the benefits for all interested stakeholders can only assist the region in addressing the resource shortages and social disruption which climate change, combined with other insecurity drivers, will inevitably bring. Some multilateral initiatives are already in place to tackle these issues. but the adverse impacts of climate change forecast by the IPCC and other international bodies suggest that collaborative initiatives to mitigate its negative effects on food and human security as well as the marine environment need to be reinforced and augmented at all levels.

---

64 Y. Huang and M. Huang, 'Implementation of the Sino-Vietnamese Fishery Agreement: Mainly Chinese Perspective', (2013) 4(3) *Beijing Law Review* p. 119.

# 6 Climate change and the law of the sea in the Asia Pacific

*Karen N. Scott*[1]

## 6.1 Introduction

As a global phenomenon, the impacts of climate change on the oceans – sea level rise, increase in water temperature and ocean acidification – will affect all regions to a greater or lesser extent.[2] However, the Asia Pacific is particularly vulnerable owing to, *inter alia*, the number of low-lying atoll islands in the Pacific, the presence of unstable coastlines such as the Mekong Delta in Vietnam, the large number of significant coral reef ecosystems and the fact that the Asia Pacific is the most disaster-prone region in the world.[3] Although this vulnerability has been recognised by States within and beyond the region, especially in the context of sea level rise, meaningful action is limited by the broader global neglect of the oceans-climate connection.[4] Until relatively recently, the oceans have been largely omitted from consideration by the climate regime established under the auspices of the 1992 United Nations Framework Convention on Climate Change (UNFCCC),[5] but equally, climate change is not directly addressed by the law of the sea, developed under the framework of the 1982 United Nations

---

1 This chapter draws on and develops work previously published as K.N. Scott, 'Climate Change and the Oceans: Navigating Legal Orders' in M.H. Nordquist, J.N. Moore and R. Long (eds), *Legal Order and the World's Oceans: UN Convention on the Law of the Sea*, Leiden: Koninklijke Brill, 2017, p. 124; K.N. Scott, 'Legal Aspects of Climate Change' in International Ocean Institute – Canada (ed), *The Future of Ocean Governance and Training: Essays in Honour of Elisabeth Mann Borgese (1918–2002)*, Leiden: Koninklijke Brill, 2018, p. 169; K.N. Scott, 'Ocean Acidification and Sustainable Development Goal 14: A Goal but No Target?' in M.H. Nordquist, J.N. Moore and R.Long (eds), *The Marine Environment and United Nations Sustainable Development Goal 14: Life below Water*, Leiden: Koninklijke Brill, 2018, p. 323.
2 See generally M. Rhein et al., 'Observations: Ocean' in T.F Stocker et al. (eds), *Climate Change 2013: The Physical Science Basis. Contribution of Working Group I to the Fifth Assessment Report of the Intergovernmental Panel on Climate Change*, Cambridge: Cambridge University Press, 2013, p. 255 [hereafter IPCC Fifth Assessment Report].
3 J.H. Hashim and Z. Hashim, 'Climate Change, Extreme Weather Events, and Human Health Implications in the Asia Pacific Region', (2016) 28 (2S) *Asia Pacific Journal of Public Health* p. 8S.
4 See Scott, 'Climate Change and the Oceans: Navigating Legal Orders', note 1, p. 124.
5 *United Nations Framework Convention on Climate Change*, 9 May 1992, 1771 UNTS 107 [hereafter *UNFCCC*].

Convention on the Law of the Sea (LOSC).[6] This relative neglect at the global level arguably opens up opportunities at the regional level for action, although developments to date have largely focussed on adaptation to, rather than mitigation of, climate change.

This chapter will explore the intersection of oceans and climate through the lenses of mitigation, exploitation and adaptation, with a particular focus on developments in the Pacific as well as South East Asia. There are obvious parallels between the two regions, particularly with respect to the nature of the threats posed to marine ecosystems, coastal regions and maritime resources. However, whereas the Pacific is emerging as a global leader with respect to climate change – both on the international stage and in terms of regional innovation – the same cannot be said for South East Asia. Through an examination of the oceans-climate regime complex, this chapter will critically discuss the global instruments of application to climate change mitigation and the exploitation of the oceans for climate-related purposes. Adaptation is addressed at both the global and regional levels, and selected examples from the Asia Pacific will be drawn on to illustrate developing practice, which demonstrates examples of regional innovation in the context of responding to the impacts of climate change on the oceans. Two innovations from the Pacific region, in relation to fisheries management and sea level rise, will be highlighted in particular to demonstrate the contrast between the two regions and to illustrate possible precedents for other regions, including South East Asia.

## 6.2 Climate change, the oceans and the Asia Pacific

The ocean and the atmosphere

> form a coupled system, exchanging at the air sea interface gases, water (and water vapour), particles, momentum and energy. These exchanges affect the biology, the chemistry and the physics of the ocean and influence its biogeochemical processes, weather and climate.[7]

Atmospheric concentration of carbon dioxide ($CO_2$) now averages more than 400 parts per million,[8] an increase from approximately 280 ppm at the onset of

---

6 United Nations Convention on the Law of the Sea, 10 December 1982, 1833 UNTS 397 [hereafter LOSC].

7 *The First Global Integrated Marine Assessment (World Ocean Assessment I) by the Group of Experts of the Regular Process under the Auspices of the United Nations General Assembly and its Regular Process for Global Reporting and Assessment of the State of the Marine Environment, including Socioeconomic Aspects* (2016), available online at www.un.org/Depts/los/global_reporting/WOA_RegProcess.htm, chapter 5, p. 1 [hereafter WOA I].

8 World Meteorological Organization, *Greenhouse Gas Bulletin* No. 12, 24 October 2016, available online at https://ane4bf-datap1.s3-eu-west-1.amazonaws.com/wmocms/s3fspublic/GHG_Bulletin_12_EN_web_JN161640.pdf?aZaKZhdpDfJdmHvtbSvLwbj6zb_PWwdz

## 96  Karen N. Scott

the Industrial Revolution.[9] The oceans operate as the largest sink for $CO_2$, and hold around 50 times more $CO_2$ than the atmosphere.[10] Approximately half of all fossil fuel emissions since the beginning of the Industrial Revolution have been absorbed by the oceans,[11] and 30% of all anthropogenic $CO_2$ is drawn down into the oceans annually.[12] About half of all anthropogenic $CO_2$ is stored in the upper 10% of the ocean.[13] As well as sequestering $CO_2$, the oceans also play an important role in mitigating the impacts of climate change by absorbing and distributing heat by means of wind and differences in water density.[14] The oceans contain around 1000 times more heat than the atmosphere[15] and have absorbed 93% of the additional heat generated by anthropogenic activities over the last 50 years.[16]

The fundamental role played by the oceans in mitigating the impacts of climate change has predictably had negative implications for their health and productivity. The upper ocean has increased in temperature by between 0.65° and 1.06° between 1880 and 2012,[17] and recent research suggests that the temperature increase is in fact at the high end of previous estimates.[18] Temperature increases impact both the biology and the chemistry of the oceans. Research suggests water temperature changes may lead to the relocation of fish and plankton species, typically towards higher latitudes or to greater depths,[19] impacting on primary production and nutrient cycles.[20] In the Western Pacific, it is predicted that tuna fisheries will move east and north between, and ultimately beyond, the exclusive economic zones (EEZs) of the Pacific island States that depend on the tuna fishery for a significant proportion of their economies.[21] Modelling predicts

---

9  M.R. Raupach et al., 'Global and regional drivers of accelerating $CO_2$ emission', (2007) 104 *Proceedings of the National Academy of Sciences* p. 10288.

10  IPCC Fifth Assessment Report, note 2, p. 260.

11  WOA I, note 7, chapter 5, p. 17.

12  IPCC Fifth Assessment Report, note 2, p. 260.

13  WOA I, note 7, chapter 5, p. 17.

14  Ibid., chapter 5, p. 7.

15  Ibid., chapter 5, p. 7.

16  IPCC Fifth Assessment Report, note 2, p. 260.

17  D.L Hartmann et al., 'Observations: Atmosphere' in T.F. Stocker et al. (eds), *Climate Change 2013: The Physical Science Basis. Contribution of Working Group I to the Fifth Assessment Report of the Intergovernmental Panel on Climate Change*, Cambridge: Cambridge University Press, 2013, p. 161.

18  L. Resplandy et al., 'Quantification of Ocean Heat Uptake from Changes in Atmospheric $O_2$ and $CO_2$ Composition', (2018) 563 *Nature* p. 105.

19  WOA I, note 7, summary, p. 13; see also A.S. Brierley and M.J. Kingsford, 'Impacts of Climate Change on Marine Organisms and Ecosystems', (2009) 19 *Current Biology* p. R608, and, with particular reference to Asia, J.C. Molinero et al., 'Interannual Change in Zooplankton Echo Subtropical and High Latitude Climate Effects in the Southern East China Sea', (2018) 13 *PloS ONE*.

20  WOA I, summary, p. 13.

21  Revenue from licensing varies from between 2% and 60% of GDP for Pacific States; see A.D. Yeeting et al., 'Implications of New Economic Policy Instruments for Tuna Management in the Western and Central Pacific', (2016) 63 *Marine Policy* p. 45; see more generally, A. McIlgorm,

Climate change 97

that up to 55% of Asian fisheries will experience a shift in ecological range, with 29% of those changes being classed as significant.[22] Higher temperatures may also impact on the metabolic and productivity rates of fish stocks.[23] Sedentary species are likely to be the first affected[24] and coral bleaching within the Asia Pacific and other regions is one of the most visible impacts of climate change on the oceans to date.[25] A further consequence of ocean warming is deoxygenation, as warmer waters hold less oxygen than colder waters[26] and this, combined with changes in salinity (resulting from ice melt and alternations of precipitation patterns), has increased ocean stratification[27] and, ironically, reduced the capacity of the ocean to absorb $CO_2$.[28]

The thermal expansion of the oceans combined with melting sea ice and glaciers is also predicted to lead to a rise in sea levels, and it is estimated that global sea levels have already risen by 0.19 m between 1901 and 2010.[29] Recent research suggests that sea levels could rise by more than 2 metres by 2100.[30] Coastal habitats are at particular risk, including mangroves, salt marshes and seagrasses, which collectively store between 50% and 71% of $CO_2$ in ocean sediments.[31] The Asia Pacific is particularly rich in mangrove and seagrass ecosystems[32] with 22% of the world's mangrove forests being located in Indonesia alone.[33] In Kiribati, mangrove forests comprise the atoll State's most productive and biologically

---

'Economic Impacts of Climate Change on Sustainable Tuna and Billfish Management: Insights from the Western Pacific', (2010) 86 *Progress in Oceanography* pp. 187, 189–191; A. Monllor-Hurtado, M.G. Pennino and J.L. Sanchez-Lizaso, 'Shift in Tuna Catches due to Ocean Warming', (2017) 12 *PLoS ONE*; J.D Bell et al., 'Effects of Climate Change on Oceanic Fisheries in the Topical Pacific: Implications for Economic Development and Security', (2013) 119 *Climatic Change* p. 213.

22 C. Costello, 'Does Climate Change Bolser the Case for Fishery Reform in Asia?', (2018) 35 *Asia Development Review* pp. 31, 33.

23 Research predicts that potential fish catches decrease by more than 3 million metric tonnes per degree of warming; see W.W.L. Cheung, G. Reygondeau and T.L. Frölicher, 'Large Benefits to Marine Fisheries of Meeting the 1.5° C Global Warming Target', (2016) 354 *Science* p. 1591.

24 Brierley and Kingsford, note 19, p. R605.

25 For an overview of climate change and global coral reefs, see C. Birkeland, 'Global Status of Coral Reefs: In Combination, Disturbances and Stressors Become Ratchets' in C. Sheppard (ed), *World Seas: an Environmental Evaluation. Volume III: Ecological Issues and Environmental Impacts*, 2nd ed., London: Academic Press, 2019, p. 35.

26 See A.J. Watson, 'Oceans on the Edge of Anoxia', (2016) 354 *Science* p. 1529.

27 WOA I, summary, p. 11.

28 Ibid.

29 IPCC Fifth Assessment Report, note 2, p. 258.

30 M. Oppenheimer and R.B. Alley, 'How High will the Seas Rise?', (2016) 354 *Science* p. 1375.

31 C. Nellermann (ed), *Blue Carbon. The Role of Healthy Oceans in Binding Carbon*, Norway: UNEP and GRID Arendel, 2009, p. 7.

32 C.E Lovelock et al., 'The Vulnerability of Indo-Pacific Mangrove Forests to Sea-Level Rise', (2015) 526 *Nature* p. 559.

33 L. Dsikowitzky et al., 'Java Island, Indonesia' in C. Sheppard (ed), *World Seas: An Environmental Evaluation. Volume II: the Indian Ocean to the Pacific*, 2nd ed., London: Academic Press, 2019, pp. 459, 467.

diverse ecosystem.[34] Sea level rise also risks coastal communities through flooding, salinisation of soil and fresh water and associated economic impacts on agriculture, aquaculture, tourism and coastal infrastructure.[35] In Vietnam, saline intrusion is already severe in the Mekong Delta region and it is estimated that sea level rise may displace almost six million people in Vietnam by 2100.[36] Of the 25 cities most vulnerable to a rise in sea level of 1 metre, 19 are located in the Asia Pacific with seven of them in the Philippines alone.[37] It is predicted that Indonesia will be most at risk from coastal flooding in South East Asia with an estimated 5.9 million people likely affected on an annual basis by 2100.[38] Fundamentally, sea level rise threatens to impact on the extent of current maritime zones as basepoints are inundated and ultimately, the very survival of low-lying nations such as Kiribati, Tuvalu and the Marshall Islands is at risk.[39] It is estimated that 55% of Kiribati will be uninhabitable by 2050 owing to inundation and storm surges[40] and Kiribati has already purchased land in Fiji in anticipation of future migration.[41] Climate-forced migration is not however, merely an issue for future policy-makers: 2600 people have already moved from the low-lying Carteret Islands to Bougainville in Papua New Guinea as a consequence of sea level rise.[42]

Ocean acidification comprises the third impact of climate change on the oceans although it is perhaps better described as a consequence of increasing levels of $CO_2$ in the oceans rather than a consequence of climate change *per se*. Ocean acidity has increased by about 30% since the onset of the Industrial Revolution,[43] a startling rise given that ocean pH had been stable for around

---

34 S. Mangubhai et al., 'Kiribati: Atolls and Marine Ecosystems' in Sheppard, note 33, pp. 807, 819.

35 R.J. Nicholls and J.A. Low, 'Benefits of Mitigation of Climate Change for Coastal Areas', (2004) 14 *Coastal Environmental Change* pp. 229, 234.

36 S. Giuliani, L.G. Bellucci and D.H. Nhon, 'The Coast of Vietnam: Present Status and Future Challenges for Sustainable Development' in Sheppard, note 33, pp. 415, 422–423.

37 I. Overland et al., *Impact of Climate Change on ASEAN International Affairs: Risk and Opportunity Multiplier*, Norwegian Institute of International Affairs and Myanmar Institute of International and Strategic Studies, 2017, available online at www.researchgate.net/publication/320622312_Impact_of_Climate_Change_on_ASEAN_International_Affairs_Risk_and_Opportunity_Multiplier, p. 5.

38 Ibid., p. 5.

39 K. Wyett, 'Escaping a Rising Tide: Sea Level Rise and Migration in Kiribati', (2014) 1 *Asia and the Pacific Policy Studies* p. 171.

40 Ibid., p. 172.

41 L. Caramel, 'Besieged by the Rising Tides of Climate Change, Kiribati buys Land in Fiji', *The Guardian Weekly*, 1 July 2014, available online at www.theguardian.com/environment/2014/jul/01/kiribati-climate-change-fiji-vanua-levu

42 For background to this controversial move, see J. Connell, 'Last days in the Carteret Islands? Climate Change, Livelihoods and Migration on Coral Atolls', (2016) 57 *Asia Pacific Viewpoint* p. 3.

43 S. Dupont and H. Pörner, 'A Snapshot of Ocean Acidification Research', (2013) 160 *Marine Biology* p. 1765.

Climate change 99

800,000 years until the beginning of the nineteenth century.[44] Although the principal cause of ocean acidification is $CO_2$ from the atmosphere (and, to a lesser extent, from land-based runoff),[45] recent research has also identified other greenhouse gases such as $SO_x$, $NO_x$ and $NH_3$ as contributing sources.[46] Lower ocean pH levels decrease the saturation of calcium carbonate ($CaCO_3$) in the oceans, which is the compound integral to the shells and skeletons of many marine species,[47] and calcifying species such as pteropods[48] and shelled molluscs[49] are particularly at risk. Of particular vulnerability within the Asia Pacific are coral reef ecosystems,[50] and ocean acidification is predicted to compound the impacts of ocean temperature rise and contribute to coral bleaching events.[51] Although the impact of ocean acidification on fish is under-researched, some experiments have indicated that low pH levels may damage key organs in the larvae of yellowfin tuna,[52] slow the development of embryos and larvae,[53] negatively impact the ability of fish to sense predators[54] or distinguish between predator and non-predator odours,[55] and change behaviour, including becoming less

44 C. Turley and J. Gattuso, 'Future Biological and Ecosystem Impacts of Ocean Acidification and their Socioeconomic-Policy Implications', (2012) 4 *Current Opinion in Environmental Sustainability*, p. 278.

45 W. Cai et al., 'Acidification of Subsurface Coastal Waters Enhanced by Eutrophication', (2011) 4 *Nature Geoscience* p. 766.

46 K. Hunter et al., 'Impacts of Anthropogenic SOx, NOx and NH3 on Acidification of Coastal Waters and Shipping Lanes', (2011) 38 *Geophysical Research Letters* p. L13602.

47 B. Hönisch et al., 'The Geological Record of Ocean Acidification', (2012) 335 *Science* pp. 1058, 1059.

48 J. Orr et al., 'Anthropogenic Ocean Acidification over the Twenty-First Century and its Impact on Calcifying Organisms', (2005) 437 *Nature* p. 681; N. Bednaršek et al., 'Pteropods on the Edge: Cumulative Effects of Ocean Acidification, Warming, and Deoxygenation', (2016) 145 *Progress in Oceanography* p. 1.

49 J. Ekstrom et al., 'Vulnerability and Adaptation of US Shellfisheries to Ocean Acidification', (2015) 5 *Nature Climate Change* p. 207.

50 O. Hoegh-Guldbert et al., 'Coral Reefs Under Rapid Climate Change and Ocean Acidification', (2007) 318 *Science* p. 1737. For example, calcification of the Great Barrier Reef has decreased by around 21% between 1988 and 2003; see S. Doney et al., 'Ocean Acidification: The Other $CO_2$ Problem', (2009) 1 *Annual Review of Marine Science* pp. 169, 175.

51 K.R.N. Anthony et al., 'Ocean Acidification Causes Bleaching and Productivity Loss in Coral Reef Builders', (2008) 105 *Proceedings of the National Academy of Sciences of the United States of America* p. 17442; P.L. Jokiel et al., 'Ocean Acidification and Calcifying Reef Organisms: A Mescocosm Investigation', (2008) 27 *Coral Reefs* p. 473.

52 A. Frommel et al., 'Ocean Acidification has Lethal and Sub-Lethal Effects on Larval Development of Yellowfin Tuna, *Thunnus Albacares*' (2016) 482 *Journal of Experimental Marine Biology and Ecology* p. 19.

53 K. Verkaik, J. Hamel and A. Mercier, 'Impact of Ocean Acidification on Reproductive Output in the Deep-Sea Annelid *Ophryotrocha sp.* (Polychaeta: Dorvilleidae)' (2017) 137 *Deep-Sea Research II* p. 368.

54 P. Munday et al., 'Replenishment of Fish Populations is Threatened by Ocean Acidification', (2010) 107 *Proceedings of the National Academy of Sciences of the United States of America* p. 12930.

55 T. Branch et al., 'Impacts of Ocean Acidification on Marine Seafood', (2013) 28 *Trend in Ecology and Evolution* pp. 178, 180.

## 100   *Karen N. Scott*

predator adverse.[56] It is predicted that the current pH of 8.1 could decrease to between 7.9 and 7.7 by 2100,[57] although the potential impact of changing ocean chemistry on species and ecosystems is largely unknown at this stage.[58] More generally, it is predicted that a low pH ocean environment has a reduced capacity to absorb further $CO_2$, weakening the ocean as a natural (or unnatural) sink for $CO_2$.[59]

The negative impacts of climate change and ocean acidification on the health and productivity of the oceans are regionally diverse but on one estimate up to 60% of ocean biomass could be affected.[60] The Asia Pacific is likely to be in the frontline of such impacts as low-lying States, unstable coastlines and coral reef ecosystems will be, and in fact are already, being negatively affected by rising sea levels, warmer waters and ocean acidification. The peoples of the Asia Pacific are also likely to be among the first (alongside the communities of the Arctic) significantly affected by climate change as valuable fish stocks such as tuna relocate, and people are forced to migrate as land becomes uninhabitable and inundated and, consequently, identity and culture risks being lost.[61] Less dramatically, but no less significant in the short to medium term, a changing climate is likely to increase the frequency of severe weather events, and, in a region that already accounts for 91, 92 and 66% of the world's tropical cyclones, floods and landslides, respectively (on a per capita basis),[62] the Asia Pacific will likely be disproportionately affected by these events. It is estimated that between 2010 and 2011, 42 million people were displaced in the Asia Pacific owing to natural disasters associated with flood and drought[63] and this figure is likely to rise in the future. The irony is not lost on these communities that, for the most part (with the exception of China), they have contributed little to the causes of

---

56  P.L. Munday et al., 'Selective Mortality Associated with Variation in $CO_2$ Tolerance in a Marine Fish', (2012) 1(1) *Ocean Acidification* p. 1.

57  Turley and Gattuso, note 44, p. 278.

58  Experiments carried out to date have largely been laboratory based and operate on the worse-case pH scenarios and all indicated mixed results with wide variations on how species might respond to low pH environments; see for example I.E. Hendriks, C.M. Durart and M. Álvarez, 'Vulnerability of Marine Biodiversity to Ocean Acidification: A Meta-Analysis', (2010) 86 *Estuarine, Coastal and Shelf Science* p. 157; J. Kavousi et al., 'Colony-Specific Investigations Reveal Highly Variable Responses Among Individual Corals to Ocean Acidification and Warming', (2015) 109 *Marine Environmental Research* p. 9; K. Lohbeck, U. Riebesell and T. Reusch, 'Adaptive Evolution of a Key Phytoplankton Species to Ocean Acidification', (2012) 5 *Nature Geoscience* p. 346.

59  V. Rérolle, C. Floquet and M. Mowlem, 'Seawater pH Measurements for Ocean-Acidification Observations', (2012) 40 *Trends in Analytical Chemistry* p. 146.

60  WOA I, note 7, summary, p. 12.

61  See T. Weir, L. Dovey and D. Orcherton, 'Social and Cultural Issues Raised by Climate Change in the Pacific Island Countries: An Overview', (2016) 17 *Environmental Change* p. 1017.

62  Hashim and Hashim, note 3.

63  M.R. Islam and N.A. Khan, 'Threats, Vulnerability, Resilience and Displacement Among the Climate Change and Natural Diaster-Affected People in South-East Asia: An Overview', (2018) 23 *Journal of the Asia Pacific Economy* p. 297.

*Climate change* 101

climate change and ocean acidification, and are generally least able to respond and adapt to its consequences.

## 6.3 The climate-oceans regime complex

The climate-oceans regime complex[64] comprises key instruments managing atmospheric pollution (namely the UNFCCC and the 1997 Kyoto Protocol[65] and 2015 Paris Agreement),[66] marine pollution (the LOSC, 1973/78 MARPOL,[67] 1972 London Dumping Convention[68] and 1996 Protocol)[69] as well as regional seas conventions and regional fisheries management organisations and arrangements (RFMO/A). The nature of the climate-oceans regime complex varies according to which regulatory lens is applied: mitigation, exploitation or adaptation. Mitigation of climate change through a reduction in greenhouse gas emissions is largely – with the exception of shipping – managed through the climate change regime developed under the auspices of the UNFCCC. Exploitation of the oceans for climate change mitigation purposes, on the other hand, is primarily regulated by the law of the sea at both the national and at the regional levels. Adaptation to the impacts of climate change on the marine and coastal environment is facilitated and managed under both the climate and the law of the sea regimes. Soft law plays a vital interstitial role bridging the regimes, and endeavours to fill the lacunae between climate law and the law of the sea. For example, in relation to ocean acidification, which is largely ignored by both the climate and the law of the sea regimes, soft targets addressing ocean acidification were established by Aichi Biodiversity Target 10[70] adopted under the auspices of the Conference of the Parties (COP) to the 1992 Convention

---

64 A 'regime complex' comprises functionally overlapping parallel regimes and institutions which are non-hierarchical but which nevertheless affect one another's sphere of operations; see further K.J. Atler and S. Meunier, 'The Politics of International Regime Complexity', (2009) 7 *Perspectives on Politics* p. 13; T. Gehring and B. Faude, 'The Dynamics of Regime Complexes: Microfoundations and Systemic Effects', (2013) 19 *Global Governance* p. 119; and K. Raustiala and D.G. Victor, 'The Regime Complex for Plant Genetic Resources', (2004) 58 *International Organisation* p. 277.

65 *Kyoto Protocol to the United Nations Framework Convention on Climate Change*, 11 December 1997, 2303 UNTS 214 [hereafter *Kyoto Protocol*].

66 *Paris Agreement*, 12 December 2015, (2016) 55 ILM 743 [hereafter *2015 Paris Agreement*]

67 *International Convention for the Prevention of Pollution from Ships, as Modified by the Protocol of 1978 Relating Thereto*, 17 February 1978, 1340 UNTS 62 [hereafter *MARPOL 73/78*].

68 *Convention on the Prevention of Marine Pollution by Dumping of Wastes and Other Matter*, 29 December 1972, 1046 UNTS 120 [hereafter *London Convention*].

69 *Protocol to the London Convention on the Prevention of Marine Pollution by Dumping of Wastes and Other Matter*, 8 November 1996, (1997) 36 ILM 1 [hereafter *London Protocol*].

70 United Nations Environment Programme, 'Decision Adopted by the Conference of the Parties to the Convention on Biological Diversity at its 10th Meeting', 29 October 2010, UN Doc. UNEP/CBD/COP/DEC/X/2, Annex.

102    *Karen N. Scott*

on Biological Diversity[71] and the UN General Assembly (UNGA) in UNGA Resolution 66/288 *The Future We Want* (2012).[72] Most recently, in Sustainable Development Goal 14, adopted by the UNGA in 2015,[73] States are urged to 'minimise and address the impacts of ocean acidification, including through enhanced scientific cooperation at all levels',[74] to conserve at least 10% of coastal and marine areas by 2020,[75] and to more generally sustainably manage and protect marine and coastal ecosystems in order to strengthen their resilience.[76] In the Asia Pacific, soft law and collaborative initiatives involving NGO and private organisations designed to protect, promote and develop mangrove forests comprise an important component of the regime complex.[77] In the Pacific, in particular, climate change is predictably a major policy interest of regional organisations such as the Pacific Islands Forum and the Secretariat of the Pacific Regional Environment Programme (SPREP) and multiple projects associated with resilience, adaptation and sea level rise comprise part of the climate-oceans regime complex in the region.[78]

For the purposes of this chapter, the climate-oceans regime complex will be outlined below within the regulatory parameters of mitigation, exploitation and adaptation. Pertinent regional initiatives will be noted with a particular emphasis on adaptation. Two legal regional developments in the Pacific demonstrating an approach to responding to the impacts of climate change based on collaboration and cooperation, in the areas of fisheries management and sea level rise, will be highlighted.

### 6.3.1 *Mitigation: reduction of greenhouse gas emissions*

The overarching goal of the UNFCCC is the stabilisation of greenhouse gas concentrations in the atmosphere at a level that prevents dangerous interference with the climate system.[79] Although as noted above, the oceans are integral to the 'climate system' and this is reflected in Article 1(3) of the UNFCCC, the focus of the regime is nevertheless on the atmosphere rather than on the oceans. This is demonstrated by the definition of 'climate change' in the Convention as

---

71  *Convention on Biological Diversity*, 5 June 1992, 1760 UNTS 79 [hereafter *Biodiversity Convention*].

72  United Nations General Assembly, 'The Future We Want', 27 July 2012, UN Doc. A/RES/66/288, (2012) [166].

73  United Nations General Assembly, 'Transforming our world: the 2030 Agenda for Sustainable Development', 25 September 2015, UN Doc. A/RES/70/1.

74  Sustainable Development Goal 14.3.

75  Sustainable Development Goal 14.5.

76  Sustainable Development Goal 14.2.

77  For example, the Blue Carbon Initiative, see details at http://thebluecarboninitiative.org; Blue Forests, see details at https://blue-forests.org; and Mangroves for the Future (MFF), see details at www.mangrovesforthefuture.org These initiatives are discussed briefly below.

78  A selected number of these initiatives are discussed below.

79  *UNFCCC*, Article 2.

*Climate change* 103

'a change of climate which is attributed directly or indirectly to human activity that alters the composition of the *global atmosphere* and which is in addition to natural climate variability observed over comparable time periods'.[80] States are currently committed to take action in order to limit the global average temperature increase to 'well below 2°C above pre-industrial levels' with the aim of limiting the increase to 1.5°C.[81] Notably, Pacific Island States played an important role in negotiating the inclusion of the aspirational target of 1.5°C in Article 2(1)(a) of the Paris Agreement in order to recognise the impact of even a 1.5°C increase on atoll islands and coral reefs.[82] Nevertheless, the Paris Agreement fails to establish an ocean pH target and, like its predecessor the Kyoto Protocol, omits to include targets for $CO_2$ emissions specifically, which are the most significant contribution to ocean acidification. More generally, even if all nationally determined contributions (NDCs) that have been pledged by States are fully implemented under the Paris Agreement, it is predicted that this will limit the temperature increase to between 2.6°C and 3°C by 2,100,[83] well beyond the 1.5°C that is predicted to significantly impact many coral ecosystems[84] and the 2°C agreed to by States under the Agreement.

With respect to emissions reductions, with the exception of shipping, the LOSC adds minimal additional commitments to support emissions reductions. The LOSC imposes a general, high-level obligation on parties to protect and preserve the marine environment[85] and, more specifically, to prevent and mitigate all sources of marine pollution.[86] However, whilst the obligations under Article 194 and the definition of pollution under Article 1(4) of the Convention are undoubtedly broad enough to encompass $CO_2$ and other greenhouse gases responsible for climate change and ocean acidification, they are expressed at a level of generality that adds little to the existing obligations adopted under

---

80  *UNFCCC*, Article 1(2) (emphasis added).
81  *Paris Agreement*, Article 2(1)(a).
82  See T. Ourbak and A.K. Magnan, 'The Paris Agreement and Climate Change Negotiations: Small Islands, Big Players', (2018) 18 *Regional Environmental Change* p. 201.
83  M. Sigmond, J.C. Fyfe and N.C. Swart, 'Ice-Free Arctic Projections Under the Paris Agreement', (2018) 8 *Nature Climate Change* p. 362; J. Rogelj et al., 'Paris Agreement Climate Proposals Need a Boost to Keep Warming Well Below 2 °C', (2016) 534 *Nature* p. 631.
84  M. Allen et al., 'Technical Summary' in V. Masson-Delmott et al. (ed), *Global warming of 1.5⁰C. An IPCC Special Report on the Impacts of Global Warming of 1.5⁰C above Pre-Industrial Levels and Related Greenhouse Gas Emission Pathways, in the Context of Strengthening the Global Response to the Threat of Climate Change, Sustainable Development, and Efforts to Eradicate Poverty*, 2018, available online at www.ipcc.ch
85  LOSC, Articles 192, 193 and 194(5); ee also *In the Matter of the Chagos Marine Protected Area Arbitration before an Arbitral Tribunal Constituted under Annex VII of the United Nations Convention on the Law of the Sea between the Republic of Mauritius and the United Kingdom of Great Britain and Northern Ireland*, PCA Case no 2011-03, Award of 18 March 2015, [535]; *In the Matter of an Arbitration before An Arbitral Tribunal Constituted Under Annex VII to the 1982 United Nations Convention on the Law of the Sea between The Republic of the Philippines and the People's Republic of China*, PCA Case no 2013-19, Award of 12 July 2016 [992–993].
86  LOSC, Article 194.

## 104   *Karen N. Scott*

the UNFCCC regime. Neither Articles 207 nor 212 of LOSC, which establish obligations relating to land-based and atmospheric pollution respectively create global standards or require parties to comply with standards established outside of LOSC.[87] The only source of greenhouse gases that is specifically regulated by the law of the sea is ship-based greenhouse gas emissions, which since 1997, have been subject to regulation under Annex VI of the 1973/78 MARPOL. These standards are applicable to all LOSC parties by virtue of Article 211(2) of the Convention.[88] Although the targets agreed to under the auspices of the UNFCCC regime might arguably be challenged as to whether they are sufficient to prevent pollution of, and other harm to, the marine environment, at this stage they undoubtedly represent the *lex specialis* in respect of mitigation of climate change through emissions reductions.

In light of this conclusion, it is important that the oceans increase their profile as an essential agenda item within the UNFCCC. Recent UNFCCC initiatives suggest that this is slowly occurring. At the 21st UNFCCC Conference of the Parties (COP) in 2015, over 40 ocean-related events were held and, in 2016 at COP 22 the ocean was designated as one of nine Global Climate Action Events. Other initiatives that were reported on in 2016 include the creation of the Global Ocean Acidification Observing Network (GOA-ON), which is a collaborative network of institutions undertaking research on ocean acidification processes in order to inform policy development.[89] A Strategic Action Roadmap on Oceans and Climate: 2016–2021 was also released in 2016 setting out six policy recommendations relating to the role of the oceans in the areas of climate, mitigation, adaptation, displacement, financing and capacity development.[90] Nevertheless, less positively, the 2016 Marrakech Action Proclamation for our Climate and Sustainable Development made no specific reference to the oceans.[91] In 2017 however, at COP 23, which incidentally was co-hosted by Fiji, the Oceans Pathway Partnership was launched. This is a significant development that comprises a two-track strategy for 2020 to (1) increase the role of ocean considerations in the UNFCCC process and (2) increase action in priority areas impacting

---

87  This is in contrast to Articles 210 and 211 of the LOSC, which requires parties to comply with external standards established under the *MARPOL* and the *London Convention* in respect of shipping pollution and dumping, respectively.

88  It is noted that ship-based emissions in East Asia accounted for 16% of global shipping $CO_2$ in 2013, an increase from 4 to 7% in 2002–2005; see H. Liu et al., 'Health and Climate Impacts of Ocean-Going Vessels in East Asia', (2016) 7 *Nature Climate Change* p. 1037.

89  See *Global Climate Action Event: Oceans*, 12 November 2016, available online at http://climateaction.unfccc.int/media/1055/gca-oceans-programme.pdf

90  B. Cicin-Sain et al., *Toward a Strategic Action Roadmap on Oceans and Climate: 2016–2021*, Washington: Global Ocean Forum, 2016, available online at https://globaloceanforumdotcom.files.wordpress.com/2013/03/strategic-action-roadmap-on-oceans-and-climate-november-2016.pdf

91  Marrakech Action Proclamation for our Climate and Sustainable Development, 17 November 2016, available online at https://unfccc.int/files/meetings/marrakech_nov_2016/application/pdf/marrakech_action_proclamation.pdf

or impacted by ocean and climate change. The co-chairs of this initiative are Sweden and Fiji and it is worth noting that the leadership group is dominated by Pacific States including Samoa, Marshall Islands, Cook Islands, New Zealand, Kiribati and French Polynesia.[92] Equally positively, 70% of the 161 States which have filed NDCs pursuant to Article 4(2) of the 2015 Paris Agreement refer to marine issues.[93] In all, 50 NDCs refer to both ocean mitigation and adaptation with 53 referring to marine adaptation only.[94] Importantly, 45 NDCs addressed mangrove conservation, restoration and management,[95] an important mechanism to exploit the ocean carbon sink in the Asia Pacific. Notably, Australia, Federated States of Micronesia and New Zealand omit any reference to marine issues in their NDCs.[96]

### 6.3.2 Exploitation of the ocean sink to mitigate climate change

The oceans have typically been viewed as a resource for exploitation whether that be for food, transport or even as a repository for the world's waste. More recently, the value of the ocean for energy generation through wave and wind power as well as ocean thermal energy conversion has been recognised, and renewable energy constitutes an important alternative to fossil fuel production. To date however, the exploitation of the oceans for renewable energy, particularly in the Asia Pacific, has not been significant.[97]

A more controversial strategy for climate change mitigation is the exploitation of the ocean water column and/or seabed for the sequestration of $CO_2$. Both strategies are now at least partially regulated by the dumping regime developed under the auspices of the London Convention and the 1996 Protocol. The 1996 Protocol was amended in 2006 to expressly permit, and create a legal basis for, the disposal of carbon dioxide in sub-seabed geological formations.[98] Parties must comply with a detailed risk assessment and management framework when undertaking sub-seabed disposal activities, and must actively consider the nature of the disposal site, processes associated with disposal and potential impacts on

---

92 'The Ocean Pathway: Towards an Inclusive UNFCCC Process', (n.d.), available online at https://cop23.com.fj/the-ocean-pathway
93 N.D. Gallo, D.G. Victor and L.A. Levin, 'Ocean Commitments Under the Paris Agreement', (2017) 7 *Nature Climate Change* p. 833.
94 Ibid., p. 834.
95 Ibid., p. 833.
96 Ibid.
97 D. Leary and M. Esteban, 'Climate Change and Renewable Energy from the Ocean and Tides: Calming the Sea of Regulatory Uncertainty', (2009) 24 *International Journal of Marine and Coastal Law* p. 617.
98 *London Protocol*, Annex I, paras. 1.8 and 4 as inserted by 'Resolution LP.1(1): On the amendment to include $CO_2$ Sequestration in sub-seabed Geological formations in Annex 1 to the London Protocol', 2 November 2006; see generally, R. Purdy, 'The Legal Implications of Carbon Capture and Storage under the Sea' (2006–2007) 7 *Sustainable Development Law and Policy* p. 22.

## 106   Karen N. Scott

biodiversity and habitats when carrying out an environmental impact assessment prior to disposal.[99] Importantly, Resolution LP.1(1) (2006) amending the 1996 Protocol emphasised that 'carbon dioxide capture and sequestration should not be considered as a substitute to other measures to reduce carbon dioxide emissions'.[100] The Protocol was further amended in 2009 so as to permit the export of $CO_2$ within streams for disposal, provided that an agreement or an arrangement has been entered into by the countries concerned confirming and allocating permitting responsibilities between the States in accordance with the Protocol.[101] The 2006 amendment entered into force in 2006 and applies to all 51 parties to the Protocol. However, the Protocol is not particularly well ratified by States within the Asia Pacific.[102]

Exploiting the ocean $CO_2$ 'sink', defined as a process, activity or mechanism which removes a greenhouse gas from the atmosphere[103] and transfers it, in this case, to the water column within the ocean, is also subject to nascent regulation under the 1996 London Protocol. The climate change regime largely ignores the capacity of the ocean as a sink for $CO_2$, focussing instead on the enhancement of terrestrial sinks through afforestation, reforestation and land-use change.[104] Exploiting or 'geoengineering' the ocean to enhance its capacity as a natural sink for $CO_2$ has nevertheless generated significant scientific, policy and, increasingly, regulatory attention outside of the UNFCCC regime.[105] Much work has focussed on ocean fertilization, an artificial process designed to stimulate the ocean's biological pump through the addition of nutrients such as iron to biologically unproductive regions in order to stimulate a plankton bloom, which, in turn, draws down $CO_2$ from the ocean surface and transfers it to the ocean depths by means of biological processes and the operation of deep

---

99  See International Maritime Organization, 'Risk Assessment and Management Framework for $CO_2$ Sequestration in Sub-seabed Geological Structures', 30 October–3 November 2006, UN Doc. LC/SG-CO2 1/7, annex 3. Additional guidelines were adopted in 2012; see International Maritime Organization, '2012 Specific Guidelines for the Assessment of Carbon Dioxide for Disposal into Sub-seabed Geological Formations', 2 November 2012, UN Doc. LC 34/15, annex 8.

100  'Resolution LP.1(1): On the amendment to include $CO_2$ Sequestration in sub-seabed Geological formations in Annex 1 to the London Protocol', 2 November 2006, preamble.

101  *London Protocol*, Article 6(2) as inserted by Resolution LP.3(4) on the amendment to Article 6 of the London Protocol (30 October 2009, not yet in force); see D. Langlet, 'Exporting $CO_2$ for Sub-Seabed Storage: The Non-Effective Amendment to the London Dumping Protocol and Its Implications', (2015) 30 *International Journal of Marine and Coastal Law* p. 395.

102  Currently, states party to the 2006 Protocol within the Asia Pacific comprise: Australia, China, Japan, Marshall Islands, New Zealand, Philippines, Tonga and Vanuatu. The 2009 amendment has been ratified by only five parties to date: Finland, the Islamic Republic of Iran, the Netherlands, Norway and the United Kingdom.

103  *UNFCCC*, Article 1(8).

104  See ibid., Article 4(2)(a) and *Kyoto Protocol*, Article 4(2)(a).

105  For an overview of geoengineering for climate change mitigation see K.N. Scott, 'Geoengineering and the Law of the Sea' in R. Rayfuse (ed), *Research Handbook on International Marine Environmental Law*, Cheltenham: Edward Elgar Publishing, 2015, p. 451.

*Climate change* 107

ocean currents.[106] There is little proof that long-term sequestration actually takes place,[107] and the risks associated with ocean fertilization include the introduction of toxic algae,[108] disruption of the ecosystem food chain,[109] oxygen depletion, ocean acidification[110] and the release of gases such as methane and nitrous oxide.[111] These activities are of potential concern to Pacific States as one of the regions identified as suitable for fertilization activities is the Equatorial Pacific. Moreover, in 2007, an ocean fertilization experiment involving urea took place in the Sulu Sea off the coast of the Philippines.[112]

Responding to both the increasing interest in ocean fertilization and the absence of any other pertinent regulatory forum, the parties to the 1996 London Protocol adopted an amendment in 2013 creating an explicit mandate for the regulation of ocean fertilization and, in the future, for other forms of marine geoengineering.[113] The amendment inserts a definition of geoengineering into the Protocol that expansively defines the activity as

> a deliberate intervention in the marine environment to manipulate natural processes, including to counteract anthropogenic climate change and/or its impacts, and that has the potential to result in deleterious effects, especially where those effects may be widespread, long lasting or severe.[114]

Whilst this arguably provides a mandate to regulate any form of marine geoengineering in the future, the Protocol, for the time being, is restricted to regulating geoengineering that involves the placement of matter into the sea from vessels, aircraft or offshore structures. Namely, that parties shall not allow the placement of such matter for ocean fertilization purposes unless the activity is authorized under a permit.[115] A permit may only be issued where

---

106 See J.H. Martin, 'Glacial-Interglacial $CO_2$ Change: The Iron Hypothesis', (1990) 5 *Paleoceanography* p. 1; see also P.W. Boyd et al., 'Mesoscale Iron Enrichment Experiments 1993–2005: Synthesis and Future Directions', (2007) 315 *Science* p. 612.
107 P. Williamson et al., 'Ocean Fertilization for Geoengineering: A Review of Effectiveness, Environmental Impacts and Emerging Governance', (2012) 90 *Process Safety and Environmental Protection* pp. 475, 477.
108 Q. Schiermeier, 'The Oresmen', (2003) 421 *Nature* pp. 109, 110.
109 A. Strong, 'Ocean Fertilization: Time to Move on', (2009) 461 *Nature* p. 347.
110 Williamson et al., note 107, pp. 480–482.
111 J. Furhman and D. Capone, 'Possible Biogeochemical Consequences of Ocean Fertilization', (1991) 36 *Limnology & Oceanography* p. 1951; M. Lawrence, 'Side-effects of Ocean Iron Fertilization', (2002) 297 *Science* p. 1993.
112 See J. Mayo-Ramsay, 'Environmental, Legal and Social Implications of Ocean Urea Fertilization: Sulu Sea Example', (2010) 34 *Marine Policy* p. 831. Urea is a nitrogen-rich organic compound that is commonly used in fertilizers.
113 'Resolution LP.4(8): On the Amendment to the London Protocol to Regulate the Placement of Matter for Ocean Fertilization and other Marine Geoengineering Activities', 18 October 2013.
114 *London Protocol*, Article 1(5)*bis* (amendment not yet in force).
115 *London Protocol*, Article 6*bis*, Annex 4.

108  *Karen N. Scott*

the activity constitutes legitimate scientific research[116] and where it accords with the detailed Assessment Framework set out in Annex 5 of the Protocol. As of 2018, however, only three States have ratified the 2013 amendment to the 1996 Protocol (Finland, Norway and the UK), and ocean fertilization is consequently currently governed by the generally applicable rules of the dumping regime; the principles on the prevention of pollution and harm to the marine environment as set out in Part XII of the LOSC; and the general principles of international environmental law, including precaution, the no harm principle (and due diligence) and process obligations such as environmental impact assessment.[117] These principles are inevitably expressed at a level of much greater generality than the regime developed under the 1996 Protocol, but their interpretation should arguably be informed by the non-binding resolutions adopted under the London Convention that broadly endorse application of the amended regime on a voluntary basis.[118]

Finally, and of direct relevance to the Asia Pacific, the exploitation of ocean vegetated habitats – mangroves, salt marshes and seagrasses for example – provides one potential mechanism to enhance $CO_2$ mitigation as well as making an important contribution to adaptation.[119] It is estimated that whilst these habitats cover less than 2% of the ocean surface, they account for almost half of the carbon stored in ocean sediments.[120] Nevertheless, they are being destroyed at a significant rate, losing more than 20% of global coverage between 1980 and 2005 alone.[121] As noted above, the Asia Pacific is particularly rich in these important, but increasingly threatened, habitats. In the Mekong Delta, mangrove forests are estimated to have decreased from around 400,000 ha in the 1940s to 269,000 ha in 1980, with only an estimated 158,000 ha remaining in 2000.[122] Whilst the use of herbicide during the Vietnam War was a significant cause of this decrease, more recently, mangrove forests have been cleared

---

116  *London Protocol*, Annex 4.

117  See K.N. Scott, 'International Law in the Anthropocene: Responding to the Geoengineering Challenge', (2013) 34 *Michigan Journal of International Law* pp. 309, 333–350.

118  'Resolution LC.LP.1: On the Regulation of Ocean Fertilization', 2008; 'Resolution LC.LP.2: On the Assessment Framework for Scientific Research Involving Ocean Fertilization', 2010. Similarly influential, but also non-binding, the parties to the *Biodiversity Convention* adopted in 2008, 2010 and 2012 resolutions recommending a moratorium on ocean fertilization and geoengineering more generally for purposes other than scientific research: 'Decision COP IX/16: Biodiversity and Climate Change', 30 May 2008, UNEP/CBD/COP/DEC/9/16, para. C.4; 'Decision adopted by the conference of the parties to the Convention on Biological Diversity at its 10th meeting: X/33 Biodiversity and climate change' 29 October 2010, UNEP/CBD/COP/DEC/X/33, para. 8(w); CBD Decision XI/20 (2012) *Climate Related Geoengineering*.

119  On the importance of mangrove forests to ecosystem services, see J.H. Primavera et al., 'The Mangrove Ecosystem' in Sheppard, note 25, p. 1.

120  C.M. Duarte, J.J. Middelburg and N. Caraco, 'Major Role of Marine Vegetation on the Oceanic Carbon Cycle', (2005) 2 *Biogeosciences* pp. 1, 2.

121  Primavera et al., note 119, p. 8.

122  R. Warner et al., 'Opportunities and Challenges for Mangrove Carbon Sequestration in the Mekong River Delta in Vietnam', (2016) 11 *Sustainability Science* pp. 661, 664.

for shrimp farming in the region.[123] Indonesia has among the highest rates of mangrove forest destruction in the world, ranging between a loss of 0.26 and 0.66% annually between 2000 and 2012.[124] Principal threats include logging, coastal development and conversion to rice fields and palm oil plantations.[125] In Thailand, in 1961, mangroves covered about 60% of its coastline.[126] This has decreased to 50% of its former coverage on the Andaman coast and to less than 10% of former coverage in the Southern Gulf Coast owing to coastal development, agriculture and shrimp farming.[127] More positively, mangrove forest coverage has been growing since 1996 in Thailand owing to domestic regulatory reforms promoting the conservation of these ecosystems and the implementation, in conjunction with NGOs, of mangrove restoration projects.[128] The situation in the Pacific is similar. In Kiribati for example, mangrove forests cover 1% of the island's land area and constitute its most productive and biologically diverse ecosystem in addition to having an estimated carbon sequestration value of US$266,533 annually, yet are under threat from deforestation for fuel, coastal development and pollution.[129]

As noted above, the climate regime largely focusses on terrestrial sinks and it is remarkable that of the 245 Clean Development Mechanism projects that were registered in Vietnam by 2016 none related to the Mekong Delta mangroves.[130] However, in parallel with the UNFCCC's increasing recognition of oceans issues,[131] 45 States have committed to the conservation, management and restoration of mangrove forests within their NDCs.[132] Vietnam, for example, has committed to 'protect, restore, plant and improve the quality of coastal forests, including mangroves, especially in coastal estuaries and the Mekong and Red River deltas' including 20,000 to 50,000 ha of additional mangrove planting.[133] Kiribati has committed to protecting and sustainably managing its mangrove resources as well as seagrass beds and predicts that these actions will represent the 'effective stewardship of more than 6 million tonnes of $CO_2$ stored, more than 100 times the current annual national emissions inventory'.[134] Less ambitiously, the restoration of mangrove forests in the context of adapta-

---

123 Giuliani, Bellucci and Nhon, note 36, p. 421.
124 Dsikowitzky et al., note 33, p. 467.
125 Ibid.
126 I.D. Lange, E. Schoenig and S. Khokiattiwong, 'Thailand' in Sheppard, note 33, pp. 491, 496.
127 Ibid.
128 Ibid., p. 497.
129 Mangubhai et al., note 34, p. 812.
130 Warner et al., note 122, p. 671.
131 As discussed above in III.A.
132 Gallo, Victor and Levin, note 93, p. 833. By contrast, only 28 NDCs make commitments in connection with coral reefs.
133 See *Intended Nationally Determined Contribution of Viet Nam*, 3 November 2016, pp. 10–11, available online at www4.unfccc.int/sites/ndcstaging/PublishedDocuments/Viet%20Nam%20First/VIETNAM%27S%20INDC.pdf
134 See *Republic of Kiribati. Intended Nationally Determined Contribution*, 21 September 2016, available online at www4.unfccc.int/sites/ndcstaging/Pages/Home.aspx

110   *Karen N. Scott*

tion is also referred to by Fiji in its NDC.[135] By contrast however, there is no reference to mangrove conservation or restoration in NDCs submitted to date by Australia, China, Indonesia, Malaysia, Papua New Guinea and the Solomon Islands.[136] Therefore, despite representing the most important location for mangrove ecosystems, the Asia Pacific would appear to be largely under-represented in the context of NDC mangrove forest-related commitments. Nevertheless, many if not most of these States are involved to some extent in a number of public-private collaborative initiatives to protect and restore mangrove forests and otherwise enhance 'blue carbon' resources. These include the Blue Carbon Initiative (coordinated by Conservation International), the International Union for Conservation of Nature (IUCN) and the Intergovernmental Oceanographic Commission of the United Nations Educational, Scientific, and Cultural Organization[137]; Blue Forests, an initiative of UNEP funded by the GEF and partners and managed by GRID-Arendal[138]; and Mangroves for the Future (MFF), which is co-chaired by the UNDP and the IUCN, and operates in India, Indonesia, Maldives, Seychelles, Sri Lanka, Thailand, Bangladesh, Cambodia, Myanmar, Pakistan and Vietnam.[139]

### 6.3.3 *Adaptation to climate change*

Adaptation has been an equal partner of mitigation since at least 2010[140] and is a key pillar of the 2015 Paris Agreement.[141] In contrast to mitigation, adaptation is also facilitated by global and regional oceans regimes and takes a myriad of forms. For example, climate change adaptation is now typically a key component of marine spatial planning and integrated coastal management in many States. Within the UNFCCC itself, adaptation is explicitly linked with the notion of integrated coastal zone management in Article 4(1)(e) of the Convention. Increasingly, the designation of marine protected areas (MPAs) is designed to enhance ecosystem resilience in responding to climate change.[142] Climate change considerations are being more slowly integrated into fisheries management, but the relocation of stocks and/or their diminishment is now discussed

---

135  See *Fiji's Intended Nationally Determined Contribution*, 22 April 2016, p. 8, available online at www4.unfccc.int/sites/ndcstaging/Pages/Home.aspx
136  All NDCs are available online at www4.unfccc.int/sites/ndcstaging/Pages/Home.aspx.
137  See details at http://thebluecarboninitiative.org
138  See details at https://blue-forests.org. Site locations include Indonesia.
139  See details at www.mangrovesforthefuture.org
140  The Cancun Adaptation Framework (CAF) was adopted at COP 16 in 2010 building on previous initiatives including the Nairobi Work Programme (COP 12, 2006) and the Least Developed Countries Work Programme (COP 7, 2001). See 'Report of the Conference of the Parties on its sixteenth session, held in Cancun from 29 November to 10 December 2010: Decision 1/CP.16', 29 November 2010, UN Doc. FCCC/CP/2010/7/Add.1.
141  *Paris Agreement*, Article 7.
142  See generally R.K. Craig, *Comparative Ocean Governance. Place-Based Protections in an Era of Climate Change*, Cheltenham: Edward Elgar, 2012.

*Climate change* 111

by a number of RFMOs. Finally, sea level rise has generated detailed analysis by scholars, the International Law Association[143] and, in 2018, was placed on the agenda of the International Law Commission for consideration.[144]

It is beyond the scope of this chapter to examine the multiplicity of measures associated with ocean and coastal adaptation to climate change in the Asia Pacific. The lead agency charged with responding to climate change in the Pacific is the Secretariat of the Pacific Regional Environmental Programme (SPREP). SPREP has established the Pacific Adaptation to Climate Change Project (PACC), which has 14 members and is strongly focussed on resilience.[145] It supports the development of Joint National Action Plans (designed to bring together climate change and disaster management)[146] as well as the development of National Adaptation Programmes of Action (NAPA) for the four least developed countries in the Pacific: Kiribati, Samoa, Solomon Islands and Vanuatu.[147] The 2016 Framework for Resilient Development in the Pacific (2017–2030) establishes a voluntary framework for integrating climate change response and disaster planning into mainstream policy-making, low carbon development and coordinated disaster response, and establishes a Pacific Resilience Partnership.[148] Climate change and collaboration is also an important policy area for the Council of Regional Organisations in the Pacific (CROP).[149] By contrast, the Pacific Islands Regional Ocean Policy, adopted in 2002 and supported by the Framework for

143 See the ILA Committee on Sea Level Rise, 'Resolution 5/2018', 19–24 August 2018, and the 2018 Report of the Committee, both available online at www.ila-hq.org/index.php/committees
144 International Law Commission, 'Report of the International Law Commission', 30 April–1 June and 2 July–10 August 2018, A/73/10, para. 29 and Annex B.
145 SPREP, 'Pacific Adaptation to Climate Change (PACC) Programme', (n.d.), available online at www.sprep.org/pacc
146 See Pacific Islands Applied Geoscience Commission, 'Guide to Developing National Action Plans. A Tool for Mainstreaming Disaster Risk Management Based on Experiences from Selected Pacific Island Countries', October 2009, available online at www.sprep.org/att/IRC/eCOPIES/Pacific_Region/507.pdf
147 For background to NAPAs within the UNFCCC framework, see United Nations Climate Change, 'National Adaptation Programmes of Action', (n.d.), available online at https://unfccc.int/topics/resilience/workstreams/national-adaptation-programmes-of-action/introduction
148 See the '2016 Pohnpei Statement: Strengthening Pacific Resilience to Climate Change and Disaster Risk', available online at www.fsmpio.fm/announcements/forum/Annex2_Strengthening_Pacific_Resilience_to_Climate_Change_and_Disaster_Risk.pdf. The new framework replaces two previous frameworks that dealt with climate change and disaster response separately.
149 See CROP, 'Collaborating to Support Effective Response to Climate Change', (2015), available online at www.spc.int/sites/default/files/wordpresscontent/wp-content/uploads/2017/01/Response-to-Climate-Change.pdf. CROP was established by the PIF in 1988 and includes, in addition to the PIF, the Forum Fisheries Agency (FFA), Pacific Islands Development Programme (PIDP), the Secretariat for the Pacific Community (SPC), SREP, the South Pacific Tourism Organisation (SPTO), the University of the South Pacific, the Pacific Power Association (PPA) and the Pacific Aviation Safety Office (PASO).

## 112  *Karen N. Scott*

a Pacific Oceanscape developed in 2010,[150] whilst providing a strong focus on ocean health, has less direct application to climate change and has struggled to facilitate regional integrated management of oceans policy.[151]

Regional ocean planning and climate change are significantly weaker in the Asian region although the Asia Pacific Adaptation Network (APAN) has been established under the auspices of the UNEP Global Adaptation Network, and is designed to manage and apply climate change adaptation knowledge in the region.[152] APAN is supporting a project on coastal zone management,[153] including responding to sea level rise, and held the 5th Asia Pacific Climate Change Adaptation Forum in 2016.[154] Similarly, the issue of sea level rise has also been a focus of the Coordinating Bodies of the Seas of East Asia (COBSEA), which held a workshop on sea level rise and coastal erosion in 2012.[155] More recently however, the COBSEA Strategic Directions 2018–2022 adopted in 2018,[156] established that marine and coastal planning and management would be one of two policy priorities for the region,[157] including the development of MPA networks with a particular focus on coral reefs, mangroves, seagrass, coastal wetlands and fishery refugia.[158] Climate change is liberally referenced throughout the document. ASEAN has also identified climate change as a priority issue and the ASEAN Climate Change Initiative and ASEAN Working Group on Climate Change were established in 2009.[159]

With respect to area protection and the enhancement and protection of ecosystems, there is unsurprisingly a strong emphasis on the protection of coral reef ecosystems in the region. References to coral reef adaptation are noted in 28 NDCs submitted under Article 4 of the Paris Agreement,[160] and the Coral Reef Triangle Initiative is the most high-profile coral reef MPA network in the region established under the auspices of the Coral Reef Triangle Initiative on

---

150  Pacific Islands Regional Ocean Policy and Framework for Integrated Strategic Action, (2005), available online at www.sprep.org/att/IRC/eCOPIES/Pacific_Region/99.pdf

151  See J. Vince et al., 'Ocean governance in the South Pacific region: Progress and plans for action', (2017) 79 *Marine Policy* p. 40.

152  See further Asia Pacific Adaptation Network, 'About APAN' (n.d.), available online at www.asiapacificadapt.net/about-us

153  See further Asia Pacific Adaptation Network, 'Coastal Zone Management' (n.d.), available online at www.asiapacificadapt.net/resources/themes/coastal-zone-management

154  For further information, see Asia Pacific Adaptation Network, '5th Asia Pacific Climate Change Adaptation Forum', (n.d.), available online at www.asiapacificadapt.net/adaptationforum/2016

155  See further COBSEA, 'Yeosu Coastal Erosion Project' (n.d.), available online at www.cobsea.org/projects/YEOSU_Coastal_Erosion_Project.html

156  Secretariat of the Coordinating Body on the Seas of East Asia (COBSEA), 'COBSEA Strategic Directions 2018–2022', 2018 [hereafter COBSEA Strategic Directions].

157  The other priority being land-based sources of pollution.

158  *COBSEA Strategic Directions*, [25–30].

159  Overland et al., note 37, p. 15. A Statement on Joint Reponse to Climate Change and an ASEAN Action Plan on Joint Response to Climate was adopted in 2010 and 2012, respectively.

160  Gallo, Victor and Levin, note 93, p. 833.

*Climate change* 113

Coral Reefs, Fisheries and Food Security (CTI-CFF).[161] The MPA network comprises 1900 MPAs covering 1.6% of the EEZs of the six States within the Coral Triangle (Indonesia, Malaysia, Papua New Guinea, Philippines, Solomon Islands and Timor-Leste) and 17.8% of coral reef habitat.[162] The MPAs range from large multi-use zones to small, strictly managed no-take zones, although a 2014 study showed that only about 6% of the MPAs were actually under effective management.[163]

Two legal innovations within the Pacific region are however, worth a particular mention as demonstrating a strong collective and pragmatic legal response to the impacts of climate change. The first is the development of collaborative fisheries management by eight Pacific States with adjoining EEZs, known as the Parties to the Nauru Agreement (PNA).[164] The 1982 Nauru Agreement has provided the framework for a number of important collaborative initiatives over the last 30 years designed to improve the bargaining power of Pacific coastal States *vis-a-vis* distant water fishing States and, less successfully, the conservation of tuna.[165] A significant innovation with particular relevance to climate change was the introduction of the Vessel Day Scheme (VDS) in 2007.[166] Rather than limiting the number of fishing vessels operating in the region, the VDS limits the number of days in a year that may be fished, essentially changing the focus from managing capacity to managing effort.[167] Importantly, the VDS also shifted the control of fishing from distant water fishing States to Pacific coastal States.[168] The PNA

---

161 Further details are available online at www.coraltriangleinitiative.org

162 A.T. White et al., 'Marine Protected Areas in the Coral Triangle: Progress, Issues and Options', (2014) 42 *Coastal Management* p. 87.

163 A. Walton et al., 'Establishing a Functional Region-Wide Coral Triangle Marine Protected Area System', (2014) 42 *Coastal Management* pp. 107, 110.

164 *Nauru Agreement Concerning Cooperation in the Management of Fisheries of Common Interest*, 11 February 1982, available online at www.pnatuna.com/sites/default/files/Nauru%20Agreement_0.pdf. The PNA States comprise the Federated States of Micronesia, Kiribati, Marshall Islands, Nauru, Palau, Papua New Guinea, Solomon Islands and Tuvalu.

165 Initiatives include the negotiation of harmonised terms and conditions of access of foreign vessels to all Pacific Island EEZs, requirements associated with foreign investment in fishing infrastructure in the Pacific and limitations on the number of purse seine vessels able to operate over the season. For an overview of regional collaboration between Pacific Island States in respect of their EEZ fisheries see C. Goodman, 'The Cooperative Use of Coastal State Jurisdiction with Respect to Highly Migratory Stocks: Insights from the Western and Central Pacific Region' in L. Martin, C. Houreas and C. Salonidis (eds), *Natural Resources and the Law of the Sea*, Huntington, NY: Juris, 2017, p. 215.

166 See generally T. Aqorau, 'Recent Developments in Pacific Tuna Fisheries: The Palau Arrangement and the Vessel Day Scheme', (2009) 24 *International Journal of Marine and Coastal Law* p. 557 and Q. Hanich, M. Tsamenyi and H. Parris, 'Sovereignty and Cooperation in Regional Pacific Tuna Fisheries Management: Politics, Economics, Conservation and the Vessel Day Scheme', (2010) 2 *Australian Journal of Maritime and Ocean Affairs* p. 2.

167 Goodman, note 165, p. 228.

168 E. Havice, 'Rights-Based Management in the Western and Central Pacific Ocean Tuna Fishery: Economic and Environmental Change Under the Vessel Day Scheme', (2013) 42 *Marine Policy* pp. 259, 261.

parties determine both Total Allowable Effort (TAE) and Party Allowable Effort (PAE) on the basis of historical effort and biomass effort at levels which are intended to support the conservation efforts of the Western and Central Pacific Fisheries Commission (WCPFC).[169] Its most significant feature, from the perspective of climate change, is that the VDS permits the transfer of PAE between Pacific States in order to take into account fluctuations in the natural distribution of the fishery.[170] It also permits the transfer of PAE to another management year within a three-year management period.[171] This flexibility was designed to manage the natural variability in tuna fisheries that occur on account of periodic shifts between El Niño (warm) and La Niña (cool) events in the eastern tropical Pacific,[172] but is clearly well-suited to respond to changes in fisheries owing to longer-term shifts in climate patterns. It is not suggested here that the VDS or indeed the broader cooperative regime for EEZ fisheries management between the Pacific States is free from criticism,[173] but the flexibility with which vessel days can be transferred between States or indeed within a three-year time scale does provide a firm and unique foundation on which to build a regulatory regime capable of responding to the relocation of fisheries as a consequence of climate change.[174]

The second development is similarly (although less formally) collaborative, and comprises an emerging Pacific consensus and practice around the establishment of fixed baselines and/or outer maritime limits that are expressly stated to remain notwithstanding future sea level rise. The traditional principle underpinning all aspects of maritime delimitation is 'the land dominates the sea'[175] and thus, applying an orthodox approach, normal baselines are ambulatory in that they move as geographical features such as coastlines, islands and rocks change or disappear altogether.[176] The threat to the maritime zones or indeed the very existence of low-lying Pacific island States has been extensively discussed elsewhere and will not be canvassed for the purposes of this chapter.[177] What will be highlighted, however, is the evolving regional practice in the Pacific

---

169 A.D. Yeeting et al., 'Implications of New Economic Policy Instruments for Tuna Management in the Western and Central Pacific', (2016) 63 *Marine Policy* pp. 45, 48.

170 Havice, note 168, p. 263.

171 Ibid.

172 See generally K. Miller, 'Climate Variability and Tropical Tuna: Management Challenges for Highly Migratory Fish Stocks', (2007) 31 *Marine Policy* p. 56.

173 See in particular, Havice, note 168.

174 Of course, the scheme will only be effective to the extent that tuna stocks move within and not beyond the EEZs of PNA States.

175 *North Sea Continental Shelf* (Germany v. Denmark; Germany v. Netherlands) [1969] ICJ Rep 3 [96].

176 This view was confirmed in the Final Report of the International Law Association Committee, 'Baselines under the International Law of the Sea', 2012, p. 31, reproduced as C. Lathrop, J.A Roach and D.R. Rothwell (eds), 'Baselines Under the International Law of the Sea', (2018) 2: 1–2 *The Law of the Sea* p. 58.

177 See for example, R. Rayfuse, 'International Law and Disappearing States – Maritime Zones and the Criteria for Statehood', (2011) 41 *Environmental Policy and Law* p. 281.

*Climate change* 115

whereby eight States to date[178] have adopted legislation establishing 'fixed' baselines and/or outer maritime limits using geographic coordinates rather than baselines. This process has been supported by the Pacific Boundaries Project in partnership with Australia.[179] Moreover, the practice of establishing fixed or permanent baselines, without considering sea level rise, has been advocated at a regional level for almost a decade.[180] The Taputapuātea Declaration on Climate Change adopted by the Polynesian Leaders Group in 2015 acknowledges

> under the United Nations Convention on the Law of the Sea (UNCLOS), the importance of the Exclusive Economic Zones of the Polynesian Island States and Territories, whose area is calculated according to emerged lands and [sic] permanently establish the baselines in accordance with the UNCLOS, without taking into account sea level rise.[181]

And, most recently, in March 2018, at the 2nd Leaders Summit of the PNA, the eight Pacific States adopted the 2018 Delap Commitment on Securing Our Common Wealth of Oceans whereby they agreed 'to pursue legal recognition of the *defined baselines* established under the United Nations Convention on the Law of the Sea to remain in perpetuity irrespective of the impacts of sea level rise'.[182] Establishing fixed or permanent baselines to mitigate – in the short to medium term – the impact of sea level rise on the maritime zones and marine resources of vulnerable States is not a new idea[183] but it is gaining increasing currency. In 2018, the ILA Committee on International Law and Sea Level Rise adopted Resolution 5/2018 endorsing the principle that where baselines and outer limits have been determined in accordance with the LOSC 'they should not be required to be recalculated should sea level change affect the geographical

---

178 Cook Islands (2013), Fiji (2007/2015), Kiribati (2015), Marshall Islands (2016), Nauru (1999), Niue (2014), Palau (2008) and Tuvalu (2013); see D. Freestone and C. Schofield, 'Current Legal Developments. Republic of the Marshall Islands', (2016) 31 *International Journal of Marine and Coastal Law* pp. 732, 733, 738–740.

179 R. Frost et al., 'Redrawing the Map of the Pacific', (2018) 95 *Marine Policy* p. 302.

180 The *Framework for a Pacific Oceanscape* published in 2010 by the Pacific Islands Forum advocated depositing coordinates and charts with the UN and engaging a 'united regional effort so that the limits cannot be challenged due to sea level rise'; see C. Pratt and H. Govan, 'Framework for a Pacific Oceanscape: A Catalyst for Implementation of Ocean Policy', November 2010, available online at www.forumsec.org/wp-content/uploads/2018/03/Framework-for-a-Pacific-Oceanscape-2010.pdf

181 Polynesian Leaders Group, 'Taputapuātea Declaration', 16 July 2015, available online at www.samoagovt.ws/wp-content/uploads/2015/07/The-Polynesian-P.A.C.T.pdf

182 ILA Committee on International Law and Sea Level Rise, 'Conference Report', 2018, p. 17, available online at www.ila-hq.org/index.php/committees

183 See, for example, D.D. Caron, 'When Law Makes Climate Worse: Rethinking the Law of Baselines in Light of a Rising Sea Level', (1990) 17 *Ecology Law Quarterly* p. 621; A.H.A. Soons, 'The Effects of a Rising Sea Level on Maritime Limits and Boundaries', (1990) 37 *Netherlands International Law Review* p. 207.

## 116 *Karen N. Scott*

reality of the coastline'.[184] It is beyond the scope of this chapter to discuss whether and to what extent the practice of fixing baselines/outer limits in the Pacific constitutes general or regional customary international law but there is no doubt that this collaborative and collective initiative, like the previous collaborative and collective initiative relating to the management of tuna fisheries, represents a very particular 'Pacific response' to the impacts of climate change on coastal and maritime entitlements.

## 6.4 Concluding remarks

The oceans-climate regime complex is rapidly evolving across the areas of mitigation, exploitation and adaptation. Soft law initiatives are playing a significant interstitial role in bridging the oceans-climate regimes, and in addressing lacunae, such as ocean acidification. The Pacific region, in particular, has championed the oceans – climate nexus, and has played an important leadership role in developing oceans-related initiatives within the climate regime. The flexibility introduced into the Paris Agreement, which allows parties to determine their own commitments designed to meet the overall objective of limiting global temperature rise to 2 (and preferably 1.5) degrees, has led to a much more significant focus on the oceans despite the fact that oceans issues are not prominently addressed within the Agreement itself. Whilst several States within the Asia Pacific have included commitments associated with the oceans within their NDCs, it is notable that many States have not, even where they are otherwise developing policies and programmes to support ocean and coastal resilience and adaptation to climate change. Given the (relative) immediacy of the impacts of climate change on Pacific island States it is perhaps unsurprising that it is in this region that practice has evolved most rapidly outside of the global oceans-climate regime. The collaborative initiatives in respect of managing variability in the tuna fishery and sea level rise represent innovative and pragmatic responses to forestall a diminution or loss of rights over marine resources, at least in the short to medium term, owing to climate change.

Whether these initiatives represent appropriate precedents for other regions, in particular, South East Asia however, is debatable. Although climate change was identified as a priority issue by ASEAN in 2007, States within the region 'remain takers rather than makers in international climate politics'.[185] This is despite the fact that four of the ten States slated to be most affected by climate change are located in South East Asia – Myanmar, the Philippines, Thailand and Vietnam[186] – and 'the special geography of Southeast Asia makes it particularly likely that climate change will affect interstate relations', particularly in respect of

---

184 Committee on International Law and Sea Level Rise, 'Resolution 5/2018' 24 August 2018, available online at www.ila-hq.org/index.php/committees
185 Overland et al., note 37, p. vi.
186 Ibid., p. 1.

maritime boundaries.[187] In contrast to the Pacific, South East Asia is not characterised by an especially collaborative approach to international politics, although ASEAN has recently agreed to 'explore the possibility of developing a harmonized approach to measuring, reporting and verifying greenhouse gas emissions as a first step towards further regional collaboration on carbon markets'.[188] Given that both regional and domestic fishing regimes are under-developed and, in many cases, outdated within South East Asia,[189] the development of principles and protocols allowing for shared jurisdiction throughout a species range, taking into consideration the implications of climate change for that range, appears unlikely, at least in the medium term. Moreover, whilst the fixing of baselines and/or outer limits to manage the implications of sea level rise in respect of territory and maritime rights is superficially attractive, the existence of multiple and live maritime disputes in South East Asia makes the development of a Pacific-style regional initiative a similarly unlikely prospect. Greater collaboration around adaptation and mitigation, particularly with respect to protecting mangrove, seagrass and coral ecosystems, is, however, eminently foreseeable. Ultimately, however, while regional initiatives can clearly support global action on climate change they cannot be an effective substitute for a global solution to what might be described as the ultimate global problem.

187 Ibid., p. 2.
188 See 'ASEAN Countries Join Forces for Climate Action', 24 October 2017, available online at https://unfccc.int/news/asean-countries-join-forces-for-climate-action
189 C. Costello, 'Does Climate Change Bolser the Case for Fishery Reform in Asia?', (2018) 35 *Asia Development Review* p. 31.

# 7 The limits of the natural state doctrine

## Rocks, islands and artificial intervention in a changing world

*Imogen Saunders*

## 7.1 Introduction

Article 121(3) of the United Nations Convention on the Law of the Sea (LOSC) sets out that 'rocks which cannot sustain human habitation or economic life of their own shall have no exclusive economic zone or continental shelf'.[1] Such rocks differ from fully entitled islands: without extended maritime zones, the benefits they bring to the States who claim them are greatly reduced, limited only to the rock itself and a 12 nautical mile territorial sea. This provision has long raised interpretative problems. It has been deemed 'problematic',[2] 'famously vague',[3] 'controversial ... the result of deliberate ambiguity'[4] and a 'perfect recipe for confusion and conflict'.[5]

Before the *South China Sea* arbitration,[6] little judicial attention had been paid to Article 121(3).[7] However, the tribunal in the *South China Sea* arbitration had no choice but to engage with the provision. In doing so, the tribunal addressed many of the disputed interpretations of Article 121(3) – including whether the provision is disjunctive or cumulative,[8] the geological requirements (if any) of 'rock'[9] and definition of both 'human habitation'[10] and 'economic life of their own'.[11]

---

1 United Nations Convention on the Law of the Sea, 10 December 1982, 1833 UNTS 397, Article 121(3) [hereafter LOSC].

2 E. Franckx, 'The Arbitral Tribunal's Interpretation of Paragraph 3 in Article 121: A First but Important Step Forward' in S. Jayakumar et al. (eds), *The South China Sea Arbitration: The Legal Dimension*, Cheltenham: Edward Elgar, 2018, pp. 154, 162.

3 N. Oral, '"Rocks" or "Islands"? Sailing Towards Legal Clarity in the Turbulent South China Sea', (2016–2017) 110 *American Journal of International Law Unbound* p. 279.

4 J. Mossop, 'The South China Sea Arbitration and New Zealand's Maritime Claims' (2017) 15 *New Zealand Journal of Public and International Law* pp. 265, 268.

5 E.D. Brown, *The International Law of the Sea*, Vol. 1, Aldershot: Dartmouth Publishing, 1994, p. 151.

6 *In the Matter of an Arbitration before An Arbitral Tribunal Constituted Under Annex VII to the 1982 United Nations Convention on the Law of the Sea between The Republic of the Philippines and the People's Republic of China*, PCA Case no. 2013-19, Award of 12 July 2016 [hereafter *South China Sea* arbitration].

7 See Franckx, note 2, pp. 160–163 for a summary of the relevant cases.

8 *South China Sea* arbitration, [493–496].

9 Ibid., [479–482].

10 Ibid., [488–492].

11 Ibid., [498–503].

*The limits of the natural state doctrine* 119

Various aspects of the tribunal's ruling have already been analysed.[12] In particular, a strict reading of the tribunal's decision suggests that high-tide maritime features will be classified as 'rocks' incapable of generating extended maritime zones *regardless of the size of those features* if the feature can neither sustain human habitation nor an economic life of their own.[13] This reading challenges existing State practice regarding the classification of certain high-tide features as fully entitled islands. This includes claims made by Australia regarding Heard and McDonald Islands[14]; Japan regarding Okinotorishima, Senkaku/Diaoyu and Takeshima/Dokdo Islands[15]; the United States regarding Johnston Atoll and other Pacific Ocean features[16]; New Zealand regarding Antipodes, Bounty and Snares Islands[17]; Brazil regarding the St Peter and St Paul Archipelago[18]; Chile regarding Isla Salas y Gomez,[19] France regarding the Kerguelen Islands[20]; and Mexico regarding Isla Socorro, Isla Clarion, Isla San Benedicto and Isla Roca Partida.[21]

Some of these claims are disputed by other States[22] but many are not.[23] As such, there are legitimate questions as to the compatibility of the arbitral tribunal's ruling with State practice,[24] as well as questions of possible acquiescence affecting the entitlements of these features.[25] This chapter, however, is concerned with a different aspect of the arbitral tribunal's ruling to those that have been previously explored: the role of artificial intervention in determining the capability of a feature to sustain human habitation or an economic life of its own. The importance of this to the South East Asian context cannot be understated: as the arbitral tribunal's decision demonstrates, artificial intervention to and on islands and rocks is common.[26] This includes the island building

---

12 See Franckx, note 2, for a consideration of the grammatical structure of Article 121(3) as well as the question of geological composition.

13 *South China Sea* arbitration, [538], [548].

14 N. Klein, 'Islands and Rocks after the *South China Sea Arbitration*', (2016) 24 *Australian Year Book of International Law* pp. 21, 28–29.

15 Ibid., p. 28.

16 Ibid.

17 Mossop, note 4, pp. 279–280.

18 Y. Song, 'The 2016 Arbitral Award, Interpretation of Article 121(3) of the UNCLOS, and Selecting Examples of Inconsistent State Practice', (2018) 49 *Ocean Development and International Law* pp. 247, 254.

19 Ibid.

20 Y. Tanaka, 'Reflections on the Interpretation and Application of Article 121(3) in the *South China Sea Arbitration* (Merits)', (2017) 48 *Ocean Development and International Law* pp. 365, 373.

21 Ibid.

22 Such as Japan's claims to the status of Okinotorishima; see Klein, note 14, p. 28.

23 D.R. Rothwell and T. Stephens, *The International Law of the Sea*, 2nd ed., Oxford: Hart Publishing, 2016, pp. 89–90.

24 See for example Song, note 18; M.H. Nordquist, 'UNCLOS Article 121 and Itu Aba in the South China Sea Final Award: A Correct Interpretation?' in S. Jayakumar et al. (eds), *The South China Sea Arbitration: The Legal Dimension*, Cheltenham: Edward Elgar, 2018, pp. 176, 188.

25 Mossop, note 4, pp. 286–290; Klein, note 14, p. 29.

26 Indeed, the creation of islands through reclamation is particularly common in the region: S.Y. Chee et al., 'Land Reclamation and Artificial Islands: Walking the Tightrope between Development and Conservation', (2017) 12 *Global Ecology and Conservation* p. 80.

## 120  *Imogen Saunders*

activities in the South China Sea, land preservation activities such as Japan's constructions around Okinotorishima since 1988,[27] and also extends to 'smaller' instances of artificial intervention such as the use of desalination plants.[28]

The question of artificial intervention is particularly pertinent in the context of the Anthropocene: the current era where human induced change – including, but not limited to, global warming – is greater than naturally occurring environmental changes.[29] Such human induced change will have (and is already having) significant effects on islands and other maritime features.[30] Again, the relevance of this to South East Asia is clear. Populations on small low-lying islands will be disproportionally affected by climate change[31]; and the effects of climate change are already being seen such as increased coastal erosion in the Sangihe Islands in Indonesia,[32] and increased typhoons causing floods and landslides on Rapu-Rapu Islands in the Philippines.[33]

Coupled with the impact of climate change on islands and maritime features is the growing recognition that technological solutions may be required to off-set the effects of climate change – whether these are mitigation technologies to protect existing features and ecosystems, or adaption technologies to adapt to new environmental realities.[34] These twin aspects of human induced climate change and human ingenuity expressed through technological advancements make increasing artificial alteration of our environment inevitable. How does such artificial intervention interact with Article 121?

The arbitral tribunal's decision used the concept of the natural state of a feature in its interpretation of Article 121(3). This approach assesses the capacity of a feature in its intrinsic or natural state, before any artificial modification or intervention: termed the 'natural state doctrine' in this chapter. This chapter will

---

27  See, for example, A.L. Silverstein, 'Okinotorishima: Artificial Preservation of a Speck of Sovereignty', (1990) 16 *Brooklyn Journal of International Law* p. 409.

28  Such as China's desalination plant on Woody Island: A. Panda, 'South China Sea: China Activates First Desalination Plant on Woody Island', *The Diplomat Online*, 4 October 2016, available online at https://thediplomat.com/2016/10/south-china-sea-china-activates-first-desalination-plant-on-woody-island/

29  See, for example, W. Steffen et al., 'The Anthropocene: Are Humans Now Overwhelming the Great Forces of Nature', (2007) 36 *AMBIO: A Journal of the Human Environment* p. 614; see generally J. Davies, *The Birth of the Anthropocene*, Oakland: University of California Press, 2016.

30  See, for example, T. Stephens, 'Warming Waters and Souring Seas: Climate Change and Ocean Acidification' in D.R. Rothwell et al. (eds), *The Oxford Handbook of the Law of the Sea*, Oxford: Oxford University Press, 2015, pp. 777, 790.

31  C.B. Field et al. (eds), Intergovernmental Panel on Climate Change, *Climate Change 2014: Impacts, Adaptation and Vulnerability*, Cambridge: Cambridge University Press, 2014, p. 1347.

32  L. Hiwasaki et al., 'Local and Indigenous Knowledge on Climate-related Hazards of coastal and small island communities in Southeast Asia', (2015) 128 *Climatic Change* pp. 35, 40.

33  Ibid., p. 41.

34  B. Metz et al. (eds), Intergovernmental Panel on Climate Change Working Group III, *Climate Change 2007: Mitigation of Climate Change*, 2007, p. 148.

## The limits of the natural state doctrine 121

explore implications of the natural state doctrine to situations outside the factual matrix of the *South China Sea* arbitration. While that case was rooted firmly in the context of China's island building activities,[35] the decision went beyond the circumstances of land reclamation, assessing Article 121(3) criteria against a baseline of the natural state. But how realistic is this doctrine in the context of the Anthropocene – both for South East Asia and the world more generally? To answer this question, this chapter will set out the arbitral tribunal's discussions on artificial modification of features. It will then explore the development of the natural state doctrine, particularly in respect of rocks and islands. The chapter will then apply the natural state approach to two circumstances where maritime features may be affected by artificial intervention: islands rendered uninhabitable because of the effects of climate change; and islands whereby the capacity to support human habitation is generated by some initial and/or ongoing artificial intervention.

## 7.2 The *South China Sea* arbitration and artificial intervention

Article 121 of the LOSC limits the regime of islands to those that are a 'naturally formed area of land'.[36] There is no further textual restriction in Article 121(3) that requires the *capacity* of a feature to 'support human habitation' and 'have an economic life of its own' to also be naturally formed. The arbitral tribunal, however, based its analysis of Article 121(3) on this restriction: asking 'does the feature *in its natural form* have the capability of sustaining human habitation or an economic life?'[37]

This restriction must be read in light of the background to the dispute, particularly the massive land reclamation that had been carried out by China, turning both low-tide elevations and tiny high-tide features[38] into artificial islands capable of supporting military personnel, airstrips and buildings.[39] This context is reflected in the tribunal's statement that:

> Just as a low-tide elevation or area of seabed cannot be legally transformed into an island through human efforts, the Tribunal considers that a rock cannot be transformed into a fully entitled island through land reclamation. The status of a feature must be assessed on the basis of its natural condition.[40]

---

35 See I. Saunders, 'The *South China Sea Award*, Artificial Islands and Territory', (2016) 24 *Australian Year Book of International Law* pp. 31, 31–32.

36 LOSC, Article 121(1).

37 *South China Sea* arbitration, [483] (emphasis added).

38 This article follows the language used by the arbitral tribunal to delineate between low-tide elevations and those maritime features dry at high tide. The latter (whether rocks or islands) are described as 'high-tide features'.

39 Office of the Secretary of Defence, *Annual Report to Congress: Military and Security Developments Involving the People's Republic of China*, 15 May 2017, p. 12. available online at www.defense.gov/Portals/1/Documents/pubs/2017_China_Military_Power_Report. PDF?ver=2017-06-06-141328-770

40 *South China Sea* arbitration, [508].

## 122  *Imogen Saunders*

In the context of land reclamation, assessing a maritime feature before the reclamation occurred is necessary. From a legal perspective, to do otherwise would mean the land being assessed would not be naturally formed: thus, it would never qualify as an island in the first place. There are also valid policy reasons for this restriction in the context of reclamation: to deter States from a 'grab and ransack' mentality, whereby large areas of water can be claimed through strategic building on otherwise uninhabitable shoals and reefs.[41] This is especially important considering the often-devastating environmental impacts of land reclamation.[42]

However, the tribunal's use of the natural state doctrine went beyond considering artificial additions to land mass. In addition to land reclamation, the tribunal classified desalination facilities, and the introduction of tillable soil as artificial interventions that could not be taken into account when assessing the capacity of the feature.[43] Thus, the tribunal stated that 'the Convention requires that the status of a feature be ascertained on the basis of its earlier, natural condition, prior to the onset of significant human modification ...'.[44]

If one accepts this doctrine, a question arises as to what qualifies as 'significant human modification'. It can be argued that most of the world *has* been subject to significant human modification over millennia through agrarian transformations.[45] Clearly, it would be nonsensical to insist on assessing land in its 'natural state' from thousands of years ago, even if such a practical determination could be made. The tribunal did add two qualifiers to the general statement which assist in this regard. First, artificial interventions are excluded from the capacity analysis where they are 'external additions or modifications intended to increase its capacity to sustain human habitation or an economic life of its own'.[46] Second, the tribunal was particularly suspect of artificial interventions that occurred *after* the establishment of extended maritime entitlements, suggesting any interventions after this date could be 'clouded by an apparent attempt to assert a maritime claim'.[47] Rather, the tribunal preferred historical evidence:

> Accordingly, the Tribunal considers historical evidence of conditions on the features – prior to the advent of the exclusive economic zone as a concept

---

41  See, for example, P.C. Jessup, *The Law of Territorial Waters and Maritime Jurisdiction*, New York: Kraus Reprint, 1970, p. 69.

42  T. Stephens, 'The Collateral Damage from China's "Great Wall of Sand": The Environmental Dimensions of the *South China Sea Case*', (2016) 24 *Australian Year Book of International Law* pp. 41, 48–52.

43  *South China Sea* arbitration, [511].

44  Ibid.

45  Nordquist, note 24, p. 196; see generally B. Pascoe, *Dark Emu Black Seeds: Agriculture or Accident?*, Broome: Magabala Books, 2014.

46  *South China Sea* arbitration, [541].

47  Ibid., [550].

The limits of the natural state doctrine 123

or the beginning of significant human modification – to represent a more reliable guide to the capacity of the features to sustain human habitation or economic life.[48]

Again, against the factual background to the dispute, these restrictions make sense. Many of the features being assessed were, in their natural state, 'miniscule and barren' and 'obviously incapable of sustaining human habitation or an economic life of their own'.[49] One feature only qualified as a high-tide feature because storm activity pushed a coral boulder onto the reef, above the high-tide line.[50] In conjunction with the unmistakable nature of the features in their natural state, the human modification undertaken on several was immense: turning former barren rocks and low-tide elevations into military outposts.[51] To assess the newly created features as they currently exist would fall foul both of the 'naturally formed' requirement in Article 121(1) *and* incentivise such reclamation behaviours more generally.

But what of artificial interventions that do not involve land reclamation? The arbitral tribunal considered this situation in the context of the disputed feature of Itu Abu. The Philippines contended Itu Abu, while bigger than other disputed features, was a rock and not a fully entitled island.[52] The arbitral tribunal assessed Itu Abu's capacity to support human habitation, and in doing so two issues of artificial intervention were considered. First was the issue of potable water. Like many islands, Itu Abu's permanent source of drinking water is supplied by a freshwater lens.[53] The tribunal recognised that this water source was negatively impacted by the building activities on Itu Abu: 'the construction of the airstrip on the feature would have reduced the soil's capacity to absorb rainwater and regenerate the freshwater lens'.[54] The tribunal accordingly assessed Itu Abu's water resources *before* the construction 'in their natural condition, whether or not that remains the case today'.[55]

---

48 Ibid., [578].
49 Ibid., [561] (in respect of Cuarteron Reef); see also [556] (in respect of Scarborough Shoal), [558] (in respect of Johnson Reef), [564] (in respect of Fiery Cross Reef) and [567] (in respect of Gaven Reef (North)).
50 Ibid., [570] (in respect of McKennan Reef).
51 Media reports in 2018 suggest the presence of cruise missiles on reclaimed land at Fiery Cross Reef, Subi Reef and Mischief Reef; and radar and communications jamming equipment on reclaimed land at Mischief Reef; see M.R. Gordon and J. Page, 'China Installed Military Jamming Equipment on Spratly Islands, U.S. Says', *Wall Street Journal Online*, 9 April 2018, available online at www.wsj.com/articles/china-installed-military-jamming-equipment-on-spratly-islands-u-s-says-1523266320; A. Macias, 'China Quietly Installed Defensive Missile Systems on Strategic Spratly Islands in Hotly Contested South China Sea', *CNBC Online*, 2 May 2018, available online at www.cnbc.com/2018/05/02/china-added-missile-systems-on-spratly-islands-in-south-china-sea.html?
52 *South China Sea* arbitration, [426].
53 Freshwater lenses are discussed in more detail below.
54 *South China Sea* arbitration, [584].
55 Ibid.

## 124    *Imogen Saunders*

Second, the tribunal assessed the capacity of the soil to support vegetation on Itu Abu, finding that although many plants were introduced, there was 'no evidence that this would have involved the importation of soil and concludes that it most likely reflects the capacity of the feature in its natural condition'.[56] Thus, it seems that if soil *had* been introduced to Itu Abu, the arbitral tribunal would not have considered any effect the introduced soil may have had on vegetation and future habitability.

Ultimately, the tribunal held that Itu Abu was not able to support human habitation (as opposed to human survival)[57] – a finding that has been questioned.[58] It is clear that the tribunal steadfastly refused to consider the *effect* of any artificial intervention at Itu Abu, including those on naturally formed, non-reclaimed land: regardless of whether such interventions positively or negatively impacted the capacity of the feature.

If one accepts the Tribunal's decision as the correct approach to Article 121(3), it follows that any assessment of the capacity of a feature to sustain human habitation and an economic life of its own should be done entirely on the natural capacity of that feature, discounting the effects of any form of artificial intervention. As set out above, this approach is not evident on the face of Article 121(3): the only natural requirement on the face of Article 121 is the naturally formed *land* requirement. The next part of this chapter will thus discuss the development of the natural state doctrine.

## 7.3 The natural state doctrine

As the arbitral tribunal recognised, there is historic support for the exclusion of artificial modifications from consideration of the capacity of maritime features.[59] This support is found in materials from the 1923 Imperial Conference held between the Government of the United Kingdom and the Governments of the self-governing Dominions: Canada, Australia, New Zealand, South Africa, Newfoundland and the Irish Free State,[60] as well as representatives from India.[61] Resolution Four of that Conference set out common policy for the British Empire, and included the definitional provision that 'the word "island" covers all portions of territory permanently above high water in normal circumstances and capable of use or habitation'.[62]

An explanatory memorandum provided to the Conference further stated

---

56  Ibid., [596].
57  Ibid., [621–622].
58  See, for example, Nordquist, note 24.
59  *South China Sea* arbitration, [522].
60  W.R. Riddell, 'The Imperial Conference of 1923' (1924) 8 *The Constitutional Review* p. 131.
61  Ibid., p. 134.
62  Imperial Conference 1923, *Report of Inter-Departmental Committee on the Limits of Territorial Waters*, 27 September 1923, extracted in Brown, note 5, p. 151.

*The limits of the natural state doctrine* 125

22. The phrase "capable of use or habitation" has been adopted as a compromise. It is intended that the words 'capable of use' should mean capable, without artificial addition, of being used throughout all seasons for some definite commercial or defence purpose, and that 'capable of habitation' should mean capable, without artificial addition, of permanent human habitation.

23. It is recognized that these criteria will in many cases admit of argument, but nothing more definite could be arrived at in view of the many divergent considerations involved. It is thought that no criteria could be selected that would not be open to some form of criticism.[63]

Thus, there is one example of State practice, from at most eight States.[64] As the arbitral tribunal further recognised, the United Kingdom proposed similar criteria – that islands must be 'capable of occupation and use'[65] – at the 1930 League of Nations Hague Codification Conference.[66] This criterion was not adopted by the preparatory committee to the conference,[67] and was not included in the definition of island in the International Law Commission's 1956 Articles Concerning the Law of the Sea.[68] The arbitral tribunal further recognised that the final wording of Article 121(3) was a 'compromise', with the drafters consistently rejecting proposals to introduce specific criteria.[69] None of the criteria proposed by States in the drafting of the LOSC included any restriction on artificial intervention or additions.[70]

Although some commentators suggest Article 121(3) *should* have included the phrase 'without artificial addition',[71] other commentators disagree. In 1983, Van Dyke and Brooks argued that 'In today's world of high technology, any land protrusion can be made "inhabitable" if a nation is willing to expend sufficient resources'.[72] Charney further argues that

Ocean features that were not capable of sustaining human habitation or did not have an economic life in the past, but subsequently developed those

---

63 Ibid.

64 There are of course questions of independence and Statehood for the Dominion States and British India.

65 League of Nations Conference for the Codification of International Law, 'Bases of Discussion for the Conference Drawn up by the Preparatory Committee', Vol II: Territorial Waters, League of Nations Doc C.74.M.39.1929.V, p. 53.

66 *South China Sea* arbitration, [523].

67 League of Nations Conference for the Codification of International Law, note 65, pp. 52–54.

68 International Law Commission, 'Articles Concerning the Law of the Sea', (1956) II *Yearbook of the International Law of the Sea* pp. 256, 257; see also *South China Sea* arbitration, [523], [524].

69 *South China Sea* arbitration, [537].

70 See M.H. Nordquist (ed), *United Nations Convention on the Law of the Sea 1982: A Commentary*, Vol. III, Dordrecht: Martinus Nijhoff, 1982, pp. 326–339.

71 Brown, note 5, p. 151.

72 J.M. Van Dyke and R.A. Brooks, 'Uninhabited Islands: Their Impact on the Ownership of the Ocean's Resources', (1983) 12 *Ocean Development and International Law* pp. 265, 267.

## 126  *Imogen Saunders*

capabilities owing to changes in economic demand, technological innovations or new human activities, would also not be Article 121(3) rocks.[73]

Technological innovations in this context would presumably be some form of artificial interventions.

Support for assessing a feature on *future* capacity rather than *historic* capacity is also found in Iran's declaration upon signing the LOSC, which relevantly states

> 5) Islets situated in enclosed and semi-enclosed seas which potentially can sustain human habitation or economic life of their own, but due to climatic conditions, resource restriction or other limitations, have not yet been put to development, fall within the provisions of paragraph 2 of article 121 concerning "Regime of Islands", and have, therefore, full effect in boundary delimitation of various maritime zones of the interested Coastal States.[74]

As such, the arbitral tribunal's expansion of the natural state restriction from matters of land formation (which Article 121 clearly textually supports) to *all* non-land forming artificial intervention (which neither Article 121 nor the *traveuax* supports) is problematic. There is limited historic State practice to support such an expansion: and limited modern contrary State practice to reject it. The policy reason behind the arbitral tribunal's decision to expand the application of the natural state doctrine is clear, and justified within the factual matrix of the dispute being considered by the tribunal. However, if the reasoning is applied more broadly, it may itself produce highly unsatisfactory results. This is the focus of the next part of this chapter.

## 7.4 Application of the natural state doctrine to features affected by artificial intervention

This section will consider two different scenarios: islands affected by climate change, and islands whereby other artificial intervention (either initially or on an ongoing basis) is necessary to sustain human habitation and an economic life of its own.

### 7.4.1 *Islands affected by climate change*

Much of the discussion surrounding islands and climate change has been centred on the loss of land due to rising sea levels: the problem of sinking island States.

---

73 J.I. Charney, 'Rocks that Cannot Sustain Human Habitation', (1999) 93 *American Journal of International Law* pp. 863, 867.

74 Declaration made by the Islamic Republic of Iran upon signature of LOSC (10 December 1982) available online at www.un.org/Depts/los/convention_agreements/convention_declarations.htm

# The limits of the natural state doctrine 127

However, climate change also has the potential to render islands uninhabitable without submergence. This could occur in three main ways.

The changing climate may disrupt and even destroy fresh water resources on many small islands, although the islands themselves may remain above water. This is particularly true for those islands which rely on freshwater lenses as their source of freshwater. A lens is a type of underground aquifer, in which a layer of fresh water floats on top of sea (salt) water. The lens is recharged through rainwater that filters down into it. As long as the rate of use of the lens is less or equal to the rate of recharge, the lens will keep replenishing and will be an ongoing source of fresh water. Such lenses are affected by climate change in two ways. First, rising sea levels has the potential to decrease the size of the freshwater lens (and thus the amount of water available).[75] Second, increased storm activity due to climate change brings increased storm surges which can result in 'salt contamination of the freshwater lens and a temporary loss of freshwater'.[76] The particular vulnerability of such freshwater resources means climate change may potentially render formerly habitable islands uninhabitable.[77]

Even before freshwater reserves are depleted, climate change may affect vegetation on shallow islands, particularly coral atolls, destroying 'deep rooted food crops' and toppling coconut trees.[78] Sand pushed onto islands by extreme weather events can also damage soil fertility and productivity, leaving island inhabitants reliant on external food supplies.[79] This has already happened to some extent on the Carteret Islands in Papua New Guinea.[80] Finally, climate change can also affect the productivity of the sea surrounding the island: coral bleaching and destruction affects the fish species that live in the coral reefs, many of which are relied upon by island communities as their main food source.

In the above situations, the effect of climate change could be that the maritime feature itself may not sink and indeed may still be a high-tide feature. However, it will have lost its capacity to support human habitation. Each of these above scenarios – the loss of freshwater, the loss of vegetation and arable soil, the loss of fish resources and the reliance on external supplies of food and provisions – tracks

---

75 S. Holding and D.M. Allen, 'From Days to Decades: Numerical Modelling of Freshwater Lens Response to Climate Change Stressors on Small Low-lying Islands', (2015) 19 *Hydrology and Earth System Sciences* p. 933.

76 Ibid.

77 See, for example, G.A. Meehl, 'Vulnerability of Freshwater Resources to Climate Change in the Tropical Pacific Region', (1996) 92 *Water, Air and Soil Pollution* pp. 203, 210; D.D. Caron, 'When Law Makes Climate Change Worse: Rethinking the Law of Baselines in Light of a Rising Sea Level', (1990) 70 *Ecology Law Quarterly* pp. 621, 627.

78 L. Yamamoto and M. Esteban, 'Vanishing Island States and Sovereignty', (2010) 53 *Ocean and Coastal Management* pp. 1, 2.

79 Ibid., p. 3.

80 Ibid.; see also D. James, 'Lost at Sea: The Race against Time to Save the Carteret Islands from Climate Change', *ABC News Online*, 4 August 2018, available online at www.abc.net.au/news/2018-08-04/the-race-against-time-to-save-the-carteret-islanders/10066958

## 128 *Imogen Saunders*

directly to elements which the arbitral tribunal emphasised as crucial in showing the ability of a feature to support human habitation.[81]

How then are such affected islands assessed under the natural state doctrine? Kaye has argued that given the human cause, climate change *itself* could be considered an artificial intervention.[82] As such, any islands affected by climate change should be assessed in their natural state pre-climate change: still with undisturbed fresh water resources, undamaged soil and intact fish stocks. While the attraction in allowing States affected by climate change to maintain their maritime entitlements is clear, there are three problems with this argument.

First, the arbitral tribunal *did* consider the situation where a previously habitable feature becomes uninhabitable due to intervening events. However, it seems this consideration was on the assumption of temporary uninhabitability:

> In such circumstances, the Tribunal should consider whether there is evidence that human habitation has been prevented or ended by forces that are separate from the intrinsic capacity of the feature. War, pollution, and environmental harm could all lead to the depopulation, for a prolonged period, of a feature that, in its natural state, was capable of sustaining human habitation.[83]

Can this same reasoning be extended to situations where depopulation is not for a prolonged period, but is irrevocably permanent?

Second, and especially in the case of uninhabitability caused by extreme weather events, it can be very hard to differentiate extreme weather events caused by climate change and extreme weather events that are naturally occurring.[84] This is the very point of the Anthropocene: 'the natural and the human are mixed up, not merely added, and their influences cannot be neatly distinguished'.[85] If an island is significantly impacted by an extreme weather event, must this now always be considered an artificial intervention? Stephens argues for some weather events it *is* possible to differentiate between those caused (or augmented) by climate change and those naturally occurring.[86] Although 'quantifying the climate change influence is more complex',[87] 'advances in attribution science mean

---

81  See *South China Sea* arbitration, [490], [550], [580–601].

82  S. Kaye, 'The Law of the Sea Convention and Sea Level Rise in the Light of the South China Sea Arbitration', (2017) 93 *International Law Studies* pp. 423, 431.

83  *South China Sea* arbitration, [549].

84  T. Stephens, 'Disasters, International Environmental Law and the Anthropocene' in S.C. Breau and K.L.H. Samuel (eds), *Research Handbook on Disasters and International Law*, Cheltenham: Edward Elgar Publishing, 2016, p. 153.

85  C. Hamilton, 'Human Destiny in the Anthropocene' in C. Hamilton et al. (eds), *The Anthropocene and the Global Environmental Crisis: Rethinking Modernity in a New Epoch*, New York: Routledge, 2015, pp. 32, 34.

86  T. Stephens, 'Wishful thinking? The Governance of Climate Change-related Disasters in the Anthropocene' in R. Lyster and R.R.M. Verchick, *Research Handbook on Climate Disaster Law: Barriers and Opportunities*, Cheltenham: Edward Elgar Publishing, 2018, pp. 31, 34–35.

87  Ibid., p. 34.

*The limits of the natural state doctrine*  129

that it is possible, at least in some cases, to determine if climate change affected the probability of an extreme weather event occurring'.[88] Given this, the natural state doctrine would *differentiate* between islands rendered uninhabitable by, on the one hand, climate change induced rising sea levels, heat waves and floods, and on the other hand, non-climate change induced earthquakes or other natural disasters. The island in the first scenario would maintain its fully entitled status, and maritime zones would remain undisturbed. The island in the second situation would be considered no longer an island, but a rock, and would lose all extended maritime zones. This would be true even if practically speaking, each island now had the same degree of uninhabitability.

This situation leads to the third problem with discounting the effects of climate change when assessing maritime features. The rationale behind Article 121(3) was, in the words of the arbitral tribunal:

> … to disable tiny features from unfairly and inequitably generating enormous entitlements to maritime space that would serve not to benefit the local population, but to award a windfall to the (potentially distant) state to have maintained a claim to such a feature.[89]

How can this policy goal be achieved if the local population no longer exists and the feature cannot ever sustain one again? Van Dyke and Brooks argue that

> The key factor must be whether the island can in fact support a stable population. Islands should not generate ocean space if they are claimed by some distant absentee landlord who now desires the island primarily because of the ocean resources around the island. Islands should generate ocean space if stable communities of people live on the island and use the surrounding ocean areas.[90]

An island decimated by climate change will not be able to support a stable population. It may be that the population of the affected island moves to other land territory in close proximity[91]; or perhaps an artificial island built for this purpose.[92] In this case, the policy justification still applies. If, however, the former population of the island is dispersed,[93] and no stable community live in

---

88 Ibid., p. 35.
89 *South China Sea* arbitration, [516].
90 Van Dyke and Brooks, note 72, p. 286.
91 Such as people being resettled from the Carteret Islands to Bougainville in Papua New Guinea; see Displacement Solutions, *The Bougainville Resettlement Initiative Meeting Report*, 11 December 2008, available online at http://displacementsolutions.org/wp-content/uploads/BG.pdf
92 Such as Hulhumalé in the Maldives; see R. Rayfuse, 'Climate Change and the Law of the Sea' in R. Rayfuse and S.V. Scott (eds), *International Law in the Era of Climate Change*, Cheltenham: Edward Elgar Publishing, 2012, pp. 147, 153; see generally J.G. Stoutenberg, *Disappearing Island States in International Law*, Leiden: Brill, 2015.
93 Most likely in the case of whole nation displacement: or where the affected island is geographically distant from the rest of the State's territory.

## 130   Imogen Saunders

the area or use the surrounding ocean area, why should the extended maritime zones prevail? Such a situation seems antithetical to the goal that oceans remain the common heritage of mankind.[94]

Yet as unsatisfactory as the argument is, the application of the natural state doctrine leads to a perfidious situation if climate change is not assessed as an artificial intervention. If the 'natural state' of islands is taken as their state post-climate change, then any artificial intervention to reduce the negative effects – both coastal protection and sea defences – must be discounted. As Kaye points out, it is the very island building activities that the arbitral tribunal disapproved of that may be instrumental to States retaining the habitability of their islands.[95]

### 7.4.2 Islands that are transformed by artificial interventions

The focus of this section is upon islands that in their natural state are unable to sustain human habitation, but through some form of artificial intervention are rendered habitable. Importantly, the focus here is on non-reclamation artificial intervention: the islands in question fulfil the naturally formed criteria of Article 121(1).

The first way that artificial intervention may transform an uninhabitable island into land capable of sustaining a human population is through terraforming. Although terraforming is often discussed in the hypothetical[96] or the virtual,[97] there is at least one example on Earth of a successfully terraformed island. Ascension Island, in the tropical south Atlantic, has been transformed by deliberate plantings of introduced species in the mid-nineteenth century.[98] The island, once described by Charles Darwin as 'entirely destitute of trees',[99] is now home to an artificially created cloud forest, described as a 'luxuriant tropical ecosystem'.[100] The artificial interventions altered the soil and hydrology of the island, and reportedly improved habitability for the population.[101] No ongoing

---

94  Van Dyke and Brooks, note 72, p. 288.

95  Kaye, note 82, p. 432.

96  Such as terraforming Mars and other celestial bodies; see, for example, M. Beech, *Terraforming: The Creation of Habitable Worlds*, New York: Springer, 2009. As an example of terraforming in science fiction, see K.S. Robinson, *Green Mars*, London: Harper Collins, 1993.

97  Such as terraforming in online games; see, for example, M. Wheeler, 'Developing the Media Zoo in Second Life', (2009) 40 *British Journal of Education Technology* pp. 427, 428–429.

98  D.M. Wilkinson, 'The Parable of Green Mountain: Ascension Island, Ecosystem Construction and Ecological Fitting', (2004) 31 *Journal of Biogeography* pp. 1, 2.

99  C. Darwin, *Journal of Researches into the Geology and Natural History of the Various Countries Visited by H.M.S. Beagle under the Command of Captain Fitzroy R.N. from 1832 to 1836*, London: Henry Colburn, 1839.

100  Wilkinson, note 98, p. 2. Although also see M. Teller, 'Ascension: The Island Where Nothing Makes Sense', *BBC News Online*, 19 April 2016, available online at www.bbc.com/news/magazine-36076411

101  See C. Fieseler, 'Mysterious Island Experiment Could Help Us Colonize Other Planets', *National Geographic Online*, 8 May 2017 available online at https://news.nationalgeographic.com/2017/05/ascension-island-terraformed-biology-evolution-conservation/

# The limits of the natural state doctrine    131

artificial intervention is required to maintain the established forest ecosystem. How then would the natural state doctrine apply to Ascension Island? Must it be assessed as it was before the artificial intervention? Or can the now established and self-sustaining ecosystem be taken into account?

The second way that artificial intervention may render previously uninhabitable islands habitable is through the uses of technology to overcome resource problems. Technological advances are making artificially assisted living feasible. For example, desalination was once considered too expensive to be used on a large scale. However, now 70% of Israel's drinking water is provided by desalination plants,[102] with plans to increase that percentage to 85%.[103] Desalination is becoming increasingly common in countries experiencing extreme water scarcity.[104] As noted above, the arbitral tribunal expressly excluded desalination plants from its consideration of the capacity of a feature to sustain human habitation. If an island is reliant on desalination for its drinking water, a strict reading of the natural state doctrine would suggest that an island may not actually fulfil the criteria of Article 121(3) regardless of its size.[105]

Another question that arises is at what point does artificial intervention become too much? For example, fresh water is available on Cabo Verde island of Santo Antao, but predominantly as ground water: there are no permanent rivers.[106] Agriculture on the island has been reliant on artificial intervention in the form of diversion dams, reservoirs and canals: first by the local farmers[107] and then through State intervention from mid-twentieth century.[108] The irrigation schemes are the 'enormous efforts of the local population to make use of limited water resources in a very hostile physical environment'.[109] Without such artificial intervention, Santo Antao would not be able to sustain its agricultural base; or its population. How is this different to an island dependent on a desalination plant? The mere *presence* of freshwater is not enough to show a capacity to support human habitation according to the arbitral tribunal.[110]

---

102 M. Lidman, 'Desalination Isn't the Magic Bullet, Water Authority Warns Israelis', *The Times of Israel Online*, 5 June 2018 available online at www.timesofisrael.com/desalination-isnt-the-magic-bullet-water-authority-warns-israelis/

103 S. Gorodeisky, 'Israel Publishes Tender for World's Biggest Desalination Plant', *Globes Online*, 29 October 2018, available online at https://en.globes.co.il/en/article-israel-publishes-tender-for-worlds-biggest-desalination-plant-1001258500

104 L.H.F. Varela, 'Challenges to the Human Right to Water and to the Sustainability of Services in Santa Cruz, Cabo Verde', (2016) 14 *Ambiente and Sociedade* pp. 207, 209.

105 The recognition of inherent capacity due to size in *South China Sea* arbitration, [548] is limited by the natural state doctrine set out earlier by the arbitral tribunal in [541].

106 B. Haagsma, 'Traditional Water Management and State Intervention: The Case of Santo Antao, Cape Verde', (1995) 15 *Mountain Research and Development* pp. 39, 40.

107 Ibid., p. 42.

108 Ibid., p. 48.

109 Ibid., p. 42.

110 The tribunal accepted that Itu Abu had freshwater resources: see *South China Sea* arbitration, [581–584].

## 132 *Imogen Saunders*

What level of human intervention in developing a resource will tip the line such that it cannot be assessed as part of the intrinsic capacity of the feature? To make this question more complicated, desalination *has* become necessary in Cabo Verde. As of 2013, 'the proportion of desalinated water in domestic consumption was equivalent to that of ground water'.[111] How would the natural state doctrine assess these two different (and necessary) types of artificial intervention?

Both Ascension Island and Cabo Verde have a population that has been sustained over time. In line with the arbitral tribunal's decision, historic evidence of population is important for determining the capacity of a feature to support human habitation.[112] However, the arbitral Tribunal warned against populations serviced from the outside, especially those 'installed ... precisely to stake a claim to the territory and the maritime zones generated by it'.[113] Would this also extend to populations reliant on artificial interventions?

This is particularly pertinent in the example of Ascension Island. The population was first established under British naval control,[114] and the population relied upon distillation of sea water as the primary freshwater resource.[115] After terraforming, a farm on the island provided food – although that has now closed and the island is reliant on external supplies.[116] Today, the island is a British Overseas Territory with no permanent right of abode: its population is mostly military and all are either on work contracts or the family of a contractor.[117] Yet, the United Kingdom claims an EEZ and continental shelf[118]: these claims have not been challenged.[119] Whether through initial distillation practices, the now terraformed island or external supply of provisions, Ascension Island has always relied on artificial interventions. A strict reading of the natural state doctrine would suggest this means it would not qualify as a fully entitled island.

---

111 Varela, note 104, p. 209.

112 *South China Sea* arbitration, [549–550].

113 *South China Sea* arbitration, [550].

114 R.A. Daly, 'The Geology of Ascension Island', (1925) 60 *Proceedings of the American Academy of Arts and Sciences* pp. 3, 6.

115 Ibid., p. 9.

116 See F. Pearce, 'US and UK Accused of "Squeezing Life Out Of" Ascension Island', *The Guardian Online*, 12 September 2013, available online at www.theguardian.com/uk-news/2013/sep/11/ascension-island-population-cut-uk-government

117 See Ascension Island Government, 'Living on Ascension', (n.d.), available online at www.ascension-island.gov.ac/working-here/living-on-ascension/

118 O. Bowcott, 'Britain Lays Claim to 200,000 sq km of the South Atlantic Seabed', *The Guardian Online*, 24 May 2008, available online at www.theguardian.com/world/2008/may/24/antarctica.arctic

119 Although the UK's claims to an extended continental shelf was rejected: Commission on the Limits of the Continental Shelf, *Summary of Recommendations of the Commission on the Limits of the Continental Shelf in Regard to the Submission Made by the United Kingdom of Great Britain and Northern Ireland in Respect of Ascension Island on 9 May 2008*, available online at www.un.org/depts/los/clcs_new/submissions_files/gbr08/gbr_asc_isl_rec_summ.pdf

## 7.5 Conclusion

It must be acknowledged that the arbitral tribunal applied the natural state doctrine in a very particular context. The arbitral tribunal was either assessing miniscule features, made habitable only by large reclamation works, or borderline cases, falling close to the line between habitability and uninhabitability. Even the borderline cases had been artificially enhanced, maintained and populated as part, it was suggested, of an overall strategy to claim sovereignty and maritime entitlements. In this particular context, the arbitral tribunal's aversion to artificial intervention is understandable. Although the arbitral tribunal supported a case-by-case application of Article 121(3),[120] the requirement that the feature 'be determined on the basis of its natural capacity, without external additions or modifications intended to increase its capacity to sustain human habitation or an economic life of its own'[121] was stated as a general rule. Applying the natural state doctrine more broadly is problematic.

First, although the naturally formed requirement for land is clear, there is no textual support for importing a natural requirement for non-land creation activities that affect the criteria in Article 121(3). Although there is a historic example of this approach, this was one example of practice within the British Empire, explicitly rejected in later international documents, and neither suggested nor included in the final text of the LOSC.

Second, insistence on the natural state doctrine for the criteria of capacity to support human habitation and the economic life of its own doctrine results in the law ignoring reality. This is the case if the law insists an island rendered uninhabitable by climate change is still intrinsically capable of supporting a population. It is equally the case if the law insists that an island populated for 200 years but always with some form of artificial support or intervention is not capable of supporting a population.

Worrying too, especially in the case of climate change, is the possibility of deeply inconsistent applications. If an island is affected by a tropical storm, the frequency and magnitude of which is affected by climate change, it could be argued the storm itself is artificially induced: and thus its impact discounted. Yet if another island is affected by another type of natural disaster, non-climate change related, its capacity is assessed against its current, post-disaster 'natural state': and in the case of extreme and permanent devastation, could possibly be downgraded from a fully entitled island to a rock. This is particularly relevant to South East Asia, where numerous islands are vulnerable to both climate change enhanced natural disasters[122] and non-climate change-related natural disasters.[123]

---

120 *South China Sea* arbitration, [546].
121 Ibid., [541].
122 See for example National Intelligence Council, *Southeast Asia and Pacific Islands: The Impact of Climate Change to 2030*, August 2009, available online at www.dni.gov/files/documents/climate2030_southeast_asia_pacific_islands.pdf
123 Such as the 26 December 2004 earthquakes off North Sumatra and the following tsunami.

## 134  Imogen Saunders

One way of resolving this tension is to follow the approach of Charney, who argues that the criteria in Article 121(3) must be assessed *at the time of the dispute*,[124] which is an approach consistent with that taken by the International Court of Justice in respect of other maritime features.[125] Yet this approach will only work if the effects of artificial intervention are taken into account: otherwise necessarily the feature will be being assessed on the basis of its historical conditions.

The arbitral tribunal emphasised that the purpose of Article 121(3) is to 'place limits on excessive and unfair claims' by States,[126] and to prevent 'encroachment on the international seabed reserved for the common heritage of mankind' and avoid the 'inequitable distribution of maritime spaces under national jurisdiction'.[127] But these are not the only views: Charney argues a teleological approach to Article 121(3) reveals twin policy goals both preserving common spaces but also rewarding 'optimal economic development through technological innovation and economic risk taking'.[128] More common, however, are those commentators agreeing with the tribunal.[129]

In the face of these policy objectives, a strict application of the natural state doctrine becomes even more puzzling. What merit is there in preserving maritime zones around a feature that, in fact, cannot sustain life let alone human habitation – even if it once could? Conversely, why should a population sustained by artificial intervention not reap the benefit of the maritime zones that are around the feature they live on? How does treating the maritime zones of two islands – both ravaged by natural disaster – differently depending on the *type* of disaster achieve equitable distribution of maritime spaces?

Some commentators have suggested that doctrines of acquiescence should apply for those features already subject to claim.[130] Others have raised notions of fixed maritime zones, which will not change even if the feature that generates them does.[131] While these doctrines may help some of the challenges identified

---

124  Charney, note 73, p. 867.

125  See, for example, the case of Fasht al Dibal in *Qatar v Bahrain*: although the feature had undergone both artificial and natural interventions, its status was assessed as it was at the time of the case: *Case Concerning Maritime Delimitation and Territorial Questions Between Qatar and Bahrain* (Qatar v. Bahrain) [2001] ICJ Rep 40, p. 93; see I. Saunders, 'Artificial Islands and Territory in International Law', (2019) 52 *Vanderbilt Journal of Transnational Law* forthcoming.

126  *South China Sea* arbitration, [550].

127  Ibid., [535].

128  Charney, note 73, p. 865.

129  See, for example, D. Guilfoyle, 'The South China Sea Award: How Should We Read the UN Convention on the Law of the Sea?', (2018) 8 *Asian Journal of International Law* p. 51; L. Diaz, 'When is a Rock an Island – Another Unilateral Declaration Defies Norms of International Law', (2007) 15 *Michigan State Journal of International Law* p. 519.

130  See, for example, Mossop, note 4.

131  See, for example, C. Schofield, 'Shifting Limits? Sea Level Rise and Options to Secure Maritime Jurisdictional Claims', (2009) 3 *Climate Change and the Law of the Sea* p. 405; J. Lisztwan, 'Stability of Maritime Boundary Agreements', (2012) 37 *Yale Journal of International Law* p. 154.

The limits of the natural state doctrine   135

above, they cannot assist with the development of previously unproductive features into those capable of supporting human habitation or an economic life of their own; nor in the case of fixed maritime zones do they reconcile law with reality. As such, the criteria in Article 121(3) still need to be understood. This chapter cannot provide a comprehensive model for how Article 121(3) should be applied in the challenges that will be faced in the Anthropocene. However, it is clear that a strict application of the natural state doctrine to matters other than 'naturally formed land' will yield inequitable and sometimes nonsensical results. In the face of inevitable environmental challenges, and the knowledge of human ingenuity that leads to technological advances, a more nuanced approach is needed.

# 8 The Law of the Sea, status and message ambiguity

*Rob McLaughlin*

## 8.1 Introduction

Messaging is often a delicate balance between perception, poise and purpose. China's 'Belt and Road Initiative' (BRI), for example, has significant maritime implications and ramifications, but ambiguities as to its purpose, mixed messages as to asset poise, and the perception of ulterior motives continue to hamper its take-up rate. Is the BRI about establishing a 'silk road, iron fist' string of dual-use facilities and pliant local governments? Or is it an investment outlet for the substantial savings held by the Chinese population? Or is it a cunning mechanism for indenturing states through the imposition and renegotiation of unmanageable debt burdens?[1] In the same way, albeit at a more granular level, clarity in on-water 'message' transmission at sea – perception, poise and purpose – hinges around the nexus between the status of the act, the status of the actor, the location and the consequence. For example, a warship transiting within 12 nm of Hughes Reef (a low-tide elevation (LTE)) in accordance with

---

1 R. Walker, 'Is China's Ambitious Belt and Road Initiative a Risk Worth Taking for Foreign Investors?', *South China Morning Post*, 11 March 2018, available online at https://www.scmp.com/business/companies/article/2136372/chinas-ambitious-belt-and-road-initiative-risk-worth-taking; P. Ferdinand, 'Westward ho – the China Dream and "One Belt, One Road": Chinese Foreign Policy Under Xi Jinping' (2016) 92 *International Affairs* p. 941; 'Gateway to the Globe', *The Economist*, 28 July 2018, pp. 13–16; 'Monsoon Squalls', *The Economist*, 10 March 2018, p. 34; 'A Chinese Lake: China has Broken its Promise, Militarized the South China Sea and Got Away with it', *The Economist*, 23 June 2018, p. 28; J. Bowen, 'Strategic Implications of China's Belt and Road Initiative Too Big to Ignore', *The Strategist*, Australian Strategic Policy Institute, 31 August 2018, available online at https://www.aspistrategist.org.au/strategic-implications-of-chinas-belt-and-road-initiative-too-big-to-ignore/; L. Johnston, 'China's 21st Century Maritime Silk Road', presentation at *Maritime Order in the Indian Ocean: Application of UNCLOS and other legal norms in the context of emerging challenges and opportunities* (Conference), Deakin University, 30 April – 1 May 2018; L. Johnston, 'The Belt and Road Initiative: What is in it for China?' (2018) 6 (1) *Asia and the Pacific Policy Studies* pp. 1, 6–8; L. Jakobson and R. Medcalf, *The Perception Gap: Reading China's Maritime Strategic Objectives in Indo-Pacific Asia*, Lowy Institute, June 2015, available online at www.lowyinstitute.org/publications/perception-gap-reading-chinas-maritime-objectives-indo-pacific-asia

*Message ambiguity* 137

the *South China Sea* arbitration[2] whilst deploying an organic helicopter[3] (or a submarine transiting whilst dived)[4] sends a very clear message about the view of the transiting vessel's sovereign as to the status of that feature. In this case, that message is that the transiting State considers the feature to be an LTE (and thus incapable of supporting a territorial sea claim),[5] and that transit is therefore in accordance with the high seas freedom of navigation.[6] By contrast, transiting in innocent passage within 12 nm of Fiery Cross Reef,[7] without prior notification to China,[8] sends a series of interlinked messages: on the one hand, that the feature is a rock which can generate a territorial sea[9] and, on the other hand, that any asserted limitations (such as a requirement for prior notice as to warship innocent passage) are not relevant. This may be because the transiting vessel's sovereign subscribes to a general rule of international law to this effect[10] or

2 *In the Matter of an Arbitration before An Arbitral Tribunal Constituted Under Annex VII to the 1982 United Nations Convention on the Law of the Sea between The Republic of the Philippines and the People's Republic of China*, PCA Case no 2013-19, Award of 12 July 2016 [hereafter *South China Sea* arbitration] [358] ('In light of all of the evidence, the Tribunal concludes that Hughes Reef is a low-tide elevation').

3 Such operations are not permitted during innocent passage: United Nations Convention on the Law of the Sea, 10 December 1982, 1833 UNTS 397, Article 19(2)(e) [hereafter LOSC].

4 Similarly, dived transit by submarines is not permitted in innocent passage (LOSC, Article 20) but is otherwise permissible in transit passage through straits used for international navigation and in archipelagic sea lanes passage, when operating in 'normal mode' (LOSC, Articles 39(1)(c) and 53(3)) and as a high seas freedom (LOSC, Article 87(1)(a)).

5 LOSC Article 13(2) – 'Where a low-tide elevation is wholly situated at a distance exceeding the breadth of the territorial sea from the mainland or an island, it has no territorial sea of its own…'.

6 It must be noted that a second possible message in a case where the status of the feature is uncertain as between an LTE or a rock, is that it is a rock capable of supporting a Territorial Sea claim, but in the absence of the transiting vessel State's acceptance of any particular nation's territorial claim to the rock, no Territorial Sea is thus in place and the area around the 'territory of no state' rock is thus not an 'activated' Territorial Sea.

7 *South China Sea* arbitration, [343]: 'The Tribunal concludes that Fiery Cross Reef, in its natural condition was encumbered by a rock that remained exposed at high tide and is, accordingly, a high-tide feature', and thus can generate a Territorial Sea (LOSC, Article 121(3)).

8 People's Republic of China, *Declaration made upon ratification of the Law of the Sea Convention 1982* (7 June 1996), para. 4: 'The People's Republic of China reaffirms that the provisions of the United Nations Convention on the Law of the Sea concerning innocent passage through the territorial sea shall not prejudice the right of a coastal State to request, in accordance with its laws and regulations, a foreign State to obtain advance approval from or give prior notification to the coastal State for the passage of its warships through the territorial sea of the coastal State…'; *Law on the Territorial Sea and the Contiguous Zone 1992* (China), Article 6: '…To enter the territorial sea of the People's Republic of China, foreign military ships must obtain permission from the Government of the People's Republic of China…', available online at http://www.un.org/Depts/los/LEGISLATIONANDTREATIES/PDFFILES/CHN_1992_Law.pdf

9 LOSC, Article 121(3).

10 US Navy, US Coast Guard and US Marine Corps, *The Commander's Handbook on the Law of Naval Operations*, August 2017 (NWP 1-14M) (*The Commander's Handbook on the Law of Naval Operations*), [2.5.2.4]: 'All warships, regardless of cargo, armament, or means of propulsion, enjoy the right of innocent passage through the territorial sea in accordance with international law, for which neither prior notification nor authorization is required'.

# 138 *Rob McLaughlin*

because the warship's sovereign, whilst recognising that a coastal State can make such laws, does not accept that the rock is in fact Chinese territory. Proceeding in accordance with innocent passage in this situation would signal merely a genuflection to the fact that there is a claimable, but not claimed or allocated, territorial sea around the rock. In this way, the 'location' of the message is fundamental to its content.

Actor and act status, however, are equally fundamental to message clarity. Given that these components of any message are more fluid, controllable and susceptible to nuanced and responsive calibration than geographic location, intentional obfuscation and consciously introduced ambiguity have a disproportionate influence on the degree of uncertainty attributable to both the status of the act and the status of the actor. In particular, if the status of the actor (sovereign vessel or private vessel?), or the act (private assault, act of policing or state use of force?) can be cast into doubt, the question can arise – was it a sovereign message at all or was it simply rogue private activity at sea?

This chapter will briefly outline and assess the ambiguities that attend the use by China of maritime militias to send messages at sea. The chapter commences with a brief examination of the possible legal nature(s) of the Chinese maritime militia. This is followed by an assessment of the possible status of maritime militia vessels under LOSC,[11] and then an examination of the potential for attribution of maritime militia conduct (and thus messaging) in accordance with the *Articles on State Responsibility*.[12] The chapter concludes with a recommendation in relation to facilitating more robust legal and diplomatic responses to the status and conduct characterisation ambiguities that attend use of a maritime militia for 'messaging' at sea.

## 8.2 The Chinese 'maritime militia'

Although there have been reports that Vietnam is 'quietly fostering a State-supported fishing boat militia to hold off China at sea' through the employment of fishing vessels and fishers as a State-sanctioned and controlled (for these purposes) militia,[13] any 'lawfare'[14]-based assessment of the practical character

---

11 As noted previously, message ambiguity and clarity at sea is often the result of a nuanced collaboration between vessel status, and the legal nature of any maritime feature or zone that provides an additional legal overlay upon the conduct – such as its location in a territorial sea or the contested (rock? low tide elevation?) status of the adjacent maritime feature. The zonal aspects of this equation are dealt with in other chapters in this volume.

12 The *Articles on State Responsibility* were initially developed by the International Law Commission prior to consideration and then acceptance by the UN General Assembly.

13 R. Jennings, 'Vietnam's Fishing "Militia" to Defend Maritime Claims Against China', *Voice of America*, 6 April 2018, available online at www.voanews.com/a/vietnam-fosters-fishing-militia-to-defend-maritime-claims-against-china/4335312.html

14 'Legal warfare' is one of the 'three warfares' of recent Chinese military doctrine: psychological warfare, public opinion warfare and legal warfare: see, for example, S. Lee, 'China's "Three Warfares": Origins, Applications, and Organizations', (2014) 37 *Journal of Strategic Studies* p. 198.

of the maritime militia, and its place (to the extent that this can be distilled) within domestic legal and organisational arrangements will inevitably focus upon China – the employer par excellence of this legally nuanced tactic. The term 'maritime militia' has recently gained significant currency. A 2017 Congressional Research Service paper, for example, assessed that the COLREGS[15] were applicable 'to military vessels, paramilitary and law enforcement (i.e. coast guard) vessels, maritime militia vessels, and fishing boats, among other vessels'.[16]

However, the main focus of analysis is inevitably China, and there appear to be two aspects to this Chinese 'maritime militia': The Peoples Armed Forces Maritime Militia (PAFMM); and the more ad hoc employment of fishing vessels and fishers on an opportunistic basis.

The first component of the Chinese maritime militia, the formally established PAFMM, is generally equipped with large steel-hulled vessels and well-trained personnel. The 2018 US Department of Defense *Annual Report to Congress* on China's military developments asserted that China employs 'the only government-sanctioned maritime militia in the world'. The PAFMM, the Report stated, 'is a subset of China's national militia, an armed reserve force of civilians available for mobilization', and 'has organizational ties to, and is sometimes directed by, China's armed forces, and is active in the South and East China Seas'.[17] The PAFMM is clearly being equipped for its dual role as an auxiliary to the armed forces and as a part time fishing fleet:

> The Hainan provincial government, adjacent to the South China Sea, ordered the building of 84 large militia fishing vessels with reinforced hulls and ammunition storage, which the militia received by the end of 2016, along with extensive subsidies to encourage frequent operations in the Spratly Islands. This particular PAFMM unit is also China's most professional, paid salaries independent of any clear commercial fishing responsibilities, and recruited from recently separated veterans.[18]

To this end, it seems clear that the PAFMM – the 'big-ship', formally recognised, and routinely employed maritime militia, whose members may in fact operate under militia discipline, and which appears to have a formal operations support role – is in effect an auxiliary Chinese Coast Guard (CCG) force.

The second component of the maritime militia appears to be fishing vessels and fishers employed on a more ad hoc basis as adjuncts to the CCG and

---

15 Being the regulations endorsed, and modified over time, in the *Convention on the International Regulations for Preventing Collisions at Sea*, 20 October 1972, 1050 UNTS 16 [hereafter *COLREGS*].

16 R. O'Rourke, *Maritime Territorial and Exclusive Economic Zone (EEZ) Disputes Involving China: Issues for Congress*, Washington: Congressional Research Service, 12 December 2017, p. 14.

17 Office of the Secretary of Defense (USA), *Annual Report to Congress: Military and Security Developments Involving the People's Republic of China 2018*, 16 May 2018, pp. 71–72.

18 Ibid., p. 72.

140   *Rob McLaughlin*

People's Liberation Army – Navy (PLA-N) – primarily in harassment and projection operations. As the US Department of Defense *Annual Report to Congress* observes, 'The government subsidizes various local and provincial commercial organizations to operate militia vessels to perform "official" missions on an ad hoc basis outside of their regular civilian commercial activities'.[19] Both prior to, and since, larger PAFMM vessels have been deployed,[20] local private fishing vessels have been regularly employed in maritime militia roles. The *Defence of Japan 2017* report observed, for example, that

> among the militia that is China's armed force other than the military forces, the so-called maritime militia is playing the role of the advance guard for supporting China's maritime interests. The maritime militia is said to operate in the South China Sea, etc. It is believed that the militia is made up of fishermen and residents of isolated islands, though the details of its actual situation have not been revealed.[21]

The report continued

> when Chinese naval and other vessels obstructed the U.S. Navy surveillance ship Impeccable on the high seas on the South China Sea in March 2009, maritime militia were said to be aboard the fishing boat that tried to take away a sonar from Impeccable. It is also pointed out that when the deepwater drilling rig Haiyang Shiyou 981 conducted prospective drilling to the south of the Paracel Islands from May to July 2014, steel-hull fishing boats maned by maritime militia also arrived as an escort fleet.[22]

The precise status of this component of the maritime militia may be more problematic than for the PAFMM because it is a true hybrid or 'dual-use' force – fishing on Monday, ad hoc opportunistic (but centrally coordinated) harassment operations on Tuesday, and back to fishing on Wednesday. That is, vessels of this 'limb' of the maritime militia tend to slide more fluidly, but also more clearly, between a private and State status.

However, and despite the growing literature on the PAFMM and on maritime militia operations and incidents more generally,[23] the precise legal status

---

19  Ibid.
20  US Navy, *China People's Liberation Army Navy (PLAN), Coast Guard, and Government Maritime Forces: 2018 Recognition and Identification Guide*, 2018, available online at www.oni.navy.mil/Portals/12/Intel%20agencies/PLANavy.jpg?ver=2018-07-16-090249-333;  see also A. Erickson, 'Exposed: Pentagon Report Spotlights China's Maritime Militia', *National Interest*, 20 August 2018, at https://nationalinterest.org/feature/exposed-pentagon-report-spotlights-china%E2%80%99s-maritime-militia-29282
21  Ministry of Defence, *Defence of Japan 2017*, 2017, p. 94, available online at www.mod.go.jp/e/publ/w_paper/2017.html
22  Ibid.
23  See, inter alia: J. Chock, 'China's Non-Military Maritime Assets as a Force Multiplier for Security', (2015) 322 *East-West Centre Asia Pacific Bulletin*, available online at www.eastwestcenter.

## Message ambiguity    141

implications of this status fluidity are still not as yet clear. Erickson's assessment is that the maritime militia has been incorporated into the chain of command, with links to the PLA-N, the CCG, Border Security Forces and the People's Armed Forces Department.[24] Tobin has drawn similar conclusions.[25] And although the major 2013 reorganisation of China's maritime law enforcement agencies (the 'Five Dragons')[26] appears to have been more focussed upon the integration of formal maritime policing agencies,[27] Yatsuzuka of the Japanese National Institute for Defence Studies has noted that China's complex system of militia laws and regulations can clearly encompass the maritime militia.[28] Similarly, although Kraska and Monti have argued that 'The hybrid civilian-naval forces [of the maritime militia] are integrated as *unofficial* constabulary and military auxiliaries into the PLAN',[29] it seems clear from the publicly

---

org/system/tdf/private/apb322.pdf?file=1&type=node&id=35314; A. Erickson and C. Kennedy, 'China's Fishing Militia Is a Military Force in All But Name', *War is Boring*, 9 July 2016, available online at https://warisboring.com/chinas-fishing-militia-is-a-military-force-in-all-but-name/; P. Pedrozo, 'Close Encounters at Sea: The USNS Impeccable Incident', (2009) 62 *Naval War College Review* p. 101; A. Erickson and C. Kennedy, 'China's Maritime Militia', *Foreign Affairs*, 23 June 2016, available online at www.foreignaffairs.com/articles/china/2016-06-23/chinas-maritime-militia; A. Cordesman and J. Kendall, 'China Military Organization and Reform', *Centre for Strategic And International Studies*, working draft 1 August 2016, available online at www.csis.org/analysis/chinese-military-organization-and-reform

24 A. Erickson, 'China's Third Sea Force, The People's Armed Forces Maritime Militia: Tethered to the PLA', *China and the World Program*, 27 March 2017, available online at https://cwp.sipa.columbia.edu/news/china%E2%80%99s-third-sea-force-people%E2%80%99s-armed-forces-maritime-militia-tethered-pla-cwp-fellow-alumni; A. Erickson, 'Understanding China's Third Sea Force: The Maritime Militia', *The Fairbank Center for Chinese Studies*, 8 September 2017, available online at https://medium.com/fairbank-center/understanding-chinas-third-sea-force-the-maritime-militia-228a2bfbbedd; A. Erickson, *Testimony before the House Armed Services Committee Seapower and Projection Forces Subcommittee Hearing on Seapower and Projection Forces in the South China Sea*, Washington, DC, 21 September 2016, p. 1, available online at https://docs.house.gov/meetings/AS/AS28/20160921/105309/HHRG-114-AS28-Wstate-EricksonPhDA-20160921.pdf

25 L. Tobin, 'Wind in the Sails: China Accelerates Its Maritime Strategy', *War on the Rocks*, 9 May 2018, available online at https://warontherocks.com/2018/05/wind-in-the-sails-china-accelerates-its-maritime-strategy/; L. Tobin, 'Underway – Beijing's Strategy to Build China into a Maritime Great Power', (2018) 71 *Naval War College Review* p. 1, 15–16.

26 Y. Mingjie, 'Sailing on a Harmonious Sea: A Chinese Perspective' (2010) 5 *Global Asia* p. 22.

27 L. Morris, 'Taming the Five Dragons? China Consolidates its Maritime Law Enforcement Agencies', (2013) 13 *China Brief*, available online at https://jamestown.org/program/taming-the-five-dragons-china-consolidates-its-maritime-law-enforcement-agencies/; Y. Chang and N. Wang, 'The Restructuring of the State Oceanic Administration in China: Moving Toward a More Integrated Governance Approach', (2015) 30 *International Journal of Marine and Coastal Law* p. 795; M.C. Huang, 'China's 2013 Reform of Maritime Law Enforcement: Progress and Unsolved Issues', (2016) 28 *Korean Journal of Defence Analysis* p. 545.

28 M. Yatsuzuka, 'China's Advance into the Sea and the Maritime Militia', (2016) Commentary No. 53 *Japanese National Institute for Defense Studies*, available online at www.nids.mod.go.jp/english/publication/commentary/pdf/commentary053e.pdf

29 J. Kraska and M. Monti, 'The Law of Naval Warfare and China's Maritime Militia', (2015) 91 *International Law Studies* pp. 450, 452 (emphasis added); see also J. Kraska, 'China's Maritime

142    *Rob McLaughlin*

available sources and analysis that there is a general consensus to the effect that the PAFMM (at the least) is certainly an integrated formal component of China's maritime forces, and that the more ad hoc elements of the maritime militia are likewise considered to be – either on a personnel basis or on a vessel basis – part of the PAFMM when they are operating under organised command in pursuit of governmental purposes.

## 8.3  Maritime militia status under LOSC

To the extent that the formal legal character of the maritime militia is thus knowable in an international law sense, the critical question for outsiders is what status these vessels should be accorded within the clear vessel characterisation and status scheme encapsulated by the LOSC. Under this scheme, sovereign immune vessels are warships,[30] government ships operated for non-commercial service[31] and authorized ships 'clearly marked and identifiable as being on government service'.[32] Non-sovereign immune vessels, by contrast, include government ships operated for commercial purposes,[33] merchant ships[34] and fishing vessels.[35] These discrete categories can overlap – a government ship operated for non-commercial purposes can also be an authorized ship (such as a Coast Guard cutter),[36] whilst a government vessel operated for commercial purposes is also a merchant vessel.

The first operationally relevant differentiation point for the purposes of vessel status, act and response characterisation is therefore whether the vessel attracts sovereign immune status. This is where maritime militia status ambiguity is most evident and exploitable because sovereign immune vessels are considered to be representatives and messengers of their sovereign: a point made clearly in the 1812 US Supreme Court case of *The Schooner Exchange v. McFaddon and Others*.[37] A more recent assessment of the principle of sovereign immunity from

---

Militia Upends Rules on Naval Warfare', *The Diplomat*, 10 August 2015, available online at http://thediplomat.com/2015/08/chinas-maritime-militia-upends-rules-on-naval-warfare/

30  LOSC, Articles 29, 32.

31  Ibid., Articles 31, 32.

32  Ibid., Articles 110(5), 111(5), 224.

33  Ibid., Part II Section 3 Sub-section B – such vessels are equated to merchant ships.

34  Ibid.

35  Ibid., Articles 42(1)(c), 62(4).

36  Noting, however, that some Coast Guards are both a military and law enforcement force, and their cutters are therefore characterisable as warships – for example, the US Navy, US Coast Guard and US Marine Corps, *The Commander's Handbook on the Law of Naval Operations*, note 10, [2.2.1].

37  *The Schooner Exchange v. McFaddon* (1812) 11 US 116 per Marshall CJ at 144: 'But in all respects different is the situation of a public armed ship. She constitutes a part of the military force of her nation; acts under the immediate and direct command of the sovereign; is employed by him in national objects. He has many and powerful motives for preventing those objects from being defeated by the interference of a foreign state. Such interference cannot take place without affecting his power and his dignity. The implied license therefore under which such vessel enters

*Message ambiguity*  143

a domestic legal perspective is found in advice by the Office of the General Counsel for the US National Oceanic and Atmospheric Administration:

> The doctrine of sovereign immunity (also known as 'jurisdictional immunity') is an 'amalgam of two quite different concepts, one applicable to suits in the sovereign's own courts and the other suits in the courts of another sovereign' ... In simplest terms, the doctrine provides an exemption from the exercise of court jurisdiction and enforcement against a sovereign entity. This immunity also extends to the property belonging to the sovereign. A government ship is a special type of property that is afforded immunity under treaty, customary international law, and domestic statute.[38]

A recent judicial expression and application of this doctrine in international law is found in the International Tribunal for the Law of the Sea (ITLOS) order in the 2012 *ARA Libertad* case:

> Considering that a warship is an expression of the sovereignty of the State whose flag it flies ... Considering that, in accordance with general international law, a warship enjoys immunity, including in internal waters...[39]

Thus, if a maritime militia vessel is considered to be sovereign immune, in the absence of any discernible indications that it is acting 'rogue',[40] then its conduct and actions can be assumed to be at the command of its sovereign.[41] This is important for understanding the message, assessing its legal nature and then calibrating any response. A forcible act by a maritime militia vessel of sovereign immune status, whether it is harassing a transiting warship,[42] blocking resupply

---

a friendly port, may reasonably be construed, and it seems to the Court, ought to be construed, as containing an exemption from the jurisdiction of the sovereign, within whose territory she claims the rites of hospitality'.

38 US National Oceanic and Atmospheric Administration, *Sovereign Immunity of Government Ships*, (n.d.), available online at www.gc.noaa.gov/gcil_sovereign.html; the quotation is from the US case *Nevada v. Hall* (1970) 440 US 410, 414.

39 *The 'ARA Libertad' Case* (Argentina v. Ghana) (Provisional Measures) (ITLOS, Case no 20, 15 December 2012) (2014) 156 ILR 186 [94-95].

40 As, for example, is the case when a mutinied warship becomes a private actor capable of committing an act of piracy: LOSC, Article 102.

41 This is why sovereign immune vessels are such useful messengers; see, for example, R. McLaughlin, 'Dangerous Waters and International Law: The Corfu Channel Case, Warships, and Sovereignty Irritants' in T. Christakis, K. Bannelier, and S. Heathcote (eds), *The Enduring Impact of a Seminal Case: Corfu Channel, the ICJ, and Modern International Law*, Milton Park, UK: Routledge, 2011, pp. 164–180.

42 See, for example, M. Green et al, 'Countering Coercion in Maritime Asia: The Theory and Practice of Gray Zone Deterrence – Case Study of Harassment of the USNS Impeccable', *Asia Maritime Transparency Initiative*, 9 May 2017, available online at https://amti.csis.org/counter-co-harassment-usns-impeccable/. Although carried out by PLA-N and CCG vessels, other examples in 2018 include: 'British navy's HMS Albion warned over South China Sea

## 144 Rob McLaughlin

of forces on a rock or LTE,[43] interfering with sovereign immune vessel operations by cutting towed array sonar cables or interdicting on the high seas a deployed hydrographic data collection system,[44] or riding off the fishing vessels of other states,[45] will need to be assessed in terms of whether it is a legitimate act of maritime law enforcement and/or a use of force.[46] If, however, the maritime militia vessel is, at the time of the conduct, operating as a 'private' merchant (including fishing) vessel, then it is not prima facie assumed to be executing the military or jurisdictional will of its sovereign, but rather to be operating in a private commercial capacity. In this case, the vessel's conduct is – at first instance – assessable as private conduct; that is, it may be piracy,[47] or an offence under the Convention for the Suppression of Unlawful Acts Against the Safety of Maritime Navigation (SUA Convention),[48] but it is not at first blush a sovereign act, and thus should not be assessed against criteria and rights – such as maritime law enforcement and use of force – that are permitted only to sovereign agents.

---

"provocation"', *BBC*, 6 September 2018, available online at www.bbc.com/news/uk-45433153; I. Ali and B. Blanchard, 'Exclusive: U.S. Warship Sails Near Disputed South China Sea Island, Officials Say', *Reuters*, 23 March 2018, at available online www.reuters.com/article/us-usa-china-southchinasea/exclusive-u-s-warship-sails-near-disputed-south-china-sea-island-officials-say-idUSKBN1GZ0VY; A. Greene, 'Australian Warships Challenged by Chinese Military in South China Sea', *ABC*, 20 April 2018, available online at www.abc.net.au/news/2018-04-20/south-china-sea-australian-warships-challenged-by-chinese/9677908; A. Greene, 'Near-Collision of US Warship and "Aggressive" Chinese Destroyer in South China Sea Captured in Photos', *ABC*, 4 October 2018, available online at www.abc.net.au/news/2018-10-03/south-china-sea-encounter-between-us-warship-and-chinese-vessel/10333096

43 As with Chinese maritime militia/fishing vessels in relation to attempts to resupply Philippines forces stationed at Second Thomas Shoal: *South China Sea* arbitration, [1161].

44 J. Borger, 'Chinese Warship Seizes US Underwater Drone in International Waters: Official Says Drone Deployed by American Oceanographic Vessel in South China Sea was Taken by Chinese Navy on Thursday', *The Guardian*, 17 December 2016, available online at www.theguardian.com/world/2016/dec/16/china-seizes-us-underwater-drone-south-china-sea

45 A. Panda, 'China Steps Up Harassment of Vietnamese Fishermen: Recent Incidents Highlight the Return of Low-Level Coercion Against Vietnamese Fishermen in Disputed Waters', *The Diplomat*, 13 July 2015, available online at https://thediplomat.com/2015/07/china-steps-up-harassment-of-vietnamese-fishermen/

46 See, for example: *In the Matter of an Arbitration before An Arbitral Tribunal Constituted under Annex VII to the 1982 United Nations Convention on the Law of the Sea between Guyana and Suriname*, PCA Case no 2004-04, Award of 17 September 2007, [445]: 'The Tribunal accepts the argument that in international law force may be used in law enforcement activities provided that such force is unavoidable, reasonable and necessary. However in the circumstances of the present case, this Tribunal is of the view that the action mounted by Suriname on 3 June 2000 seemed more akin to a threat of military action rather than a mere law enforcement activity ... Suriname's action therefore constituted a threat of the use of force in contravention of the Convention, the UN Charter and general international law...'; see also, P.J. Kwast, 'Maritime Law Enforcement and the Use of Force: Reflections on the Categorisation of Forcible Action at Sea in the Light of the Guyana/Suriname Award' (2008) 13 *Journal of Conflict and Security Law* p. 49.

47 LOSC, Article101.

48 *Convention for the Suppression of Unlawful Acts Against the Safety of Maritime Navigation*, 10 March 1988, 1678 UNTS 221, Article 3(1)(3): '...destroys a ship or causes damage to a ship or to its cargo which is likely to endanger the safe navigation of that ship...'.

## 8.4 The maritime militia and state responsibility

There is a second operationally relevant legal option that may come into play in seeking to assess what ostensibly appears to be 'fishing vessel' conduct. The potential for attribution of the conduct of the vessel in accordance with the 2002 *Articles on the Responsibility of States for Internationally Wrongful Acts* (*ASR*) can transform what otherwise appear to be the acts of private vessels into conduct that is legally characterisable as an expression of the will of that vessel's sovereign. The first possibility is to assess the conduct of a possible maritime militia vessel by reference to *ASR* Article 5:

> Article 5. Conduct of persons or entities exercising elements of governmental authority
>
> The conduct of a person or entity which is not an organ of the State under article 4 but which is empowered by the law of that State to exercise elements of the governmental authority shall be considered an act of the State under international law, provided the person or entity is acting in that capacity in the particular instance.[49]

As the *ASR Commentary* observes, this article is designed to 'take account of [inter alia] the increasingly common phenomenon of para-statal entities, which exercise elements of governmental authority in place of State organs'.[50] As Crawford notes, the key assessment in an *ASR* Article 5 analysis (and, as discussed below, a significant differentiating condition between *ASR* Article 5 attribution and *ASR* Article 8 attribution), is that 'the internal law of the State has conferred on the entity in question the exercise of certain elements of the governmental authority'.[51] In the case of ad hoc maritime militia, it would thus be domestic legal indicia such as legislative descriptions of fishers and fishing vessels as auxiliaries to the armed forces or CCG, or the subjection of crew members to any form of militia discipline that would be key. The example provided in the *ASR Commentary* is a useful comparative point:

> Thus, for example, the conduct of a railway company to which certain police powers have been granted will be regarded as an act of the State under international law if it concerns the exercise of those powers, but not if it concerns other activities (e.g. the sale of tickets or the purchase of rolling-stock).[52]

The correlation with possible maritime militia conduct is readily apparent. If the conduct involves supporting the CCG in a power projection or harassment

---

49 United Nations General Assembly, 'Responsibility of States for Internationally Wrongful Acts', 28 January 2002, UN Doc. A/RES/56/83, [hereafter *ASR*].
50 J. Crawford, *The International Law Commission's Articles on State Responsibility: Introduction, Text and Commentaries*, Cambridge: Cambridge University Press, 2002, p. 100 para. 1.
51 Ibid., p. 101 para. 5.
52 Ibid.

## 146 *Rob McLaughlin*

operation, and this role or duty is mandated under Chinese domestic law, then the conduct of that vessel will be 'maritime militia' conduct and attributable to the State. If the conduct is fishing, even if it is carried out under the apparent protection of CCG cutters, then it is private commercial conduct, and is not attributable to the State by virtue of *ASR* Article 5. However, the delinquent conduct of the government vessels in tolerating the unlawful conduct of the fishing vessels is of course still directly attributable to the State.[53]

The other possible State responsibility pathway is for attribution of maritime militia conduct via *ASR* Article 8:

> Article 8 Conduct directed or controlled by a State
> The conduct of a person or group of persons shall be considered an act of a State under international law if the person or group of persons is in fact acting on the instructions of, or under the direction or control of, that State in carrying out the conduct.[54]

In this situation, however, the analytical starting point is different to that for *ASR* Article 5 attribution in that Article 5 concerns 'entities which are empowered by internal law to exercise governmental authority'.[55] *ASR* Article 8 attribution, by contrast, concerns 'a specific factual relationship between the person or entity engaging in the conduct and the State' such that there is sufficient evidence of 'private persons acting on the instructions of the State in carrying out the wrongful conduct ... [or] the more general situation where private persons act under the State's direction or control'.[56] A key consideration is the 'degree of control', an assessment that hinges around (as the *ASR Commentary* notes) jurisprudence, including the *Nicaragua* case.[57] Thus, as the *ASR Commentary* concludes, 'It is clear ... that a State may, either by specific directions or by exercising control over a group, in effect assume responsibility for their conduct'.[58] Furthermore, each potential case of *ASR* Article 8 attribution must be assessed on its facts,[59] and in this regard the indicia of 'instructions', 'direction' or 'control', as opposed to domestic legislative arrangements, are the critical discriminators. For Article 8 attribution of maritime militia conduct,

---

53 See, for example, *South China Sea* arbitration, [721], [735–757]; for example [757]: '...the Tribunal finds that China has, through the operation of its marine surveillance vessels in tolerating and failing to exercise due diligence to prevent fishing by Chinese flagged vessels at Mischief Reef and Second Thomas Shoal in May 2013, failed to exhibit due regard for the Philippines' sovereign rights with respect to fisheries in its exclusive economic zone. Accordingly, China has breached its obligations under Article 58(3) of the Convention'.

54 *ASR*, Article 8.

55 Crawford, note 50, p. 101 para. 7

56 Ibid., p. 110 para. 1.

57 *Case Concerning the Military and Paramilitary Activities in and Against Nicaragua* (Nicaragua v. United States of America) [1986] ICJ Rep 14, [109], [115].

58 Crawford, note 50, p. 113 para. 7.

59 Ibid.

consequently, the analytical focus will not be upon domestic legal arrangements but rather upon the indicia of an on-water 'maritime militia overlay' on the vessel and its conduct: indicia such as the presence and apparent coordinating role of warships or cutters, the fulfilment of government stated roles or the fact that a group of fishing vessels are acting in pre-planned concert to achieve a particular non-fisheries-related objective.[60]

## 8.5 Conclusion: status ambiguity and 'message' transmission

Navies and Coast Guards are expensive, so a responsive maritime militia presents an attractive and cost-effective option for force projection, force support and message transmission. Indeed, as many analyses of the Chinese maritime militia point out, their inclusion in the Chinese maritime 'order of battle' (with the PLA-N and the CCG) makes the combined Chinese 'blue water' force the largest in the world.[61] Additionally, maritime militia acts, because their ambiguous LOSC and use of force status can be legally spun as 'private', can nevertheless send clearly sovereign political messages about status, location, intentions and resolve. Ambiguity in relation to maritime militia status, and the legal characterisation of their conduct, will thus continue to create opportunities for governments to do things that should not be done (in the interests of conflict avoidance) with 'formal' State vessels. This ambiguity will also for the foreseeable future usefully serve the interests of 'less' confronting and attributable force projection, and even formal deniability if the State declares the conduct to be that of 'private' actors. This will make actor-act-status-consequence assessments, and the legally appropriate and paradigmatically coherent (State attributable use of force or piracy?) structuring and shaping of responses, more challenging, particularly as the fundamental first assessment question generally asked is whether the act is that of a private vessel or a sovereign. This opacity will continue to create uncertainty and delay, manifesting as a preference for tentative responses in the face of political risk. This is especially the case given that the employment of maritime militias based upon fishing vessels leaves open a legally viable counter-narrative that paints any response to their harassment or forcible measures as aggressive and unwarranted interference with 'a poor and industrious order of men'.[62]

How, then, might on-water and diplomatic responses to maritime militia operations be better structured? The first priority is for interested States to

---

60 C. Kennedy and A. Erickson, 'Riding A New Wave of Professionalization and Militarization: Sansha City's Maritime Militia', *Centre for International Maritime Security*, 1 September 2016, available online at http://cimsec.org/riding-new-wave-professionalization-militarization-sansha-citys-maritime-militia/27689; A. Erickson and C. Kennedy, 'China's Maritime Militia', *Centre for Naval Analyses*, (n.d.), pp. 6, 10–12, 17–18, available online at www.cna.org/cna_files/pdf/chinas-maritime-militia.pdf

61 For example, Erickson, 'Understanding China's Third Sea Force: The Maritime Militia', note 24.

62 *The Paquete Habana* (1900) 175 US 677, per Gray J at 708.

## 148 *Rob McLaughlin*

devote some effort to analysing the domestic regulatory arrangements that surround the Chinese maritime militia; indeed, the ongoing uncertainty as to the status of maritime militia vessels, personnel and acts remains the central enabler in this nuanced Chinese use of lawfare and the primary legal reason for ambiguity and timidity in response. A clearer understanding of mandate, role and arrangements will facilitate more definitive conclusions as to the legal status and character of the various components of the maritime militia. This will then allow affected States to define and refine the response options available based upon sound assessments as to the applicable legal regime (sovereign act of maritime law enforcement or use of force? private act of piracy or a SUA offence?) and the relevant indicia and pathways (sovereign vessel status under the LOSC? ASR Article 5? ASR Article 8?) for attributing maritime militia conduct to any State. Whilst greater certainty in this regard will not necessarily alter tactical on-water responses to maritime militia conduct, it will allow States, in those situations where attribution is established, to more robustly characterise the conduct and message as both sovereign and unfriendly, thus opening the door to otherwise legally unavailable counter-measure options.

# 9 The United Nations Convention on the Law of the Sea in South East Asia

## Smooth sailing or stormy seas?

*Tim Stephens*

## 9.1 Introduction

South East Asia is one of the world's most dynamic regions. Bookended to the east and west by the world's most populous nations – China and India – the region comprises a rich diversity of peoples, cultures and environments. South East Asia's rapid economic and strategic transformation is increasingly viewed as a portent of the 'Asian Century' or 'Indo-Pacific Century'.[1] As the twentieth century was the 'American Century', and the nineteenth century was the 'British Century', so the twenty-first century is witnessing the emergence of Asia as a predominant power. Moreover, the growing influence of Asian States is increasingly being projected through South East Asia's complex and expansive maritime domain.

In 1995, Crawford highlighted several reasons why the Asia Pacific region, which he defined as

> the area of the Pacific, north and south of the equator, bordered to the west by the countries of east Asia, south east Asia and Australia ... and [including] the whole of east Asia, the Association of Southeast Asian Nations (ASEAN) countries, the independent Pacific islands and Australasia,[2]

holds such significance for the law of the sea. Crawford observed that the region includes fast growing economies, major maritime trading nations, sensitive and important marine environments most archipelagic zones, the largest areas of geomorphological continental shelf beyond 200 nautical miles, and many unresolved sovereignty and maritime boundary issues. Crawford was writing before the 1982 United Nations Convention on the Law of the Sea[3] (LOSC) had

---

1 Australian Government, *Australia in the Asian Century*, Canberra: Commonwealth of Australia, 2012.

2 J. Crawford, 'Introduction' in J. Crawford and D.R. Rothwell (eds), *The Law of the Sea in the Asian Pacific Region*, Dordrecht: Martinus Nijhoff, 1995, pp. 1–2.

3 United Nations Convention on the Law of the Sea, 10 December 1982, 1833 UNTS 397 [hereafter LOSC].

## 150 *Tim Stephens*

entered into force, but he did foresee that the Convention would bring greater certainty to the law of the sea in the region. Almost 25 years later, it is now possible to assess whether the LOSC has lived up to its promise both for the Asia Pacific generally and for South East Asia specifically.

Much recent commentary on the law of the sea issues in the region has been consumed by the *South China Sea*[4] arbitration. However, that controversy, as significant as it is, represents only one part of a broader picture in which there has been increasing and mostly positive engagement by governments in South East Asia with LOSC rules and institutions. Nonetheless, it is clearly not altogether smooth sailing for the LOSC in South East Asia, and several challenges, from relatively confined and technical points to much larger questions including persistent maritime disputes, present 'stormy seas' that will require careful navigation to maintain the relevance and legitimacy of the LOSC.

## 9.2 Smooth sailing – support for the LOSC in South East Asia

### 9.2.1 *The South East Asian region*

Geographers refer to South East Asia as comprising two parts: the northern part of the region as 'Mainland South East Asia' and the southern part as 'Maritime South East Asia'.[5] The region includes some of the world's most complex and contested maritime areas which have a long history and have given rise to significant State practice in the law of the sea. Between the Indian and Pacific Oceans, these areas include (from west to east) the Andaman Sea, South China Sea, Java Sea, Sulu Sea, Savu Sea, Flores Sea, Celebes Sea, Sibuyan Sea, Visayan Sea, Timor Sea, Banda Sea, Arafura Sea, Ceram Sea, Molucca Sea, Bohol Sea, Camotes Sea, Samar Sea, East China Sea, Philippine Sea, Coral Sea, Solomon Sea and Bismarck Sea. The region also features a range of important straits, including the Straits of Malacca and Singapore (Indonesia/Malaysia/Singapore) and Sunda and Lombok Straits (Indonesia).[6] ASEAN States have a combined coastline length of over 100,000 km and a total Exclusive Economic Zone of

---

4 *In the Matter of an Arbitration before An Arbitral Tribunal Constituted under Annex VII to the 1982 United Nations Convention on the Law of the Sea between The Republic of the Philippines and the People's Republic of China*, PCA Case no. 2013-19, Award on Jurisdiction and Admissibility of 29 October 2015; *In the Matter of an Arbitration before an Arbitral Tribunal Constituted Under Annex VII to the 1982 United Nations Convention on the Law of the Sea between The Republic of the Philippines and the People's Republic of China*, PCA Case no. 2013-19, Award of 12 July 2016 [hereafter *South China Sea* arbitration].

5 See generally R. Hill, *Southeast Asia: People, Land and Economy*, Sydney: Allen & Unwin, 1995.

6 These straits have differing legal statuses under the law of the sea. The Straits of Malacca and Singapore are straits used for international navigation under Part III of the LOSC, whereas Sunda and Lombok Straits are routes within Indonesia's archipelagic waters normally used for international navigation and have been designated as archipelagic sea lanes and air routes under Part IV of the LOSC.

## Smooth sailing or stormy seas? 151

about 11 million sq km.[7] The coastal and marine environments of ASEAN are mega-diverse, supporting 75% of global coral species and 51 of 70 mangrove species, but are under increasing pressure from a range of threats.[8]

South East Asian States have made a major contribution to the development of the law of the sea over many centuries, presenting a challenge to the view that the law of the sea is a purely European construct. Pointing to the 'precedent of Asian practice of free navigation and trade' to which Grotius referred in *Mare Liberum*, Anand argued that 'whatever may be said about some other rules of international law, freedom of the seas, which has been the pith and substance of the modern law of the sea, is one principle which Europe acquired from Asia through Grotius'.[9] In subsequent centuries, States in Asia and elsewhere saw the freedom of the seas become an 'unequal freedom or freedom for the few', even a form of 'tyranny', used by maritime powers, predominantly from the West, to facilitate a colonial expansion and enable overfishing.[10] However, following the 'disintegration of colonialism', Asian, African and Latin American States took 'concerted action for the protection of their interests' through successive United Nations conferences on the law of the sea.[11] This action culminated in the conclusion of the LOSC which reflected aspects of the 'New International Economic Order' called for by developing countries, including those in South East Asia. As a result, in the LOSC era, South East Asian States have become fully enmeshed within the contemporary global order of the seas.

This chapter's analysis will focus on Brunei Darussalam, Cambodia, Timor-Leste, Indonesia, Laos, Malaysia, Myanmar, Philippines, Singapore, Thailand and Vietnam. With the exception of Timor-Leste, all of these States are members of ASEAN, which was established in 1967 to promote development, trade, peace and stability in the region. Timor-Leste made a formal application to join the Association in 2011, and views the attainment of ASEAN membership as 'the cornerstone' of its foreign policy.[12] Although they play a prominent role in South East Asian affairs, China, Japan and South Korea are not ASEAN members; however, they have been included in the 'ASEAN Plus Three' process which is described by ASEAN as 'the main vehicle towards the long-term goal of building an East Asian community'.[13] While there is conflicting comment regarding China's status as a South East Asian State, and India is geographically

---

7 ASEAN, *Fifth ASEAN State of the Environment Report*, Jakarta: ASEAN Secretariat, 2017, p. 150.

8 Ibid.

9 R.P. Anand, 'Maritime Practice in South-East Asia until 1600 AD and the Modern Law of the Sea' (1981) 30 *International and Comparative Law Quarterly* pp. 440, 448.

10 Ibid., p. 452.

11 Ibid., p. 453.

12 B. Strating, 'Timor-Leste's Critical Window on ASEAN', *The Interpreter*, 17 August 2017, available online at www.lowyinstitute.org/the-interpreter/timor-leste-critical-window-asean

13 See ASEAN, 'Overview of ASEAN Plus Three Cooperation', June 2017, available online at asean.org/storage/2017/06/Overview-of-APT-Cooperation-Jun-2017.pdf

## 152 Tim Stephens

not a South East Asian State, the rising influence of China and India inevitably casts a lengthening shadow over law of the sea practice in the region.[14]

### 9.2.2 South East Asian State membership of the LOSC

With the exception of landlocked Laos, all ASEAN members have maritime interests of varying extents. Singapore, for instance, has the second shortest coastline among ASEAN States; however, it is very heavily invested in the legal order of the oceans because of its insular status and location at a global maritime crossroads between the Indian Ocean and the South China Sea.[15] As is well known, Singapore helped facilitate the successful negotiation and conclusion of the LOSC thanks to the efforts of Ambassador Tommy Koh.[16]

All members of ASEAN except Cambodia are parties to the LOSC and to the 1994 Implementing Agreement[17] which adjusted the Convention's provisions relating to deep seabed mining (see Table 9.1, below).[18] However, only Indonesia and the Philippines, the major archipelagic States in the region, are parties to the second LOSC implementing agreement: the 1995 Fish Stocks Agreement[19] (see Table 9.1, below). It is a similar picture in relation to other multilateral fisheries treaties, despite the importance of fishing and the fishing industry to South East Asian States. The Philippines is the only ASEAN member that is party to the 1993 Agreement to Promote Compliance with International Conservation and Management Measures by Fishing Vessels on the High Seas,[20] and only Indonesia, Philippines and Thailand are parties to the 2009 Agreement on Port State Measures to Prevent, Deter, and Eliminate Illegal Unreported and Unregulated Fishing.[21]

Expanding the range of vision from South East Asia to the wider Asia Pacific, there is a generally positive record of adherence to the LOSC and the 1994

---

14 On East Asia, see H. Nasu and D.R. Rothwell, 'Re-evaluating the Role of International Law in Territorial and Maritime Disputes in East Asia', (2014) 4 *Asian Journal of International Law* p. 55; K. Zou, *Law of the Sea in East Asia*, London: Routledge, 2005.

15 Z. Sun, 'Implementation of the United Nations Law of the Sea Convention in Singapore' in S. Lee and W. Gullett (eds), *Asia-Pacific and the Implementation of the Law of the Sea: Regional Legislative and Policy Approaches to the Law of the Sea Convention*, Leiden: Brill Nijhoff, 2016, p. 104.

16 T.T.B. Koh, 'Negotiating a New World Order for the Sea', (1984) 24 *Virginia Journal of International Law* p. 761.

17 *Agreement Relating to the Implementation of Part XI of the United Nations Convention on the Law of the Sea of 10 December 1982*, 28 July 1994, 1836 UNTS 42.

18 Cambodia signed the LOSC on 1 July 1983 but has not yet ratified the convention.

19 *Agreement for the Implementation of the Provisions of the United Nations Convention on the Law of the Sea of 10 December 1982 Relating to the Conservation and Management of Straddling Fish Stocks and Highly Migratory Fish Stocks*, 4 August 1995, 2167 UNTS 88 [hereafter 1995 Fish Stocks Agreement].

20 *Agreement to Promote Compliance with International Conservation and Management Measures by Fishing Vessels on the High Seas*, 24 November 1993, 2221 UNTS 91.

21 *Agreement on Port State Measures to Prevent, Deter and Eliminate Illegal, Unreported and Unregulated Fishing*, 22 November 2009, [2016] ATS 21.

*Table 9.1* Ratifications by ASEAN Members and Timor-Leste of the LOSC and Its Implementing Agreements

| | LOSC | 1994 Implementing Agreement | 1995 Fish Stocks Agreement |
|---|---|---|---|
| Brunei | Yes, 5 November 1996 | Yes, 5 November 1996 | No |
| Cambodia | No | No | No |
| Indonesia | Yes, 3 February 1986 | Yes, 2 June 2000 | Yes, 28 September 2009 |
| Laos | Yes, 5 June 1998 | Yes, 5 June 1998 | No |
| Malaysia | Yes, 14 October 1996 | Yes, 14 October 1996 | No |
| Myanmar | Yes, 21 May 1996 | Yes, 21 May 1996 | No |
| Philippines | Yes, 8 May 1984 | Yes, 23 July 1997 | Yes, 24 September 2014 |
| Singapore | Yes, 17 November 1994 | Yes, 17 November 1994 | No |
| Thailand | Yes, 15 May 2011 | Yes, 15 May 2011 | No |
| Timor-Leste | Yes, 8 January 2013 | Yes, 8 January 2013 | No |
| Vietnam | Yes, 25 July 1994 | Yes, 27 April 2006 | No |

Implementing Agreement. Most of the 21 members of the Asia-Pacific Economic Cooperation (APEC) forum are members of the LOSC and the 1994 Implementing Agreement, and there is also strong support for the 1995 Fish Stocks Agreement which reflects the interests of many APEC countries that possess large Exclusive Economic Zones (EEZs) and productive fisheries. In addition, all of the State members of the Pacific Community (the SPC),[22] except the United States, are parties to the LOSC (Table 9.2).

In formal terms, therefore, the picture of support by States in the Asia Pacific and South East Asian sub-region for the fundamental norms of the law of the sea is encouraging. While not all of these States were actively engaged in the negotiations of the Convention (or, in the case of Timor-Leste, even existed at the time), there has been a strong level of backing for the LOSC. However, as discussed below, this formal adherence masks some areas of disagreement and divergence from the substantive norms of the LOSC.

In addition to the LOSC and other overarching multilateral treaties applicable to the oceans, South East Asian States are also parties to an array of bilateral maritime boundary treaties, many of which have been concluded since the LOSC was finalised and ratified by the relevant parties. The LOSC has clearly had a significant and positive influence on many of these maritime boundary agreements, as seen for example in Vietnam's delimitation agreements with Thailand, China and Indonesia which 'demonstrate its practical application of [the LOSC] to help enrich international practice in maritime delimitation'.[23]

22 The Pacific Community is the main scientific and technical organisation in the Pacific region. Founded originally as the South Pacific Commission in 1947, it was renamed the Pacific Community in 1997 to encompass the organisation's broader Pacific membership. The abbreviation 'SPC' has been kept because of its broad recognition in the region.
23 N.T. Giang, 'Implementation of the United Nations Law of the Sea Convention in Vietnam' in Lee and Gullett, note 15, pp. 130, 141.

## 154 *Tim Stephens*

*Table 9.2* Ratifications by APEC Members of the LOSC and Its Implementing Agreements

| | LOSC | 1994 Implementing Agreement | 1995 Fish Stocks Agreement |
|---|---|---|---|
| Australia | Yes, 5 October 1994 | Yes, 5 October 1994 | Yes, 23 December 1999 |
| Brunei | Yes, 5 November 1996 | Yes, 5 November 1996 | No |
| Canada | Yes, 7 November 2003 | Yes, 7 November 2003 | Yes, 3 August 1999 |
| Chile | Yes, 25 August 1997 | Yes, 25 August 1997 | Yes, 11 February 2016 |
| China | Yes, 7 June 1996 | Yes, 7 June 1996 | No |
| Hong Kong | – | – | – |
| Indonesia | Yes, 3 February 1986 | Yes, 2 June 2000 | Yes, 28 September 2009 |
| Japan | Yes 20 June 1996 | Yes, 20 June 1996 | Yes, 7 August 2006 |
| South Korea | Yes, 29 January 1996 | Yes, 29 January 1996 | Yes, 1 February 2008 |
| Malaysia | Yes, 14 October 1996 | Yes, 14 October 1996 | No |
| Mexico | Yes, 18 March 1983 | Yes, 10 April 2003 | No |
| New Zealand | Yes, 19 July 1996 | Yes, 19 July 1996 | Yes, 18 April 2001 |
| Papua New Guinea | Yes, 14 January 1997 | Yes, 14 January 1997 | Yes, 4 June 1999 |
| Peru | No | No | No |
| Philippines | Yes, 8 May 1984 | Yes, 23 July 1997 | Yes, 24 September 2014 |
| Russia | Yes, 12 March 1997 | Yes, 12 March 1997 | Yes, 4 August 1997 |
| Singapore | Yes, 17 November 1994 | Yes, 17 November 1994 | No |
| Taiwan | – | – | – |
| Thailand | Yes, 15 May 2011 | Yes, 15 May 2011 | No |
| USA | No | No | Yes, 21 August 1996 |
| Vietnam | Yes, 25 July 1994 | Yes, 27 April 2006 | No |

### 9.2.3 South East Asian participation in law of the sea dispute settlement

Another means by which to assess the level of support for the LOSC in the region is to examine the use by South East Asian States of the LOSC dispute settlement system. Under Part XV of the LOSC, parties are given a choice of means for resolving disputes under the Convention, with arbitration the default option, and both the International Tribunal for the Law of the Sea (ITLOS) and the International Court of Justice (ICJ) also available to them to use.[24]

ITLOS has had a total of 27 cases in its docket, and three South East Asian governments have been represented among the litigants. Malaysia and Singapore litigated a dispute over marine environmental issues in the Strait of Johor[25] while Myanmar was a party to a maritime boundary delimitation dispute with

---

24 LOSC, Article 287.
25 *Land Reclamation by Singapore in and around the Straits of Johor* (Malaysia v Singapore) (Provisional Measures) (2003) 126 ILR 487.

Bangladesh.[26] The ICJ has also been tasked with disputes with maritime dimensions involving South East Asian States. Singapore and Malaysia are parties to a (still unresolved) dispute over sovereignty over Pedra Branca/Pulau Batu Puteh, Middle Rocks and South Ledge,[27] and Indonesia and Malaysia have litigated a sovereignty dispute over Pulau Ligitan and Pulau Sipadan.[28] If the scope is broadened to include the Asia Pacific, the list grows to include, among others, the whaling dispute between Australia and Japan.[29]

In Annex VII Arbitration, which is the default procedure for resolving LOSC disputes where the parties have not agreed on another forum, there have been two cases involving South East Asian States: the *South China Sea* arbitration between the Philippines and China, and the discontinued *Straits of Johor* arbitration[30] between Malaysia and Singapore. In addition, States in the region have been the very first to make use of the conciliation procedure under Article 298 and Annex V of the LOSC with Timor-Leste and Australia successfully resolving a long-standing maritime boundary dispute through this process.[31]

South East Asian States are self-evidently not heavy users of the LOSC dispute resolution system. But neither can it be said that these States universally prefer diplomatic over judicial methods of dispute settlement for the resolution of their law of the sea disputes. There has been cooperative and consensual use of the LOSC and other dispute settlement frameworks and, more exceptionally, unilateral institution of proceedings. The openness of South East Asian, and Asia Pacific States more generally, to use the LOSC dispute settlement and (for the most part) to abide by decisions produced through it signals a degree of acceptance that the LOSC supplies a legal order in which the peaceful settlement of law of the sea disputes is as important as the LOSC's substantive rules themselves.

### 9.2.4 South East Asian participation in the commission on the limits of the continental shelf

In contrast to the LOSC's dispute settlement mechanisms, South East Asian States have been somewhat less actively engaged with another regime established by the LOSC: the Commission on the Limits of the Continental Shelf (CLCS).

---

26 *Delimitation of the Maritime Boundary between Bangladesh and Myanmar in the Bay of Bengal* (Bangladesh/Myanmar) (2012) 51 ILM 844.

27 *Sovereignty over Pedra Branca/Pulau Batu Puteh, Middle Rocks and South Ledge* (Malaysia v. Singapore) [2008] ICJ Rep 12.

28 *Sovereignty over Pulau Ligitan and Pulau Sipadan* (Indonesia/Malaysia) [2002] ICJ Rep 625.

29 *Whaling in the Antarctic* (Australia v Japan; New Zealand Intervening) [2014] ICJ Rep 226.

30 *Land Reclamation by Singapore in and around the Straits of Johor* (Malaysia v Singapore) (Provisional Measures) (2003) 126 ILR 487.

31 *In the Matter of the Maritime Boundary between Timor-Leste and Australia before a Conciliation Commission constituted under Annex V of the 1982 United Nations Convention on the Law of the Sea between the Democratic Republic of Timor-Leste and the Commonwealth of Australia*, PCA Case no. 2016-10, Report and Recommendations of the Compulsory Conciliation Commission between Timor-Leste and Australia on the Timor Sea of 9 May 2018.

## 156 *Tim Stephens*

*Table 9.3* Submissions to the Commission on the Limits of the Continental Shelf by ASEAN Members and Timor-Leste

| | *Date of Submission to CLCS* | *CLCS Recommendations Adopted* |
|---|---|---|
| Brunei | 12 May 2009 (preliminary information) | – |
| Cambodia | Not LOSC party | – |
| Indonesia | 16 June 2008 (North West of Sumatra Island) | 28 March 2011 |
| Laos | N/A | – |
| Malaysia | 6 May 2009 (joint submission with Vietnam in southern part of South China Sea) | – |
| Myanmar | 16 December 2008 | – |
| Philippines | 8 April 2009 (in Benham Rise region) | 12 April 2012 |
| Singapore | N/A | N/A |
| Thailand | – | – |
| Timor-Leste | – | – |
| Vietnam | 6 May 2009 (joint submission with Malaysia in southern part of the South China Sea), 7 May 2009 (in North Area, VNM-N) | – |

The CLCS considers information submitted by LOSC parties on the outer limits of their continental shelf and makes recommendations as to those limits based upon the formulae set out in Article 76 (Table 9.3).

Of the ten ASEAN members plus Timor-Leste, only four have made submissions of data to the CLCS, and all but one of these submissions have been for partial areas of outer continental shelf. Moreover, Brunei has only submitted 'Preliminary Information', an option made available to developing States not in a position to submit continental data within the timeframe set by the LOSC.[32]

There are several reasons for this less than complete record of continental data submission to the CLCS, including complex maritime geography which means that there are multiple overlapping areas of shelf requiring coordination between two or more States in the submission process, ongoing sovereignty and maritime boundary disputes, and technical and other capacity constraints among ASEAN members. One of the major benefits of the CLCS process is that it has shone a light on law of the sea practice in South East Asia as CLCS submissions often include details of basepoints and baselines even when these have not yet been formally proclaimed by the submitting State, as in the case of Malaysia.

## 9.3 Stormy seas – South East Asian challenges for the LOSC

Simply tallying the number of LOSC ratifications, CLCS submissions and the degree of participation in LOSC-related cases provide an important but

32 LOSC, Annex II, Article 44.

*Smooth sailing or stormy seas?* 157

*Table 9.4* LOSC Declarations by ASEAN Members and Timor-Leste

| | LOSC Declaration | Areas of Inconsistency with the LOSC |
|---|---|---|
| Brunei | No | – |
| Cambodia | N/A | – |
| Indonesia | No | – |
| Laos | N/A | – |
| Malaysia | Yes | Consent required for military exercises/manoeuvres in EEZ; Advance authorization for passage of nuclear-powered vessels or vessels carrying nuclear material or other similar material through territorial sea pending conclusion of international agreements regulating their passage; under Article 74 and Article 83 delimitation of exclusive economic, continental shelf or other maritime zones is to be the median line unless agreement otherwise; any objects of archaeological and historical nature within 'maritime zones over which it exerts sovereignty or jurisdiction' shall not be removed without prior notification and consent |
| Myanmar | No | – |
| Philippines | Yes | The concept of archipelagic waters is similar to the concept of internal waters under the Constitution of the Philippines, and removes straits connecting these waters with the economic zone or high sea from the rights of foreign vessels to transit passage for international navigation |
| Singapore | No | – |
| Thailand | Yes | Enjoyment of freedom of navigation in the EEZ excludes any 'non-peaceful use' without the consent of the coastal State, in particular military exercises |
| Timor-Leste | Yes | – |
| Vietnam | Yes | – |

incomplete picture of the extent to which South East Asian States have supported the LOSC regime. Formal adherence by most South East Asian States to the LOSC and support for its institutions masks some practice that diverges from the LOSC, including several declarations that are at odds with the convention (see Table 9.4) and a number of excessive maritime claims.

To gain a complete picture of the fidelity of ASEAN States to the LOSC, governments in the region could do more to deposit official charts and coordinates and provide due publicity, as required by the LOSC.[33] Only Indonesia, Myanmar, Philippines and Vietnam have deposited charts.[34] In the absence of full transparency from governments, there have been efforts by commentators

33 LOSC, Article 16.
34 Details available online at www.un.org/Depts/los/LEGISLATIONANDTREATIES/depositpublicity.htm

## 158    Tim Stephens

and non-governmental organisations to understand and analyse the extent of maritime claims in the region and their consistency with the LOSC. Prominent among these is the work of the Asia Maritime Transparency Initiative (AMTI) which maintains a web page with interactive maps showing maritime claims in South East Asia.[35]

As Roach and Smith observe, '[t]he stability of [the LOSC] regime is undermined by claims to exercise jurisdiction, or to interfere with navigational rights and freedoms, that are inconsistent with the terms of [the LOSC]'.[36] They catalogue a number of excessive maritime claims by South East Asian coastal States including improperly drawn baselines, impermissible assertions of jurisdiction over innocent passage, claims to contiguous zone jurisdiction beyond the limits of the LOSC, limitations on navigation and other uses of the EEZ by other States, and excessive archipelagic claims. Taking each ASEAN State and Timor-Leste in turn, a number of examples of practice consistent with and contrary to the LOSC may be identified.

### 9.3.1 Brunei

Brunei has a short coastline (of just 161 km) and is enclaved within the Malaysian state of Sarawak. Brunei is a party to the LOSC and its limited law of the sea practice appears to be in conformity with the convention.

### 9.3.2 Cambodia

Cambodia, by contrast, has much more significant maritime interests and shares borders with Thailand and Vietnam in the Gulf of Thailand. Cambodia is not a party to the LOSC (although it has signed the Convention), and its applicable maritime law (a decree issued in 1982) has several aspects inconsistent with the LOSC, including the drawing of extravagant straight baselines which use insular features too far offshore.[37]

### 9.3.3 Indonesia

Indonesia is one of the world's great archipelagic States and has had a major influence on the development of the unique archipelagic regime in the LOSC. Initially, Indonesia was somewhat circumspect towards the LOSC because its historic claim to full sovereignty over the areas within its archipelago exceeded the more limited concept of archipelagic waters under the Convention. Despite this, Indonesia subsequently proclaimed archipelagic baselines and has adopted

35  Details available online at amti.csis.org/
36  J. Ashley Roach and Robert W. Smith, *Excessive Maritime Claims*, 3rd ed., Leiden: Martinus Nijhoff, 2012, p. 4.
37  C. Schofield and M. Tan-Mullins, 'Maritime Claims, Conflicts and Cooperation in the Gulf of Thailand' (2008) 22 *Ocean Yearbook* pp. 75, 85.

*Smooth sailing or stormy seas?* 159

laws and policies applicable to its maritime zones which are largely consistent with the LOSC. One ongoing point of disagreement is with respect to archipelagic sea lanes, a core element of the LOSC archipelagic regime. The International Maritime Organization has accepted Indonesia's 'partial designation' of three north-south archipelagic sea lanes.[38] However, Indonesia's Regulation No. 37 of 2002 purports to restrict archipelagic sea lanes passage through other routes even though this is permitted under the LOSC in respect of routes normally used for international navigation.

### 9.3.4 Malaysia

Malaysia's Baselines of Maritime Zones Act 2006 provides for the declaration of baselines. However, no basepoints or baselines have yet been declared, so it is difficult to assess the conformity of Malaysia's baseline practice with the LOSC. Schofield has noted that a map included in Malaysia and Vietnam's joint submission to the CLCS depicts lengthy straight baselines along the coastlines of Sabah and Sarawak that may be open to legal challenge.[39] Malaysia's Exclusive Economic Zone Act 1984 also has several features inconsistent with the LOSC, namely a general limitation on the construction of *any* artificial island, installation and structure in the EEZ, and not just those used for economic purposes, without Malaysian government authorization. Malaysia also does not permit foreign military exercises in its EEZ.[40] As with other similar claims to regulate or prohibit foreign military activities, this position has attracted protest from the United States and other governments.[41]

### 9.3.5 Myanmar

Myanmar, which has an extensive coastline fronting the Bay of Bengal and Andaman Sea, maintains several straight baselines on the Arakan Coast, Gulf of Martaban and the Tenesserim Coast that are inconsistent with Article 7 of the LOSC.[42] Additionally, the Territorial and Maritime Zones Act 1977 has several provisions at odds with the LOSC jurisdictional regime and navigational rights and freedoms. The Act purports to require foreign warships to obtain permission to pass through the territorial sea and asserts that Myanmar may exercise a general security jurisdiction in the contiguous zone.[43]

---

38  Resolution MSC 72(69) (19 May 1998).
39  C. Schofield, 'Trouble over the Starting Line: The Practice Concerning Baselines in the South China Sea' in S. Wu, M. Valencia and N. Hong (eds), *UN Convention on the Law of the Sea and the South China Sea*, London: Routledge, pp. 123, 136.
40  Roach and Smith, note 36, p. 22.
41  See generally, R. Pedrozo, 'Military Activities in the Exclusive Economic Zone: East Asia Focus', (2014) 90 *International Law Studies* p. 514.
42  Roach and Smith, note 36, pp. 116–118.
43  Ibid., pp. 154–155.

160 *Tim Stephens*

### 9.3.6 *The Philippines*

The Philippines, as noted above, submitted an understanding on signature of the LOSC which purported to assimilate the notion of archipelagic waters under the LOSC and the notion of internal waters under the Philippines Constitution.[44] Subsequently, however, the Philippines adopted legislation which protects the rights of innocent passage and archipelagic sea lanes passage conformably with the LOSC.[45] That legislation also adopts a system of archipelagic baselines that appear to meet the requirements of the LOSC. A comprehensive Maritime Zones Act and the adoption of archipelagic sea lanes remain a work in progress for the Philippines Congress with several bills under consideration in the House of Representatives and Senate.

### 9.3.7 *Singapore*

Singapore has asserted an entitlement to a territorial sea and EEZ, but has not stipulated the precise limits of its claims and has not yet adopted legislation on maritime zones.[46] Singapore uses a normal baseline system that is in conformity with the LOSC. Sun observes that Singapore's strong support for the LOSC and 'actions with respect to the implementation of the LOSC – whether viewed domestically, regionally or internationally – demonstrate that Singapore as a small State believes in the power of law in the governance of the world's oceans'.[47]

### 9.3.8 *Thailand*

Thailand, with its lengthy coast on the Malay Peninsula facing the Gulf of Thailand, has established straight baselines along four parts of its coast that are inconsistent with the LOSC. Several of these baselines are drawn to islands that are some distance from the coast and are not fringing islands, and it cannot reasonably be argued that the area enclosed is so closely linked to the mainland to be considered internal waters.[48] Schofield and Tan-Mullins observe that 'it is something of a mystery why Thailand chose to adopt such a seemingly excessive additional claim to straight baselines' but that '[i]t is possible that the claim was made to counter Cambodia's (and Vietnam's) similarly "maximalist" straight baseline systems'.[49]

### 9.3.9 *Timor-Leste*

Timor-Leste's baselines and maritime zones are defined in Law No. 7/2002 which appears to conform with the LOSC both in relation to its baseline and

---

44 Ibid., pp. 214–215.
45 Republic Act No. 9522 (2009) (amending Republic Act No. 3046 (1961)).
46 Sun, note 15, p. 109.
47 Ibid., p. 129.
48 Schofield and Tan-Mullins, note 37, p. 88.
49 Ibid.

jurisdictional provisions. Timor-Leste has been engaged in a long-standing dispute with Australia over continental shelf and EEZ boundaries in the Timor Sea. However, following compulsory conciliation under Part XV of the LOSC, in March 2018 Australia and Timor-Leste concluded a treaty establishing permanent maritime boundaries in the Timor Sea.[50] Timor-Leste's ongoing challenge is the resolution of its maritime boundaries with Indonesia.

### 9.3.10 Vietnam

Vietnam's straight baseline system, which has been asserted since 1977, is well known as it joins a number of isolated islands lying a significant distance from shore. The extensive straight baseline system encloses the coastline from the Gulf of Thailand, through to the South China Sea, and north to the island of Cồn Cỏ in the Gulf of Tonkin. These baselines are not in the immediate vicinity of the coast, are excessively long, and have attracted protest from the United States and Thailand.[51] Historically, Vietnam maintained other practice that was inconsistent with the LOSC, such as the requirement set out in a 1980 decree that foreign warships seek permission before entering Vietnam's contiguous zone or territorial sea, and the assertion of a security jurisdiction in the contiguous zone.[52] However, following Vietnam's ratification of the LOSC and promulgation of the Law of the Sea of Vietnam in 2012, the consent requirement has been dropped (although there remains a requirement, which is not enforced, of prior notification), and a security jurisdiction is no longer claimed in the contiguous zone.[53] This is another illustration of the way in which South East Asian States have generally sought to bring their law of the sea practice in line with the LOSC.

## 9.4 Conclusion

The LOSC regime remains, in many respects, a work in progress and its effective operation depends on the active and positive participation by its 168 parties across the globe. A relatively small but influential number of these parties are found in the South East Asian region. There is significant political and legal diversity among States in South East Asia and this complicates the task of identifying a distinctive and homogenous South East Asian approach to the law of the sea. Nonetheless, the growing economic and strategic importance of the area means that the practice of South East Asian States carries global implications for the ongoing development and implementation of the LOSC and a regionally focussed assessment is fully merited.

---

50 *Treaty between Australia and The Democratic Republic of Timor-Leste Establishing their Maritime Boundaries in the Timor Sea*, 6 March 2018, [2018] ATNIF 4.
51 Roach and Smith, note 36, p. 99.
52 Ibid., p. 156.
53 Ibid., p. 256.

## 162   *Tim Stephens*

In assessing the performance of the LOSC in South East Asia, it is important not to lay broader diplomatic and legal failures at the feet of the LOSC. For instance, the rules and institutions of the LOSC should not be subject to criticism for failing to resolve sovereignty disputes such as those that beset the South China Sea. While these disputes have significant maritime dimensions, and the LOSC and the *South China Sea* arbitration have contributed to their clarification (if not their resolution), at their heart these controversies hinge on contested territorial claims that can never be addressed exclusively under the LOSC.

As has been seen in this chapter, South East Asian States have, in general, been supportive of the LOSC and its institutions. Moreover, there is evidence that this support is growing rather than retreating over time and that there is no breakout of State practice starkly inconsistent with the LOSC. Some South East Asian States have been more active and engaged than others with the LOSC, while some governments that have been initially circumspect towards the Convention have, over time, provided greater support for the Convention and its institutions. Indonesia and the Philippines are good examples of this, having brought their practice and domestic law increasingly into line with the letter and spirit of the LOSC. While there are no guarantees that this trend will continue across the region, the indications are positive, not least because the LOSC is seen as a key element of the regional order, as reflected in the ASEAN Chairman's Statement at the 30th ASEAN summit in 2017, which expressly referenced LOSC in reaffirming a 'shared commitment to maintaining and promoting peace … in accordance with the universally recognized principles of international law'.[54]

---

54 See ASEAN, 'Chairman's Statement 30th ASEAN Summit' (30 April 2017), available online at asean.org/chairmans-statement-30th-asean-summit/

# 10 'Do As I Do, Not As I Say' – navigational freedom and the Law of the Sea Convention

*Dale Stephens and Timothy Quadrio*[φ]

## 10.1 Introduction

The 1982 United Nations Convention on the Law of the Sea (LOSC)[1] might be rightly characterised as a world charter for maritime governance.[2] The Third United Nations Conference on the Law of the Sea (UNCLOS III)[3] lasted from 1973 until 1982 and produced one of the most comprehensive multilateral treaties ever negotiated. The LOSC provides layered avenues of maritime regulation and covers an extremely broad scope of subject matter. Most ambitiously, it created a comprehensive and largely compulsory dispute settlement framework where multiple mechanisms for resolution of disputes are made available.[4] This regime promised much for resolving maritime disputes peacefully. It signalled to some a significant and propitious moment in the history of international relations where old antagonisms might be overcome in a constructive and holistic manner according to the rule of law.[5] Despite the innovation of compulsory dispute resolution, the LOSC did significantly provide an

---

φ Lieutenant Quadrio's contribution to this chapter is made in his personal capacity and does not represent the official policy of the Australian Defence Force or the Australian Government.

1 United Nations Convention on the Law of the Sea, 10 December 1982, 1833 UNTS 397 [hereafter LOSC].

2 Admiral James Watkins, testimony before the Foreign Relations Committee (2003) as found in J.T. Oliver, 'Implications of U.S. Acceptance of the 1982 Law of the Sea Convention and the 1994 Agreement: National Security and the U.N. Convention on the Law of the Sea: U.S. Coast Guard Perspectives', (2009) 15 *ILSA Journal of International and Comparative Law* pp. 573, 576 (describing the LOSC as establishing 'the foundation of public order of the oceans').

3 See generally United Nations 'Codification Division Publications – Diplomatic Conferences', available online at http://legal.un.org/diplomaticconferences/1973_los/

4 LOSC, Article 287(1) provides for multiple forums of resolution comprising the International Tribunal for the Law of the Sea, the International Court of Justice, an Arbitral Tribunal constituted under the LOSC and a special Arbitral Tribunal established under the LOSC.

5 For example, note the highly optimistic comment of Phillip Allott, 'Power Sharing in the Law of the Sea', (1983) 77 *American Journal of International Law* p. 1, where he states 'The United Nations Convention on the Law of the Sea is a fact. It exists. Whether or not it becomes a fully operational treaty ... it is and will be the cause of significant effects. Its very existence modifies political, economic, and legal relationships in countless ways whose direction and intensity we can predict only in a most speculative way'.

optional exception for military activities.[6] Not surprisingly perhaps, a number of States made declarations upon ratification of the LOSC under Article 298 that they would not accept compulsory dispute resolution for the settlement of disputes relating to military activities.[7] Accordingly, the settlement of disputes for these activities required resorting to more traditional and diffuse means of international legal procedure.

One key area where there has been ongoing dispute in the context of military activities in maritime zones is the issue of navigational rights and obligations relating to warships. This has found particular expression in the realm of the innocent passage regime through a coastal State's territorial sea and activities that may be conducted by warships within a coastal State's archipelagic waters and exclusive economic zone (EEZ). This chapter will examine these issues in view of the provisions of the LOSC and explore the background context under which the relevant LOSC provisions were agreed. Despite the apparent wording of the LOSC on these issues, some States in the Asia Pacific region have made strident statements regarding their understanding of the meaning of the relevant LOSC provisions and seek to restrict navigational freedom for warships. Such views are strongly opposed by other States. Such a scenario is not unusual within international law and the manner in which States have subsequently opposed or acquiesced and their actual conduct in this respect since 1982 carries its own legal significance. A case will be made that over the last few decades there has been a growing convergence of understanding regarding such warship rights and obligations in the territorial sea, archipelagic waters and EEZ of coastal States. Moreover, it will be contended that methodologies advanced by the International Law Commission (ILC) to discern relevant State practice do assist in drawing conclusions concerning both the interpretation of treaty provisions as well as parallel rights and obligations under customary international law. In this regard, a view will be advanced that it is what States do, rather than what they say, that has the most legal significance. Accordingly, it will be concluded that an interpretation of the LOSC that accords greater navigational freedom for warships has become the predominant view.

Such a conclusion will draw on experiences in the Asia Pacific region which necessarily have resonance in South East Asia, the focus of this volume. It is in South East Asia that rights concerning archipelagic status, territorial sea claims and EEZ rights have found particular expression. To this end, State practice in the Asian region, especially South East Asia, has the most potential to condition broader understandings of global navigational rights under the LOSC.

---

6 LOSC, Article 298(1)(b) ('disputes concerning military activities, including military activities by government vessels and aircraft engaged in non-commercial services...').

7 Available online at www.un.org/depts/los/convention_agreements/convention_declarations.htm

## 10.2 Innocent passage by warships and rights under the LOSC

Article 19 of the LOSC outlines those activities of a military nature that are not deemed to be innocent passage.[8] By implication therefore, it is clear that warships have the right of innocent passage within another State's territorial sea (as do submarines subject to the conditions outlined in Article 20).[9] To this extent at least, Article 19 simply reinforces the general view that the International Court of Justice provided in the *Corfu Channel* case[10] that there was nothing intrinsic about warships that meant they were not capable of undertaking innocent passage.[11] What is potentially problematic, however, is the assertion by some States that warships require prior authorization, or need to provide prior notification, before they may undertake innocent passage in another State's territorial sea.

The issue of prior authorization and prior notification is one that has been around for many decades. During the first United Nations Conference on the Law of the Sea (UNCLOS I), a number of States did hold the view that these were relevant obligations under international law. In fact, a draft Article was submitted during UNCLOS I, proposing that prior notification for warship passage in the territorial sea was required. That proposal was defeated[12] and the resulting *1958 Convention on the Territorial Sea and Contiguous Zone*[13] accordingly makes no mention of this requirement. During the UNCLOS III negotiations, a number of States again held disparate views about these apparent requirements, but again these views were not pressed in the drafting of Article 19. On the one hand, this settles the issue given the lack of language that conveys such prohibitions. Alternatively, it might be argued that such requirements are silently implicit in any attempted exercise of innocent passage activity under the LOSC, hence a condition precedent to the exercise of the right as outlined in Article 19.

A small minority of States made declarations upon ratification of the LOSC which reflected their view that the regime of innocent passage in the Territorial Sea is only available to warships following the granting of an authorization permission by the coastal State.[14] The LOSC does not generally allow for res-

---

8 LOSC, Article 19 provides that 'Passage is innocent so long as it is not prejudicial to the peace, good order or security of the coastal State...' and enumerates those activities that are not permitted as including 'any threat or use of force', 'any exercise or practice with weapons...' and/or 'the launching, landing or taking on board any aircraft [or any military device]'.

9 LOSC, Article 20 provides 'In the territorial sea, submarines and other underwater vehicles are required to navigate on the surface and to show their flag'.

10 *Corfu Channel* (Merits) (United Kingdom v. Albania) [1949] ICJ Rep 4.

11 Although the transit in that instance was through what would now be considered an international strait.

12 R. McLaughlin, *United Nations Naval Peace Operations in the Territorial Sea*, Boston: Martinus Nijhoff, 2009, p. 100.

13 *Convention on the Territorial Sea and Contiguous Zone*, 29 April 1958, 516 UNTS 206.

14 China, Bangladesh, Croatia, Egypt, Iran, Malta, Montenegro and Oman are examples of States that made declarations to this effect at the time of their ratification of LOSC; see D.R. Rothwell and T. Stephens, *The International Law of the Sea* 2nd ed, Oxford: Bloomsbury, 2016, p. 238.

# 166 *Dale Stephens and Timothy Quadrio*

ervations; hence, such declarations are relied upon by States to reflect their understanding of the operation of the Convention. As with reservations however, such declarations cannot operate to defeat the object and purpose of the LOSC.

Under the LOSC, it would seem unlikely that the application of a requirement for prior authorization could withstand even textual muster. Article 24(a) of the LOSC provides that the coastal State 'shall not: (a) impose requirements on foreign ships which have the practical effect of denying or impairing the right of innocent passage'. Clearly, any purported assertion of a right to exercise a discretion by a coastal State as to whether to permit (or not) warships to undertake innocent passage necessarily has such a 'practical effect'. Accordingly, it is difficult to conceive of any claim that might be successfully advanced by a State party to the LOSC given such a prohibition.

As to the requirement of prior notification, the issue may be more ambiguous. It would seem that on a textual reading of the Articles of the LOSC no right is being impaired *per se*; rather the coastal State merely seeks to have prior knowledge of such passage. However, it became clear through the negotiations of UNCLOS I and III that the right of innocent passage was established as an international navigational right, not a coastal State concession.[15] To this end, there would be no entitlement that could be implied as a matter of law that a coastal State was entitled to be informed of such passage. Despite this, it is useful to undertake both an interpretative assessment of Article 19 and to also track relevant State practice as to this possible obligation.

## 10.2.1 Interpretation of the LOSC – the role of state practice

The 1969 *Vienna Convention on the Law of Treaties*[16] (VCLT) provides the necessary starting point when approaching the interpretation of the LOSC, or indeed any treaty after 1980. Article 31 of the VCLT requires that a treaty shall be interpreted in good faith in accordance with the ordinary meaning to be given to the words of the treaty in their context and in light of its object and purpose. The *Golder* case[17] establishes a unity of approach regarding these separate elements. While these elements are easily stated, their application in the context of the LOSC presents a particular challenge.

The terms of Article 19 do nothing to either confirm or deny the rights of coastal States to obtain prior authorization/prior notice of warship innocent passage through their territorial sea. To that end, understanding 'ordinary meaning' or even 'context' on the face of the treaty becomes impossible as there appear to be no words in the relevant Article that advance a particular view either way.

---

15 McLaughlin, note 12, p. 101.
16 *Convention on the Law of Treaties*, 23 May 1969, 1155 UNTS 331.
17 *Golder v The United Kingdom* [1975] 1 EHRR 524.

'Do As I Do, Not As I Say' 167

Accordingly, recourse must be taken to locating relevant State practice to provide meaning to Article 19 with respect to this question of prior permission or notice. The location of relevant State practice in this regard is different from identifying State practice in the more familiar context of ascertaining customary international law in that there does not need to be any corresponding *opinio juris* identified. The goal is not to establish a customary international legal right or obligation, but rather, to understand how States parties to the treaty have applied various provisions in practice. Therefore, Article 31(3)(b) of the VCLT, which allows recourse to 'any subsequent practice in the application of the treaty which establishes the agreement of the parties regarding the interpretation of the treaty...' becomes critical in discerning contemporary meaning.

In identifying the reach of Article 31(3)(b) of the VCLT, the ILC, in its study of 'subsequent state practice'[18] acknowledged that there was the possibility of either a narrow view or a broad view that can be taken as to the impact of Article 31(3)(b). The narrow view restricts the operation of Article 31(3)(b) to first identifying whether an agreement at the time of negotiations was manifested. Hence, this narrow view pre-supposes the existence of an agreement that facilitated the drafting process and accordingly subsequent State practice is examined to either confirm or deny that agreement. In contrast, the broad view extends beyond the temporal limitations of the treaty development process and seeks to locate relevant subsequent State practice following the conclusion of the agreement to discern meaning for provisions that are invoked over time to gauge meaning. In respect of this broad view, the ILC concluded that '[f]or the purpose of treaty interpretation "subsequent practice" consists of conduct, including pronouncements, by one or more parties to the treaty after its conclusion regarding its interpretation or application'.[19] It is this broad interpretation of State practice that the ILC has come to identify as being relevant for discerning meaning.

Hence, in accepting the broad view, the ILC has noted that relevant State practice includes 'official statements concerning the treaty's meaning, protests against non-performance, or tacit consent to statements or acts by other parties'.[20] According to the ILC, the State practice need not necessarily be a repeated pattern of frequency, but can also include single events, although in viewing single events the ILC observed that the evidentiary and normative value of such single events are to be weighted accordingly.[21]

Significantly, the ILC observed that there need not be a universal convergence of State practice to permit a conclusion as to established meaning. The ILC

---

18 International Law Commission, 65th session, A/CN.4/660 (2013) 'First report on subsequent agreements and subsequent practice in relation to treaty interpretation', (Georg Nolte, Special Rapporteur) (hereafter First ILC Report).
19 Ibid., 45 (draft conclusion 3).
20 Ibid., [110, 43].
21 Ibid., [109, 42–43].

168  *Dale Stephens and Timothy Quadrio*

commented, however, that there is still a 'high threshold'.[22] It noted that a number of international courts and tribunals have been satisfied where there is a 'vast majority view',[23] 'emerging consensus'[24] or a 'discernable pattern'[25] that can be identified. The task is to find a common understanding that has accorded meaning to a term. In this regard, the ILC noted that the value of subsequent practice will largely depend on whether it is 'concordant, common and consistent'.[26] Importantly, the ILC also concluded that where there is a common understanding on a treaty term as manifested by subsequent State practice, an outlier State cannot itself undermine such a conclusion; indeed, the ILC approvingly quoted a WTO Appellate Body statement in *Sempra Energy International v Argentine Republic (Award)* that 'the view of one State does not make [or deny] international law'.[27]

### 10.2.2 State practice and warship exercise of innocent passage

Academic views on the issue of prior authorization and/or prior notification have tended to emphasise the existence of a significant divergence of views and associated State practice. Such apparent divergence certainly fuels academic discourse and allows for great speculation as to the nature of rights and obligations in the context of military maritime operations. Klein, for example, suggests that 'state practice continues to be ambivalent' on the question of prior authorization and/or prior notification.[28] A frequently cited study conducted by Roach and Smith in 1994 suggested 40 States had a requirement for either prior notification or authorization for warships entering the territorial sea.[29] Such a number would represent a significant minority of the 168 parties to the LOSC and thus would represent meaningful State practice for the purposes of Article 31(3)(b) of the VCLT. A more contemporary academic estimate published in 2016 by Rothwell and Stephens suggests 39 States require either require prior notification or authorization for warships entering the territorial sea.[30]

---

22 International Law Commission, 66th session, A/CN.4/671 (2014) 'Second report on subsequent agreements and subsequent practice in relation to the interpretation of treaties', (Georg Nolte, Special Rapporteur) (hereafter Second ILC Report), [45, 21].

23 First ILC Report, note 18, [98, 38–39].

24 Ibid., [98, 39].

25 Second ILC Report, note 22, [48, 23].

26 Ibid.

27 First ILC Report, note 18, [107, 42].

28 N. Klein, *Maritime Security and the Law of the Sea*, Oxford: Oxford University Press, 2011, p. 38.

29 See J.A. Roach and R.W. Smith, 'Excessive Maritime Claims', (1994) 66 (1) *International Law Studies* pp. 158–159, table 10.

30 The States listed as requiring prior authorization are as follows: Algeria, Antigua and Barbuda, Bangladesh, Barbados, Brazil, Cambodia, Cape Verde, China, Congo, Denmark, Grenada, Iran, Maldives, Myanmar, Oman, Pakistan, Philippines, Poland, Romania, St Vincent and the Grenadines, Somalia, Sri Lanka, Sudan, Syria, United Arab Emirates, Vietnam and Yemen. The States listed as requiring prior notification are as follows: Bangladesh, Croatia, Denmark, Egypt,

'Do As I Do, Not As I Say' 169

In comparing the lists of States compiled by Roach and Smith in 1994 against Rothwell and Stephens' list from 2016 (and accounting for States that have either ceased to exist or changed names since 1994), it becomes clear that several States have abandoned their requirements for prior authorization or notification. These States include Albania, Bulgaria, Finland, Indonesia, the Seychelles and Sweden. The numerical similarity between these lists is actually based on the fact that the Rothwell and Stephens' list includes the following States that were not accounted for in the 1994 research: Croatia, Estonia, Nigeria, South Korea, Serbia and Montenegro and the United Arab Emirates. Hence taking into account this anomaly, the actual number of States that formally assert such rights has dropped in real terms in the past 25 years.

Klein suggests that there is 'some evidence' that the prior authorization/notification requirement has been complied with by other States seeking to have their warships engage in innocent passage. As a matter of State practice, Klein notes that this is manifested through the use of 'low-level' briefings by naval attaché officers before warships enter the territorial sea of a coastal State.[31] However, this claim is not substantiated by, and appears to run counter to, contemporary naval practice and/or doctrine. Indeed, in 2001, at a time of heightened tension between China and the United States of America (US) regarding the EP-3 incident, Australian warships without prior permission or providing prior notification, undertook passage in the Taiwan Strait in the purportedly claimed Chinese territorial sea, causing diplomatic and naval reaction by the Chinese Government. At exactly the time where 'low-level' consultations would have been most likely to occur, they did not.[32]

In contrast to these assertions by academic commentators, there is empirical evidence that the vast majority of States do not require prior authorization or notification before warships undertake innocent passage within another State's territorial sea, and several States that did once hold that view, no longer do so. Rather, State practice appears to be trending towards the cessation of purported prior permission/prior notification demands or the failure to follow-up these previously stated demands by practical State action.

A significant development in this regard was the 1989 agreement between the Union of Soviet Socialist Republics (USSR) and the United States that resulted in the *Joint Statement on the Uniform Interpretation of Rules of International Law Governing Innocent Passage*.[33] This Statement expressly provides that

---

Estonia, Guyana, India, Libya, Malta, Mauritius, Nigeria, Serbia, Montenegro and South Korea; see Rothwell and Stephens, note 14, p. 291.

31 Klein, note 28, p. 39 citing S. Bateman 'Security and the Law of the Sea in East Asia: Navigational Regimes and Exclusive Economic Zones' in D. Freestone, R. Barnes and D. Ong (eds), *The Law of the Sea: Progress and Prospects*, Oxford: Oxford University Press, 2006, pp. 365, 368.

32 'Stand-Off in the Taiwan Strait', *BBC News*, 29 April 2001, available online at http://news.bbc.co.uk/2/hi/asia-pacific/1303037.stm

33 USA- USSR *Joint Statement on the Uniform Interpretation of Rules of International Law Governing Innocent Passage*, 23 September 1989, (1989) 14 *Law of the Sea Bulletin* p. 13.

## 170   Dale Stephens and Timothy Quadrio

prior authorization/notification for warships engaged in innocent passage is not required as a matter of law.[34] As the two dominant global naval powers in 1989, this Statement carried considerable weight as it reflects resolution of this issue between two major naval powers. Moreover, this Statement is consistent with the views of the vast majority of States party to the LOSC who have not made any declaration as to the issue of prior authorization/notification.

The *1989 Joint US-USSR Statement* does represent relevant state practice in this field, as does the consistent and common practice of the majority of States parties to the LOSC with respect to the issue of prior authorization/notification. As outlined above, the significance of State practice in the realm of maritime rights and obligations under the LOSC has particular purchase given the resident ambiguity of many of the provisions of that treaty.[35] While traditional mechanisms of interpretation as outlined under VCLT Article 31(1) have permitted great progress in discerning meaning for multiple treaty interpretations in various fields of international law, the ambiguity and 'package deal' nature of the LOSC can limit such modalities of interpretation. In this regard what States do in terms of relevant practice in giving effect to their obligations and asserting their rights under the terms of a contested provision does provide a sounder manner of locating meaning.

It is notable that China is listed by both Roach and Smith, and Rothwell and Stephens, as a key State that requires prior permission from a foreign warship before engaging in innocent passage within Chinese territorial waters. As China is a contemporary major maritime nation, its practice and attitude towards the question of prior authorization or notification is particularly significant. While it is true that Chinese domestic law requires such permission, the actions of the People's Liberation Army-Navy have sometimes gone in the opposite direction. Significantly, in 2015, five Chinese warships undertook innocent passage through the US territorial sea near the Aleutian Islands. The passage complied precisely with the requirements of innocent passage as mandated under Article 19 of the LOSC and was tracked by the United States at the relevant time.[36] Critically, the passage was undertaken without obtaining prior permission or providing prior notification, namely the very same features that Chinese internal law seems to require in China's territorial sea. Such actions by the Chinese warships are entirely consistent with the concordant views of the overwhelming majority of States party to the LOSC and hence carry with them significant legal and normative weight that supports such rights as being consistent with Article 19 of the LOSC.

---

34 Ibid., Article 2 states: 'All ships, including warships, regardless of cargo, armament or means of propulsion, enjoy the right of innocent passage through the territorial sea in accordance with international law, for which neither prior notification nor authorization is required'.

35 See generally G. Walker and J. Noyes, 'Definitions for the 1982 Law of the Sea Convention' (2002) 32 (2) *California Western International Law Journal* p. 343 who identify over 60 particularly ambiguous terms of significance.

36 S. LaGrone, 'Chinese Warships Made 'Innocent Passage' Through U.S. Territorial Waters off Alaska', *USNI News*, 3 September 2015, available online at https://news.usni.org/2015/09/03/chinese-warships-made-innocent-passage-through-u-s-territorial-waters-off-alaska

### 10.2.3 Naval activities in the EEZ and state practice

The dominant interpretation of Article 58 of the LOSC is that it provides States the right to conduct naval activities in the EEZ of other States, without any requirement for their consent or permission. The overwhelming majority of States support this interpretation of Article 58 and this is confirmed by the state practice of major maritime States and declarations made by Germany, Italy, the Netherlands and the United Kingdom.[37]

Nevertheless, the dominant interpretation of Article 58 has been disputed, at least in what they say, by a minority of States. At the time of their signature or ratification of the LOSC, eight States made declarations to the effect that military exercises or manoeuvres were not permitted in the EEZ without the consent of the coastal State.[38] Kraska and Pedrozo have identified a further ten States that have attempted to regulate or prohibit military activities in their EEZ, taking the total number of 'dissenting' States to 18, in addition to six States that have attempted to claim a 200 nautical mile territorial sea and restrict military activities in that zone.[39] What this small minority of States have said about the legality of naval activities in the EEZ is, however, at odds with what almost all States do, through their navies by conducting naval activities in the EEZ of other States without seeking their prior permission or consent. This State practice is captured by Yo and Piao, who describe the 'general practice' of coastal States to 'tolerate those military activities of other states in their EEZ' so long as those activities do not constitute a threat.[40]

China has been described as an 'unfortunate stand out' from this zeitgeist of contemporary State practice on this issue,[41] particularly following the interactions at sea between Chinese naval assets and US special mission ships USNS *Bowditch*[42] in 2001 and USNS *Impeccable* in the vicinity of Hainan Island within China's claimed EEZ in 2009.[43] However, China's contemporary State

---

37 M. Hayashi, 'Military Activities in the Exclusive Economic Zones of Foreign Coastal States' (2012) 27 *The International Journal of Marine and Coastal Law* pp. 795, 800.

38 Bangladesh (27 July 2001), Brazil (10 December 1982), Cabo Verde (10 December 1982), India (29 June 1995), Malaysia (14 October 1996), Pakistan (26 February 1997), Thailand (15 May 2011), Uruguay (10 December 1982); 'United Nations Convention on the Law of the Sea: Declarations made upon signature, ratification, accession or succession or anytime thereafter', available online at www.un.org/Depts/los/convention_agreements/convention_declarations.htm

39 Burma (Myanmar), China, Indonesia, Iran, Kenya, Maldives, Mauritius, North Korea, the Philippines and Portugal; see J. Kraska and R. Pedrozo, *International Maritime Security Law*, Leiden: Martinus Nijohff, 2013, pp. 238–239.

40 Y.-D. Yo and W.-J. Piao, 'Legal Study of Military Activities in the EEZ with a Focus on Foreign Military Activities in the EEZ of P.R China' (2011) 3(2) *International Journal of Maritime Affairs and Fisheries* pp. 163, 168.

41 Kraska and Pedrozo, note 39, p. 240.

42 For a description of this incident see Rothwell and Stephens, note 14, pp. 296–297.

43 See generally M. Green et al., 'Counter-Coercion Series: Harassment of the USNS Impeccable', *Asia Maritime Transparency Initiative*, 9 May 2017, available online at https://amti.csis.org/counter-co-harassment-usns-impeccable/

172 *Dale Stephens and Timothy Quadrio*

practice may indicate otherwise. In 2017, China conducted naval operations in Japan's EEZ, it deployed an Auxiliary General Intelligence (AGI) ship into the United States' EEZ near the Aleutian Islands while another Chinese AGI ship monitored a multinational naval exercise in Australia's EEZ.[44] Such State practice is consistent with the dominant interpretation of States' rights in the EEZ of other States. It represents a convergence in what China does, as against what it says, that indicates an alignment with the dominant understanding of a right to conduct naval activities in the EEZ of other States.

The contemporary State practice of India may also demonstrate convergence in terms of what it does, as against what it says, to the dominant understanding of a State's right to conduct naval activities in the EEZ of other States. India's declaration on ratification of the LOSC in 1995 said it understood 'military exercises or manoeuvres' in the EEZ to require the consent of the coastal State.[45] However, the Indian Navy appears to regularly operate in the EEZs of other States, particularly in the Andaman Sea and the Bay of Bengal.[46] While the precise nature of these naval activities, particularly whether they involve coastal State consent is not clear, there have been no accompanying statements made by India that State consent has been obtained. Indeed, silence on this key point is significant and the actions India undertakes at sea are likely to be more consistent with the dominant understanding of a State's right to conduct naval activities in the EEZ without the need for permission.

## 10.3 Navigational rights in archipelagic waters: the recent state practice of the Philippines

Together with Indonesia, the Philippines was a leading force in the development of the legal regime of archipelagic States in the second half of the twentieth century. In 1955 the Philippines claimed 'exclusive sovereignty' over 'all waters around, between and connecting different islands' of their archipelago.[47] This

---

44 Department of Defense (USA), 'Annual Report to Congress: Military and Security Developments Involving the People's Republic of China', 16 May 2018, pp. 67–68, available online at https://media.defense.gov/2018/Aug/16/2001955282/-1/-1/1/2018-CHINA-MILITARY-POWER-REPORT.PDF

45 India (29 June 1995), 'United Nations Convention on the Law of the Sea: Declarations made upon signature, ratification, accession or succession or anytime thereafter', available online at www.un.org/Depts/los/convention_agreements/convention_declarations.htm

46 Speaking about the present areas of interest for Indian naval operations, Admiral Sunil Lanba, Chief of Naval Staff has been reported as saying: 'We started off by having a ship deployed permanently in Andaman Sea and approaches to the Malacca straits. Then we have mission based deployments in the North Arabian Sea, Gulf of Oman and Persian Gulf. Similarly, in the Northern part of Bay of Bengal and we are enhancing our surveillance in the South part, near Sri Lanka. We are also sending ships to the Lombok and Sunda straits'; see D. Peri, 'Full Text of Interview with Admiral Sunil Lanba, Chief of Naval Staff', *The Hindu* (online), 4 November 2017, available at www.thehindu.com/opinion/interview/interview-with-admiral-sunil-lanba-chief-of-naval-staff/article19982347.ece

47 This was contained in a *note verbale* to the United Nations dated 7 March 1955; see D.P. O'Connell, 'Mid-Ocean Archipelagos in International Law' (1971) 45 *British Yearbook of International Law* pp. 1, 27–28.

'Do As I Do, Not As I Say' 173

claim was followed by a pattern of State practice to support this claim, with a particular focus on restricting the movement of foreign warships through the Philippine archipelago. For example in 1968, the Philippines made diplomatic representations to Australia stating that it did not recognise the 'so-called right of innocent passage' and that it required an application for clearance to be made at least seven days in advance of any expected passage of an Australian warship through the Philippines.[48] The text of the 1973 Philippines constitution was equally forward leaning on the characterisation of the water space between its islands, declaring that the 'waters around, between, and connecting the islands of the archipelago ... form part of the internal waters of the Philippines'.[49] This classification of 'internal waters' remains in the present text of the Philippines Constitution.[50]

Given the Philippines' historical view on the classification of archipelagic waters, it is not surprising that the Philippines were not entirely satisfied with the 'package deal' outcome of UNCLOS III. Upon signature and ratification of the LOSC, the Philippines lodged a declaration saying 'the concept of archipelagic waters is similar to the concept of internal waters'. The declaration also purported to remove the 'rights of foreign vessels to transit passage' through the routes ordinarily used for international navigation within the archipelago, despite these rights to 'archipelagic sea lanes passage' being explicitly granted by Article 53 of the LOSC.[51] This declaration remains on the record, suggesting what the Philippines says about navigational rights in archipelagic waters has not changed.

However, the State practice of the Philippines since ratification of the LOSC demonstrates a significant shift in the Philippines' position on these matters. In the past decades, the Philippines have not sought to restrict or challenge the movement of warships through the archipelago, even when warships of the United States (and others) have transited their archipelagic waters without seeking prior permission or authorization.

At the same time, the jurisprudence of the Philippines' judicial branch appears to have swung into line with the dominant norms of the LOSC. Indeed, in a 2011 case concerning the constitutionality of executive orders delimiting archipelagic boundaries, the Supreme Court of the Philippines found

> ...the Philippines exercises sovereignty over the body of water lying landward of the baselines ... The fact of sovereignty, however, does not preclude ... unimpeded, expeditious international navigation, consistent with the international law principle of freedom of navigation ... international law norms, now codified in UNCLOS III, operate to grant innocent passage rights over

---

48 Ibid., p. 35.
49 Article 1, *Constitution of the Republic of the Philippines* (1973).
50 Article 1, *Constitution of the Republic of the Philippines* (1987).
51 The Philippines understanding made upon signature (10 December 1982) and confirmed upon ratification (8 May 1984), available online at www.un.org/depts/los/convention_agreements/convention_declarations.htm#Philippines

174  *Dale Stephens and Timothy Quadrio*

the territorial sea or archipelagic waters, subject to the treatys [sic] limitations and conditions for their exercise. Significantly, the right of innocent passage is a customary international law, thus automatically incorporated in the corpus of Philippine law.[52]

In step with developments in the judicial branch, the actions of the legislative branch of the Philippines government also indicate State practice consistent with the dominant regional (and international) view of navigational rights and obligations. Legislation to establish archipelagic sea lanes through the Philippine archipelago has been introduced into both houses of the Philippine legislature.[53] Although no bill has yet passed into law, the delineation of archipelagic sea lanes appears to be a high priority for the Philippines. The National Security Policy released in 2017 details that the 'enactment of laws pertaining to ... archipelagic sea lanes and all other matters necessary for the country's commitments and obligations under international law is urgent and imperative'.[54]

The acquiescence of the executive branch of the Philippines government to assertions of navigational freedoms also demonstrates a convergence to the dominant legal norms contained within the LOSC. Through its Freedom of Navigation (FON) programme,[55] the United States has made operational assertions to the Philippines' claim of archipelagic waters as internal waters, with US warships transiting through Philippine archipelagic waters without notice. Although the United States has made operational assertions in 1999, 2010, 2012 and 2016, there has been no public objection to these assertions made by the Philippines government. Indeed, in response to a 2017 United States Navy (USN) operational assertion carried out by the USS *John S. McCain* near Mischief Reef (a feature the Philippines claim sovereignty over), a spokesperson for the Armed Forces of the Philippines said 'freedom of navigation is guaranteed and anyone can do it ... and as long as it is within the bounds set forth by

---

52  *Magallona et al. v Ermita et al.* (July 16, 2011) Supreme Court of the Philippines, available online at http://sc.judiciary.gov.ph/jurisprudence/2011/august2011/187167.html#sdfootnote44anc

53  House Bill No. 4153 and Senate Bill No. 2738, identically titled 'An Act to Establish the Archipelagic Sea Lanes in the Philippines Archipelagic Waters, Prescribing the Rights and Obligations of Foreign Ships and Aircrafts exercising the Right of Archipelagic Sea Lanes Passage through the established Archipelagic Sea Lanes and providing for the associated protective measures therein'; and 17th Congress Senate Bill No. 92 'Philippine Archipelagic Sea Lanes Act' filed on 30 June 2016; see discussion at Melissa Luz T. Lopez, 'House bill assigning routes for foreign ships, planes approved on 2nd reading', *Business World Online*, March 23, 2015, available online at www.bworldonline.com/content.php?section=Nation&title=house-bill-assigning-routes-for-foreign-ships-planes-approved-on-2nd-reading&id=104820

54  Republic of the Philippines, *National Security Policy for Change and Well-Being of the Filipino People (2017–2022)*, (April 2017), p. 13, available online at www.nsc.gov.ph/attachments/article/NSP/NSP-2017-2022.pdf?bcsi_scan_320ea08b1835f508=2o2u5yUvmi/kOnibJq9Xtu/J3RwBAAAABrPIAA==&bcsi_scan_filename=NSP-2017-2022.pdf

55  Discussed below in Section 4.

international law, then it is all right'.[56] These words are consistent with those of a presidential spokesperson who said in 2017 that 'the Philippines has no objection regarding the presumed innocent passage of sea craft'.[57] Additionally, it was reported in February 2019 that the Philippines National Security Adviser said 'If the US, United Kingdom, Japan, Australia, France and New Zealand and even India would want to patrol the South China Sea, then that is alright with us if the only intent is to show freedom of navigation'.[58]

These developments in all three branches of the Philippines government demonstrate a significant shift in its national application of the LOSC. Over three decades, the Philippines have developed from a State that objected to the LOSC concept of 'archipelagic waters' to one that sees the need to promulgate archipelagic sea lanes as an 'urgent and imperative' national security priority.

## 10.4 State reticence and action

Because of its decentralised nature, international law has always relied heavily upon tracing the actions (and reactions) of States themselves when evaluating the nature of international legal rights and obligations claimed or rejected. Accordingly, against this background, the US in 1979 first developed its FON programme. The FON programme is a multi-layered 'whole of Government' effort to safeguard and reinforce US views of what international law provides by way of freedom of navigation rights.[59] Such assertions of navigational freedom are shared by many nations who perhaps enjoy the benefit of such assertions without the attendant risk of undertaking such actions themselves. Hence, such assertions, representative of State practice, are routinely and methodically made to lend credibility to the normative weight of legal navigational rights being asserted. The actions and reactions by States are thus meticulously recorded and made public through the *US Maritime Claims Reference Manual*.[60] These FON assertions are not intended to be any kind of 'force projection' or represent an abuse of right under international law, but rather they provide the necessary evidence of acceptance (or not) of maritime claims. Organisations such as the International Law Association acknowledge that such assertions are critical to

---

56 N. Corrales, 'Despite China's Protest, PH has no Objection to US Ship's 'Innocent Passage'', *Inquirer.Net*, August 11, 2017, available online at http://globalnation.inquirer.net/159642/despite-chinas-protest-ph-no-objection-us-ships-innocent-passage

57 Ibid.

58 National Security Adviser Hermogenes Esperon Jr., reported in 'Increase of US Navigation Patrols No Problem', *The Philippines Star*, February 19, 2019, p. 4.

59 See generally, R.J. Grunawalt, 'Freedom of Navigation in the Post-Cold War Era' in D.R. Rothwell and S. Bateman (eds), *Navigational Rights and Freedoms and the New Law of the Sea*, The Hague: Martinus Nijhoff, 2011, pp. 11, 15.

60 U.S. Navy Judge Advocate General's Corps, *Maritime Claims Reference Manual* (May 2018), available online at www.jag.navy.mil/organization/code_10_mcrm.htm

## 176 *Dale Stephens and Timothy Quadrio*

calibrating legal rights under international law.[61] Such State practice establishes a level of acquiescence regarding the interpretation of the LOSC that reinforces a reading that promotes navigational freedom.

The FON programme relies upon its legal efficacy on the actual physical undertaking of maritime transits in contested areas. There has been a long debate within international law about the legal significance of words versus actions. Hence, the question rhetorically (and practically) asked is whether it is more relevant to weight what a State does or what it says when discerning State practice? Of course, everything turns on context and studies such as the ILC 'subsequent state practice' study discussed above[62] will notionally accord equal weight to each. However, it seems inescapable that where a State actually expends physical effort in practically championing a legal right or obligation, that such exertion carries with it greater explanatory power of a State's position concerning the veracity of its claim.

Certainly, authors such as D'Amato have long held that a State's actions are to be accorded more significance. He has consistently argued that State practice is more significant if represented by acts rather than words, noting that 'acts are visible, real and significant; it crystallizes policy and demonstrates which of the many possible rules of law the acting State has decided to manifest'.[63] In his view, words by States often represent a prediction on how international law may be shaped. Everything is contingent on State reaction as it is an 'interactive process'.[64] When words are followed by actions, there is a fulfilment of a normative 'move' regarding the progression of international law. As far as words go, he notes 'If you focus just on what governments say, then ... you accept what governments say as the reality. But Governments can tell you anything. Governments can dissemble and invent just as much as anybody else'.[65] In contrast, when States act, they are doing so 'purposively', acting in an intentionally 'normative' fashion.[66] Taking the Security Council as his example he observes that

---

61 Committee on Formation of Customary (General) International Law, International Law Association, 'Final Report of the Committee', London Conference (2000), p. 10, available online at The 2000 Final Report of the International Law Association's Committee on Formation of Customary (General) Law, available online at www.ila-hq.org/index.php/committees stating: 'Thus if State A expressly claims the right to exclude foreign warships from passing through its territorial sea, and State B sends a warship through without seeking the permission of A, this is an implicit claim on the part of B that A has no right to prohibit the passage. If A fails to protest this infringement, this omission can, in its turn, constitute a tacit admission of the existence of a right of passage after all'.

62 First ILC Report, note 18.

63 A. D'Amato, *The Concept of Custom in International Law*, Ithaca, NY: Cornell University Press, 1971, p. 88.

64 A. D'Amato, 'The Theory of Customary International Law' (1988) 82 *American Society of International Law Proceedings* pp. 242, 258.

65 Ibid., p. 257.

66 Ibid., p. 258.

'Do As I Do, Not As I Say' 177

I don't take the words as significant, but I take them as indicating where people may be going. These declarations may be starting to prepare us for what states are intending to do. If that's so, and it plays out – if … practice actually follows what was said in the U.N. resolutions – then we really have something.[67]

Such an observation enables closer assessment to be made of States' actions or lack of action when understanding the nature of the international law and international relations interplay. India, for example, has been consistent in its claims (based on national law) that foreign warships obtain prior permission before undertaking innocent passage and that foreign naval activities in the Indian EEZ are subject to greater national jurisdiction. The US FON programme has undertaken innocent passage transits within the Indian territorial sea and undertaken activities not consistent with Indian national claims concerning EEZ use.[68] Sometimes, these FON actions have been protested by the Indian Government and sometimes not. Despite such verbal protests, there have been no symbolic actions by the Indian Navy or any other arm of government to reinforce such claims.

Perhaps this is consistent with the D'Amato view that this is a contingent claim on behalf of India, and that the crystallisation of such a claim awaits actual action. It may be that internal legal views are unfolding and the lack of consistency means the position regarding navigational rights is not firmly settled as a matter of Indian assessments of international law. Such a proposition may also be underpinned by Indian criticism of Chinese claims in the Pacific that are said to amount to the unjustified 'territorialisation' of such water spaces.[69] It is naturally hard to reconcile apparent Indian claims of greater national control of their maritime zones with its criticism of similar claims by China. Moreover, there seems little attempt to publicly differentiate such a stance or to provide any kind of substantive articulation of views from the standpoint of the LOSC, especially given India's own naval actions themselves as outlined above, appear to be inconsistent with its claims.

The lack of a public reconciliation of apparent disparate views is a contemporary phenomenon. In modern times, there seems to be a growing reticence by States to say things publicly, at least anything that has a deep articulated legal basis that is outlined in detail. Hence, Schmitt and Watts have observed that in the context of international humanitarian law (IHL)

---

67 Ibid., p. 259.
68 Department of Defense (USA), *Annual Freedom of Navigation (FON) Reports*, available online at https://policy.defense.gov/OUSDP-Offices/FON/ in fiscal years 2017, 2016, 2015, 2014, 2013, 2012, 2011 (#), 2010, 2009, 2008 and 2007 indicate the USN has made operational assertions relating to India's prior requirement for military exercises or manoeuvres in the EEZ.
69 I. Rehman, 'India, China, and differing conceptions of the maritime order', Project on International Order and Strategy, Brookings, June 2017, pp. 1–2, available online at www.brookings.edu/research/india-china-and-differing-conceptions-of-the-maritime-order/

## 178   Dale Stephens and Timothy Quadrio

> One no longer finds regular expressions of IHL *opinio juris*. Nor does one regularly find comprehensive and considered responses by States to the proposals and pronouncements of non-State IHL participants. In many respects ... the guns of State IHL *opinio juris* have fallen silent.[70]

Moreover, they note that this lacuna in State legal pronouncements is sometimes filled with third party non-State commentators, willing to substitute their interpretation for legal analysis that may or may not align with a State view. Hence, Schmitt and Watts further observe that

> The IHL contributions of the international legal academy have been particularly voluminous. Some are of exceptional quality. However, academia has also incentivized the production of decidedly unconventional IHL perspectives. While useful to illustrate or deconstruct normative architecture, many such efforts not only eschew rigorous legal analysis, but also display deep insensitivity to the realities of battle in favor of interpretative creativity or innovation.[71]

Such an observation, it is submitted, applies not only to IHL but all facets of international law practice, including that of maritime operations under the LOSC.

This is not to say that government legal advisors have failed in their duties to undertake legal analysis of State actions. In fact, in the context of national security matters, there has generally been a substantial increase in the human resources dedicated to legal assessment of State actions. However, such considerable effort occurs 'off stage' and such analysis does not often get presented publicly. Former Principal Legal Adviser for the United Kingdom Foreign and Commonwealth Office, Daniel Bethlehem, has in fact described this growing practice as the 'secret life of international law'. He reveals that within government there is considerable analysis and detail incorporated into assessing State actions (and words) and yet very little of it is made public.[72] Bethlehem observes that international law is taken very seriously internally. Hence, State actions and reactions, naturally including those relating to navigational rights, are reviewed and parsed very carefully by teams of lawyers within government; however, this activity and exposition of legal rights and obligations is usually shielded from public view. Such reticence necessarily fuels disquiet about a State's position from an external audience perspective. In such circumstances therefore, it becomes critical to locate and appreciate the legal significance of actual State actions that are not so shielded and to accord them greater normative weight when understanding a State's position on contentious issues. The international community

---

70  M. Schmitt and S. Watts, 'The Decline of International Humanitarian Law Opinio Juris and the Law of Cyber Warfare', (2015–2016) 50 *Texas International Law Journal* pp. 189, 191.

71  Ibid., p. 192.

72  D. Bethlehem, 'The Secret Life of international law', (2012) 1 *Cambridge Journal of International and Comparative Law* pp. 23, 24.

has no choice but to discern meaning in these actions, which provide tangible signals of State views. In this regard, the unmistakable trend within international State practice is to recognise that States do enjoy navigational freedoms in the territorial sea, archipelagic waters/sea lanes and EEZ and that such freedoms fundamentally inform meaning under the LOSC. This inescapable outcome is manifested in what States are doing more than what they are saying and, as argued in this chapter, such an analysis enjoys methodological confidence given the relevance of actions rather than words within international legal process.

## 10.5 Conclusion

The purpose of this chapter has been to critically examine the empirical evidence of State practice in the area of warship navigational rights and obligations within a coastal State's maritime zones. In the absence of meaningful adjudication of these rights and correlative obligations, legal meaning has to be discerned from actual State practice. Such practice forms an intrinsic part of the interpretative enterprise as reflected in the VCLT, and hence such methodology is a reliable and orthodox mechanism for discerning meaning. It is abundantly clear since the entry into force of the LOSC that there has been a discernible reduction in the number of States that purport to restrict navigational freedom of warships under the LOSC, especially in South East Asia. Even within the smaller number of States that still maintain conditions on the exercise of warship freedom in their maritime zones, there is evidence that some of them have asserted similar freedoms in others' zones. To this end, this chapter has argued that when understanding what constitutes relevant 'subsequent state practice', it is critical to look at what States do, more than what they say. Examples such as those exhibited by the Philippines and Indonesia in South East Asia, and more broadly by China and India that lie just to the east and west of South East Asia, provide significant normative impact on the shaping of the law. While acknowledging the claim of a dynamic, but closed doors, 'secret life of international law', it is only when States undertake specific public actions that behaviour can be reliably located and recorded. In this context, the unmistakable trend has been the effective acknowledgement of warship navigational freedom in the various zones examined in this chapter. Such a conclusion accords perfectly with the architecture of the LOSC that sought to reflect that balanced freedom in its very terms.

# 11 Regimes of navigation and maritime security in South East Asia

*Hitoshi Nasu*

## 11.1 Introduction

The maritime space in South East Asia is an important transit route between the Pacific and Indian Oceans, which makes uninterrupted navigation of vessels a critical issue of maritime security. The 1982 United Nations Convention on the Law of the Sea (LOSC)[1] provides four different legal regimes for navigation of ships: innocent passage in the territorial sea or archipelagic waters of a coastal state,[2] transit passage and overflight in straits used for international navigation,[3] archipelagic sea lanes passage and overflight,[4] and freedom of navigation and overflight on the high seas.[5] In South East Asia all of these four legal regimes of navigation are present, which sets a complex legal context in which international shipping operates while confronting multiple regional maritime security issues, such as piracy and armed robbery at sea.

The complexity of legal regimes of navigation is not in itself an issue that gives rise to any security concern in the maritime context. Rather, the cause for security concern lies in different interpretations that are adopted in the actual practice of implementing these legal regimes. The situation is further exacerbated in South East Asia due to the concentration of territorial and maritime disputes in the South China Sea, where over 250 maritime features of diverse types are scattered, many of which are subject to competing territorial and maritime claims among the claimant states, namely Brunei, Malaysia, the Philippines, People's Republic of China and Vietnam.[6] These disputes create legal uncertainty as to the mode of navigation that all ships, warships and merchant vessels alike, are required to take in different areas of the ocean. The potential eruption of armed

---

1 United Nations Convention on the Law of the Sea, 10 December 1982, 1833 UNTS 397 [hereafter LOSC].
2 Ibid., Articles 17, 52.
3 Ibid., Article 38.
4 Ibid., Article 53(2).
5 Ibid., Article 87.
6 Note that the Republic of China (Taiwan) also maintains the same claims as the People's Republic of China.

_Navigation and maritime security_ 181

hostilities or violence adds further instability to the implementation of these regimes of navigation in the region.

This chapter unravels these complications for navigation of ships as a maritime security challenge in South East Asia, with a view to establishing a holistic picture of legal issues that confront the navigation of international shipping passing through this region. To that end, this chapter examines the following: (a) traditional issues of navigation that arise in the context of the law of the sea as relevant to the region; (b) contemporary issues that affect the applicability and legal effect of regimes of navigation due to various territorial and maritime disputes that persist in the region; and (c) new legal issues that are emerging on the horizon, with a potential impact upon navigation of ships. This holistic analysis will demonstrate that the legal complexities regarding navigation of ships in South East Asia are not confined to the law of the sea regime alone, but are rather due to an increased level of interplay between the Convention regime and customary international law, the law governing territorial title, the law of armed conflict and international human rights law, as well as international law's response to technological issues such as cyber security and the use of autonomous technologies in the maritime domain. The issue of overflight in different regimes of navigation is tangentially mentioned where relevant but does not form a substantial part of the analysis.

## 11.2 Traditional legal issues of navigation

The navigational right of ships, which originates from the medieval notions of freedom of passage, is invariably subject to conditions under each of the different navigational regimes.[7] The regime of innocent passage, which is the most restrictive of the four regimes, requires the passage to be continuous and expeditious navigation for the purpose of merely traversing the territorial sea,[8] or proceeding to or from internal waters, or a call at a roadstead or port facility.[9] Additionally, the passage of ships must be carried out in a manner that is not prejudicial to the peace, good order or security of the coastal State.[10] Unlike transit passage through straits used for international navigation or archipelagic sea lanes passage, the right of innocent passage excludes activities that are incidental to the normal modes of navigation, such as underwater navigation by submarines and overflight by aircraft.

---

7 See generally, Y. Tanaka, 'Navigational Rights and Freedoms' in D.R. Rothwell et al. (eds), _The Oxford Handbook of the Law of the Sea_, Oxford: Oxford University Press, 2015, p. 536; E.D. Brown, _The International Law of the Sea_, Vol. 1, Aldershot: Dartmouth Publishing, 1994, pp. 52–72 (innocent passage through the territorial sea), pp. 80–96 (passage through straits used for international navigation), pp. 117–122 (rights of passage through archipelagic waters), pp. 286–314 (freedom of navigation on the high seas); T. Treves, 'Navigation' in R. Dupuy and D. Vignes (eds), _A Handbook on the New Law of the Sea_, Vol. 2, Dordrecht: Martinus Nijhoff, 1991, p. 835.
8 LOSC, Article 18(1)(a).
9 Ibid, Article 18(1)(b).
10 Ibid, Article 19.

182   *Hitoshi Nasu*

The catalogue of non-innocent activities in the territorial sea is provided in Article 19 of the LOSC, which is generally considered as an exhaustive list of activities incompatible with innocent passage.[11] However, the use of opaque language such as 'any other activity not having a direct bearing on passage',[12] as well as the coastal State's right to adopt laws and regulations relating to innocent passage,[13] has permitted different interpretations as to which mode of passage may be regarded as non-innocent. Particularly controversial has been the entitlement of warships to exercise the right of innocent passage,[14] with divergent State practice regarding the requirement of authorization or notification prior to the passage of warships in the territorial sea.[15] The tension over this matter, once prevalent in South East Asia, has somewhat subdued as Indonesia ceased to apply the requirement of prior notification with the adoption of the 1996 *Law on Indonesian Waters*,[16] whereas Vietnam amended the requirement of prior authorization to prior notification in January 2013.[17] Myanmar still requires foreign warships to obtain permission prior to entry into its territorial sea,[18] and so does China in the contested areas of the South China Sea.[19]

South East Asia is also home to two of the most important straits used for international navigation – the Strait of Malacca and the Singapore Strait – due to their strategic locations at 'choke' points for maritime traffic. While the legal status of these straits is not in dispute, the right of transit passage is subject to a set of navigational safety measures established by the International Maritime Organization (IMO), which have been adopted in consultation with Indonesia, Malaysia and Singapore.[20] In addition to these regulatory measures, calls have been made for consideration to the designation of the Straits of Malacca and Singapore as Particularly Sensitive Sea Areas with a view to the introduc-

---

11  See, for example, US Navy, US Coast Guard and US Marine Corps, *The Commander's Handbook on the Law of Naval Operations*, August 2017 (NWP 1-14M), Section 2.5.2.1; R.R. Churchill and A.V. Lowe, *The Law of the Sea*, 3rd ed, Manchester: Manchester University Press, 1999, p. 86. Cf R.A. Barnes, 'Section 3: Innocent Passage in the Territorial Sea' in A. Proelss (ed), *United Nations Convention on the Law of the Sea: A Commentary*, London: Hart, 2017, pp. 176, 190–196.
12  LOSC, Article 19(2)(l).
13  Ibid., Article 21.
14  See, for example, N. Klein, *Maritime Security and the Law of the Sea*, Oxford: Oxford University Press, 2011, pp. 25–43; K. Zou, 'Innocent Passage for Warships: The Chinese Doctrine and Practice', (1998) 29 *Ocean Development and International Law* p. 195; B.H. Oxman, 'The Regime of Warships under the United Nations Convention on the Law of the Sea', (1984) 24 *Virginia Journal of International Law* p. 809; D.D. Froman, 'Uncharted Waters: Non-innocent Passage of Warships in the Territorial Sea', (1984) 21 *San Diego Law Review* p. 625.
15  See K. Hakapää and E.J. Molenaar, 'Innocent Passage – Past and Present', (1999) 23 *Marine Policy* pp. 131, 143.
16  Law No. 6/1996 (Indonesia).
17  *Law of the Sea of Vietnam*, Law No. 18/2012/QH13 (Vietnam).
18  *Territorial Sea and Maritime Zones Law* No. 3/1977 (Myanmar).
19  See below Section 11.3.
20  For details, see, for example, J.H. Ho, 'Enhancing Safety, Security, and Environmental Protection of the Straits of Malacca and Singapore: The Cooperative Mechanism', (2009) 40 *Ocean Development and International Law* p. 233.

*Navigation and maritime security* 183

tion of a compulsory pilotage regime.[21] Difficulties are expected, however, due to the considerable impact on navigation, as has been the case with Australia's introduction of a compulsory pilotage regime in the Torres Strait.[22]

The legal status of waters enclosed by archipelagic States has remained uncertain, primarily due to the delay with the designation of archipelagic sea lanes in accordance with the relevant clauses of the LOSC. While, as a default rule, foreign vessels are entitled to the right of innocent passage in archipelagic waters,[23] the Philippines has not made clear that the waters enclosed by archipelagic baselines it has established are archipelagic waters rather than internal waters.[24] The *Philippine Maritime Zones Act*, introduced in 2011 to clarify the legal status of the enclosed waters, remains to be enacted at the time of writing. Having declared archipelagic status based on the LOSC in 1996,[25] Indonesia designated its archipelagic sea lanes in 2002.[26] However, due to protests from maritime states such as Australia and the United States, Indonesia's submission of the archipelagic sea lanes designation to the IMO was declared only a 'partial designation'.[27] This has left uncertainty regarding the legal status of the remaining archipelagic waters that are normally used for international navigation, particularly with regard to east-west archipelagic sea lanes through the southern part of the Indonesian archipelago.[28]

Where purported restrictions apply to freedoms of navigation and overflight under any of these navigational regimes, there is uncertainty as to what legal consequences might follow from a failure to comply with local laws and regulations of the coastal State. Questions arise whether a breach of local laws and regulations of the coastal State (e.g. possession or use of weapons and firearms)

---

21 See, for example, M.H. bin Mohd Rusli, 'The Application of Compulsory Pilotage in Straits Used for International Navigation: A Study of the Straits of Malacca and Singapore', (2011) 3 *Asian Politics and Policy* p. 501.

22 For details, see D.R. Rothwell, 'Compulsory Pilotage and the Law of the Sea: Lessons Learned from the Torres Strait' in S. Wu and K. Zou (eds), *Securing the Safety of Navigation in East Asia: Legal and Political Dimensions*, Oxford: Chandos, 2013, pp. 51, 56–66; R. Beckman, 'Australia's Pilotage System in the Torres Strait: A Threat to Transit Passage?', *Institute of Defence and Strategic Studies Commentary No. 125*, 7 December 2006, available online at www.rsis.edu.sg/wp-content/uploads/2014/07/CO06125.pdf

23 LOSC, Article 52.

24 *Republic Act No. 9522 of 2009* (Philippines). For analysis, see, US Department of State, 'Philippines: Archipelagic and Other Maritime Claims and Boundaries', (2014) 142 *Limits in the Seas* pp. 1, 4–5.

25 *Law on Indonesian Waters*, Law No. 6/1996 (Indonesia).

26 Indonesian Government Regulation No. 37 on the Rights and Obligations of Foreign Ships and Aircraft Exercising the Right of Archipelagic Sea Lane Passage through Designated Archipelagic Sea Lanes (28 June 2002), reproduced in (2003) 52 *Law of the Sea Bulletin* p. 20.

27 For details, see, for example, S. Bateman, 'Security and the Law of the Sea in East Asia: Navigational Regimes and Exclusive Economic Zones' in D. Freestone, R. Barnes and D. Ong (eds), *The Law of the Sea: Progress and Prospects*, Oxford: Oxford University Press, 2006, pp. 365, 374–375; C. Johnson, 'A Rite of Passage: The IMO Consideration of the Indonesian Archipelagic Sea-Lanes Submission', (2000) 15 *International Journal of Marine and Coastal Law* pp. 317, 325–329.

28 D.M. Sodik, 'The Indonesian Legal Framework on Baselines, Archipelagic Passage, and Innocent Passage', (2012) 43 *Ocean Development and International Law* pp. 330, 335.

184  *Hitoshi Nasu*

necessarily renders the passage non-innocent and, under such circumstances, whether the coastal State is entitled to use forcible means against the non-compliant ship.[29] Under the *Arms Offences Act* (Singapore), for example, un-authorized possession of firearms and ammunition is criminalised within the Republic of Singapore including its territorial waters,[30] while its Port Authority has the powers to refuse entry into, and direct any vessel to leave, Singapore's territorial waters in the public interest.[31] This issue has significant implications for the operation of commercial ships, particularly when their security measures against piracy (a crime that by definition occurs outside the territorial sea) and armed robbery at sea are compromised as a result of compliance with local laws and regulations regarding the possession and use of firearms.[32]

While the coastal State is required not to hamper the innocent passage of foreign ships in the territorial sea except in accordance with the LOSC,[33] there is room for subjective assessment to be made by the coastal State in exercising criminal jurisdiction over matters that arise on board the ship during its pas-sage.[34] This is because of two vaguely worded exceptions to the prohibition on the coastal State's exercise of criminal jurisdiction over a foreign ship passing through the territorial sea without entering or leaving its internal waters, namely 'if the consequences of the crime extend to the coastal State' and 'if the crime is of a kind to disturb the peace of the country or the good order of the territorial sea'.[35] Depending on how the nature of the matter is perceived by the coastal State's authorities, the innocent passage of a foreign ship could be subject to disruption due to an exercise of the coastal State's criminal jurisdiction.

## 11.3 Issues arising from territorial and maritime disputes

The large concentration of territorial and maritime disputes in the South China Sea constitutes an additional layer of complexity in the application of the legal

---

29  Compare, for example, F. Ngantcha, *The Right of Innocent Passage and the Evolution of the Inter-national Law of the Sea*, London: Pinter Publishers, 1990, p. 176; with Froman, note 14, p. 660.

30  *Arms Offences Act 1973* (Singapore); see also, J. Kraska, 'Excessive Coastal State Jurisdiction: Shipboard Armed Security Personnel' in H. Ringbom (ed), *Jurisdiction over Ships: Post-UNCLOS Developments in the Law of the Sea*, Leiden: Brill, 2015, pp. 167, 186.

31  *Maritime and Port Authority of Singapore Act 1996* (Singapore), Sections 48, 49.

32  Indeed, the arrest of two Italian marines on board *M/V Enrica Lexie* by Indian authorities over the alleged killing of two Indian fishermen in India's Exclusive Economic Zone at a distance of approximately 20.5 nautical miles off the Indian coast has resulted in a jurisdictional dispute between Italy and India, which is at the time of writing subject to arbitral proceedings under Annex VII of LOSC: *In the Matter of an Arbitration before an Arbitral Tribunal Constituted under Annex VII of the 1982 United Nations Convention on the Law of the Sea between the Italian Republic and the Republic of India concerning the 'Enrica Lexie' Incident*, PCA Case no. 2015-28, Order of 29 April 2016.

33  LOSC, Article 24(1).

34  See W.K. Agyebeng, 'Theory in Search of Practice: The Right of Innocent Passage in the Territorial Sea', (2006) 39 *Cornell International Law Journal* pp. 371, 386.

35  LOSC, Articles 27(1)(a) and (b), respectively.

regimes of navigation. These territorial and maritime disputes directly challenge the exercise of sovereign authority in disputed maritime areas, which leaves the applicable regimes of navigation open to question and challenge by other States. Uncertainty as to the applicable regimes of navigation arises in three different types of disputes: (a) where territorial title over coastal land is contested; (b) where the legal classification of a maritime feature is disputed; and (c) where a claim to maritime zones made by the coastal State is considered excessive.[36] These types of dispute primarily affect navigation of warships when they assert freedoms of navigation and overflight in disputed waters, but commercial ships navigating in these maritime areas of South East Asia may also be subject to uncertainty as to whether, and to what extent, domestic law and regulations of coastal States may apply to them.

First, there are maritime areas where the applicability of a particular regime of navigation is disputed because of a territorial dispute. A large number of maritime features in the South China Sea are subject to competing territorial claims, over which different claimant States exercise effective control. It is contentious whether the purported exercise of sovereign authority over disputed territory generates a legal entitlement to claim a territorial sea, in which the regime of innocent passage would be the applicable basis for navigation. The fact that the very basis for exercising sovereignty is contested could mean that no State is entitled to exercise *de jure* sovereignty, leaving adjacent maritime areas open to freedom of navigation until the dispute is settled in one way or another. Unresolved territorial status remains the cause for instability, which could be exploited by insurgents and other extremist activities. In 2013, 200 followers of Jamalul Kiram III, the self-proclaimed Sultan of Sulu, clashed with Malaysian security forces when they attempted to take control of the Lahad Datu district of Sabah under Malaysia's occupation.[37] This event led to the establishment of the Eastern Sabah Security Zone with restrictions on the passage of civilian vessels inside the Zone.[38]

Second, some of the maritime features in the South China Sea are subject to different assessment as to their capacity to generate maritime zones. The arbitral tribunal, established under Annex VII of the LOSC in relation to the South China Sea dispute, declared that Hughes Reef (Dongmen Jiao), the southern part of Gaven Reef (Nanxun Jiao), Subi Reef (Zhubi Jiao), Mischief Reef (Meiji Jiao) and Second Thomas Shoal (Ren'ai Jiao) were low-tide elevations incapable

---

36 This categorisation of disputes, and the following discussion in the remainder of this section, draws from the author's earlier work, H. Nasu, 'The Regime of Innocent Passage in Disputed Waters', (2018) 94 *International Law Studies* p. 241, but with illustrations specific to South East Asia.

37 G. Poling, P. DePadua and J. Frentasia, 'The Royal Army of Sulu Invades Malaysia', *Center for Strategic and International Studies*, 8 March 2013, available online at www.csis.org/analysis/royal-army-sulu-invades-malaysia

38 M. Hart, 'Eastern Sabah: Malaysia's Frontline Against Militancy', *The Diplomat*, 31 January 2018, available online at https://thediplomat.com/2018/01/eastern-sabah-malaysias-frontline-against-militancy/

## 186  Hitoshi Nasu

of generating any maritime zone.[39] However, the tribunal acknowledged methodological difficulties in measuring the tidal pattern and level of adjacent waters,[40] which were arguably fraught with outdated and inadequate surveys that could have carried little probative value in establishing the geographical condition of these features.[41]

Likewise open to controversy is the legal classification of maritime features that remain above water at high tide. The regime of islands under the LOSC prescribes the legal capacity of high-tide features to generate all the maritime zones to which the coastal state is entitled. However, if the features are incapable of sustaining human habitation or economic life of their own, they are classified as rocks which are only entitled to a territorial sea.[42] In the *South China Sea* arbitration, the arbitral tribunal declared that Scarborough Shoal (Huangyan Dao), Johnson Reef (Chigua Jiao), Cuarteron Reef (Huayang Jiao), Fiery Cross Reef (Yongshu Jiao), the northern part of Gaven Reef (Nanxun Jiao) and McKennan Reef (Ximen Jiao) were rocks.[43] The decision has been subject to controversy as to the way in which the tribunal interpreted the criteria in determining whether high-tide features are capable of sustaining human habitation or economic life of their own.[44]

The applicable regime of navigation in a large portion of the South China Sea is subject to further uncertainty due to the ambiguity of the legal claim laid by China – the most powerful and dominant claimant in the region – purporting to extend its sovereignty over the entire maritime space within the so-called Nine-Dash Line.[45] The *South China Sea* arbitration acknowledged, but then dismissed, the possibility of interpreting China's position as asserting the enclosure of the Spratly Islands 'within a system of archipelagic or straight baselines,

---

39 *In the Matter of an Arbitration before An Arbitral Tribunal Constituted under Annex VII to the 1982 United Nations Convention on the Law of the Sea between the Republic of the Philippines and the People's Republic of China*, PCA Case no. 2013-19, Award of 12 July 2016, [1203.B.(3)-(7)] [hereafter *South China Sea* arbitration].

40 Ibid. For assessment, see Y. Lyons, L.Q. Hung and P. Tkalich, 'Determining High-tide Features (or Islands) in the South China Sea under Article 121(1): A Legal and Oceanography Perspective' in S. Jayakumar et al. (eds), *The South China Sea Arbitration: The Legal Dimension*, Cheltenham: Edward Elgar, 2018, p. 128.

41 Chinese Society of International Law, 'The South China Sea Arbitration Awards: A Critical Study', (2018) 17 *Chinese Journal of International Law* pp. 207, 511–512.

42 LOSC, Article 121.

43 *South China Sea* arbitration, [1203.B.(6)-(7)].

44 See, for example, Chinese Society of International Law, note 41, pp. 520–551; Y. Song, 'The July 2016 Arbitral Award, Interpretation of Article 121(3) of the UNCLOS, and Selecting Examples of Inconsistent State Practices', (2018) 49 *Ocean Development and International Law* p. 247; M.H. Nordquist, 'UNCLOS Article 121 and Itu Aba in the South China Sea Final Award: A Correct Interpretation?' in Jayakumar, note 40, p. 176.

45 See, for example, 'Statement of the Government of the People's Republic of China on China's Territorial Sovereignty and Maritime Rights and Interests in the South China Sea', (2016) 15 *Chinese Journal of International Law* pp. 903, 904; Ministry of Foreign Affairs of the People's Republic of China, 'Position Paper of the Government of the People's Republic of China on the Matter of Jurisdiction in the South China Sea Arbitration Initiated by the Republic of the Philippines', (2016) 15 *Chinese Journal of International Law* pp. 431, 432–433.

*Navigation and maritime security* 187

surrounding the high-tide features of the group, and accorded an entitlement to maritime zones as a single unit'.[46] This alternative legal claim in relation to customary international law,[47] if it were found to be valid,[48] could have a potential to restrict freedom of navigation and overflight within more precisely defined archipelagic units consisting of the Pratas Islands (Dongsha Qundao), Paracel Islands (Xisha Qundao), Macclesfield Bank (Zhongsha Qundao) and Spratly Islands (Nansha Qundao).

The disputed status of the claim of sovereignty over a large portion of the South China Sea, or alternatively more precisely defined archipelagic units, may mean that non-Chinese flagged ships are arguably entitled to legitimately assert freedoms of navigation in disputed waters. However, as has proven to be the case in the past,[49] the exercise of navigational freedom in disputed waters often results in confrontation with Chinese authorities. For commercial ships including fishing vessels, this means the risk of being arrested by Chinese authorities for allegedly operating in breach of Chinese laws and regulations.[50]

Third, the outer reach of a territorial sea drawn by the coastal State according to its application of straight baselines may be considered as excessive.[51] In South East Asia, this has been the case with the straight baselines that have been established by Cambodia,[52] Myanmar (particularly a single straight baseline segment of 222.3 nautical miles across the Gulf of Martaban),[53] Thailand,[54] and

---

46 *South China Sea* arbitration, [573].
47 See Chinese Society of International Law, note 41, pp. 479–506.
48 There is a considerable number of protests against the claim of offshore archipelagos enclosed by straight baselines: see J.A. Roach, 'Offshore Archipelagos Enclosed by Straight Baselines: An Excessive Claim?', (2018) 49 *Ocean Development and International Law* pp. 176, 179–182; see also, C. Lathrop, J.A. Roach and D.R. Rothwell (eds), 'Baselines under the International Law of the Sea: Reports of the International Law Association Committee on Baselines under the International Law of the Sea' (2018) 2(1–2) *The Law of the Sea*, pp. 110–112 [89]–[92].
49 For a collection of maritime incidents in the South China Sea, see Centre for Strategic and International Studies, 'China Power: Are Maritime Law Enforcement Forces Destabilizing Asia', 18 August 2016, available online at https://chinapower.csis.org/maritime-forces-destabilizing-asia/
50 There are many reported cases of disruption of fishing activities in disputed waters: see, for example, P.L. Viray, 'Chinese Coast Guard Continue to Harass Filipino Fishermen in Scarborough – Report', *Philstar*, 8 June 2018, available online at www.philstar.com/headlines/2018/06/08/1822747/chinese-coast-guard-continue-harass-filipino-fishermen-scarborough-report; E. Shim, 'Chinese Boats Attack Vietnamese Fishermen in South China Sea', *United Press International*, 29 June 2017, available online at www.upi.com/Chinese-boats-attack-Vietnamese-fishermen-in-South-China-Sea/8561498755312/
51 See discussion by Rothwell in Chapter 2.
52 *Decree of the Council of State of 13 July 1982* (Cambodia), Annex I.
53 *Decree of 15 November 1968* (Myanmar), reproduced with English translation in (1970) 14 *International Boundary Study: Limits in the Seas 1*, p. 2; *Territorial Sea and Maritime Zones Law No. 3/1977* (Myanmar), Annex.
54 Announcement of the Office of the Prime Minister Concerning Straight Baselines and Internal Waters of Thailand Area 4, 17 August 1992, reproduced in (1994) 25 *Law of the Sea Bulletin* pp. 82–84.

## 188   *Hitoshi Nasu*

Vietnam.[55] The United States, most notably, has been challenging these maritime claims as excessive and invalid under international law.[56] The validity of these straight baselines is disputable as an interpretive issue under the LOSC between the Convention Parties, whereas against a non-Party State such as the United States, it is subject to acceptance under customary international law as it evolves. The disputed status of these waters leaves uncertainty as to whether foreign ships can enjoy freedoms of navigation and overflight, or even should be compelled to exercise such freedoms in order to retain the legitimate claim of disputing the status.

Uncertainty regarding the applicable navigation regime means that ships navigating in these disputed waters have to navigate themselves through these legal conundrums as well. A critical difference to the traditional legal issues concerning navigation is that restrictions on the freedoms of navigation and overflight are purported to be in place due to the *de facto* exercise of sovereign authority. Compliance with such restrictions may be seen as favouring the interest of the coastal State, for example, in reinforcing continued and peaceful display of its sovereign authority as evidence of title to the disputed territory or maritime features,[57] or as subsequent practice that establishes general agreement with the particular interpretation and application of the baseline rules in the LOSC.[58] Further difficulties arise in deciding which of the competing national authorities should be approached for granting permission on various activities associated with navigation, such as fishing and marine scientific research, in these disputed areas of the ocean.

## 11.4 New issues on the horizon

In addition to the traditional and contemporary challenges, there are other issues that are emerging on the horizon with a potential impact on the regulation of navigation in South East Asia. These issues arise depending on: (a) the development of geopolitical tensions between China and the United States in the region; (b) the application of technological advances in the maritime context; and (c) the extension of jurisprudence in the area of international human rights law. None of these factors have yet caused any immediate challenge, but rather posit the broader picture of the regimes of navigation in a changing context.

---

55 *Law of the Sea of Vietnam, Law No. 18/2012/QH13* (Vietnam); Vietnam, *Statement of 12 November 1982 on the Territorial Sea Baseline of Vietnam*, 12 November 1982, available online at www.un.org/Depts/los/LEGISLATIONANDTREATIES/PDFFILES/VNM_1982_Statement.pdf

56 U.S. Navy Judge Advocate General's Corps, *Maritime Claims Reference Manual* (May 2018), available online at www.jag.navy.mil/organization/code_10_mcrm.htm

57 See, for example, *Sovereignty over Pedra Branca/Pulau Batu Puteh, Middle Rocks and South Ledge* (Malaysia v. Singapore) [2008] ICJ Rep 12, [62–69]; *Frontier Dispute* (Burkina Faso v. Mali) [1986] ICJ Rep 554, [63]; *Legal Status of Eastern Greenland* (Denmark v. Norway) [1933] PCIJ (Ser A/B) No. 53, pp. 45–46; *Island of Palmas* (Netherlands v. US) (1928) 2 RIAA 829, p. 846.

58 Vienna *Convention on the Law of Treaties*, 23 May 1969, 1155 UNTS 331, Article 31(3)(b).

*Navigation and maritime security* 189

First, the geopolitical tension between major powers, particularly China and the United States, could, as it did in the past,[59] manifest itself in the maritime context as navigational confrontation in the South China Sea,[60] where the United States conducts Freedom of Navigation Operations (FONOPs) to challenge China's assertion of sovereignty in the disputed maritime space.[61] An escalation of this tension, as a result of navigational confrontation, could disrupt commercial ships' freedom and safety of navigation. In the event that confrontation triggers an international armed conflict between two States, the navigation of ships is subject to restrictions in accordance with rules governing naval warfare.[62] However, in cases where non-State actors engage in a de-centralised network of hostile operations,[63] a legal 'grey zone' could be created due to the different criteria that apply to the classification of armed conflicts as the basis for implementation of various rules of the law of armed conflict.[64] Indeed, the maritime context presents a unique set of difficulties in distinguishing incidents at sea from hostilities.[65] In such situations of legal uncertainty, the defending coastal State authorities may assert the right of belligerent search and visit, which may disrupt the navigation of ships in, and in the vicinity of, the scene of confrontation.

Second, commercial pressure and demands for inter-connected logistics management systems have led to modern shipping being highly dependent

---

59 A notable example is the *Impeccable* incident: see, R. Pedrozo, 'Close Encounters at Sea: The USNS Impeccable Incident', (2009) 62 *Naval War College Review* p. 101.

60 See the discussion by Stephens and Quadrio in Chapter 10.

61 It is important to note that FONOPs target multiple states to challenge maritime claims that the US government considers excessive and invalid. For details of FONOPs, see, for example, J. Kraska, *Maritime Power and the Law of the Sea: Expeditionary Operations in World Politics*, Oxford: Oxford University Press, 2011, pp. 397–403; W.J. Aceves, 'The Freedom of Navigation Program: A Study of the Relationship Between Law and Politics', (1995) 19 *Hastings International and Comparative Law Review* p. 259; S.A. Rose, 'Naval Activities in the EEZ – Troubled Waters Ahead?', (1990) 39 *Naval War Review* pp. 67, 85–90; G. Galdorisi, 'The United States Freedom of Navigation Program: A Bridge for International Compliance with the 1982 United Nations Convention on the Law of the Sea?', (1996) 27 *Ocean Development and International Law* p. 399.

62 See L. Doswald-Beck (ed), *San Remo Manual on International Law Applicable to Armed Conflict at Sea*, Cambridge: Cambridge University Press, 1995.

63 China has been known for reinforcing a network of fishing vessels organised into a maritime militia in protecting its national interest in disputed waters: see, for example, M.D. Armour, 'The Chinese Maritime Militia: A Perfect Swarm?', (2016) 10 *Journal of Defence Studies* pp. 21–39. Vietnam has also reportedly been reinforcing its maritime militia forces: N.K. Giang, 'Vietnam's Response to China's Militarised Fishing Fleet', *East Asia Forum*, 4 August 2018, available online at www.eastasiaforum.org/2018/08/04/vietnams-response-to-chinas-militarised-fishing-fleet/

64 For detailed analysis by the author elsewhere, see H. Nasu, 'Challenges of Hybrid Warfare to the Implementation of International Humanitarian Law in the Asia-Pacific' in S. Linton, T. McCormack and S. Sivakumaran (eds), *Asia-Pacific Perspectives on International Humanitarian Law*, Cambridge: Cambridge University Press, forthcoming.

65 W. Heintschel von Heinegg, 'The Difficulties of Conflict Classification at Sea: Distinguishing Incidents at Sea from Hostilities', (2016) 98 *International Review of the Red Cross* p. 449.

## 190   Hitoshi Nasu

on information technology and computerised systems, such as automatic identification systems. The widespread use of information technology and computerised systems increases the risk of cyber-attack, which could lead to collisions or ships running aground.[66] The *Tallinn Manual 2.0* notes that vessels engaged in innocent passage may undertake cyber activities that are necessary to ensure their safety and security, such as monitoring its cyber infrastructure and receiving patches to fix vulnerabilities.[67] However, views are divided as to whether non-intrusive cyber activities such as passive assessment of wireless networks by vessels are compatible with innocent passage.[68] Certain measures of cyber security may also be prohibited under the coastal State's domestic laws and regulations, which as discussed above, may affect an exercise of the right of innocent passage depending on how the coastal State interprets the relevant provisions of the LOSC.

Further technological innovation enabling autonomous navigation of vessels is also expected to increase efficiency and safety in international shipping. Yet, the use of unmanned autonomous technology raises a question regarding the entitlement of such objects under relevant regimes of navigation.[69] For example, if a coastal State adopts the view that such objects do not enjoy the right of innocent passage within its territorial sea, the unmanned vehicle may be subject to arbitrary capture or interruption of passage without any legal protection. Indeed, the status of such an object became a subject of international dispute when a Chinese navy vessel seized an unmanned underwater vehicle the *USNS Bowditch* deployed for oceanographic survey, despite United States protests that the vehicle was entitled to sovereign immunity as a government vessel.[70] While the vehicle was later returned to the United States, this episode demonstrated the potential for different approaches to the classification of unmanned autonomous vessels and their entitlement under different regimes of navigation. The issue also affects the ability to deploy small swarm boats to protect commercial ships from various maritime security threats such as piracy and armed robbery at sea.

Third, while the safety of navigation has been at the forefront of the maritime security agenda for many years, the increase in more diverse activities associated with shipping has changed the legal landscape in this area,[71] with a potential

---

66 United Nations Conference on Trade and Development, 'Review of Maritime Transport 2017', 2017, UN Doc. UNCTAD/RMT/2017, pp. 85–86.

67 M.N. Schmitt (ed), *Tallinn Manual 2.0 on the International Law Applicable to Cyber Operations*, Cambridge: Cambridge University Press, 2017, p. 243 [11].

68 Ibid., 243 [8].

69 See, for example, R. McLaughlin, 'Unmanned Naval Vehicles and the Law of Naval Warfare' in H. Nasu and R. McLaughlin (eds), *New Technologies and the Law of Armed Conflict*, The Hague: Springer, 2014, pp. 229, 238–242.

70 See, for example, J. Borger, 'Chinese Warship Seizes US Underwater Drone in International Waters', *The Guardian*, 16 December 2016, available online at www.theguardian.com/world/2016/dec/16/china-seizes-us-underwater-drone-south-china-sea

71 See, for example, United Nations General Assembly, 'Ocean and the Law of the Sea: Report of the Secretary-General', 29 August 2003, UN Doc. A/58/65/Add.1, paras. 31–48.

*Navigation and maritime security* 191

extra-territorial application of international human rights law.[72] A range of safety issues in navigation could be turned into human rights issues, including the positive obligation to protect the right to life at sea, the right to liberty and security of the person, and the prohibition of torture and cruel, inhuman or degrading treatment.[73] A potential point of controversy is the issue of 'jurisdiction' for the purpose of applying international human rights law. Is it the flag State that is considered to be exercising sufficient control over a vessel by virtue of its obligation under the LOSC to 'effectively exercise its jurisdiction and control in administrative, technical and social matters over ships flying its flag'?[74] Or, could it be another State that in fact exercises effective control over the vessel or the individuals on board, for example, through instructions issued by the port authorities?[75] The actual extent and scope of human rights obligations may also differ according to the human rights treaty instrument(s) each State is party to.

South East Asia remains, by and large, conservative towards international commitments to human rights protection. Six of the ten ASEAN member States have either ratified or acceded to the International Covenant on Civil and Political Rights,[76] but Brunei, Myanmar, Malaysia and Singapore are not parties. However, the region has gradually become more amenable to civil society's advocacy for greater human rights protection,[77] with the adoption of the ASEAN *Human Rights Declaration* in 2012,[78] and the establishment of the ASEAN Inter-Governmental Commission on Human Rights.[79] The growth in awareness of human rights issues arising in the maritime domain and the potential for extra-territorial application of human rights obligations in that context, therefore, could impose additional legal obligations on the part of the flag State, the

---

72 For discussion, see, for example, U. Khaliq, 'Jurisdiction, Ships and Human Rights Treaties' in Ringbom, note 30, p. 324.

73 *International Covenant on Civil and Political Rights*, 19 December 1966, 999 UNTS 171, Articles 6, 7 and 9, respectively.

74 LOSC, Article 94(1); *Hirsi Jamaa and Others v Italy* (European Court of Human Rights, Grand Chamber, Application No. 27765/09, 23 February 2012) [77] (observing that the principle concerning the exclusive jurisdiction of the flag state 'has led the Court to recognise, in cases concerning acts carried out on board vessels flying a State's flag, in the same way as registered aircraft, cases of extraterritorial exercise of the jurisdiction of that State').

75 Cf *Medvedyev and Others v France* (European Court of Human Rights, Grand Chamber, Application No. 3394/03, 29 March 2010) [67] (determining that the non-flagged vessel *Winner* and its crew were within the jurisdiction of France for having exercised, de facto, full and exclusive control over them).

76 Acceded to by Cambodia on 26 May 1992, Indonesia on 23 February 2006, Thailand on 29 October 1996 and Vietnam on 24 September 1982; ratified by Lao PDR on 25 September 2009 and the Philippines on 23 October 1986.

77 H. Tan, 'Persistent Engagement and Insistent Persuasion: The Role of the Working Group for an ASEAN Human Rights Mechanism in Institutionalising Human Rights in the Region' in H. Nasu and B. Saul (eds), *Human Rights in the Asia-Pacific Region: Towards Institution Building*, Abingdon: Routledge, 2011, p. 127.

78 Adopted at the 21st ASEAN Summit, Phnom Penh, Cambodia, 18 November 2012.

79 See generally, H. Tan, *ASEAN Intergovernmental Commission on Human Rights: Institutionalising Human Rights in Southeast Asia*, Cambridge: Cambridge University Press, 2011.

## 192 *Hitoshi Nasu*

coastal State or even a third State to which the conduct of the vessel is considered attributable for the purpose of the application of human rights law.

## 11.5 Concluding observations

The navigation of ships in South East Asia faces multiple challenges as they sail through the region's geopolitical tension and technological transformation. Many of the traditional issues of navigation under the law of the sea remain unresolved due to interpretive differences, leaving uncertainty as to the precise scope of freedom of navigation and commerce at sea. Moreover, as this chapter has demonstrated, the geopolitical tension associated with the territorial and maritime disputes in the region, as well as technological advances relevant to navigation have added complexity to the legal regimes of navigation at the intersection between the law of the sea regime, the law governing territorial title, the law of armed conflict and international human rights law.

As maritime security threats arise or increase, commercial ships will be required to be aware of various legal limitations on the ways in which they can seek protection from those security threats. Such limitations include areas where navy or government vessels encounter legal sensitivities in conducting operations; the range of options available to them to protect themselves from maritime security threats under different local laws and regulations that may apply in different coastal states; and legal uncertainty as to whether unmanned autonomous vessels can be considered ships entitled to the right of innocent passage, transit passage or archipelagic sea lanes passage under the relevant regimes of navigation.

# 12 Crossing the Rubicon

## Singapore's evolving relations with China in the context of the 2016 arbitral award

*See Seng Tan*

This chapter examines the evolution of Singapore's increasingly difficult relationship with China against a convoluted backdrop of developments, including the landmark ruling by the arbitral tribunal on 12 July 2016, denying Chinese claims to huge swathes of the South China Sea. Since both countries normalised ties in 1990, Singapore has nurtured a robust economic and diplomatic relationship with China as part of a broader foreign policy of strategic hedging whilst deepening its partnership with the United States at the same time – friend to all and enemy to none, as Singapore Foreign Minister Vivian Balakrishnan has put it.[1] However, with growing Chinese impatience at Singapore's conduct undertaken at China's expense (or so thought), Singapore's ability to hedge has been called into question. Crucially, China's present assertiveness is reflective of a changing distribution of power and influence in the Indo-Pacific region. China's newfound status and self-awareness, and its consequent expression of that – marked by the attitudinal and policy shift from Deng Xiaoping's 'keep a low profile' strategy to Xi Jinping's 'China dream' – can therefore be understood as the crossing of a critical juncture, beyond which Chinese tolerance for what Beijing fairly or otherwise perceives as Singaporean policies pursued at China's expense can no longer be presumed.

According to Bull, international order (or society) is made and kept through a number of mechanisms or institutions, including international rules and conventions and the balance of power.[2] From the Singaporean perspective, there are at least two things over which Singapore and China seem to disagree with respect to how regional order in the Indo-Pacific should be constructed and maintained. The first involves Singapore's firm support for and advocacy of international law and a rules-based regional order; a logical decision for small and/or weak States for whom principle offers a normative bulwark against the raw political-military

---

1 D. Cheong, 'Vivian Balakrishnan Outlines Core Principles Guiding Singapore's Foreign Policy', *The Straits Times,* 18 July 2017, p. A6.
2 H. Bull, *The Anarchical Society: A Study of Order in World Politics,* New York: Columbia University Press, 1977.

## 194   See Seng Tan

power of larger and more powerful nations.[3] The second involves Singapore's conviction that the regional stability and security of the Indo-Pacific is best kept by way of an effective balance of power between China and the United States. The sustained commitment by both major powers to maintaining that balance also allows Singapore to continue its hedging strategy.[4] Before delving into those two issues, the chapter will begin with a review of the changing nature of Singapore ties with China.

## 12.1  Singapore-China relations: 'special' no more?

As Singapore's founding premier Lee Kuan Yew (hereafter 'LKY') once conceded, China has had (and continues to have) a profound influence on Singapore. The 'Lion City' has approached its relationship with China with care, whilst enjoying a sort of special dispensation from Beijing on the tacit basis of Singapore's predominantly ethnic Chinese population and the close interpersonal ties between Singapore's first-generation leaders and their Chinese counterparts. It was presumably on that same basis that Chinese leaders 'tolerated' Singapore's close security ties with the United States and its unique relationship with Taiwan – which has long provided Singapore with training facilities for the Singapore Armed Forces (SAF) – which the Chinese acknowledge within the terms of their 1990 normalisation agreement with Singapore. This 'special relationship' has progressed significantly in the post-Mao era, bolstered by the interest of succeeding Chinese leaders since Deng in Singapore as a governance model that China could presumably emulate.[5] As Xi Jinping reportedly told LKY when they met at the 2008 Beijing Olympic Games, 'We will need you for a long time. I have been to Singapore, I know what you have and our people want to learn. We get more from you than from America'.[6]

   Arguably, the two countries have continued to maintain a warm relationship ever since the beginning of international *détente* in the 1970s, in part because 'there are no outstanding issues and no areas of open conflict' between them.[7] Singapore vigorously pursued economic engagement with China in an effort to

---

3  T. Koh, 'International Law Serves as Shield and Sword but Small Countries must also be Self-Reliant', *The Straits Times*, 4 July 2017, available online at www.straitstimes.com/opinion/small-countries-must-be-self-reliant

4  See, C.C. Kuik, 'The Essence of Hedging: Malaysia and Singapore's Response to a Rising China', (2008) 30 *Contemporary Southeast Asia* p. 159; S.S. Tan, 'Mailed Fists and Velvet Gloves: The Relevance of Smart Power to Singapore's Evolving Defense and Foreign Policy', (2015) 38 *Journal of Strategic Studies* p. 332.

5  C. Huang, 'Communist Party Journal Suggests it Could Learn from Singapore's PAP', *South China Morning Post*, 23 October 2012, available online at www.scmp.com/news/china/article/1067561/communist-party-journal-suggests-it-could-learn-singapores-pap

6  Cited in Y. Zheng, 'The Special Relationship with China', *Today*, 23 March 2015.

7  J. Wong, 'Sino-Singapore Relations: Looking Back and Looking Forward', *Singapore China Friendship Association*, (n.d.), available online at www.singapore-china.org/profile/selected2.shtml

*Crossing the Rubicon* 195

develop the so-called 'second wing' of regional and global market expansion to complement its existing West-oriented approach.[8] The strategy provided added incentives for Singapore, whose economy complements China's, to exploit growing economic opportunities in China.[9] For the most part, Singapore, the first Asian country to sign a free trade agreement with China, has been Beijing's largest trading partner among the ASEAN economies.[10] Accordingly, Singapore has incessantly sought to render itself 'relevant to China's development by sharing its experiences and best practices' – as evidenced by the establishment of joint projects in China such as the China-Singapore Suzhou Industrial Park, Sino-Singapore Tianjin Eco-city, Sino-Singapore Guangzhou Knowledge City, Singapore-Chengdu High-Tech Park and Sino-Singapore Jilin Food Zone.[11] Despite all this, the two countries have arguably not fully reaped the expected benefits in terms of capital inflows and outflows.[12] Nor has mutual admiration and cooperation precluded their perception of each other as economic competitors.[13] Moreover, Singapore's investments in China considerably outweigh China's investments in Singapore.[14] Finally, Singapore's military-security ties with China have been recent and relatively minor, but since 2009, the SAF and the People's Liberation Army (PLA) have conducted counterterrorism exercises in Gulin and Singapore and army drills in Nanjing. When Chinese defence minister General Chang Wanquan visited Singapore in February 2018, both he and his Singaporean counterpart promised to 'step up bilateral defence cooperation'.[15]

However, over the past couple of years, Singapore-China relations endured turbulence unmatched by anything since both sides normalised ties in 1990. When LKY passed away in March 2015, China responded with a rare

---

8  S.P. Kim, 'Singapore-China Special Economic Relations: In Search of Business Opportunities', (2005) 3 *Ritsumeikan International Affairs* p. 151.

9  Economic engagement with advanced economic and industrial powers and markets has long been a key strategy for Singapore. As LKY explained in 1996, 'We had decided soon after independence to link Singapore up with the advanced countries and make ourselves a hub or nodal point for the expansion and extension of their activities'; cited in M. Leifer, *Singapore's Foreign Policy: Coping with Vulnerability*, London: Routledge, 2000, p. 12.

10  'Singapore, China to sign free trade pact in Beijing', *Channel News Asia*, 21 October 2008, available online at www.channelnewsasia.com/stories/singaporelocalnews/view/384360/1/.html

11  Zheng, note 6.

12  L. Wang, 'China's Expanding Outward Investment in Singapore', (2012) 4 *East Asian Policy* pp. 73–84.

13  Y. Liu, 'Facing the Challenge of Rising China: Singapore's Responses', (2009) 29 *Journal of Policy Modeling* p. 505; F. Herschede, 'Asian Competition in Third-Country Markets', (1991) 31 *Asian Survey* p. 434. For a contrarian view, see, J. Ravenhill, 'Is China an Economic Threat to Southeast Asia?' (2006) 46 *Asian Survey* pp. 653–674.

14  N. Aggarwal, 'S'pore is China's Largest Investor', *The Business Times*, 6 November 2015, available online at www.iesingapore.gov.sg/Media-Centre/News/2015/11/S-pore-is-China-s-largest-investor

15  'Singapore and China armies to step up defence cooperation', *Channel News Asia*, 5 February 2018, available online at www.channelnewsasia.com/news/singapore/singapore-and-china-armies-to-step-up-defence-cooperation-9929100

196  *See Seng Tan*

high-profile treatment of Lee's funeral. When Chinese President Xi Jinping held his landmark summit with his then-Taiwanese counterpart, Ma Ying-jeou, in November 2015, it made perfect sense that the meeting took place in Singapore. Since those high points in Singapore-China relations, mistrust between the two countries has grown, spurred by a litany of divisive issues. First, Chinese anger over Singapore's response to the *South China Sea* arbitration.[16] Second, Chinese allegations that Singapore sought to include mention of the *South China Sea* arbitration in the final communiqué of the 2016 Non-Aligned Movement summit in Venezuela (a charge which Singapore has denied). Third, Singapore's long-standing security partnership with America and its persistent advocacy of the United States rebalance to Asia strategy, which China views as directed against its rise, has become a source of friction between Singapore and Beijing. Fourth, Chinese criticism of Singapore's ties with Taiwan since Tsai Ing-wen became President, which presumably led to the seizure in Hong Kong of Singapore's armoured military vehicles bound for home after a training stint in Taiwan in late 2016.[17] Lastly, the lack of a formal invitation to Singapore Prime Minister Lee Hsien Loong (hereafter 'LHL') to the inaugural Belt and Road Forum in Beijing in May 2017.[18]

Both sides have sought to reset ties. This much is clear with the positive developments of the Joint Council for Bilateral Cooperation (JCBC), an annual convention between China and Singapore. On their part, some Chinese pundits have portrayed the JCBC developments as indication that bilateral relations are 'back on track after a chilling spell'.[19] Likewise, leaders on both sides have sought to cast bilateral ties in positive terms.[20] Presumably, Singapore-China relations will continue to stay 'a step ahead of China's ties with other ASEAN countries', as President Xi intimated to LHL in Beijing in November 2014.[21] But in all probability, a qualitative change has occurred in their relationship as a consequence of the growing number of differences highlighted above. According to one Chinese view, Singapore is not unlike a deceptive 'overseas relative' because even though China willingly granted business priorities to

---

16  *In the Matter of an Arbitration before An Arbitral Tribunal Constituted Under Annex VII to the 1982 United Nations Convention on the Law of the Sea between The Republic of the Philippines and the People's Republic of China*, PCA Case no 2013-19, Award of 12 July 2016.

17  M. Chan, 'How Singapore's Military Vehicles Became Beijing's Diplomatic Weapon', *South China Morning Post*, 3 December 2016, available online at www.scmp.com/week-asia/politics/article/2051322/how-singapores-military-vehicles-became-beijings-diplomatic

18  B. Jaipragas, 'What New Silk Road Snub Means for Singapore's Ties with China', *South China Morning Post*, 18 May 2017, available online at www.scmp.com/week-asia/geopolitics/article/2094781/what-belt-and-road-snub-means-singapores-ties-china

19  L. Fan, 'China-Singapore Ties Back on Track After a Chilling Spell', *Global Times*, 1 March 2017, available online at www.globaltimes.cn/content/1035434.shtml

20  'Singapore, China Reaffirm 'Good and Warm' Relations', *Channel News Asia*, 28 February 2017, available online at www.channelnewsasia.com/news/singapore/singapore-china-reaffirm-good-and-warm-relations-7617246

21  K.B. Kor, 'Xi Offers Vision of "Asia-Pacific Dream"', *The Straits Times*, 11 November 2014, available online at www.asiaone.com/asia/xi-offers-vision-asia-pacific-dream

Singapore, it has been disappointed with Singapore's 'military alliance' with the United States, 'which may contain "the great rejuvenation of the Chinese nation"'.[22] As a Singaporean pundit has warily noted, the city-state's post-LKY relations with China 'will challenge Singapore's long-held strategy of making friends with all, and demands on the island nation to choose sides could be on the horizon. In this new normal, nothing will be easy'.[23] Why that would appear to be the case, this chapter suggests, is due to at least two things elaborated below.

## 12.2 Towards rules-based governance

As articulated by its Foreign Minister in a July 2017 address, the core principles of Singapore's foreign policy include the promotion of a global order governed by the rule of law, international norms and the peaceful resolution of disputes.[24] Singapore has worked with other like-minded countries to strengthen the rule of law, as evidenced in the role played by Singaporean diplomacy in delivering the 1982 United Nations Convention on the Law of the Sea (LOSC).[25] In late 2016, LHL identified freedom of navigation and overflight in the region as well as the establishment and maintenance of a rules-based regional and international order 'that upholds and protects the rights and privileges of all states and shows full respect for legal and diplomatic processes in the resolution of disputes' as key interests for Singapore.[26] The challenge was not only to get the Chinese to agree to that but also to persuade them to stick with it – particularly when shorter-term interests and the perceived costs incurred dis-incentivises against one's sustained commitment to that rules-based order. As LHL has conceded, China's rise and continued adherence to a rules-based international order is not a given in the context of ongoing major strategic shifts and the anxieties and pushbacks they engender.[27] Thus understood, as a rising – if not risen – power, the temptation to not play by the rules can prove overpowering, but one which China would do well to resist.

---

22 X. Sun, 'China and Singapore are Distant Relatives at Best', *The Globalist*, 20 December 2015, available online at www.theglobalist.com/china-and-singapore-are-distant-relatives-at-best/

23 S.H. Peh, 'Commentary: The New Normal of Singapore's Relations with China', *Channel News Asia*, 26 October 2016, available online at www.channelnewsasia.com/news/asiapacific/commentary-the-new-normal-of-singapore-s-relations-with-china-7761312

24 Cheong, note 1.

25 United Nations Convention on the Law of the Sea, 10 December 1982, 1833 UNTS 397 [hereafter LOSC]; see discussion in J.K. Sebenius and L.A. Green, *Tommy Koh: Background and Accomplishments of the 'Great Negotiator, 2014'*, Cambridge: Harvard Business School, 2014, pp. 3–4.

26 'Transcript of PM Lee Hsien Loong's Remarks at the Joint Press Conference with PM Shinzo Abe in Tokyo, Japan', Singapore Ministry of Foreign Affairs, 30 September 2016, available online at www.pmo.gov.sg/mediacentre/transcript-pm-lee-hsien-loongs-remarks-joint-press-conference-pm-shinzo-abe-tokyo-japan

27 'PM Lee Hsien Loong's interview with ABC Radio', Singapore Prime Minister's Office, 3 June 2017, available online at www.pmo.gov.sg/newsroom/pm-lee-hsien-loongs-interview-abc-radio

198 *See Seng Tan*

Notwithstanding Beijing's rejection of the *South China Sea* arbitration, Chinese officials and academics have averred their continued support for international law whilst paradoxically questioning its rationale and seeking to reshape it to better reflect Chinese interests and preferences.[28] Speaking on the side lines of the 2017 Shangri-La Dialogue in Singapore, PLA Lieutenant-General He Lei, responding to the allegation rendered by the United States and others that Chinese actions in the SCS contravene rather than uphold the rules-based order, countered that China (and the Chinese government) is in fact 'a protector and follower of international and regional rules' but also insisted that 'regional rules should represent the interest of the majority of the countries of the region'[29] – a non-too-subtle hint, perhaps, that the United States is not truly part of 'the region'. Granted, this sort of ambivalence is not unique to China alone; after all, great powers tend to see themselves as makers of international rules and laws rather than takers.[30] Be that as it may, the Chinese perspective of the nexus between rule and law is itself intriguing, not least because the development of law and governance in China is not as straightforward as it seems.[31] It has often been suggested that for the Chinese, it is rule *by* law, rather than rule *of* law, that truly matters because of the relative absence within Chinese polity and society of acceptance for natural law.[32] However, if law is treated by the Chinese as predominantly positive rather than natural, then it raises the possibility that there could be times when rule by law might be supplanted – or at least contested or complicated by – rule by man.[33] While Chinese dynasties have traditionally featured a mixture of those two ideas – rule by man and rule by law – throughout China's history, the notion that the ruling elite – whether the dynastic emperors of yore or the CCP since its takeover of the Chinese mainland in 1949 – should themselves be restrained by laws has however never been seriously considered.[34]

---

28 J. deLisle, 'China's Approach to International Law: A Historical Perspective', (2000) 94 *Proceedings of the Annual Meeting of the American Society of International Law* pp. 267–275.

29 Lieutenant-General He, Vice President of the PLA's Academy of Military Sciences, speaking on the side lines of the Shangri-La Dialogue, 3 June 2017, Singapore; cited in E. Ng, 'China upholds rules-based order, says Chinese general in response to US', *Today*, 3 June 2017, available online at www.todayonline.com/world/china-upholds-rules-based-order-says-chinese-general-response-us

30 As Allison has mused, 'Great powers do not recognize the jurisdiction of these courts – except in particular cases where they believe it is in their interest to do so': G. Allison, 'Heresy to say great powers don't bow to tribunals on Law of the Sea?', *The Straits Times*, 16 July 2016, available online at www.straitstimes.com/opinion/heresy-to-say-great-powers-dont-bow-to-international-courts

31 Y. Zheng, 'From Rule by Law to Rule of Law? A Realistic View of China's Legal Development', (1999) 25 *China Perspective* pp. 31–43.

32 The observation was rendered by Professor Wang Gungwu, former vice-chancellor of the University of Hong Kong and chairman of the East Asia Institute in Singapore, in his distinguished dinner address to the 19th Asia-Pacific Program for Senior Military Officers (APPSMO), 7 August 2017, Village Hotel Changi, Singapore, available at www.rsis.edu.sg/wp-content/uploads/2017/11/ER171130_APPSMO2017_WEB.pdf pp. 26–27.

33 L.K. Jenko, '"Rule by Man" and "Rule by Law" in Early Republican China: Contributions to a Theoretical Debate', (2010) 69 *The Journal of Asian Studies* pp. 181–203.

34 J. Chin, '"Rule of Law" or "Rule by Law"? In China, a Preposition Makes All the Difference', *The Wall Street Journal*, 20 October 2014, available online at https://blogs.wsj.com/

*Crossing the Rubicon*   199

Far from exclusive, Singapore's robust advocacy for rules-based governance can also be seen against a regional backdrop of growing awareness of, and appreciation for, the same. Reflecting on the SCS disputes, Singapore's Tommy Koh made this claim: 'with the exception of China, Asians do not have a negative attitude towards settling their disputes by arbitration or adjudication. China should therefore reconsider its position in order to conform to the best Asian and international practice'.[35] While not incorrect, the claim is arguably extravagant since South East Asia's record in rules-based management of regional security has at best been patchy. Despite the existence of the ASEAN Charter, South East Asia still has a long way to go in emulating the legal character of more advanced international organisations (if indeed that is what South East Asians aim to do).[36] There are compelling reasons that argue against that, furnished by 'path-dependence' explanations of ASEAN regionalism.[37] As a former secretary-general of ASEAN once lamented, comparisons between ASEAN and the European Union are neither fair nor judicious, especially if they are motivated by the assumption that South East Asian regionalists not only aspire to attain the institutional and legal standards and practices adhered to by their European counterparts, but that they should therefore be held accountable to those expectations.[38]

What does the historical and contemporary record suggest about South East Asia's engagement with rules? Two broad observations are noteworthy. First, the ASEAN Charter[39] appears to underscore the ASEAN member countries'

---

chinarealtime/2014/10/20/rule-of-law-or-rule-by-law-in-china-a-preposition-makes-all-the-difference/

35 T. Koh, 'The Asian Way to Settle Disputes', *The Straits Times*, 10 June 2015, available online at www.straitstimes.com/opinion/the-asian-way-to-settle-disputes

36 In this regard, there is a conceptual distinction between mimicry and emulation. To the extent ASEAN now has a charter and boasts a vision for building an ASEAN Community with economic, political-security and socio-cultural pillars – the language is reminiscent of the European Community (EC) and the EU – one can say ASEAN is mimicking the EU in terms of the superficial borrowing of lexicon and institutional conventions. On the other hand, emulation involves greater effort and deep internalization of the principles, norms and practices of the organisation the emulating actor seeks to emulate. At this point, it is safe to say ASEAN is a mimicker of more advanced institutions, but whether it successfully evolves into an emulator of such remains to be seen. On mimicry/mimicking and emulation, see, A.I. Johnston, *Social States: China in International Institutions, 1980–2000*, Princeton: Princeton University Press, 2008, pp. 45–73.

37 O. Fioretos, 'Historical Institutionalism in International Relations', (2011) 65 *International Organization* p. 367.

38 As Rodolfo C. Severino, Jr., Secretary General of ASEAN from 1998 to 2002, has written: 'Will ASEAN be like the EU? Most likely not. At least not exactly. As the EU itself acknowledges, it is unique as a regional organization and will probably remain so. But we can expect domestic and external forces, the logic of globalization and the imperatives of regionalism to move ASEAN to resemble the EU more closely than it does today, and as ASEAN evolves, more closely than we can foresee today'; see, R.C. Severino, 'Will ASEAN be Like the EU? Remarks at the European Policy Center Brussels, 23 March 2001', in *ASEAN Today and Tomorrow*, Selected Speeches of Rodolfo C. Severino, Jr Secretary-General of ASEAN, (2002) available online at http://unpan1. un.org/intradoc/groups/public/documents/apcity/unpan010349.pdf, p. 235.

39 *Charter of the Association of Southeast Asian Nations*, 20 November 2007, 2624 UNTS 223.

## 200    See Seng Tan

evident preference for norms and principles such as 'respect for the independence, sovereignty and territorial integrity of member states', 'peaceful settlement of disputes', 'non-interference in member states' internal affairs', 'right to live without external interference' – hallmarks of the 'ASEAN Way'.[40] For some, this development is arguably regressive since it amounts essentially to a codification of *existing* agreements and norms, and burnishing them with a legal patina.[41] Others welcome the Charter but lament ASEAN's inability to achieve its own targets in regional economic integration.[42] Noting how the Charter's drafters had ignored many important recommendations from the Eminent Persons Group (EPG) commissioned to provide recommendations to the drafters – recommendations which countries like Singapore and Indonesia lobbied hard to include, but ultimately conceded to conservative members due to ASEAN-style consensus[43] – an analyst concluded that 'the document reaffirms a state-centric ASEAN and institutionalizes age-old values of consensus and non-interference. It lacks clear mechanisms for dispute settlement, accountability and redress'.[44] On the other hand, the Charter's architects argue that the Charter constitutes an important achievement upon which further institutional developments and embellishments could and would be made. As Tommy Koh, Singapore's appointed representative to the High-Level Task Force which drafted the Charter, observed

> Negotiation on a protocol to implement the chapter in the Charter on dispute settlement is the most important unfinished business. One of ASEAN's past failings was a culture of not taking its commitments seriously. The Charter seeks to change that by giving the Secretary-General the responsibility to monitor the compliance of member-states with their commitments. In the event of a dispute between two states over their commitments, the Charter sets out an ASEAN dispute settlement mechanism. Such an arrangement will give assurance to partners entering into agreements with ASEAN.[45]

40  As Walter Woon, who was involved in the work of drafting the charter, has clarified, the chapter in the charter on the settlement of disputes only concerns *interstate* disputes: W. Woon, *The ASEAN Charter: A Commentary*, Singapore: National University of Singapore Press, 2016, p. 165.

41  B. Desker, 'Is the ASEAN Charter Necessary?', *RSIS Commentaries* CO08077,17 July 2008, available online at www.rsis.edu.sg/publications/Perspective/RSIS0772008.pdf

42  R. Severino, 'ASEAN Beyond Forty: Towards Political and Economic Integration', (2007) 29 *Contemporary Southeast Asia* p. 406.

43  On the politics behind the establishment of the ASEAN Charter and Singapore's role in that process, see, S.S. Tan, 'Herding Cats: The Role of Persuasion in Political Change and Continuity in the Association of Southeast Asian Nations (ASEAN)', (2013) 13 *International Relations of the Asia-Pacific* pp. 11–20.

44  T.T.H. Dang, *Examining the Engagement Between Civil Society and ASEAN in the ASEAN Charter Process*, Munich: GRIN Verlag, 2008, p. 24.

45  T. Koh, 'ASEAN Charter at One: A Thriving Tiger Cub', *Think Tank*, 9 December 2009, available online at lkyspp.nus.edu.sg/ips/wp-content/uploads/sites/2/2013/04/pa_tk_think-tank_Asean-Charter-at-one-A-thriving-tiger-pup_0912091.pdf

Thus understood, the Charter represents a work in progress, a first step in a long process towards building a culture of compliance to commitments. In 2010, ASEAN leaders adopted two legal instruments – the Rules for Reference of Unresolved Disputes to the ASEAN Summit and the Rules of Authorization for Legal Transactions under Domestic Laws – both of which were critical to the realisation of the Charter. At the same time, there were worrying signs that ASEAN could be hampered by what its previous Secretary-General, the late Surin Pitsuwan, once called 'problems in implementation'.[46] In this regard, the apparent failure of member countries to implement collective agreements and follow through on institutional commitments is a concern that could derail ASEAN's putative quest for a rules-based order. In 2010, the ASEAN senior official with oversight for the AEC implored urgently for concerted action by all ASEAN member States to move towards a 'results-based regionalism'.[47] Likewise in 2011, Surin urged member States to replace ASEAN's extant 'centrality of goodwill' with a 'centrality of substance'.[48]

The gap between ASEAN's legal aspiration and reality has not significantly improved a decade following the ratification of the Charter. For example, in 2016, members of the ASEAN Parliamentarians for Human Rights (APHR) criticised the apparent slowness with which their respective national governments are pursuing the improvement of the region's human rights record as pledged in the Charter.[49] A recent effort at Charter reform by ASEAN engendered only four proposals calling for relatively minor changes. Yet all this does not necessarily imply that ASEAN member countries are not adhering to rules, if by that one means the older diplomatic conventions of the ASEAN Way rather than the commitments specified in the ASEAN Charter. More crucially, despite falling short in its efforts to persuade and rally its fellow ASEAN countries to deliver a high-quality Charter, Singapore remains undeterred in its commitment to developing a rules-based regionalism.[50]

Second, how Singapore and its ASEAN neighbours have been settling disputes between and among themselves is perhaps more telling of the region's

---

46  Y.R. Kassim, 'ASEAN Community: Losing Grip over Vision 2015?', *RSIS Commentaries*, 2 June 2011, available online at www.rsis.edu.sg/publications/Perspective/RSIS0872011.pdf

47  S. Pushpanathan, 'Opinion: No place for passive regionalism in ASEAN', *The Jakarta Post*, 7 April 2010, available online at www.thejakartapost.com/news/2010/04/07/no-place-passive-regionalism-asean.html

48  Cited in M. Singh, 'ASEAN must do more to boost competitiveness: Surin', *Business Times*, 2 June 2011, available online at www.lkyspp.nus.edu.sg/aci/wp-content/.../20110602_ACR_Launch-Business_Times.pdf

49  'ASEAN MPs: Action must follow Sunnylands commitments', *ASEAN Parliamentarians for Human Rights*,18 February 2016, available online at aseanmp.org/2016/02/18/action-must-follow-sunnylands-commitments/

50  As Singapore's PM Lee urged at the ASEAN Foreign Ministers' meeting in early August 2018. N.A.M. Salleh, 'Asean Must Stay the Course and Press on with Economic Integration and Innovation: PM Lee', *The Straits Times*, 2 August 2018, available online at www.straitstimes.com/politics/asean-must-stay-the-course-and-press-on-with-economic-integration-and-innovation-pm-lee

## 202  *See Seng Tan*

incremental creep towards rules-based management of regional security than the preceding ambivalent account of the ASEAN Charter's evolution. Crucially, a frustrated regionalism has not precluded some ASEAN countries from relying on third-party adjudication to settle disputes involving trade and/or territorial jurisdiction, albeit still very much on a selective basis. In the area of trade-related disagreements, the dispute settlement mechanism of the World Trade Organization (WTO) has been underutilised by ASEAN countries by and large. That said, the first complaint lodged under this provision when it was introduced involved Singapore and Malaysia – two ASEAN members, no less – over import prohibitions on polyethylene and polypropylene, a case that was eventually resolved without WTO adjudication.[51] Furthermore, ASEAN countries have not shied away from settling their territorial disputes through bilateral negotiation or bringing their island disputes before the International Court of Justice (ICJ). Two oft-cited cases are the dispute over Ligitan and Sipadan islands between Indonesia and Malaysia, which Malaysia eventually won, and the dispute over Pedra Branca island between Malaysia and Singapore, which Singapore eventually won.[52] In the former case, the ICJ ruled in Malaysia's favour by virtue of the 'effective occupation' and/or 'effective administration' which Malaysia historically exercised over the islands.[53] In the latter case, the ICJ ruled in favour of Singapore on the basis of Malaysia's historical failure to respond to Singapore's conduct *à titre de souverain*, that is, its concrete manifestations of the display of territorial sovereignty over Pedra Branca.[54] However, the ICJ disagreed with Singapore's claim that Pedra Branca, Middle Rocks and South Ledge comprised a single entity and awarded the latter two formations to Malaysia instead. In July 2017, Malaysia applied to the Court to review its 2008 ruling but subsequently withdrew its application when the new Pakatan Harapan government led by Mahathir Mohamad took over in 2018.

The long-standing dispute between Cambodia and Thailand over the Preah Vihear promontory led Cambodia in April 2011 to seek an interpretation of the ICJ concerning its 1962 ruling, which had awarded the temple to Cambodia.

---

51 'DS1: Malaysia—Prohibition of Imports of Polyethylene and Polypropylene', *World Trade Organization*, available online at www.wto.org/english/tratop_e/dispu_e/cases_e/ds1_e.htm. For a discussion on WTO-related arbitration and adjudication cases involving ASEAN states, see, S.S. Tan, 'The Institutionalization of Dispute Settlements in Southeast Asia: The Legitimacy of the Association of Southeast Asian Nations in De-Securitizing Trade and Territorial Disputes' in H. Nasu and K. Rubenstein (eds), *Legal Perspectives on Security Institutions*, Cambridge: Cambridge University Press, 2015, pp. 256–259.

52 J.G. Merrill, 'Sovereignty over Pulau Ligitan and Pulau Sipadan (Indonesia v Malaysia), Merits, Judgment of 17 December 2002', (2003) 52 The International and Comparative Law Quarterly *pp. 797–802*; S. Jayakumar and T. Koh, *Pedra Branca: The Road to the World Court*, Singapore: National University of Singapore Press, 2009.

53 D.A. Colson, 'Sovereignty over Pulau Ligitan and Pulau Sipadan (Indonesia/Malaysia)', (2003) 97 American Journal of International Law *p. 398*.

54 See *Sovereignty over Pedra Branca/Pulau Batu Puteh, Middle Rocks and South Ledge* (Malaysia v. Singapore) [2008] ICJ Rep 12, [39].

Fighting broke out between Cambodian and Thai forces in February 2011, after which the Foreign Ministers of both countries appeared before the UN Security Council. Following Cambodia's request in April that year to the ICJ for an interpretation 'on the meaning and scope of the 1962 ruling',[55] Indonesia tried to mediate between the two conflicting parties at the sidelines of the ASEAN Summit in May 2011 – pursued at Jakarta's discretion in its role as chair of ASEAN – but its efforts proved inconclusive. In July 2011, the ICJ ruled that both countries were to withdraw their troops from a newly defined provisional demilitarised zone around the temple area and to allow ASEAN-appointed observers to enter the zone.[56] Further, the two claimant States were to continue working with ASEAN with the latter playing a 'facilitating' role in the resolution of the conflict. In November 2013, the ICJ unanimously upheld its 1962 ruling and clarified that the disputed territory belonged to Cambodia.[57] Both countries have indicated their respective governments and militaries would honour the ICJ's decision.[58]

The aforementioned successes notwithstanding, there remain stubborn bilateral disputes such as the Indonesia/Malaysia dispute over the Ambalat region, a sea block in the Celebes Sea off the coast of Indonesian East Kalimantan and southeast of Sabah in East Malaysia. Reportedly rich in oil and natural gas, the issue erupted following the decision by Petronas, the Malaysian State-owned oil company, to grant a concession for oil and gas exploration to its subsidiary, Petronas Caligari, and to the Anglo-Dutch oil giant, Shell, in a part of the Sulawesi Sea which Jakarta claims as its exclusive economic zone (EEZ) based on Articles 76 and 77 of the LOSC, which defines the rights and responsibilities of countries regarding their use of the world's oceans and marine natural resources.[59] In 2009, the Indonesian armed forces (TNI) accused Malaysia of having 'breached the law' by entering the disputed zone on no less than nine occasions in 2009 alone.[60] Further, a map produced by Malaysia in 1979, which depicted Ambalat or at least a large portion of it as under Malaysian sovereignty, evoked objections not only from Indonesia but some of its ASEAN neighbours as well as China. The dispute raised questions over whether Indonesia, having 'lost'

---

55 See *Request for Interpretation of the Judgement of 15 June 1962 in the Case concerning the Temple of Preah Vihear* (Cambodia v. Thailand), [2013] ICJ Rep 281, [64].

56 *Request for Interpretation of the Judgement of 15 June 1962 in the Case Concerning the Temple of Preah Vihear* (Cambodia v Thailand) (Provisional Measures), [2011] ICJ Rep 537, p. 151.

57 'UN court rules for Cambodia in Preah Vihear temple dispute with Thailand', *UN News Centre*, 11 November 2013, available online at www.un.org/apps/news/story.asp?NewsID=46461#. V2jTW00kqM8

58 S. Vong, 'Thai and Cambodian Rulers Agree to Civility', *The Phnom Penh Post*, 18 June 2013, available online at www.phnompenhpost.com/national/thai-and-cambodian-rulers-agree-civility

59 Y.R. Kassim, 'ASEAN Cohesion: Making Sense of Indonesian Reactions to Bilateral Disputes', *RSIS Commentaries*, 6 April 2005, available online at www.rsis.edu.sg/rsis-publication/rsis/676-asean-cohesion-making-sense-o/

60 'TNI moves to secure Ambalat', *The Jakarta Post*, 31 May 2009, available online at www.thejakartapost.com/news/2009/05/31/tni-moves-secure-ambalat.html

## 204 *See Seng Tan*

Ligitan and Sipadan to Malaysia, would subsequently prove twice as shy to bring the Ambalat dispute and/or other territorial disputes it has with Malaysia to the ICJ or other legal body. In June 2013, it was reported that both countries were prepared to shelve their dispute in favour of joint exploration of natural resources in the region.[61] In February 2015, following the lack of progress despite technical teams from both countries having met 26 times, both countries appointed 'special envoys' to initiate 'exploratory' negotiations over the dispute.[62]

Thus understood, Singapore's emphasis on rules-based governance is not entirely unique to itself, even if it is likely the most progressive among the ASEAN States on that score. Far from a regional imperative – no definitive Asian way of dispute settlement exists as such[63] – the development of a rules-based order in South East Asia remains at best embryonic. At the very least, it suggests that the Philippines' decision to seek international adjudication and Singapore's advocacy of international law are by no means *ex nihilo* actions given the regional context in which they have taken place.

## 12.3 Balance of power and US 'indispensability'

A second fundamental point of potential difference appears to be the notion that a stable balance of power is essential for ensuring the peace and security of the Asia Pacific. As an analyst has observed, LKY was 'remarkably consistent in his views about the balance of power'.[64] As LKY contended in 2013,

> Prudence dictates that there should be a balance of power in the Asia-Pacific region. This is reflected in a widely held consensus that the US presence in the region should be sustained. A military presence does not need to be used to be useful. Its presence makes a difference and makes for peace and stability in the region. This stability serves the interests of all, including those of China.[65]

For LKY, the role of the United States as the 'offshore balancer' is central – a position not entirely natural for Lee to adopt given his initial reservations about Washington's motives, commitment and fortitude.[66] Singapore has continued

---

61 T. Mattangkilang, 'Ambalat Border Dispute Ignored for Joint Indonesia/Malaysia Exploration Efforts', *Jakarta Globe*, 17 June 2013, available online at jakartaglobe.beritasatu.com/news/border-dispute-ignored-for-joint-exploration-efforts-2/

62 A. Panda, 'Here's How Malaysia and Indonesia Plan to Resolve Their Territorial Disputes', *The Diplomat*, 10 February 2015, available online at thediplomat.com/2015/02/heres-how-malaysia-and-indonesia-plan-to-resolve-their-territorial-disputes/

63 Koh, note 35.

64 C.G. Ang, *Lee Kuan Yew's Strategic Thought*, Abingdon: Routledge, 2012.

65 Cited in G. Allison and R. Blackwill, 'Interview: Lee Kuan Yew on the Future of US-China Relations', *The Atlantic*, 5 March 2013, available online at www.theatlantic.com/china/archive/2013/03/interview-lee-kuan-yew-on-the-future-of-us-china-relations/273657/

66 LKY's change of heart is discussed in S.S. Tan, 'America the Indispensable Power: Singapore's Perspective of America as a Security Partner', (2016) 8 *Asian Politics and Policy* p. 119.

*Crossing the Rubicon* 205

to maintain a durable and robust security partnership with the United States. Both countries share a bilateral free trade agreement and a security framework agreement that, for all intents and purposes, make them 'allies' in kind but not in name. In regional security terms, Singapore sees America as the present-day indispensable power for balancing against revisionist powers (the USSR during the Cold War, China in the post-Cold War period) and restraining potential ones (Japan through a bilateral security alliance).[67] Singaporeans and Americans see a strong confluence of interests, not least the maintenance of navigational freedom, access to markets and global financial stability.[68]

But unlike the Philippines and Thailand, Singapore has opted against a formal alliance with America; in 2003, Singapore reportedly declined an offer from the United States to be a major non-NATO ally.[69] Singapore opted instead to be a 'major security cooperation partner of the United States' provided for under the Strategic Framework Agreement for a Closer Cooperation Partnership in Defence and Security (SFA) signed in July 2005 between LHL and President George W. Bush. Reportedly born out of a shared desire to address common threats such as terrorism and the proliferation of weapons of mass destruction, the SFA extended and deepened already extensive areas of bilateral defence and security cooperation. These include those sanctioned under the 1990 Memorandum of Understanding Regarding United States Use of Facilities in Singapore and its 1998 Addendum, which grant the US military access to the air base at Paya Lebar, the Changi Naval Base (big enough to dock aircraft carriers even though Singapore does not own any), and the port of Sembawang in Singapore to where Commander, Logistics Group Western Pacific (COMLOG WEST-PAC) – the unit responsible for coordinating US Pacific Command (PACOM) military exercises – relocated in 1991 from the Philippines. These facilities were amply appropriated by US forces going to-and-from Afghanistan throughout Operation Enduring Freedom.

As part of President Barack Obama's rebalance strategy,[70] the SFA was subsequently reinforced by the launch in February 2012 of the Singapore-US Strategic Partnership Dialogue (SPD), a formal annual dialogue described by a former US ambassador to Singapore as a 'move up a weight class' in bilateral relations.[71] From 2014 onwards, Singapore began facilitating the rotational

---

67 Tan, note 4, p. 338.

68 R. Sokolsky, A. Rabasa and C.R. Neu, *The Role of Southeast Asia in US Strategy Toward China*, Santa Monica: RAND, 2001, p. 33.

69 T. Huxley, 'Singapore and the US: Not Quite Allies', *The Strategist*, 30 July 2012, available online at www.aspistrategist.org.au/singapore-and-the-us-not-quite-allies/

70 For an extended treatment of Singapore's support of the US rebalance, see, S.S. Tan, 'Facilitating the US Rebalance: Challenges and Prospects for Singapore as America's Security Partner', (2016) 12 (3) *Security Challenges* p. 20.

71 D. Adelman, 'The US-Singapore Strategic Partnership: Bilateral Relations Move Up a Weight Class', (Spring 2012) *The Ambassadors REVIEW*, available online at www.americanambassadors. org/publications/ambassadors-review/spring-2012/the-us-singapore-strategic-partnership-bilateral-relations-move-up-a-weight-class

deployments of US Navy littoral combat ships (LCSs) and, in 2015, P-8A Poseidon military reconnaissance aircraft.[72] Both these developments have been regarded by the Chinese as a clear indication of Singapore's robust support for America's rebalancing strategy. Finally, the city-State has also worked assiduously to cultivate and ensure America's continued involvement in the region through the East Asia Summit (EAS) and – until President Donald Trump withdrew the US from it in January 2017 – the Trans-Pacific Partnership (TPP) trade pact. It has been suggested that such deliberate support of US engagement have been viewed by the Chinese as a betrayal especially in the context of the ostensible special relationship Singapore has hitherto had with China.[73] As Singapore's former top diplomat Bilahari Kausikan once mused,

> Singapore has a very good relationship with China. But Chinese leaders and officials, despite our repeatedly correcting them, persistently refer to Singapore as a 'Chinese country' and say that we should therefore 'understand' them better, meaning of course that we more than other countries should know our position in life and show deference even at the cost of our own interests.[74]

Fundamentally, Singapore's view of US indispensability and its proactive facilitation of the US rebalance have been taken by the Chinese, fairly or otherwise, to connote Singaporean support for what Beijing considers amounts to a US-led containment of China. In Chinese eyes, comments by LHL like the following strongly imply that Singapore favours the United States as the undisputed preponderant power and strategic guarantor of the Asia Pacific and would like to keep it that way:[75]

> Singapore and the US are close friends and strategic partners. Our relationship is excellent and covers many areas, from trade to defence and counterterrorism. The friendship has endured because it is rooted in shared interests and compatible international perspectives ... America continues to play a vital role in Asia's stability and prosperity. You have important interests here that needs to be nurtured, amidst your many other commitments worldwide. Singapore looks forward to greater US engagement in this part of the world, and I believe so do many other South East Asian countries ... Your steadfast leadership has helped to anchor this effort to make the world a better and safer place for us all.[76]

---

72 Singapore is not the only ASEAN country that has offered to host US Navy P-8A Poseidon aircraft; so too has Malaysia; see T. Moss, 'Malaysia Offers to Host U.S. Navy Aircraft', *The Wall Street Journal*, 12 September 2014, available online at www.wsj.com/articles/malaysia-offers-to-host-u-s-navy-aircraft-military-official-says-1410524618

73 Author's personal communications with Chinese scholars based in Singapore.

74 B. Kausikan, 'Dealing with an Ambiguous World Lecture II: US-China Relations: Groping Towards a New Modus Vivendi', IPS-Nathan Lectures, 25 February 2016.

75 Singapore's (and presumably the region's) ostensible preference for the United States to stay as the 'top dog' is assessed in E. Goh, 'Great Powers and Hierarchical Order in Southeast Asia: Analyzing Regional Security Strategies', (2007/08) 32 *International Security* p. 113.

76 Cited in J. Leong, 'Singapore: Review of Major Policy Statements', (2007) 11 *Singapore Yearbook of International Law* p. 294.

Also, as LHL averred at the 2015 Shangri-La Dialogue:

> The US remains the dominant Pacific power. The Pacific Command and the US 7th Fleet are a powerful force in being, and a key factor for peace and stability in the region. America's core interest in Asia has not changed and that is a stable region that is open to do business with all countries and a regional order that enables all major powers to engage constructively in Asia. America has played this benign role in Asia since the [Second World] War. Its presence is welcomed by many regional countries which have benefited from it, including Singapore.[77]

In other words, Singapore's long-held insistence over the importance of maintaining a stable regional balance of power and the perceived indispensability of the United States as the quintessential balancer – and its insinuation that 'many regional countries' feel the same way about the United States – is regarded by the Chinese as gratuitous endorsement of US hegemony – by way of the containment of China. This suspicion over Singapore's ostensible duplicity is equally characteristic of aspects of the Chinese media. For example, LKY once complained about the unfortunate predilection of the conservative Chinese press to translate his employment of the phrase 'to balance' as 'to conscribe', hence denoting containment. Such 'mistakes' have stirred Chinese anger unnecessarily.[78] Yet, this challenge and the difficulties discussed above have neither diluted nor dissuaded the firm belief and commitment which Singapore has invested in, and to, the US rebalance. But it is also such unremitting reliance on the United States that has aroused Chinese suspicions that despite its declared insistence on the balance of power as the prerequisite for regional stability, Singapore has in fact moved from its long-standing policy of strategic hedging and effectively sided with the Americans – an allegation vehemently denied by Singaporean leaders.[79] In an interview with the British Broadcasting Corporation in February 2017, LHL surprised many with his blunter-than-usual admission that his country's friendships with both Beijing and Washington could one day be tested. Conceding what many analysts have long been warned, PM Lee said

> If America, China relations become very difficult, our position becomes tougher because then we will be coerced to choose between being friends with America and being friends with China. That's a real worry. Right now

---

77 'Transcript of keynote speech by Prime Minister Lee Hsien Loong at the Shangri-La Dialogue', Singapore Prime Minister's Office, 29 May 2015, available online at www.pmo.gov.sg/mediacentre/transcript-keynote-speech-prime-minister-lee-hsien-loong-shangri-la-dialogue-29-may-2015
78 Tan, note 70, p. 32.
79 During a visit to the Chinese foreign ministry by a Singaporean Track 1.5 delegation in May 2017 (at which this author was present), the then Chinese vice-minister for foreign affairs, Liu Zhenmin, said as much in blunt comments to the Singaporeans.

we are friends with both – it's not that we don't have issues with either, but we are generally friends with both, and the relationships are in good working order.[80]

Chinese commentators are far from convinced, however. For instance, a *Global Times* op-ed article made much of the lavish reception – usually reserved for leaders of big countries and US allies – which President Obama gave LHL during a state visit by the latter in early August 2016. First, the article noted that Obama referred to Singapore as an 'anchor' of the US presence in Asia – a word, its author insisted, that has only been used to describe either Australia or Japan.[81] Singapore was also described by Obama as a 'solid-rock' partner.[82] Second, the article averred that since the US rebalance is (in the Chinese view) to a large extent directed against China, LHL's robust support for the rebalance implies Singapore has taken sides despite its protestations to the contrary. 'We understand [Singapore] has to survive among big countries', as Jin Yinan of the PLA's National Defence University has put it. 'But now Singapore is not seeking balance among big countries – it is playing big countries off against each other … this is playing with fire'.[83] The allusion to Singapore's support for a regional *im*balance of power that favours the United States, at China's expense, is unmistakable.

## 12.4 Conclusion

This chapter has sought to examine Singapore's evolving relations with China in light of the latter's rise and rivalry with the United States and changing expectations of its bilateral ties with Singapore. It has suggested that Singapore's present difficulties with China are due in no small part to the city-State's emphasis on rules-based diplomacy, which in itself can be seen against the backdrop of South East Asia's still embryonic but growing experimentation with rules and its advocacy for the balance of power in the Indo-Pacific region, which has been interpreted by Chinese audiences as unwarranted legitimation of US preponderance and containment of China. As the above discussion has sought to show, such actions have landed Singapore in trouble with China – a concern

---

80 Cited in N. Chandran, 'Singapore PM Offers Blunt Assessment of US Relationship', *CNBC*, 29 February 2017, available online at www.cnbc.com/2017/02/28/singapore-pm-on-us-china-relationship-we-must-choose-sides.html

81 The said article is discussed at length in a blog, 永久浪客/Forever Vagabond, 'China warns PM Lee over South China Sea', *The Independent*, 7 August 2016, available online at www.theindependent.sg/china-warns-pm-lee-over-south-china-sea/

82 J. Au Yong, 'Singapore a Solid-Rock Partner, says US President Obama', *The Straits Times*, 3 August 2016, available online at www.straitstimes.com/world/united-states/singapore-a-solid-rock-partner-obama

83 Cited in 'China should make Singapore pay over South China Sea dispute, says PLA adviser', *The Straits Times*, 1 October 2016, available online at www.straitstimes.com/asia/east-asia/china-should-make-singapore-pay-over-south-china-sea-dispute-says-pla-defence-adviser

that has evoked intense debate among the city-State's doyens of foreign policy regarding how Singapore should approach its relations with China. For example, counselling that 'small states must always behave like small states', former top diplomat turned academic dean Kishore Mahbubani argued that post-LKY Singapore must learn to be more discreet and exercise restraint in commenting on matters involving great powers – as it did (imprudently, in his view) over the *South China Sea* arbitration.[84] Others have offered stinging rebuttals. Admitting his 'profound disappointment' that Mahbubani 'should advocate subordination as a norm of Singapore foreign policy', Bilahari Kausikan has insisted that

> Independent Singapore would not have survived and prospered if they always behaved like the leaders of a small state as Kishore advocates. They did not earn the respect of the major powers and Singapore did not survive and prosper by being anybody's tame poodle.[85]

The public nature of that debate – rare for the Singaporean establishment – has not escaped international attention. At the very least, it should invite commensurate reflection among the Chinese on how best their country should relate to Singapore. According to one Chinese perspective, 'China would be better off if it viewed Singapore more rationally and objectively rather than as some prodigal son refusing to come home'.[86] That might not be a bad place to begin.

84 K. Mahbubani, 'Qatar: Big Lessons from a Small Country', *The Straits Times*, 1 July 2017, available online at www.straitstimes.com/opinion/qatar-big-lessons-from-a-small-country
85 Cited in 'Minister Shanmugam Backs Bilahari's "Brilliant" Response to Kishore's Article on Small States', *Channel News Asia*, 2 July 2017, available online at www.channelnewsasia.com/news/singapore/minister-shanmugam-backs-bilahari-s-brilliant-response-to-8997092
86 Sun, note 22.

# 13 Saving the South China Sea fishery*

*Marina Tsirbas*

## 13.1 Introduction

The South China Sea is the subject of sensitive, complex and competing territorial and maritime claims. Over the last five to ten years these have increasingly drawn international media attention and, at times, become the subject of nationalistic sentiment and politicisation. The territorial and maritime jurisdictional issues in the South China Sea are sometimes best understood by reference to a map,[1] but not all of the competing claims and jurisdictional issues can be explained in this way.[2] There are a number of islands and rocks in the South China Sea, and different features are claimed by multiple States.[3] Some of the disputes relate to which State has territorial sovereignty over an island or rock (and therefore the associated maritime jurisdiction generated by that feature), but there are also disputes with respect to China's Nine-Dash Line and the extent of maritime zones such as the Exclusive Economic Zone (EEZ) and the continental shelf.[4]

---

\* The chapter expands upon and is an updated version of M. Tsirbas, 'Saving the South China Sea fishery: time to internationalise', Australian National University National Security College Policy Options Paper No. 3, (June 2017), available online at https://nsc.crawford.anu.edu. au/department-news/10725/saving-south-china-sea-fishery-time-internationalise. The chapter represents work presented by the author at the 2017 Centre for Military and Security Law Conference, with editorial update/amendment and reflects the author's own personal views.

1 See Figure 1.1 in Chapter 1.

2 However, as other chapters in this book have identified, the situation in the South China Sea is more complex than the rather simplified picture depicted in Figure 1.1; see in particular Schofield in Chapter 3.

3 For example, the Spratlys are subject to claims by Brunei, China, Malaysia, Philippines, Vietnam and Taiwan; the Paracels are subject to claims by China and Vietnam; China and the Philippines also contest claims to other maritime features. See generally R. Beckman, 'The UN Convention on the Law of the Sea and the Maritime Disputes in the South China Sea', (2013) 107 *American Journal of International Law* pp. 142–163.

4 For example, Malaysia and Vietnam lodged a formal submission to the Commission on the Limits of the Continental Shelf defining the outer limits of their extended continental shelf in the South China Sea, and that submission was disputed by China by third person note; see 'Communications received with regard to the joint submission made by Malaysia and Viet Nam to the Commission on the Limits of the Continental Shelf: China' CML/17/2009 (7 May

The United Nations Convention on the Law of the Sea (LOSC)[5] stipulates that States negotiate their EEZ boundaries, in essence, where they are within 200 nm of an opposite or adjacent coastline,[6] but in the South China Sea most States have not done so.[7] Adding to the complexity of the South China Sea claims has been the nature of the 'Nine-Dash Line' which China has used to support its rights in the region.[8] The precise nature of the claims that China seeks to make in reliance of the Nine-Dash Line is not clear, and it is highly contentious whether the continued reliance by China on any maritime claims arising from the Nine-Dash Line would form a valid basis to found maritime rights and entitlements under contemporary international law.[9]

Much of the attention of commentators and media over the last five years has been focussed on the creation of artificial islands and the strategic importance of the South China Sea for world shipping lanes and access to North Asian markets. However, this chapter posits that the state of the fisheries in the South China Sea is an equally important issue that requires urgent attention. It is estimated that 12% of the global fish catch comes from the South China Sea,[10] but those fisheries are headed for collapse.[11] This will have important national security implications for South China Sea regional countries and further afield. The ensuing security tensions may be exacerbated by increasing instances of 'fishing nationalism', whereby States focus on sovereignty in relation to fish.[12] Establishing a 'sovereignty neutral' international fisheries management regime could help to avoid those tensions,

---

2009), available online at www.un.org/Depts/los/clcs_new/submissions_files/mysvnm33_09/chn_2009re_mys_vnm_e.pdf

5 United Nations Convention on the Law of the Sea, 10 December 1982, 1833 UNTS 397 [hereafter LOSC].

6 LOSC, Article 74.

7 China and Vietnam have delimited their maritime boundaries in the Gulf of Tonkin; Malaysia and Brunei have delimited their boundaries; see discussion by Schofield in Chapter 3.

8 For an evaluation of China's nine-dash line see: Rothwell in Chapter 2; M. Tsirbas, 'What Does the Nine-dash Line Actually Mean?', *The Diplomat*, 2 June 2016, available online at https://thediplomat.com/2016/06/what-does-the-nine-dash-line-actually-mean/; and J. Ku, 'Is the Nine Dash Line a Super-sized Exclusive Economic Zone?', *Lawfare*, 25 March 2016, available online at www.lawfareblog.com/nine-dash-line-super-sized-exclusive-economic-zone

9 See the findings of the Annex VII LOSC arbitral tribunal *In the Matter of an Arbitration before An Arbitral Tribunal Constituted under Annex VII to the 1982 United Nations Convention on the Law of the Sea between The Republic of the Philippines and the People's Republic of China*, PCA Case no. 2013–19, Award of 12 July 2016 [261–262] [hereafter *South China Sea* arbitration].

10 U.R. Sumaila and W.L. Cheung, *Boom or Bust: the Future of Fish in the South China Sea*, Vancouver: University of British Columbia, 2015, available online at www.oceanrecov.org/news/ocean-recovery-alliance-news/boom-or-bust-the-future-of-fish-in-the-south-china-sea.html

11 See generally L.S.L. Teh et al., 'What is at Stake? Status and Threats to South China Sea Marine Fisheries', (2017) 46 *Ambio* pp. 57–72.

12 See for example, the discussion by L. Wijaya, 'The Rise of Indonesian Nationalism in Response to Illegal Fishing', *The Conversation*, 25 January 2018, available online at https://theconversation.com/the-rise-of-indonesian-nationalism-in-response-to-illegal-fishing-86947

## 212 Marina Tsirbas

manage the South China Sea fisheries resources and encourage habits of co-operation amongst claimants in the South China Sea. In order to achieve this outcome, there are a number of existing Regional Fisheries Management Organisations (RFMOs) that serve as useful precedents to draw from. In this respect, it needs to be observed that RFMOs are specifically provided for under the 1995 Fish Stocks Agreement[13] to the LOSC.

This chapter does not seek to make an assessment of how politically complex it may be to find a successful resolution to the fisheries management challenges that exist in the South China Sea. However, the chapter does provide a number of ideas for consideration by States that could reduce the current level of tensions regarding fish harvesting in the South China Sea while also providing some possibilities for future cooperation and harmonised activity among, and between, South China Sea States.

## 13.2 South China Sea fisheries

### 13.2.1 Managing South China Sea fisheries to promote security

The South China Sea fishery is being depleted at an unsustainable rate and in a destructive manner. The use of cyanide, dynamiting and reef destruction is not uncommon.[14] One study predicts a 50% decline in key fish stocks (as measured by catch) by 2045.[15] The individual 'sovereignty-based approach' in the claimant rich South China Sea will impede management of this valuable resource. Increased scarcity and fishing nationalism pose the threat of clashes and conflict. This issue is something that the international community and civil society should care about. States like Australia, and other like-minded States, which have traditionally played a strong role in the development of sustainable fisheries regimes internationally, should encourage key South East Asian States to look at a binding mechanism to manage the stocks, drawing on examples elsewhere in the world.[16] A legally binding fisheries management

---

13 *Agreement for the Implementation of the Provisions of the United Nations Convention on the Law of the Sea of 10 December 1982 Relating to the Conservation and Management of Straddling Fish Stocks and Highly Migratory Fish Stocks*, 4 December 1995, 2167 UNTS 88 (hereafter *Fish Stocks Agreement*), Articles 8–10.

14 *2016 South China Sea* arbitration, [829, 818]; see also L. Jing, 'Fish and Reefs under Siege as Feuding South China Sea Claimants Refuse to Cooperate', *South China Morning Post*, 10 June 2016, available online at www.scmp.com/news/china/policies-politics/article/1961538/fish-and-reefs-under-siege-feuding-south-china-sea

15 Sumaila and Cheung, note 10.

16 Regional States have set up a number of non-binding mechanisms or forums to try to manage marine environmental issues such as the ASEAN Working Group on Coastal and Marine Environment, the ASEAN Maritime Forum, United Nations Environment Programme (UNEP) programs such as the Coordinating Body on the Seas of East Asia (COBSEA), the Expanded ASEAN Maritime Forum and others. There is the Asia-Pacific Fishery Commission (APFIC), originally established as the Indo-Pacific Fisheries Council in 1948 by the UN's Food and Agriculture Organization (FAO). However, it has an advisory and information sharing role.

*Saving the South China Sea fishery*   213

regime would be the optimal result or tool. It would need to bring in key export destination States (the United States, Japan, China and the European Union (EU)), fishing States and entities (China, Taiwan,[17] Vietnam and Thailand) and the littoral States.

Acknowledging that achieving this would not be easy and would take a long time, steps could be taken down this path to build support. Greater transparency in highlighting fisheries practices, marine environment destruction and stock depletion in the South China Sea by civil society and others would be useful. A number of nations would have valuable expertise to lend in the development of such a framework given their long experience in establishing RFMOs in the Western Pacific, Southern Ocean and beyond.

### 13.2.2 Potential conflict brewing over fish

Fish stocks in the South China Sea are already a fraction of what they once were (down to as little as 5% of 1950s levels) and catch per unit of effort is a third of what it was 30–40 years ago.[18] Trend lines indicate that a collapse of a wide range of fish stocks is on the horizon. The undeniable situation is that what should be a renewable resource has been made finite.

Some of the South China Sea fish species are making their way onto the International Union for Conservation of Nature's 'red list' of threatened species in the near extinct category. More public focus on fish species and the impact of their disappearance would be useful.[19] Large parts of populations in coastal States (Philippines, Indonesia and Vietnam) rely on fish protein in their diet, and fishing makes a significant contribution to the economies of China, Vietnam, Thailand and Indonesia.[20]

Depleting fishing grounds in the South China Sea will force those who usually fish in those seas to travel further south into other States' maritime zones with implications for the environment and border security. For example, there have already been increasing numbers of Vietnamese fishing vessels straying into

---

17  Taiwan's engagement in many RFMOs and related fisheries instruments is commonly undertaken in its capacity as a 'fishing entity'; see *Convention on the Conservation and Management of Highly Migratory Fish Stocks in the Western and Central Pacific Ocean*, 5 September 2000, 2275 UNTS 43 (hereafter *WCPFC*), Annex I; and generally A. Serdy, 'Bringing Taiwan into the International Fisheries Fold: The Legal Personality of a Fishing Entity', (2005) 75 *British Yearbook of International Law* pp. 183–221.

18  Sumaila and Cheung, note 10, pp. 2, 4.

19  This conclusion was drawn by comparing the species of fish listed by Sumaila and Cheung, note 10, to the list of species listed by IUCN in the region and which category they were in according to their categories of endangerment; see IUCN, 'The IUCN Red List of Threatened Species', available online at www.iucnredlist.org/

20  Sumaila and Cheung, note 10, pp. 5, 8, 19, noting that 'Fish is the primary source of protein for the majority of Thailand's population.' (p. 5); '55% [of the world's fishing vessels] are in the South China Sea.' (p. 8); and 'In many poor fishing communities, fish catch is often a primary source of dietary protein' (p. 19).

## 214    *Marina Tsirbas*

Australian waters in search of fish over the last few years as they are pushed out of their traditional fishing grounds.[21]

As fish become scarcer, the risk of increased 'fishing nationalism' in the region rises. Domestic political pressure from disenfranchised fishermen or industries provides one of the key potential sources of pressure to governments in the region; which could lead to conflict. The reactions by Indonesian President Widodo in 2016 to incursions by Chinese vessels into the EEZ adjacent to the Natunas,[22] and Malaysia's concerns over Thai fishing vessels in its EEZ[23] are examples of the action taken by States to deal with such incursions. Fishing nationalism has also been used as a vehicle to support national maritime and territorial claims in the South China Sea, with China in particular leveraging its fishing fleet in this manner.[24] However, nationalist sentiment over fish has also run high in the Philippines and Indonesia over the last five years. It would be prudent to manage tensions over fish in the South China Sea to avoid escalation of these tensions. The sinking of a large Chinese flagged vessel fishing illegally in Argentina's EEZ in March 2016[25] is a reminder of how big the stakes around fishing can be.

Unless something is done, fish will disappear and the marine environment will continue to be degraded. China has been the major culprit by sheer size of effort over recent years but is not the only nation that seems to have engaged in destructive fishing practices.[26]

21 T. Kippen, 'Illegal Vietnamese Fishermen Getting Treated Like Heroes', *Daily Mercury*, 26 June 2017, available online at www.dailymercury.com.au/news/illegal-vietnamese-fishermen-getting-treated-like-/3193787/; T. Annett, '"Harsh": Ringleader of Gladstone's Illegal Fishermen Locked Up', *The Observer*, 10 March 2017, available online www.gladstoneobserver.com.au/news/breaking-illegal-cucumber-poachers-jailed-after-gl/3153541/; D. Bateman, 'Vietnamese Fishermen to be Detained for Illegally Fishing Off FNQ Coast', *Cairns Post*, 30 March 2016, available online at www.cairnspost.com.au/news/crime-court/vietnamese-fishermen-to-be-detained-for-illegally-fishing-off-fnq-coast/news-story/b404cf5f39ec995bfbb25781df667765?nk=f9dd05752 4b175564b9992d530f1a855-1547598940

22 See, for example, Y. Kwok, 'Indonesian President Jokowi Visits the Natuna Islands to Send a Strong Signal to China', *Time*, 23 June 2016, available online at http://time.com/4379401/indonesia-china-jokowi-natuna-sovereignty-maritime-fishing-dispute/; 'South China Sea: Indonesian Leader Visits Natuna Islands Amid Growing Tensions, *ABC News*, 23 June 2016, available online at www.abc.net.au/news/2016-06-23/joko-widodo-visits-south-china-sea-amid-tension-with-china/7539164. Widodo reportedly stated that 'there is no compromise on sovereignty': P. Hartcher and J. Topsfield, 'Indonesian President Joko Widodo says "no compromise on sovereignty"', *The Sydney Morning Herald*, 4 November 2016, available online at www.smh.com.au/world/indonesia-president-joko-widodo-says-no-compromise-on-sovereignty-20161104-gsi6yh.html

23 S. Panjarat, *Sustainable Fisheries in the Andaman Sea Coast of Thailand*, New York: United Nations Division for Ocean Affairs and the Law of the Sea, United Nations, 2008, p. 98.

24 See H. Zhang and S. Bateman, 'Fishing Militia, the Securitization of Fishery and the South China Sea Dispute', (2017) 39 *Contemporary Southeast Asia* pp. 288–314; and generally on this point McLaughlin in Chapter 8.

25 'Argentina sinks Chinese fishing boat Lu Yan Yuan Yu 010', *BBC News*, 16 March 2016, available online at www.bbc.com/news/world-latin-america-35815444

26 On destructive fishing practices generally in the South China Sea, see C.L. Wilkinson et al., *South China Sea* (Global International Waters Assessment 54), Kalmar: UNEP/University of Kalmar, 2005, p. 42ff.

*Saving the South China Sea fishery*   215

### 13.2.3 Why collective action?

As noted above,[27] there are different claimants in the South China Sea for different groups of maritime features. Unfortunately, there has also been a tendency to conflate the concepts of jurisdiction and sovereignty. While States have sovereignty over their territorial sea,[28] EEZ and continental shelf rights give to coastal States *jurisdiction* and *sovereign rights* with respect to certain matters in those zones but not sovereignty.[29] Nevertheless, there is a tendency to territorialise the EEZ and this serves to increase tensions and fuel public nationalist sentiment in South China Sea littoral States.[30]

An individual sovereignty-based approach will not work to preserve the marine environment and fish sustainability in the South China Sea. It is also out of step with the type of measures that have been taken globally to manage fragile marine ecosystems and fish stocks which straddle jurisdictions, such as the Fish Stocks Agreement, and it lacks the urgency that the situation demands. The Food and Agriculture Organisation (FAO) has estimated that a 50%–60% reduction in fishing effort would allow the fish to recover.[31] International momentum on protecting the world's oceans is gathering.[32] Optimally, the international community and regional States could look at setting up a RFMO and management frameworks with legally enforceable rules.

Given the strong market forces which are driving fishing in the South China Sea, the cooperation of regional States and those beyond is needed. For example, key target markets such as Japan, China, the United States and EU would need to take action on imports. A multiparty/regional organisation certification regime would offer the best prospect of success and avoid some of the loopholes that make Illegal, Unreported and Unregulated (IUU) fishing a problem globally. It would also avoid the risk of one nation 'certifying' unilaterally all of their catch.[33] States with marine and fisheries management experience could offer

---

27  See the discussion by Rothwell and Letts in Chapter 1, and Rothwell in Chapter 2.

28  LOSC, Article 2.

29  LOSC, Articles 55 and 76.

30  See generally on this phenomena I. Townsend-Gault, 'The "Territorialisation" of the Exclusive Economic Zone: A Requiem for the Remnants of the Freedom of the Seas?' in C.H. Schofield, S. Lee and M-S. Kwon (eds), *The Limits of Maritime Jurisdiction*, Leiden: Brill, 2013, pp. 65–76.

31  Sumaila and Cheung, note 10, p. 7.

32  As evidenced by the work under UN auspices on negotiations on a convention to manage and protect biodiversity beyond national jurisdiction; see 'International legally binding instrument under the United Nations Convention on the Law of the Sea on the conservation and sustainable use of marine biological diversity of areas beyond national jurisdiction' UNGA Res 72/249 (24 December 2017), which would in effect have application to high seas pockets in the South China Sea.

33  The EU already has a catch documentation and import prohibition scheme which might serve as an example; see *Council Regulation (EC) No 1005/2008 of 29 September 2008 Establishing a Community System to Prevent, Deter and Eliminate Illegal, Unreported and Unregulated Fishing* [2008] OJ L 286/1, available online at https://eur-lex.europa.eu/legal-content/EN/TXT/PDF/?uri=CELEX:02008R1005-20110309&from=EN; and *Council Regulation (EC) No. 1010/2009 of 22 October 2009 Laying Down Detailed Rules for the Implementation of Council*

## 216   *Marina Tsirbas*

capacity-building assistance to the region, ranging from enhanced maritime domain awareness to expertise on sustainable fisheries management, certification and catch accounting.

An example of a successful RFMO can be found in the Western and Central Pacific Fisheries Convention (WCPFC),[34] which draws in Pacific Island nations (and their EEZs); distant water fishing nations and entities; and others involved in the fishing supply chain, including port States and target markets.[35] The WCPFC focusses on the long-term conservation and sustainable use of highly migratory fish stocks, such as tunas, billfish and marlin in the western and central Pacific.[36] The WCPFC's terms are explicitly without prejudice to issues of sovereignty, stating that nothing within the Convention 'shall constitute recognition of the claims or positions of any of the members of the Commission concerning the legal status and extent of waters and zones claimed by any such members'.[37] Such an approach would seem particularly apposite to the South China Sea. Key distant water fishing States and entities like China, Japan, Taiwan and the EU, all with massive fishing fleets, are members. Another example is the Convention for the Conservation of Antarctic Marine Living Resources (CCAMLR),[38] which applies to the Southern Ocean. Following this approach would involve adopting ecosystem management, catch documentation and vessel monitoring schemes, surveillance, enforcement and market control measures.

In the South China Sea, the regime would need to encompass major fishing, claimant, trans-shipment and target market States. As a first and urgent step consideration of 'whitelisting',[39] or a moratorium by all nations and consumers on imports caught in that part of the world unless they are suitably certified as sustainably caught, could be considered. Certification should be multiparty

---

*Regulation (EC) No. 1005/2008* [2009] OJ L 280/5, available online at https://eur-lex.europa. eu/legal-content/EN/TXT/PDF/?uri=CELEX:02009R1010-20130917&from=EN

34  *WCPFC*, note 17.

35  As at 1 January 2019, the members of the WCPFC are: Australia, China, Canada, Cook Islands, European Union, Federated States of Micronesia, Fiji, France, Indonesia, Japan, Kiribati, Republic of Korea, Republic of Marshall Islands, Nauru, New Zealand, Niue, Palau, Papua New Guinea, Philippines, Samoa, Solomon Islands, Chinese Taipei, Tonga, Tuvalu, United States of America, Vanuatu; with American Samoa, Commonwealth of the Northern Mariana Islands, French Polynesia, Guam, New Caledonia, Tokelau, Wallis and Futuna as 'Participating Territories'; and Ecuador, El Salvador, Nicaragua, Panama, Liberia, Thailand, Vietnam as 'Cooperating Non-Members'.

36  A map of the *WCPFC* areas shows it as extending to the East Asian seaboard and the South China Sea, but in effect the Convention area does not include the South China Sea; see Western and Central Pacific Fisheries Commission, 'Convention Area Map' available online at www.wcpfc. int/doc/convention-area-map

37  *WCPFC*, Article 3 (2).

38  *Convention for the Conservation of Antarctic Marine Living Resources*, 20 May 1980, 1329 UNTS 47 (hereafter *CCAMLR*).

39  Which has been described as 'establishing a record of vessels authorised to operate in an' area such as an RFMO: J. Swan, *Implementation of the International Plan of Action to Prevent, Deter and Eliminate Illegal, Unreported and Unregulated Fishing: Relationship to, and Potential Effects on, Fisheries Management in the Mediterranean*, Rome: FAO, 2005, p. 19.

certification or through a regional organisation to prevent unilateralism. Nations like Australia with recognised and long-standing marine and fisheries management experience and expertise could offer capacity-building assistance to those States that do not have such expertise. In another context, Bergin[40] has argued for continued training and support in 'maritime intelligence' to parties to the Regional Plan of Action to Promote Responsible Fishing Practices (the RPOA-IUU)[41] which could also be adopted in the South China Sea.

The precise area bounded by such an RFMO would need to be informed by technical and scientific research on the fish species, their habitat and geographical distribution. It would also be the subject of negotiations by States Parties. The WCPFC notional area in the Western Pacific might be a starting point subject to a proper scientific analysis of the key species, their habitat, numbers, which are most in danger and demand the most urgent attention. It may be that the process would be incremental as well.

While whitelisting, or an import moratorium, may seem extreme, negotiating any cooperative management or legally binding regime would likely take many years given the lack of trust and competing claims in the South China Sea region. Along with trust, key member States and other players would need to build an appreciation of the gravity of the situation sufficient to enable claimants to accept the idea that, without prejudice to sovereignty, the need to cooperate to preserve the marine environment and fisheries, rather than engage in fishing nationalism, is urgent. The scope of the RFMO may well need to go beyond the South China Sea and encompass the South East Asian region to be effective given that some of the fish species are straddling.

Civil society should become alert to the implications for the environment, and the food security issues of failing to act.[42] An urgent step would be to further publicise the fate of the fishery. Previously, transparency initiatives related to island-building activities were effective[43] and there is no reason to doubt that

---

40 A. Bergin, 'Australia's Approach to Indian Ocean Fisheries: Towards Closer Regional Engagement', (2018) 14 *Journal of the Indian Ocean Region* pp. 100, 106–107.

41 Regional Ministerial Meeting on Promoting Responsible Fishing Practices including Combating IUU Fishing in the Region, 'Joint Ministerial Statement' (Bali, 4 May 2007) available online at www.rpoaiuu.org/joint-ministerial-statement/; the ROPA-IUU was endorsed by Ministers responsible for fisheries in Bali, Indonesia, May 2007 and has 11 member States (Australia, Brunei Darussalam, Cambodia, Indonesia, Malaysia, Papua New Guinea, Philippines, Singapore, Thailand, Timor-Leste and Vietnam).

42 Sumaila and Cheung, note 10: Fish is the primary source of protein for the majority in Thailand, especially people in remote villages (p. 5); Marine megafauna were once prevalent in SCS but are now rare, coral reefs are declining at a rate of 16%/decade (p. 2).

43 In particular, note the role played by the Asia Maritime Transparency Initiative (AMTI), available online at https://amti.csis.org/. The AMTI states that it is an 'interactive, regularly-updated source for information, analysis, and policy exchange on maritime security issues in Asia. AMTI aims to promote transparency in the Indo-Pacific to dissuade assertive behavior and conflict and generate opportunities for cooperation and confidence building'. AMTI has been gathering satellite imagery on island-building, documenting current status and changes; available online at

218  *Marina Tsirbas*

transparency around marine environment destruction and over-fishing could also effectively be done by civil society and highlighted in international fora.

Other relevant provisions of the WCPFC that could be drawn on provide that members are to take into account the precautionary approach[44]; an application of this approach would be most useful in the South China Sea. This could include action such as the establishment of a scientific committee, each member furnishing data to it to assist with compiling a picture of the fishery and setting catch limits. However, such an organisation would be stymied if the consensus principle applied to binding decisions or actions. In this respect, it needs to be observed that a number of RFMOs have moved away from using such a mode for decision-making. For example, the Commission for the CCAMLR, the Indian Ocean Tuna Commission and the WCPFC have adopted or modified their decision-making processes.[45] Particular attention would need to be given to voting instructions. In this respect, it should be noted that WCPFC voting allows for some decisions not to be taken by consensus.[46] This would be difficult in the South China Sea, but international negotiators would take their time in developing arcane voting provisions to protect their nations' interests.

The possibility of Antarctic Treaty principles being applied in the South China Sea has been the subject of some comment and analysis by scholars.[47] While

---

https://amti.csis.org/island-tracker/. AMTI is a sub-branch of the US 'think tank' Center for Strategic and International Studies (CSIS).

44  *WCPFC*, Article 6.
45  See *CCAMLR*, Article XII:

  1  Decisions of the Commission on matters of substance shall be taken by consensus. The question of whether a matter is one of substance shall be treated as a matter of substance.
  2  Decisions on matters other than those referred to in paragraph 1 above shall be taken by a simple majority of the Members of the Commission present and voting.

In the case of the Indian Ocean, Tuna Commission conservation and management measures are binding if adopted by 2/3 majority of members present and voting, although individual members objecting to decision are not bound. Non-binding recommendations can be adopted by simple majority; see www.fao.org/fishery/rfb/iotc/en. See also *Rules of Procedure 2014*; available online at www.iotc.org/documents/indian-ocean-tuna-commission-rules-procedure-2014, R. XII, which states:

(5) Recommendations and proposals of the sub-commissions can be adopted by simple majority. However, the preference would be to take the decision by consensus. Each member of the sub- commission will have the right to have its opinion included in the report.

See also *International Convention for the Conservation of Atlantic Tunas*, 14 May 1966, 673 UNTS 63, Article III (3):

Except as may otherwise be provided in this Convention, decisions of the Commission shall be taken by a majority of the Contracting Parties, each Contracting Party having one vote. Two-thirds of the Contracting Parties shall constitute a quorum.

46  *WCPFC*, Article 20.
47  For example, S.V. Scott, 'What Lessons Does the Antarctic Treaty System Offer for the Future of Peaceful Relations in the South China Sea?' (2018) 87 *Marine Policy* pp. 295–300 and articles cited therein.

*Saving the South China Sea fishery*   219

CCAMLR operates quite differently from the WCPFC and gives the Commission significant powers, the sovereignty neutral principles are useful.[48] In this respect, it is particularly noteworthy that Article IV of CCAMLR provides:

2   Nothing in this Convention and no acts or activities taking place while the present Convention is in force shall:

  a   constitute a basis for asserting, supporting or denying a claim to territorial sovereignty in the Antarctic Treaty area or create any rights of sovereignty in the Antarctic Treaty area;

  b   be interpreted as a renunciation or diminution by any Contracting Party of, or as prejudicing, any right or claim or basis of claim to exercise coastal state jurisdiction under international law within the area to which this Convention applies;

  c   be interpreted as prejudicing the position of any Contracting Party as regards its recognition or non-recognition of any such right, claim or basis of claim;

  d   affect the provision of Article IV, paragraph 2, of the Antarctic Treaty that no new claim, or enlargement of an existing claim, to territorial sovereignty in Antarctica shall be asserted while the Antarctic Treaty is in force.

In 2017 the Asia Maritime Transparency Initiative (AMTI), proposed a 'Blueprint for Fisheries Management and Environmental Cooperation in the South China Sea'.[49] That blueprint recognises the difficulties and sensitivities associated with establishing an RFMO. Relevantly, it also notes that the involvement by parties in the establishment and enforcement of the management area will be without prejudice to existing territorial and maritime claims and cannot be construed as recognition by any party of the claims of others. It also proposes scientific mapping of fisheries zones with the involvement of key States.

## 13.3  The *South China Sea* arbitration and its consequences for fisheries

The *South China Sea* arbitration[50] provided some important clarity on which of the South China Sea maritime features that comprise the area generally referred to as the 'Spratly Islands' are 'water' for the purposes of law, namely low-tide elevations (some), which are rocks (some) generating a 12 nautical mile territorial

---

48  For comment on this aspect of *CCAMLR* see A. Serdy, 'Antarctic Fisheries Management' in E.J. Molenaar, A.G. Oude Elferink and D.R. Rothwell (eds), *The Law of the Sea and the Polar Regions: Interactions between Global and Regional Regimes*, Leiden: Martinus Nijhoff, 2013, pp. 217, 222–224.

49  See CSIS Expert Working Group on the South China Sea, 'A Blueprint for Fisheries Management and Environmental Cooperation in the South China Sea', 13 September 2017, available online at https://amti.csis.org/coc-blueprint-fisheries-environment/

50  *South China Sea* arbitration, note 9.

220  *Marina Tsirbas*

sea, or islands (none) under the LOSC.[51] A consequence of the reasoning of the LOSC Annex VII arbitral tribunal's award is that none of the features generate an EEZ of 200 nm with the associated right to regulate and licence fishing around the Spratlys, other than within an adjacent territorial sea, which means that there is a large pocket of 'high seas' in the South China Sea for fishing purposes. This also gives rise to associated international obligations under the LOSC,[52] to manage the fisheries resources sustainably and collectively. In addition, irrespective of which State has sovereignty over the Spratly rocks (on which the arbitral tribunal did not rule), an EEZ near them could only be generated by another land mass such as that of Malaysia or Vietnam. China, as is known, rejected the ruling and continues to insist on its 'Nine-Dash Line' as having some level of unspecified importance in relation to South China Sea maritime zones.[53]

The LOSC Annex VII arbitral tribunal's award that China had breached the Convention's environmental obligations through some of its island-building activities provides additional support for action.[54] It has provided substance to the obligation upon States to protect and preserve the marine environment.[55] The offending behaviour by China, according to the Philippines submissions, involved using enormous vessels to reach down below the water line, slice up submerged reefs and deposit rubble, mixed with cement, on top of features to raise them above water and expand them.[56]

## 13.4 Other developments internationally

IUU fishing is of course not a new phenomenon and is a global concern. At its base, there is a strong commercial element.[57] The role and impact of fisheries subsidies has also been the subject of ongoing work in the World Trade Organisation

---

51  *South China Sea* arbitration, [281–648].
52  LOSC, Articles 116 and 117.
53  See *Statement of the Ministry of Foreign Affairs of the People's Republic of China on the Award of 12 July 2016 of the Arbitral Tribunal in the South China Sea Arbitration Established at the Request of the Republic of the Philippines*, 12 July 2016, available online at www.fmprc.gov.cn/mfa_eng/zxxx_662805/t1379492.shtml stating that China 'declares that the award is null and void and has no binding force … China's territorial sovereignty and maritime rights and interests in the South China Sea shall under no circumstances be affected by those awards'.
54  *South China Sea* arbitration, [815–993]; see the detailed assessment in T. Stephens, 'The Collateral Damage from China's "Great Wall of Sand": The Environmental Dimensions of the South China Sea Case' (2016) 34 *Australian Year Book of International Law* pp. 41–52.
55  LOSC, Article 192.
56  *South China Sea* arbitration, [852–859].
57  The FAO describes IUU fishing as being:

> one of the greatest threats to marine ecosystems due to its potent ability to undermine national and regional efforts to manage fisheries sustainably as well as endeavours to conserve marine biodiversity. IUU fishing takes advantage of corrupt administrations and

*Saving the South China Sea fishery* 221

(WTO). In the 2018 UN resolution on the Conservation and Management of Straddling Fish Stocks and Highly Migratory Fish Stocks, the UN expressed its support for accelerating work to complete the ongoing negotiations in the WTO to strengthen the disciplines on subsidies in the fisheries sector, including through the prohibition of certain forms of fisheries subsidies that contribute to overcapacity and overfishing.[58] Operative paragraph 83 of that resolution also relevantly provided:

> Reaffirms the need to strengthen, where necessary, the international legal framework for intergovernmental cooperation, in particular at the subregional and regional levels, in the management of fish stocks and in combating illegal, unreported and unregulated fishing, in a manner consistent with international law.[59]

## 13.5 Concluding remarks

Failing to act to preserve the fisheries of the South China Sea will have serious implications for regional States and the broader international community. Resolution of the disputes seems a long way off, but developing 'habits of cooperation'[60] may make it more likely to enter into LOSC provisional arrangements for the exploitation of resources pending the setting of permanent maritime boundaries.[61] The establishment of an RFMO to preserve the fish stocks of the South China Sea is an option that warrants close attention. Other States with experience with RFMOs and sustainability regimes and technical expertise, such as Australia, would be in a position to offer practical support on fisheries

---

exploits weak management regimes, in particular those of developing countries lacking the capacity and resources for effective monitoring, control, and surveillance (MCS).
FAO, 'Illegal, Unreported and Unregulated (IUU) Fishing', (n.d.), available online at www.fao.org/iuu-fishing/en/

58 'Sustainable fisheries, including through the 1995 Agreement for the Implementation of the Provisions of the United Nations Convention on the Law of the Sea of 10 December 1982 relating to the Conservation and Management of Straddling Fish Stocks and Highly Migratory Fish Stocks, and related instruments' (11 December 2018) UNGA A/RES/73/125, [123–125].
59 Ibid., [83].
60 See K.M. Campbell, 'East Asia and the Pacific: Maritime Territorial Disputes and Sovereignty Issues in Asia', Testimony before the Senate Foreign Relations Committee Subcommittee on East Asian and Pacific Affairs, Washington, DC, 20 September 2012, available online at https://china.usc.edu/east-asia-and-pacific-maritime-territorial-disputes-and-sovereignty-issues-asia, where Kurt M. Campbell, Assistant Secretary of the Bureau of East Asian and Pacific Affairs, Department of State (USA), commented, 'Joint exploration would not only allow claimants to reap material benefits, but could also help to build the habits of cooperation and collaboration that will ultimately be needed to resolve these disputes'.
61 Such arrangements are envisaged under LOSC, Articles 74(3) and 83(3).

management to regional countries. Civil society should promote, and governments could support, greater transparency and awareness on fishing practices and marine degradation in the region. Finally, trust and habits of cooperation that are built in addressing this issue may facilitate more trust in managing broader tensions and other disputes in the South China Sea, thereby contributing to the strengthening of maritime security in the region.

# 14 Dispute resolution and the law of the sea following the *South China Sea* arbitration

*Natalie Klein*[*]

## 14.1 Introduction

Given the long-standing, and seemingly intractable, territorial sovereignty disputes and contested maritime rights that persist in the South China Sea, the availability of feasible dispute settlement mechanisms is essential. Primarily, the key coastal States have emphasised the use of negotiations to address flashpoints and to provide a means to address longer-term governance. Yet a notable divergence from this practice emerged when the Philippines instituted compulsory arbitration against China under the United Nations Convention on the Law of the Sea (LOSC).[1]

The *South China Sea* arbitration[2] is an important showcase for dispute resolution and the law of the sea in South East Asia for several reasons. First, it was a clear reminder that a formal legal process of third-party dispute resolution with legally binding outcomes may be commenced by States within the region because of their status as parties to the LOSC. Second, due to China's insistence that there was no jurisdiction for this dispute to be resolved under the LOSC, the *South China Sea* arbitration highlighted the varied avenues of dispute resolution that were available to States in the region and how those avenues interacted with the LOSC dispute settlement regime. Third, the remedies and outcomes of the *South China Sea* arbitration further prompt interesting lessons for dispute resolution in the region in the future. The precise contribution of the arbitration may be difficult to discern given that there are a number of actors and issues at stake. Nonetheless, some influence must still be anticipated.

---

[*] Thanks to Jessie Zhang for research assistance and Matthew Kingsland for editorial assistance in the preparation of this chapter. Any remaining errors are of course my own.

1 *United Nations Convention on the Law of the Sea*, 10 December 1982, 1833 UNTS 397 [hereafter LOSC].

2 *In the Matter of an Arbitration before An Arbitral Tribunal Constituted Under Annex VII to the 1982 United Nations Convention on the Law of the Sea between The Republic of the Philippines and the People's Republic of China*, PCA Case no 2013-19, Award on Jurisdiction and Admissibility of 29 October 2015 [hereafter *2015 South China Sea (Jurisdiction) Award*]; *In the Matter of an Arbitration before An Arbitral Tribunal Constituted Under Annex VII to the 1982 United Nations Convention on the Law of the Sea between The Republic of the Philippines and the People's Republic of China*, PCA Case no 2013-19, Award of 12 July 2016 [hereafter *South China Sea* arbitration].

224  *Natalie Klein*

This chapter will identify the diverse disputes and assess the different modes of dispute resolution States may use in the future in relation to varied South China Sea issues: territorial sovereignty, maritime boundaries, navigation and overflight, fisheries and the marine environment. In relation to the different means of dispute resolution, the chapter will assess the utility of different regional mechanisms and agreements, such as the emerging Code of Conduct and the Code for Unplanned Encounters at Sea (*CUES*). It will be seen that conflict avoidance has been a key feature beyond formal dispute settlement mechanisms. The value of compulsory arbitration under the LOSC will be assessed in light of the Philippines' experience. The lessons learned from the latter experience may provide some indication as to the key ways forward in resolving both ongoing and future law of the sea disputes in South East Asia.

## 14.2 Types of disputes

As highlighted in the preceding chapters in this volume, there are a variety of tensions and conflicts that currently exist or could well emerge among South East Asian States as well as those States that have interests and act in the region. In briefly summarising these disputes, it is important to note that many are interconnected. Moreover, actors in the region do not all necessarily agree that there are 'disputes',[3] and/or would characterise the issue differently. Further, some disputes may arise or flare up because of short-term actions, whereas others are long-standing tensions or more slowly escalating disputes. As noted by McLaughlin and Nasu, '[The South China Sea] is surrounded by deep-seated intra-regional suspicions as to each other parties' broader objectives'.[4] Each of these dynamics as to the particular disputes implicates how they might be resolved, which will be addressed subsequently in the chapter.

### 14.2.1 Territorial sovereignty disputes

There are two primary issues of territorial sovereignty persisting in South East Asia. The first relates to ownership of a number of maritime features within the South China Sea (and the East China Sea).[5] Claimants to the small land features in the South China Sea include Brunei, China, Malaysia, Indonesia, the Philippines, Taiwan and Vietnam. The territorial rights over these small land features have been viewed as critical questions of national sovereignty, and are important for the marine resources lying in the waters around the land features. It is the coastal State that exercises sovereignty or sovereign rights over the adjacent maritime areas, and

---

3 Whether there is a 'dispute' may be a legal question for resolution in assessing whether a court or tribunal should exercise jurisdiction. For discussion, see Y. Tanaka, *Peaceful Settlement of International Disputes*, Cambridge: Cambridge University Press, 2017, pp. 8–9.

4 R. McLaughlin and H. Nasu, 'The Law's Potential to Break–Rather Than Entrench–the South China Sea Deadlock', (2015) 21 *Journal of Conflict and Security Law* pp. 305–337.

5 This chapter focusses on the South China Sea disputes.

Dispute resolution    225

so determining which State is actually the 'coastal State' is a critical first step for making and enforcing claims to marine resources. In addition, the location of these land features is viewed with increasing importance for military purposes, especially as China moves to militarise the settlements it has constructed on some of these features.[6]

The second territorial sovereignty question that persists in the region and has implications for dispute resolution and maintaining peaceful relations concerns Taiwan. Taiwan is not recognised as a State and its ongoing relationship with China is a source of tension as between Taiwan and China, as well as between other States that need to engage with each of Taiwan and China. Taiwan's status as a 'Fishing Entity' has facilitated its engagement in fisheries governance outside the South China Sea,[7] but how it might engage more broadly remains a question of debate.[8] In the context of the *South China Sea* arbitration, Taiwan's actions on Itu Aba/Taiping Island were placed under scrutiny when the Tribunal assessed whether any of the features in the Spratly Islands generated extended maritime zones and would have therefore limited the Tribunal's jurisdiction.[9]

### 14.2.2 Maritime boundary disputes

In the face of uncertainty as to sovereignty over small islands and rocks, the delimitation of maritime boundaries poses challenges and these disputes remain unresolved in the South China Sea.[10] States are unable to settle the outer limits of their maritime zones or demarcate boundaries of overlapping maritime zones where the land features may affect the drawing of the maritime boundary and it is not known which State may claim maritime rights from those features. With uncertainty as to the extent of the maritime rights of any particular coastal State, there are consequential difficulties in knowing which State may regulate maritime activities and enforce its laws in an area.[11]

---

6 See, for example, T. Phillips, 'Photos Show Beijing's Militarisation of South China Sea in New Detail', *The Guardian*, 6 February 2018, available online at www.theguardian.com/world/2018/feb/06/photos-beijings-militarisation-south-china-sea-philippines

7 See, for example, Z. Scanlon, 'Incorporating Taiwan in International Fisheries Management: The Southern Indian Ocean Fisheries Agreement Experience', (2017) 48 *Ocean Development and International Law* p. 35.

8 Song has proposed, for example, a memorandum of understanding between Beijing and Taipei to facilitate participation in discussions on a Code of Conduct; see Y. Song, 'The Declaration on the Conduct of Parties and a Code of Conduct in the South China Sea: Recent Actions Taken by ASEAN', in S. Lee and H.E. Lee (eds), *Northeast Asian Perspectives on International Law: Contemporary Issues and Challenges*, Leiden: Brill, 2013, pp. 29, 62.

9 *South China Sea* arbitration, [577–625].

10 A number of maritime boundaries in South East Asia have been agreed between the States concerned in the absence of territorial sovereignty disputes; see further discussion by Schofield in Chapter 3.

11 See N. Klein, 'Resolving Disputes under UNCLOS when the Coastal and User States are Disputed', in N. Hong and G. Houlden (eds), *Maritime Order and the Law in East Asia*, New York: Routledge, 2018, p. 253.

## 226 *Natalie Klein*

Related to maritime boundary disputes are other contested claims to maritime space that may be generated from claimed historic titles or the promulgation of straight baselines that are questioned for their conformity with the requirements of the LOSC.[12] As was amply demonstrated in the *South China Sea* arbitration, States have also questioned the entitlement of certain land features to extended maritime zones on the basis that the features in question are rocks, which only generate a territorial sea,[13] or low-tide elevations, which only have relevance for maritime rights when located within the territorial sea of a coastal State.[14] The presence of artificial islands and claimed rights generated from those features have also proven contestable in the South China Sea.

### 14.2.3 Navigation and overflight disputes

The uncertainty resulting from undefined maritime boundaries and contested sovereignty claims has implications for what rights of navigation and overflight may be exercised by States within the maritime areas of the South China Sea. For example, the United States, Australia and the United Kingdom have all engaged in exercises based on their claimed navigational rights in the South China Sea, despite China's protests against such activities.[15] While the conduct of different military activities in the EEZ remains polemic,[16] the rights of navigation and overflight have fundamental economic importance. One estimate is that '[m]ore than 10,000 vessels of greater than 10,000 dwt move southward through the South China Sea annually, with well over 8,000 proceeding in the opposite direction'.[17]

Navigation and overflight disputes also emerge where a coastal State may be seeking to restrict rights of navigation or overflight in ways viewed as incompatible with the rights that State has in the relevant maritime zone. For example, Indonesia or the Philippines may contest the right of a third State to engage in archipelagic sea lanes passage where those States differ on what constitutes a route 'normally used for international navigation'.[18]

In the context of overflight in particular, concerns emerged regarding China's declaration of an Air Defence Identification Zone and whether it could apply to both civil and military aircraft traversing the Zone without entering the

---

12 See discussion by Rothwell in Chapter 2.

13 By negative implication from Article 121(3) of the LOSC. It is also usually assumed on the same basis that rocks are entitled to a contiguous zone; see LOSC, Article 121(3).

14 LOSC, Articles 13(1), 13(2).

15 See, for example, A. Greene, 'Top Chinese Army officer Assures Australia free navigation in South China Sea "Never a Problem"', *ABC News*, 3 October 2018, available online at www.abc.net.au/news/2018-09-18/south-china-sea-free-navigation-never-a-problem-chinese-military/10260934

16 These debates are canvassed in Z. Keyuan, 'Navigation in the South China Sea: Why Still an Issue?', (2017) 32 *International Journal of Marine and Coastal Law* pp. 243, 253–259.

17 Ibid., p. 244.

18 LOSC, Article 53(12).

*Dispute resolution* 227

sovereign airspace of China.[19] There were also questions as to whether such a Zone could operate over disputed territories or when there were overlapping Zones.[20] Overflight disputes may be complicated by the interplay of regulations applying through the International Civil Aviation Organisation, the freedom of overflight recognised in the LOSC, and customary international law concerning rights of territorial sovereignty, the principle of non-interference, and the prohibition on the threat or use of force.

### 14.2.4 Environmental disputes

As discussed in the chapters by Warner and Scott in this volume, environmental governance and responses to climate change will be critical for States in South East Asia (and elsewhere) in the years ahead. In the *South China Sea* arbitration, the tribunal emphasised the core obligation enshrined in Article 192 of the LOSC to protect and preserve the marine environment. The tribunal considered that 'Article 192 thus entails the positive obligation to take active measures to protect and preserve the marine environment, and by logical implication, entails the negative obligation' not to degrade the marine environment'.[21] It further stated that this obligation must be 'informed by the other provisions of Part XII and other applicable rules of international law'.[22] Within South East Asia, degradation caused by land reclamation activities, the construction of artificial islands, harmful fishing activities, especially those that damage the marine ecosystem and different forms of marine pollution must therefore all be assessed by reference to core environmental principles. In this regard, claims may be made against States in the region for their harmful activities as well as their failures to act when required to protect the marine environment.

### 14.2.5 Resources disputes

It has been estimated that 20% of the world's fishery resources are located in the South China Sea.[23] Fisheries disputes are already prevalent within South East Asia, especially in the South China Sea, and, as Tsirbas indicates in her chapter, are likely to persist and deepen in the years ahead if cooperative mechanisms cannot be successfully implemented. While estimates vary, there are also predictions that the South China Sea holds 11.2 billion barrels of oil and 190 trillion cubic feet of natural gas reserves.[24] Exploration and exploitation activities are

---

19 For discussion see, for example, J. Su, 'The East China Sea Air Defense Identification Zone and International Law', (2015) 14 *Chinese Journal of International Law* p. 271; M. Vanhullebusch and W. Shen, 'China's Air Defence Identification Zone: Building Security through Lawfare', (2016) 16 *China Review* p. 121.

20 Su, note 19, pp. 298–302.

21 *South China Sea* arbitration, [941].

22 Ibid.

23 H. Min and Z. Aizhu, 'Cooperation in the South China Sea under International Law, (2014) 44 *China International Studies* pp. 88, 94.

24 See, for example, ibid.

228  *Natalie Klein*

already underway in the area,[25] but have caused controversy – especially evident with China's installation of oil platforms in areas claimed by Vietnam.[26] These competing economic interests may be exacerbated by the territorial sovereignty and maritime boundary disputes, as well as challenging strategic interests in this maritime region.

### 14.2.6 Other ocean uses

The scope of different disputes that may arise in a region, especially one dominated by a semi-enclosed sea, is potentially enormous. Depending on prevailing economic, political or social conditions, issues may emerge in responding to transnational crime with maritime elements, such as people smuggling, drug trafficking, fuel theft, hostage-taking, armed robbery and piracy.[27] The laying and protection of submarine cables for telecommunications and transfer of data between countries may become a maritime security issue. If relationships deteriorate between the littoral States, restrictions on navigation and overflight, as well as varied military activities, may become controversial. In each instance, rights and obligations under the LOSC and customary international law are implicated, and it is vital for the States concerned to have the necessary means to resolve their disputes peacefully. These avenues are addressed below.

## 14.3  Means to resolve law of the sea disputes

The variety of dispute settlement mechanisms available to States to resolve their disputes peacefully is encapsulated in Article 33 of the *Charter of the United Nations*, which highlights that States should seek 'a solution by negotiation, enquiry, mediation, conciliation, arbitration, judicial settlement, resort to regional agencies or arrangements, or other peaceful means of their own choice'.[28] These methods are not necessarily, or even usually, used in isolation and it may further be the case that different aspects of a dispute are resolved in distinct ways. This section highlights some of the legal avenues that are relevant for South East Asian States, as well as other States with interests in the region. In doing so, it assumes that peaceful means of dispute settlement are a primary concern and a preference for all concerned States. While incidents involving force have occurred in the region on occasions, they have usually fallen short of constituting a situation of armed conflict and there would likely be a disinclination to engage in provocative actions that might result in collisions and the sinking of vessels, with accompanying loss of lives.[29]

---

25  Ibid (estimating 2000 oil wells in operation in the region).

26  See M. York, 'ASEAN's Ambiguous Role in Resolving South China Dispute', (2015) 12 *Indonesian Journal of International Law* pp. 286, 298–299; see also Song, note 8, pp. 31–33.

27  For further background to maritime security threats in the region, see the discussion by Letts in Chapter 4.

28  *Charter of the United Nations*, 26 June 1945, 1 UNTS XVI, Article 33.

29  See generally D. Letts, 'A Review of Selected Measures for Reducing Potential Conflict Among Naval Vessels in the South China Sea', in J. Schildknecht et al. (eds), *Operational*

*Dispute resolution* 229

### 14.3.1 The LOSC framework for dispute settlement

For maritime disputes, the LOSC affirms the obligation to resolve disputes peacefully, and to use the variety of methods set out in Article 33 of the *UN Charter*.[30] When a dispute concerning the interpretation or application of the LOSC emerges, State parties to the LOSC are to proceed expeditiously to an exchange of views as to the means of dispute settlement,[31] and in some instances the dispute may be referred for resolution under a different treaty if certain criteria are met.[32] States are able to select any form of peaceful means of dispute settlement under their own agreement,[33] which may include the use of voluntary conciliation under Annex V of the LOSC.

Once these steps are considered and resolved, a State party may refer a dispute to compulsory procedures entailing binding decisions under Section 2 of Part XV of the LOSC. In doing so, the States potentially have a choice of procedure in selecting either the International Court of Justice, the International Tribunal for the Law of the Sea (ITLOS), ad hoc arbitration under Annex VII of the LOSC or special arbitration under Annex VIII, which involves experts in specific maritime areas being used to resolve the dispute.[34] If a State party has not selected a preferred forum, or the States in dispute have selected different fora, ad hoc arbitration under Annex VII is the default mechanism to be used.[35] When proceedings are instituted, one of the parties may seek the prescription of provisional measures to preserve its rights pending the outcome of the arbitral or adjudicative proceedings.[36]

A court or tribunal constituted under the LOSC has jurisdiction to resolve any dispute concerning the interpretation or application of that Convention,[37] and it may apply 'other rules of international law not incompatible' with the LOSC in so doing.[38] If there is any dispute as to the jurisdiction of the court or tribunal, that court or tribunal is competent to resolve this question.[39] There are a limited number of disputes that may be excluded from the subject matter jurisdiction of a court or tribunal operating under the LOSC, which are set out in Section 3 of Part XV of the Convention.[40] Some limitations apply in relation to

---

*Law in International Straits and Current Maritime Security Challenges*, Cham: Springer, 2018, pp. 143–160.

30  LOSC, Article 279.

31  LOSC, Article 283; *In the Matter of the Chagos Marine Protected Area Arbitration before an Arbitral Tribunal Constituted under Annex VII of the United Nations Convention on the Law of the Sea between the Republic of Mauritius and the United Kingdom of Great Britain and Northern Ireland*, PCA Case no 2011-03, Award of 18 March 2015, [378].

32  See LOSC, Articles 281, 282.

33  Ibid., Article 280.

34  Ibid., Article 279.

35  Ibid., Article 279.

36  Consistent with LOSC, Article 290.

37  LOSC, Article 288.

38  Ibid., Article 293.

39  Ibid., Article 288(4).

40  Ibid., Articles 297, 298.

## 230 Natalie Klein

all State parties, such as coastal State actions in relation to the conservation and management of marine living resources in the EEZ,[41] others apply at the option of a State party when joining the LOSC or any time thereafter.[42] The latter exceptions may include disputes concerning military activities,[43] or sea boundary delimitations of the territorial sea, EEZ or continental shelf pursuant to Articles 15, 74 and 83 of the LOSC, respectively.[44] Where a State has excluded these maritime boundary disputes, there is still a possibility of the dispute being referred to compulsory conciliation provided a range of conditions are met.[45]

Decisions of a court or tribunal constituted under the LOSC on jurisdiction and on the merits of the case are final and binding.[46] The LOSC provides that any decision 'shall be complied with by all the parties to the dispute',[47] but there is no formal enforcement mechanism available in the event of non-compliance.[48] As will be discussed further below, these features of the dispute settlement process available under the LOSC were tested to varying degrees during the *South China Sea* arbitration.

### 14.3.2 Regional agreements with ASEAN

Within South East Asia, there have been initiatives to reach both political and legal agreements to better manage their relationships in the maritime domain, particularly through the Association of South East Asian Nations (ASEAN).[49] As various disputes have become intractable, conflict management or conflict avoidance among actors in the region have been preferred techniques, especially in the face of unilateral action. McLaughlin and Nasu have described the current approach as

---

41  Ibid., Article 297(3).

42  Ibid., Article 298(1).

43  Ibid., Article 298(1)(b).

44  Ibid., Article 298(1)(a).

45  See Ibid., Article 298(1)(a). This option was pursued in the LOSC Annex V conciliation between Australia and Timor-Leste: *In the Matter of the Maritime Boundary between Timor-Leste and Australia before a Conciliation Commission constituted under Annex V of the 1982 United Nations Convention on the Law of the Sea between the Democratic Republic of Timor-Leste and the Commonwealth of Australia*, PCA Case no 2016-10, Report and Recommendations of the Compulsory Conciliation Commission between Timor-Leste and Australia on the Timor Sea of 9 May 2018.

46  LOSC, Article 296.

47  Ibid., Article 296(1).

48  Particularly when compared to the mechanisms available under the World Trade Organisation's Dispute Settlement Understanding; see *Marrakesh Agreement Establishing the World Trade Organization*, 15 April 1994, 1867 UNTS 3, Annex 2 ('*Understanding on Rules and Procedures Governing the Settlement of Disputes*'), Articles 3, 19, 22.

49  Four members of ASEAN are also claimants to maritime areas in the South China Sea. Although Indonesia is not a formal claimant, there have been recent confrontations between Indonesia and Chinese fishing vessels in relation to Indonesia's claimed EEZ of its Natuna Islands; see N. Kipgen, 'ASEAN and China in the South China Sea', (2018) 49 *Asian Affairs* pp. 433, 444. ASEAN also has to balance the interests of non-claimant States that have favourable relationships with China (Myanmar, Laos and Cambodia); see M. Majumdar, 'The ASEAN Way of Conflict Management in the South China Sea', (2015) 39 *Strategic Analysis* pp. 73, 76, 77.

*Dispute resolution*    231

One of stagnated cooperation – which can be characterized as being driven, at the strategic level, by the use of (predominantly) ASEAN's consensual and collective processes to balance the Chinese "divide and conquer" policy, uncomfortably buttressed at the tactical level by the use of unilateral tactics on-water, such as the militarization of islets and rocks, and clashes between fishing, coast guard and naval units.[50]

The ASEAN approach to managing relations between members is typified in documents such as the *Treaty of Amity and Cooperation in Southeast Asia (TAC)*.[51] This Treaty affirms principles of sovereignty and territorial integrity, including the principles of non-interference in domestic affairs and non-use of force.[52] The *TAC* reaffirms the obligation to settle disputes by peaceful means,[53] and requires consultation and discussion. Cooperative modes of conduct are also encouraged.[54] China became a party to the *TAC* in 2003,[55] and has also engaged with ASEAN on South China Sea issues through the ASEAN Regional Forum.[56]

An important recent initiative in this regard has been renewed focus on a Code of Conduct for ASEAN members and China, which is to build on a 2002 Declaration of Conduct (*DOC*).[57] The latter document was very much designed to promote conflict management and avoidance; 'a product of the perceived necessity for the Southeast Asian claimants to address the security dilemma caused by the increasingly unequal power distribution in the area'.[58] However, the *DOC* does not address any of the questions of territorial sovereignty or maritime claims. Instead, it requires cooperation in relation to marine environmental protection, marine scientific research, safety of navigation and communication at sea, search and rescue, and combating transnational crime.[59] There is no enforcement mechanism, but States are to resolve their 'territorial and jurisdictional disputes ... through friendly consultations and negotiations'.[60]

Discussions on developing a framework for the implementation of this *DOC* were subsequently pursued with the adoption of Guidelines in 2011.[61] The

---

50 McLaughlin and Nasu, note 4, p. 307.
51 *Treaty of amity and co-operation in Southeast Asia*, 24 February 1976, 1025 UNTS 316 [hereafter *TAC*].
52 Ibid., Article 2.
53 Ibid.
54 See Majumdar, note 49, p. 73.
55 Song, note 8, p. 43.
56 See Majumdar, note 49, p. 76.
57 *Declaration on the Conduct of Parties in the South China Sea*, 4 November 2002, available online at https://asean.org/?static_post=declaration-on-the-conduct-of-parties-in-the-south-china-sea-2 [hereafter *DOC*]. For discussion on the drafting of the *DOC*, see Song, note 8, pp. 39–41.
58 McLaughlin and Nasu, note 4, p. 315.
59 *DOC*, Article 6.
60 Ibid., Article 4.
61 Embassy of the People's Republic of China in the Lao People's Democratic Republic, 'Guidelines for the Implementation of the Declaration of Conduct', 4 August 2011, available online at http://la.china-embassy.org/eng/news/t845898.htm

## 232  Natalie Klein

Guidelines highlighted steps that could be taken to allow for activities within the South China Sea, emphasising clear identification of those activities, the need for dialogue and consultations, and for consensus among the parties for any concrete measures to be taken.[62] However, a proposal that ASEAN consultations were required prior to meetings with China was dropped and has been viewed as a validation of China's approach to create disunity within ASEAN through bilateral approaches.[63] ASEAN subsequently reaffirmed its commitment in 2012 to the core tenets of the *DOC* in a Six Point Statement, which included support for the early conclusion of a Code of Conduct.[64]

In 2017, a framework for the Code of Conduct was agreed.[65] The proposed Code of Conduct is primarily intended to manage tension and build trust but the precise mechanisms for doing so remain to be determined at time of writing.[66] As negotiations progress on developing the Code of Conduct, concerns have been raised about a number of outstanding issues. Valencia identifies the following:

> who gets to sign it? ASEAN and China, or China and each of the ASEAN members individually, or even "outsiders" that use the area? What is the area to be covered by the COC – the legally disputed areas remaining after the Hague arbitration decision rejecting both China's nine-dash line claim and any EEZ or continental shelf for any of the Spratly features; the overlap of China's original claim with that of others'; the maritime zones around the Paracels; or just the Spratlys? And the most important unanswered question is whether the COC is binding and has dispute settlement and enforcement mechanisms.[67]

At the very least, the Code of Conduct is intended to elucidate what the claimant States may and may not do within the South China Sea.[68] The United States, Australia and Japan have called for a binding and effective code that is consistent

---

62 See discussion in Kipgen, note 49, p. 442.

63 See Majumdar, note 49, pp. 79–80.

64 ASEAN Foreign Ministers, 'Statement of the ASEAN Foreign Ministers: ASEAN's Six Point Principles on the South China Sea', 20 July 2012, available online at www.asean.org/storage/images/AFMs%20Statement%20on%206%20Principles%20on%20SCS.pdf; see also York, note 26, p. 305.

65 R. Cabato and J.C. Gotinga, 'ASEAN, China Adopt Framework for South China Sea Code of Conduct', *CNN Philippines*, 6 August 2017, available online at http://cnnphilippines.com/news/2017/08/06/asean-china-framework-south-china-sea-code-of-conduct.html

66 See M.J. Valencia, 'A South China Sea Code of Conduct? Don't Get Your Hopes Up', *The Diplomat*, 30 May 2017, available online at https://thediplomat.com/2017/05/a-south-china-sea-code-of-conduct-dont-get-your-hopes-up/

67 Ibid.

68 E.P. Santos, 'China, ASEAN Agree to Move Forward with Negotiations on South China Sea Code of Conduct', *CNN Philippines*, 29 June 2018, available online at http://cnnphilippines.com/news/2018/06/29/China-ASEAN-negotiations-South-China-Sea-code-of-conduct.html

*Dispute resolution* 233

with international law.[69] The Chinese Foreign Minister has said 'all the 11 countries, once they put their signatures on the document, they shoulder responsibilities and they need to observe the document'.[70] Yet in the absence of a formal dispute settlement procedure beyond negotiations, there remains a lacuna in relation to an effective regional mechanism for dispute resolution in the event the terms of the Code of Conduct are not observed.

### 14.3.3 Bilateral agreements and arrangements

Although the South China Sea dispute is very much multilateral in nature, this factor has not precluded the conclusion of bilateral agreements and arrangements to address more focussed issues of concern. China has preferred bilateral engagement on joint development proposals, but its efforts have been criticised as an effort to entrench its own preferred position at the expense of its neighbours.[71] China has, for example, engaged with Vietnam and concluded the Agreement on the Basic Principles Guiding the Resolution of Maritime Issues.[72] A Memorandum of Understanding on Marine Cooperation has also been signed between China and Indonesia,[73] as have other bilateral agreements between China and the other South China Sea claimants.[74] While the scope of these bilateral agreements may vary, there is a strong emphasis on cooperation and incremental improvements on issues of shared concern, such as marine research, resource exploration and disaster prevention and mitigation. China's position has been that bilateral negotiations are the best way to resolve disputes relating to the South China Sea.[75] As such, these agreements reflect efforts to avoid disputes and provide a mechanism to promote dialogue in relation to the identified issues in the agreements. These sorts of dispute settlement mechanisms are discussed further below.

## 14.4 Conflict avoidance

One of the most important techniques for conflict avoidance between military forces in the South China Sea has been adopted in the *CUES*.[76] An important function of the *CUES* is to set out a communications plan and manoeuvring instructions for when naval ships and aircraft encounter each other unexpectedly. The *CUES* also capture safety measures and procedures, which are drawn from

---

69 See Kipgen, note 49, p. 442.
70 Cited in ibid., n 24 (citing Chinese Foreign Minister Wang Yi).
71 McLaughlin and Nasu, note 4, p. 320; Majumdar, note 49, p. 77.
72 Discussed in Min and Aizhu, note 23, p. 97.
73 First in 2007 and another in 2012; see discussion in ibid., pp. 99–100.
74 Discussed in ibid., pp. 100–101.
75 Song, note 8, p. 53 (referring to comments of Chinese Foreign Minister Yang Jiechi in 2010).
76 The CUES were adopted at the 14th Western Pacific Naval Symposium, April 2014, available online at www.jag.navy.mil/distrib/instructions/CUES_2014.pdf

234 *Natalie Klein*

the International Regulations for Preventing Collisions at Sea.[77] The *CUES* are limited both as a non-binding legal instrument, and because they cannot prevent a situation where the military forces of one State decide to take steps that are considered deliberately provocative by another State. ASEAN and China adopted a joint statement to apply the *CUES* in the South China Sea in 2016.[78]

Other regional mechanisms have been mooted as possible models for managing aspects of the South China Sea disputes. For example, Oegroseno has pointed to the Coral Triangle Initiative, which requires cooperation for environmental protection even in the face of undelimited maritime boundaries, and the cooperation concerning the Straits of Malacca and Singapore, which also involves contested maritime boundaries but cooperation on burden-sharing and a shared interest in responding to maritime crime.[79]

Maritime confidence-building measures are also deployed to moderate tensions in the South China Sea as a non-confrontational mechanism. They thereby create a maritime environment conducive to the ongoing flow of international trade. These measures help 'to build maritime regimes that provide good order at sea … and … they serve as "building blocks" for habits of cooperation and dialogue that reduce tensions and promote peace and stability'.[80] The communications that result between navies allow for greater exchange of ideas and understandings as well as fostering relationships at an operational level.[81] One concrete example of this effort is the Guidelines for Hotline Communications among Senior Officials of the Ministries of Foreign Affairs of ASEAN Member States and China in Response to Maritime Emergencies in the Implementation of the *DOC*.[82] Guidelines such as these are seen as another step towards formalising a Code of Conduct as well as providing an additional avenue of communication between the parties concerned. Maritime exercises consistent with the *CUES* further fall into this category of confidence-building measures to promote regional maritime stability.[83]

Finally, it should be noted that provisional arrangements are contemplated as a means to regulate this maritime area without having to resolve definitively

---

77 *Convention on the International Regulations for Preventing Collisions at Sea*, 20 October 1972, 1050 UNTS 16 (hereafter *COLREGS*).

78 Joint Statement on the Application of the Code for Unplanned Encounters at Sea in the South China Sea, 7 September 2016, available online at www.fmprc.gov.cn/nanhai/eng/zcfg_1/P020170413336454220678.pdf

79 A.H. Oegroseno, 'State Practices in Southeast Asia: Possible Collaboration Amongst Claimants in the South China Sea Dispute', (2017) 32 *International Journal of Marine and Coastal Law* pp. 364, 371–372.

80 Australian Strategic Policy Institute, *Special Report – Maritime confidence building measures in the South China Sea conference*, 27 September 2013, available online at www.aspi.org.au/report/special-report-maritime-confidence-building-measures-south-china-sea-conference, pp. 9–10, cited in Letts, note 29, p. 155.

81 See Letts, note 29, p. 155.

82 Discussed in Keyuan, note 16, p. 266.

83 See K.S.L. Collin, 'Inaugural ASEAN-China Maritime Exercise: What to Expect', (2018) 131 *RSIS Commentaries*, available online at http://hdl.handle.net/10220/45495

*Dispute resolution* 235

key territorial sovereignty and boundary disputes.[84] There are many instances of joint developments between coastal States in situations where maritime boundaries are disputed.[85] Yet prospects of agreeing on joint development initiatives in the South China Sea remain remote in light of the competing claims between the different States. One commentator from the region has noted that key stumbling blocks in this regard include the precise location of any joint development zone; burden and profit-sharing, as well as who would operate the joint development activities.[86] China's willingness to engage in this regard is limited to joint exploration and economic activities, provided that such action does not reflect any notion of joint sovereignty.[87]

## 14.5 Lessons learned from the *South China Sea* arbitration

The previous discussion has demonstrated that there are diverse means of dispute settlement available to States in South East Asia to address divergent claims relating to the law of the sea. Moreover, it has been possible to identify various ways that States can avoid disputes, or avoid disputes escalating, through different governance arrangements, compliance mechanisms or interim solutions. Yet even with these options available, the Philippines opted in 2013 to institute legal proceedings against China within the framework of the LOSC's dispute settlement regime. This course of action was one of many possibilities for dispute resolution under the law of the sea available to the Philippines, and received only muted support from other ASEAN members.[88] States will undoubtedly engage in very careful calculations in any decision to refer a dispute to a third-party through litigation. Having pursued this option, the Philippines' experience in the *South China Sea* arbitration provides some important lessons for future dispute resolution of law of the sea disputes generally, and in South East Asia specifically. The elements to consider in this regard concern the scope of jurisdiction of any court or tribunal constituted under the LOSC; the significance of a State not participating in litigation; what remedies might be sought and are available; and the outcome following litigation.

### 14.5.1 Scope of jurisdiction

The first broad lesson to be drawn from the *South China Sea* arbitration is that jurisdiction is more likely to be exercised than not within LOSC arbitration or adjudication. As noted above, there are exceptions and limitations to

---

84 McLaughlin and Nasu, note 4, pp. 319 (n 60), 321.
85 See examples cited in Min and Aizhu, note 23, p. 92.
86 See Oegroseno, note 79, p. 370.
87 See York, note 26, p. 297.
88 C. Roberts, 'The South China Sea: Beijing's Challenge to ASEAN and UNCLOS and the Necessity of a New Multi-tiered Approach', *RSIS Working Paper No 307*, 29 August 2017, available online at www.rsis.edu.sg/wp-content/uploads/2017/08/WP307.pdf, pp. 4–5.

236  *Natalie Klein*

the exercise of compulsory jurisdiction in the LOSC dispute settlement procedures.[89] In this regard, the *South China Sea* tribunal considered the array of alternative dispute settlement options available to the Philippines and China to resolve their law of the sea disputes but considered that none of these trumped the option of the Philippines resorting to arbitration.[90] Moreover, although China had taken the required steps to place maritime boundary disputes outside compulsory arbitration or adjudication,[91] the Philippines successfully framed its case to address issues that were considered a first, but distinct, phase of boundary delimitation.[92] The Philippines did this by focussing on discrete provisions of the LOSC, concerning the meaning of islands and rocks, and low-tide elevations, and arguing that these questions of interpretation were not covered by China's exception to compulsory procedures and hence could be resolved through arbitration. This approach also ensured that the dispute remained within the subject matter of a 'dispute concerning the interpretation or application' of the LOSC,[93] rather than being conceived as a dispute relating to territorial sovereignty over the land features that were generating maritime zones.[94]

Despite the potential restrictions on the exercise of jurisdiction in the *South China Sea* arbitration, the tribunal determined that almost none of these applied.[95] If the reasoning of the *South China Sea* arbitration is to be followed in future cases, it is apparent that the dispute settlement clauses of other international agreements will not prevail over the dispute settlement regime available under the LOSC. Further, the exceptions to subject matter jurisdiction, as set out in Articles 297 and 298 of the LOSC, will be read narrowly so as to allow for a court or tribunal to resolve a large variety of international law of the sea disputes concerning the interpretation or application of the LOSC, as well as disputes concerning the interaction of the Convention with another instrument or body of law.[96]

### 14.5.2 Absence of a party

Consistent with the terms of the LOSC, an arbitration may proceed even in the absence of one of the parties.[97] In the *South China Sea* arbitration, China returned the Philippines' application and advised that it would not participate in

---

89  As indicated in LOSC, Article 286.
90  Such a possibility is seen in the operation of LOSC, Articles 281 and 282; neither of which were held to apply in this case.
91  Pursuant to LOSC, Article 298(1)(a).
92  *2015 South China Sea (Jurisdiction) Award*, [146].
93  LOSC, Article 286.
94  *2015 South China Sea (Jurisdiction) Award*, [152].
95  One exception was the military activities exception; see *South China Sea* arbitration, [1161].
96  *2015 South China Sea (Jurisdiction) Award*, [168].
97  LOSC, Annex VII, Article 9.

*Dispute resolution* 237

the proceedings in any way.[98] One consequence of this decision was that China did not appoint its own arbitrator but instead the President of ITLOS had the power to do so.[99] As a result, China denied itself the opportunity of a dissenting voice within the tribunal, if the Chinese-appointed arbitrator had agreed with China's legal position.

China's approach was to communicate certain views via a published Position Paper, as well as letters from Chinese ambassadors to the tribunal.[100] The tribunal was required to ensure that it had jurisdiction and that the Philippines' claims were well founded in fact and law.[101] To meet these standards, the tribunal carefully sought out and studied diverse evidence,[102] as well as recruiting experts to assist on specific questions.[103] The tribunal may well have utilised its best efforts in this regard, but China's refusal to participate possibly made it more difficult to refute the Philippines' claims or establish defences. For example, there were questions as to whether there was any actual (or sufficient) environmental impact assessment that may have been undertaken in relation to China's dredging and construction activities.[104] The tribunal determined that China violated its obligation under Article 206 to conduct and communicate an environmental impact assessment on the basis that China never communicated such an assessment to a 'relevant international organisation' for wider distribution as needed under Article 205.[105]

Any State party that refuses to participate in arbitration or adjudication under the LOSC procedures must therefore make an assessment as to whether its interests are better served acting within the regime or outside it. It cannot necessarily be assumed that the findings in the *South China Sea* arbitration would have been any different even if China had appointed its own arbitrator and otherwise contributed to the composition of the tribunal, nor if China had fully participated in the proceedings. It is nonetheless notable that even with China's formal non-participation, the arbitration still served as a catalyst for China to take some steps to clarify its positions publicly because of the proceedings.[106]

---

98 *South China Sea* arbitration, [29].
99 LOSC, Annex VII, Article 3(e).
100 *South China Sea* arbitration, [127].
101 LOSC, Annex VII, Article 9.
102 The tribunal's efforts in this regard are set out in the Award; see *South China Sea* arbitration, [121], [130–142].
103 Ibid., [136] (referring to the tribunal's decision 'to appoint coral reef ecology experts to provide their independent opinion on the impact of Chinese construction activities on the coral reef systems in the Spratly Islands'), [138] (referring to the tribunal commissioning an expert to 'review the available documentary material and draw independent conclusions' in relation to the Philippines' allegations of dangerous manoeuvring by Chinese law enforcement vessels).
104 Ibid., [989] ('Despite China's repeated assertions by officials at different levels, that it has undertaken thorough environmental studies, neither the Tribunal, the Tribunal-appointed experts, the Philippines, nor the Philippines' experts have been able to identify any report that would resemble an environmental impact assessment that meets the requirements of Article 206').
105 Ibid., [991].
106 McLaughlin and Nasu, note 4, p. 313.

## 238 Natalie Klein

### 14.5.3 Remedies

Pursuing litigation against a State party to the LOSC may present opportunities to seek reparations for violations of that treaty. Reparations are primarily intended to return the parties to the situation that existed prior to the commission of the internationally wrongful act.[107] In the *South China Sea* arbitration, the final decisions of the tribunal were reflected in a series of declarations as to whether China's actions had violated the LOSC.[108] To this end, the tribunal commented:

> The root of the disputes presented by the Philippines in this arbitration lies not in any intention on the part of China or the Philippines to infringe on the legal rights of the other, but rather – as has been apparent throughout these proceedings – in fundamentally different understandings of their respective rights under the Convention in the waters of the South China Sea. In such circumstances, the purpose of dispute resolution proceedings is to clarify the Parties' respective rights and obligations and thereby to facilitate their future relations in accordance with the general obligations of good faith that both governments unequivocally recognise.

The tribunal's views in this regard reflect support for States acting in good faith in their international relationships. While there may be disagreement as to whether States do conduct themselves in good faith in all instances, the tribunal was correct in its observation that clarifying the rights and obligations of the parties is an extremely important dimension to the resolution of international disputes through litigation.

There are two other notable dimensions to the lessons learned about remedies derived from this litigation under the LOSC. The first concerns the tribunal's holding that China was under an obligation not to aggravate the dispute between it and the Philippines once the case had been instituted.[109] This obligation was based on 'a principle of international law that is applicable to States engaged in dispute settlement as such',[110] rather than a specific provision of the LOSC. The tribunal did not, however, require China to take steps to reverse any actions that had caused the aggravation of the dispute.

Moreover, the other notable dimension is that the tribunal did not require China to provide reparations, either in the form of restitution or compensation, for any of its violations of international law. Indeed, as noted above, the Philippines had not requested any such form of reparations.[111] The approach of the Philippines may have made political sense in terms of assessing the minimal likelihood of compliance with any order to return artificial islands to their natural

---

107 *Factory At Chorzów* (Germany v. Poland) [1928] PCIJ (ser A) No 17, p. 47.
108 *South China Sea* arbitration, [1203].
109 Ibid., [1173].
110 Ibid.
111 The Philippines sought a declaration in its Submission 15 that would have required China to conform to the LOSC, but the tribunal did not consider it was necessary or appropriate to so order: ibid., [1201].

*Dispute resolution* 239

state or any order to compensate for environmental harm. Yet as an obvious legal response to violations relating to the protection and preservation of the marine environment, it may be a disappointing result for advocates supporting the restoration and preservation of the marine environment in the South China Sea.

The *South China Sea* arbitration at least did not rule out the possibility of ordering restitution or compensation in this situation. The decision of the International Court of Justice in *Costa Rica v. Nicaragua* demonstrates that States may be required to pay compensation for environmental harm caused in violation of international legal obligations.[112] For a State seeking compensation, it will need to establish clearly what losses and/or costs have been incurred to warrant a monetary payment. Some leeway may exist, though, as the Court stated, 'absence of adequate evidence as to the extent of material damage will not, in all situations, preclude an award of compensation for damage'.[113] The *Costa Rica v. Nicaragua* decision has highlighted the potential for compensation to be awarded by a State occupying disputed territory and causing damage to that territory through its activities prior to the sovereignty dispute being resolved.[114]

### 14.5.4 Outcomes of the arbitration

As the remedies in the *South China Sea* arbitration were ultimately limited to statements concerning the interpretation and application of the LOSC in relation to China's conduct, it fell to the parties to follow up on any further consequences in light of the tribunal's findings. China's position was that the tribunal's decision was null and void and should have no legal impact at all.[115] In subsequent negotiations with China, the Philippines secured the removal of Chinese military from Scarborough Shoal.[116] Otherwise, it does not appear that the Philippines has sought any further change in China's conduct in the area based on the award.[117] Similarly, the member States of ASEAN were largely circumspect in responding to the arbitration's award.[118] Given China's stated

---

112 *Certain Activities Carried out in the Border Area* (Costa Rica v. Nicaragua) [2017] ICJ Rep 97.
113 Ibid., [35].
114 See further Klein, note 11.
115 Ministry of the Foreign Affairs of the People's Republic of China, 'Statement of the Ministry of Foreign Affairs of the People's Republic of China on the Award of 12 July 2016 of the Arbitral Tribunal in the South China Sea Arbitration Established at the Request of the Republic of the Philippines', 12 July 2016, available online at www.fmprc.gov.cn/mfa_eng/zxxx_662805/t1379492.shtml
116 'South China Sea: Philippines says Chinese vessels have left Scarborough Shoal following Duterte visit', *ABC News*, 29 October 2016, available online at www.abc.net.au/news/2016-10-29/philippines-says-china-vessels-have-left-scarborough-shoal/7976964
117 'South China Sea tribunal ruling clings to relevance: experts', *Viet Nam News*, 18 July 2018, available online at https://vietnamnews.vn/opinion/451973/south-china-sea-tribunal-ruling-clings-to-relevance-experts.html#2Rlk4IIxD1pryfTt.97
118 Among ASEAN members, only the Philippines, Vietnam and Malaysia welcomed the *South China Sea* award; ibid. One commentator notes that 'ASEAN and China worked feverishly to tamp down tensions' following release of the award: Collin, note 83; see also Roberts, note 88, p. 7.

## 240 *Natalie Klein*

position, there would not appear to be any political benefit for any other State in the region to persist in the application of the tribunal's decision in further interactions regarding conduct and claims in the South China Sea.

Although only strictly binding on the Philippines and China,[119] the reasoning and findings of the *South China Sea* arbitration will nonetheless draw attention as other States party to the LOSC consider what the interpretations mean for their own understanding of their rights and obligations under that treaty. States may choose to adjust their behaviour to conform with the legal standards elucidated therein, or may choose to maintain a particular practice until challenged by other States parties either diplomatically or through litigation where those States rely on the views espoused in the *South China Sea* arbitration. Different aspects of the ruling may ultimately have greater longevity and influence than others. Each State in the region will need to decide to what extent they wish to rely on the ruling in their ongoing interactions in resolving law of the sea disputes.

## 14.6 Concluding remarks

In light of the complex range of disputes existing in relation to the South China Sea, it is evident that diverse dispute settlement and dispute management techniques must be deployed to ensure that tensions do not escalate further. Some commentators consider it unlikely that military hostilities amounting to an act of aggression will eventuate between China and the other claimants in the South China Sea.[120] To date, the emphasis in managing the dispute has been on confidence-building measures and managing the conflict between ASEAN and China, with varying degrees of involvement from other stakeholders. While emphasis is often placed on the role of ASEAN in addressing China's claims in the region, 'ASEAN's inability to build one united front on the South China Sea dispute is a major challenge for the regional bloc'.[121] The continued engagement of non-ASEAN members is thus critical, despite China's preference to restrict the issue to the littoral States. Preventive diplomacy, trust-building and peaceful modes of dispute settlement appear to remain cornerstones in the steps required to resolve ongoing and outstanding disputes in this region.

Although the significance of these political mechanisms to avoid disputes is undeniable, it is also important to note that these initiatives must still occur within an agreed legal framework, most particularly the legal framework established under the LOSC. The claims and counter-claims of the parties are drawn from their views of their legal rights in this region, and as such, the LOSC as the central treaty for defining these rights must be regarded as a critical avenue for

---

119 LOSC, Article 296(2).
120 See, for example, York, note 26, p. 302.
121 Kipgen, note 49, p. 445; see also Majumdar, note 49, p. 82.

*Dispute resolution* 241

resolving disputes. The LOSC dispute settlement regime is all the more important as a tool to reduce power differences that otherwise exist between States.[122] Hence it is important to understand how the LOSC dispute settlement procedures have been used in the *South China Sea* arbitration and to contemplate the lessons to be drawn from that experience in seeking to maintain peaceful relationships between stakeholders in the future.

122 Roberts, note 88, p. 21.

# 15 Challenges for the law of the sea in South East Asia

## Resolving current controversies and addressing horizon threats

*David Letts and Donald R. Rothwell*

## 15.1 Introduction

The law of the sea in South East Asia is currently facing many challenges. These challenges arise not so much from the law itself but from the consequences of the law of the sea for the region and how South East Asian States have responded to the law. As has been demonstrated throughout this book,[1] South East Asian States have been beneficiaries and strong supporters of the law of the sea, as framed around the 1982 United Nations Convention on the Law of the Sea (LOSC).[2] This is unsurprising, given that the two largest archipelagic States, Indonesia and the Philippines, are located within the region. However, while the LOSC has conferred many benefits upon South East Asian States it has also created new challenges. The most self-evident of these has been the need to negotiate an array of maritime boundaries in a tightly congested and contested maritime domain. Another consequence has been the greater entitlements of coastal States to the living and non-living natural resources of the seas and oceans within South East Asia. This has created a higher level of economic and food security for some States but has also resulted in some competition for these resources and associated management issues. In this regard another factor is Taiwan, its unique status and its needs and interests as a fishing entity. A final factor creating challenges for implementing the law of the sea in the region is that the LOSC confirms the status of South East Asian waters as ones in which certain freedoms of navigation apply. These freedoms extend from the waters of the Straits of Malacca and Singapore, where transit passage rights apply, to archipelagic sea lanes in Indonesia and the Philippines to the general freedoms of navigation for the ships of all States in exercising innocent passage and high seas freedoms in both the exclusive economic zone (EEZ) and the high seas. These navigational rights and freedoms are the lifeblood of trade and commerce throughout South East Asia and have been pivotal in the growth of regional economies.

---

1 See Rothwell and Letts in Chapter 1, and Stephens in Chapter 9.
2 United Nations Convention on the Law of the Sea, 10 December 1982, 1833 UNTS 397 [hereafter LOSC].

_Challenges for the law of the sea_   243

This chapter assesses the challenges confronting the law of the sea in South East Asia by first considering current and known controversies and how the law of the sea has responded to and is shaping those controversies. Consideration will then move to an assessment of known, assumed and potential horizon threats for the law of the sea in South East Asia.

## 15.2  Resolving current controversies

### 15.2.1  Territorial and maritime claims

Reflecting upon the dynamics of South East Asia's maritime domain noted above, a characteristic of the region is how unresolved territorial disputes have implications for the law of the sea which create an impediment for the resolution of maritime boundaries and related maritime issues. There is no greater example of this impasse than in the South China Sea, especially the claims and counter-claims made to territory in the Spratly Islands group. A failure to resolve these territorial issues will only further escalate existing nationalistic tensions throughout the region, which, in many instances, may result in a hardening of resolve to not make concessions. To that end, a critical issue is attaining a precise understanding of the maritime entitlements of the disputed features. In this regard, the _South China Sea_ arbitration[3] is instructive in that while the LOSC Annex VII Tribunal had no jurisdiction to resolve the territorial disputes, it was competent to pronounce upon the entitlements of the various maritime features that it was assessing, ranging from Article 121 islands, to Article 121 (3) rocks, to Article 13 low-tide elevations. While China has consistently rejected the authority of the _South China Sea_ arbitration, it remains the most authoritative decision of any international court or tribunal on this matter and is the only decision of its type with respect to the South China Sea. The _South China Sea_ arbitration is a legitimate basis upon which to characterise the various maritime features in the region, which may have the effect of neutralising aspects of the territorial disputes if a feature is found to be a low-tide elevation incapable of generating any independent maritime zone.

A resolution of the status of these maritime features is important for resolving maritime boundaries throughout greater South East Asia. While there is a developing track record with respect to the negotiation of maritime boundaries,[4] more boundaries remain in need of resolution in order to bring greater certainty to South East Asia's maritime domain. Other factors are also at play in this regard, including the assessment of Article 76 outer continental shelf claims before the Commission on the Limits of the Continental Shelf (CLCS), some

---

3  _In the Matter of an Arbitration before An Arbitral Tribunal Constituted Under Annex VII to the 1982 United Nations Convention on the Law of the Sea between The Republic of the Philippines and the People's Republic of China_, PCA Case no 2013-19, Award of 12 July 2016 [hereafter _South China Sea_ arbitration].

4  See the discussion by Schofield in Chapter 3.

## 244 *David Letts and Donald R. Rothwell*

of which may be significantly delayed as a result not only of the backlog in the Commission's work but also because of the Commission's refusal to consider applications where territorial disputes exist. In this regard, it needs to be recalled that LOSC Article 83 permits States to enter into 'provisional arrangements of a practical nature',[5] which may present some States with an opportunity to move ahead with the interim settlement of continental shelf boundaries pending resolution of CLCS submissions.

### 15.2.2 *Marine resources*

Whilst the LOSC has generated substantial maritime entitlements in South East Asia, it has also resulted in increased resource conflict over living and non-living resources. The high level of dependence within the region upon fisheries and other marine living resources as a food source has created increased competition for those limited resources resulting in significant challenges for EEZ resource management, including the policing of illegal, unreported and unregulated (IUU) fishers. This issue has increasingly gained prominence within the Association of South East Asian Nations (ASEAN), and in 2017 the ASEAN Regional Forum adopted a statement seeking to address regional IUU fishing challenges.[6] However, while some South East Asian States have given this issue increased attention,[7] responses have been variable.[8] In addressing this challenge, increased acceptance and rigorous implementation of the global, regional and sub-regional fisheries management frameworks is one foundation. New policy responses to meet this challenge are also essential,[9] some of which will require greater collaboration between neighbouring States akin to measures adopted in Europe and the South West Pacific. Ultimately, there is a need for a shared sense of regional fisheries stewardship and diminished competition.

With respect to South East Asian marine oil and gas reserves, a regional characteristic is that vast reserves are largely untapped due to ongoing maritime boundary disputes and claims and counter-claims over the South China Sea. It has been estimated that the South China Sea holds about 190 trillion cubic feet of natural gas and 11 billion barrels of oil in proved and probable reserves,[10]

---

5  LOSC, Article 83(3).
6  *ASEAN Regional Forum Statement on Cooperation to Prevent, Deter and Eliminate Illegal, Unreported, and Unregulated Fishing*, 7 August 2017, available online at www.asean2017.ph/wp-content/uploads/8.ARF-Statement-on-Cooperation-to-Prevent-Deter-and-Eliminate-IUU-Fishing-_Adopted.pdf
7  This has particularly been the case in Indonesia, see M. Tennesen, 'Blowing Up Illegal Fishing Boats Helps Indonesian Fishers', *Scientific American*, 6 August 2018, available online at www.scientificamerican.com/article/blowing-up-illegal-fishing-boats-helps-indonesian-fishers/
8  See M.J. Williams, 'Will New Multilateral Arrangements Help Southeast Asian States Solve Illegal Fishing?', (2013) 35 *Contemporary Southeast Asia* pp. 258–283.
9  See the discussion by Tsirbas in Chapter 13.
10  US Energy Information Administration, 'South China Sea', 7 February 2013, available online at www.eia.gov/beta/international/regions-topics.php?RegionTopicID=SCS

*Challenges for the law of the sea* 245

while in 2010 the US Geological Survey estimated an additional undiscovered 160 trillion cubic feet of natural gas and 12 billion barrels of oil.[11] With these estimates, it is unsurprising that the region has a record of maritime clashes over oil and gas exploration and development which have only served to heighten regional tensions.[12] Nevertheless, there are examples of South East Asian States working cooperatively on offshore oil and gas ventures within joint development frameworks as envisaged by the LOSC.[13] China, as the largest regional State and the one with the greatest energy needs, has begun to explore cooperative bilateral arrangements with Brunei and the Philippines.[14] Joint development of offshore oil and gas has a long-standing track record and can with political will and robust mechanisms bring about mutually beneficial results for all parties.[15] In the face of unresolved EEZ and continental shelf boundaries, joint development provides a way forward,[16] though the development of such a regime in the South China Sea poses complex legal and geopolitical issues.[17]

### 15.2.3 Marine environment

South East Asia has a complex marine environment which is facing multiple challenges.[18] Some of these, such as climate change, are global in nature, while others exist as a result of individual State actions that arise from land reclama-

---

11 US Geological Survey, 'Assessment of Undiscovered Oil and Gas Resources of Southeast Asia, 2010' Fact Sheet 2010–3015, June 2010, available online at http://pubs.usgs.gov/fs/2010/3015/pdf/FS10-3015/pdf

12 Numerous clashes have occurred between China and Vietnam with respect to offshore oil and gas exploration off the Vietnamese coast and in the South China Sea; see, for example, L. Murdoch, 'South China Sea: Vietnam Accuses China of dragging Oil Rig into its Waters' *The Sydney Morning Herald*, 21 January 2016, available online at www.smh.com.au/world/south-china-sea-vietnam-accuses-china-of-dragging-oil-rig-into-its-waters-20160121-gmafr1.html; R. Jennings, 'Vietnam Faces New Oil Dispute With China After Beijing Cuts Visit Short', *Voice of America*, 26 June 2017, available online at www.voanews.com/a/vietnam-faces-new-oil-dispute-with-china-after-beijing-cuts-visit-short/3915859.html

13 This includes the Malaysia-Thailand Joint Authority which operates in the Gulf of Thailand; for details see www.mtja.org/home.php.

14 M.A Kuo, 'The Geopolitics of Oil and Gas in the South China Sea', *The Diplomat*, 12 December 2018, available online at http://the diplomat.com/2018/12/the-geopolitics-of-oil-and-gas-in-the-south-china-sea/

15 For a discussion of some of the relevant processes, see C. Schofield, 'Defining Areas for Joint Development in Disputed Waters' in S. Wu and N. Hong (eds), *Recent Developments in the South China Sea Dispute: The Prospects for a Joint Development Regime*, London: Routledge, 2014, pp. 78–98.

16 See the collection of papers on this issue in R.C. Beckman, I. Townsend-Gault and C. Schofield (eds), *Beyond Territorial Disputes in the South China Sea: Legal Frameworks for the Joint Development of Hydrocarbon Resources*, Cheltenham: Edward Elgar, 2013.

17 See R. Emmers, 'China's Influence in the South China Sea and the Failure of Joint Development' in E. Goh (ed), *Rising China's Influence in Developing Asia*, Oxford: Oxford University Press, 2016, pp. 155–173.

18 See the discussion by Warner in Chapter 5 and Scott in Chapter 6.

## 246 David Letts and Donald R. Rothwell

tion and the building of artificial islands. To that end, one of the challenges for the region has been reconciling sustainable development with the legitimate economic and development aspirations of South East Asian peoples. In this respect, the complexity of the regional marine environment needs to be acknowledged. Indonesia and the Philippines as vast archipelagic States encompassing thousands of islands enjoy sovereignty over a maritime domain that is predominantly within their national limits. Singapore's maritime domain, on the other hand, is shared with Indonesia and Malaysia with the consequence that transnational marine environmental issues have implications for its bilateral relations.[19] South East Asian marine environmental issues have been given greater prominence as a result of China's artificial island building and land reclamation in the South China Sea. Whilst China's conduct was the subject of detailed assessment in the *South China Sea* arbitration,[20] notwithstanding the tribunal's findings that China's activities were the cause of significant environmental impact in breach of the LOSC, China did not cease its island building activities. More regional initiatives are therefore required to address challenges faced by the South East Asian marine environment, including the impacts of climate change. The launch in 2018 of the 'Marine Environment Protection for Southeast Asian Seas (MEPSEAS) Project' under the auspices of ASEAN and the International Maritime Organization (IMO)[21] is, in that regard, a welcome step; however, there remains a need for distinctive regional initiatives to deal with ship-sourced and land-based marine pollution, and the impacts of land-based pollution.

### 15.2.4 Navigational rights and freedoms

One of the highest profile ongoing law of the sea issues confronting the region relates to the freedom of navigation in the South China Sea. In that respect, it needs to be observed that while there have previously been disagreements regarding the exercise of navigational rights and freedoms throughout South East Asian straits and archipelagos,[22] various forms of mutual accommodation have been reached to resolve those issues within the LOSC framework. In the

---

19 As highlighted by the issues arising from Singapore's land reclamation in its relations with Malaysia in *Land Reclamation by Singapore in and around the Straits of Johor* (Malaysia v Singapore) (Provisional Measures) (2003) 126 ILR 487.

20 *South China Sea* arbitration, [815–993]; see the detailed assessment in T. Stephens, 'The Collateral Damage from China's 'Great Wall of Sand': The Environmental Dimensions of the South China Sea Case' (2016) 34 *Australian Year Book of International Law* pp. 41–52.

21 International Maritime Organisation 'MEPSEAS Project Launched to Protect South-East Asia Marine Environment', 26 June 2018, available online at www.imo.org/en/MediaCentre/PressBriefings/Pages/11-MEPSEASLAUNCH.aspx

22 See, for example, I. Shearer, 'Navigation Issues in the Asian Pacific Region' in J. Crawford and D.R. Rothwell (eds), *The Law of the Sea in the Asian Pacific Region*, Dordrecht: Martinus Nijhoff, 1995, pp. 199–222; and generally D.R. Rothwell and S. Bateman (eds), *Navigational Rights and Freedoms and the New Law of the Sea*, The Hague: Martinus Nijhoff, 2000.

*Challenges for the law of the sea*  247

South China Sea, however, an ongoing source of tension between China and the United States relates to the exercise of navigation rights by US warships and military vessels, especially whilst engaged in 'freedom of navigation' operations (FONOPS).[23] In this respect, it needs to be recalled that the LOSC's navigation regimes apply to all ships, whether commercial or government vessels (including warships)[24] and in some cases these regimes also include overflight by aircraft. The South China Sea and more generally South East Asia can also be considered unique in the sense that all of the LOSC's four navigation regimes are present in what is a relatively confined geographic region.[25] Commercial ships navigating in these waters should be aware that there are different views and practices among States regarding each of these navigation regimes. First, there are maritime areas where the applicability of a particular navigation regime is disputed due to a territorial or maritime dispute, leading to differences of opinion regarding when a vessel is required to undertake 'innocent passage' in the relevant territorial sea or whether more permissive passage rights can be exercised. Second, the legality of various activities associated with navigation is subject to different interpretations, including disagreement as to whether a violation of local law and regulations of the coastal State necessarily renders the passage as non-innocent. Third, with the increased use of unmanned autonomous vessels for commercial purposes, there is a question regarding the navigational entitlement of such vessels.

Notwithstanding these ongoing disagreements regarding the application and interpretation of the LOSC, it needs to be emphasised that to date there has not been any significant interference with commercial shipping in the South China Sea. Any such interference would clearly be counter-productive to the freedom of trade in the region and possibly have global ramifications, making it unlikely that any State would contemplate direct interference with passage of a commercial vessel in the ordinary course of events. China, in particular, would be mindful of the implications arising from any impact upon the freedom of navigation of commercial shipping for its Belt and Road Initiative.

### 15.2.5 Status of the South China Sea arbitration

In addition to the matters noted above, lingering issues arise from the 2016 *South China Sea* arbitration. China's insistence that it will not recognise the award as the outcome of the arbitration does not change the fact that a legitimately constituted LOSC Annex VII tribunal handed down the award which is 'final and without appeal'.[26] The Philippines as the applicant in the proceedings

---

23 See the discussion by Stephens and Quadrio in Chapter 10.
24 LOSC, Articles 17–26, 38, 52, 87.
25 Those being LOSC, Article 17 (innocent passage), Article 38 (transit passage), Article 53 (archipelagic sea lanes passage), and Article 87 (high seas freedom of navigation); see also Nasu in Chapter 11.
26 LOSC, Annex VII, Art 11; which does provide for an appeal process if the parties had so agreed; however, no agreement to that effect was reached in this instance.

248   *David Letts and Donald R. Rothwell*

is the State with both the moral, legal and political authority to seek to have the award enforced; however, it has not sought to do so. In this respect, it needs to be recalled that President Rodrigo Duterte took office on 1 July 2016, just weeks before the tribunal handed down the award and accordingly his administration inherited proceedings commenced by his predecessor, Benigno Aquino III. President Duterte has also consistently taken a low-key approach towards the 2016 award, preferring to advance bilateral relations between China and the Philippines, and in November 2018 a joint statement was issued following a visit by Chinese President Xi Jinping to Manila, stating that

> Both sides agree to exercise self-restraint in the conduct of activities in the South China Sea that would complicate or escalate disputes and affect peace and stability. Both sides also note the importance of confidence-building measures to increase mutual trust and confidence.[27]

South China Sea issues between China and the Philippines would therefore appear to have been settled through diplomatic manoeuvring and attempts to enforce the award appear to be remote. That does not mean that the award's finding with respect to China's assertion of the Nine-Dash Line will be ignored, as there are other States within South East Asia and more broadly who accept the award and its finding that there is no basis in the law of the sea for the Nine-Dash Line. While China's insistence upon recognition of the Nine-Dash Line will more than likely continue, it can be expected that irrespective of the Philippines' position China will continue to experience opposition in its efforts to seek to enforce the claim. More than likely however, the status of the Nine-Dash Line will become mingled with China's efforts to assert other aspects of its South China Sea maritime claims offshore its territories.

### 15.2.6 Dispute resolution

A notable feature of South East Asia and the law of the sea is the number of cases that have been taken before international courts and tribunals in recent years. This has resulted in a range of formal dispute resolution mechanisms having been utilised, ranging from the International Court of Justice[28] to the International Tribunal for the Law of the Sea[29]; LOSC Annex VII Arbitration[30]; and, on the margins of South East Asia, the LOSC Annex V Compulsory

---

27 'Joint statement of the Philippines and China', *Philippines Star*, 21 November 2018, available online at www.philstar.com/headlines/2018/11/21/1870517/full-text-joint-statement-philippines-and-china#SAPYh3S1tThKvajt.99

28 *Sovereignty over Pedra Branca/Pulau Batu Puteh, Middle Rocks and South Ledge* (Malaysia/Singapore) [2008] ICJ Reps 12.

29 *Land Reclamation by Singapore in and around the Straits of Johor* (Malaysia v Singapore) (Provisional Measures) (2003) 126 ILR 487.

30 As occurred in the *South China Sea* arbitration.

*Challenges for the law of the sea*  249

Conciliation between Timor-Leste and Australia.[31] South East Asian States have therefore become familiar with a range of formal mechanisms to resolve their law of the sea disputes, which has resulted in confidence-building with respect to the capacity of those mechanisms to bring about a successful resolution of the dispute when diplomatic means have not succeeded. In that regard, it is notable that even following its rejection of both the 2015 decision on jurisdiction[32] and the subsequent 2016 decision on the merits in the *South China Sea* arbitration, China has continued to work with ASEAN members to finalise the proposed 'Code of Conduct' (CoC) for the South China Sea. There continue to be great expectations associated with the CoC; however, its negotiation has been exceptionally slow, and doubts remain regarding its capacity to bring about a resolution of South China Sea disputes and associated tensions, including whether the instrument will be legally binding.[33]

With the exception of the CoC, there is no other apparent diplomatic initiative on the table for the resolution of maritime and associated territorial disputes in the region. The apparent impasse over the South China Sea suggests the time is ripe for innovative diplomatic solutions, raising the prospect of a South China Sea Commission. A 15-member Commission with a mandate to facilitate mediation, conciliation and ultimately arbitration of the disputes would provide both an informal and formal third-party mechanism capable of dealing with the disputes at both a bilateral and regional level. Under this model, each of the six South China Sea claimants would appoint a Commission member, with the remaining nine members appointed from outside the region. The Commission's reach could extend to both land and maritime disputes, including islands, rocks and other small maritime features such as reefs and shoals. Its mandate could also extend to determining maritime entitlements and maritime boundaries consistently with the LOSC, with the exception of the continental shelf beyond 200 nm which falls within the remit of the CLCS. Commission members would be diplomats and jurists with expertise in territorial and maritime disputes, assisted by a staff of permanent technical experts including geographers, historians, hydrographers and marine scientists. The Commission could be established by a negotiated treaty framework, whereby each State gives its consent.

---

31 *In the Matter of the Maritime Boundary between Timor-Leste and Australia before a Conciliation Commission Constituted under Annex V to the 1982 United Nations Convention on the Law of the Sea between the Democratic Republic of Timor-Leste and the Commonwealth of Australia*, PCA Case no 2016-10, Report and Recommendations of the Compulsory Conciliation Commission between Timor-Leste and Australia on the Timor Sea of 9 May 2018.

32 *In the Matter of an Arbitration before An Arbitral Tribunal Constituted Under Annex VII to the 1982 United Nations Convention on the Law of the Sea between The Republic of the Philippines and the People's Republic of China*, PCA Case no 2013-19, Award on Jurisdiction and Admissibility of 29 October 2015.

33 See, for example, M.J. Valencia, 'A South China Sea Code of Conduct? Don't Get Your Hopes Up', *The Diplomat*, 30 May 2017, available online at https://thediplomat.com/2017/05/a-south-china-sea-code-of-conduct-dont-get-your-hopes-up/

## 250  *David Letts and Donald R. Rothwell*

A South China Sea Commission would be entirely consistent with Article 33 of the Charter of the United Nations[34] which encourages regional solutions to disputes and would add to the already extensive range of peaceful means and methods of dispute resolution that are available.[35] However, unlike those bodies which are mainly located in Europe, a South China Sea Commission would be located within South East Asia. Commission members could predominantly come from within the region. Contentious issues of consent would have been addressed by each individual State having signed and agreed to support the Commission. Creative legal solutions could be found through the flexibility of mediation or conciliation, with legally binding arbitration a last resort. Such an approach could be a regional solution for a regional problem.

## 15.3 Addressing horizon threats

Trying to predict how future maritime threats in South East Asia will arise, and subsequently be addressed, is an inherently difficult process that involves a mixture of considered speculation combined with calculated assessment of likely future events and behaviour. Nevertheless, undertaking a brief evaluation of a number of scenarios that may eventuate in the future provides a way of rounding out the discussion that has been provided in this book while leaving scope for future research and discourse in subsequent years.

### *15.3.1 Excessive maritime claims*

Resolution of maritime claims that do not conform to the legal regimes set out in the LOSC is one area that could realistically be progressed in South East Asia. However, to achieve this, a fundamental re-assessment by States of their publicly articulated position in relation to these non-conforming claims would be needed, and there would also have to be recognition by States that it is clearly in their national interest to do so. If this does not occur, then the prospect for additional unilateral declarations by States that do not accord with the LOSC, such as the Air Defence Identification Zone declared by China in November 2013,[36] will remain at least a credible possibility. There is, of course, the possibility that a 'snowball' effect of claims that do not conform to the LOSC could become the norm in South East Asia, with States perhaps taking cognisance of those excessive claims that already exist[37] as well as China's response to the *South China Sea* arbitration.[38] It is hoped that the future does not take that

---

34 *Charter of the United Nations*, 26 June 1945, 1 UNTS XVI.
35 See the discussion by Klein in Chapter 14.
36 See the explanatory statement at Embassy of the People's Republic of China in the United States of America, 'Defense Ministry Spokesman on China's Air Defense Identification Zone', 4 December 2013, available online at www.china-embassy.org/eng/zt/dhfksbq2/
37 See the discussion by Rothwell in Chapter 2 and Tim Stephens in Chapter 9.
38 See the discussion by Klein in Chapter 14.

*Challenges for the law of the sea* 251

path, however, consolidated action will be required from regional States, perhaps with ASEAN involvement, to advocate LOSC compliance including responding to compliance fractures that may start to appear. In this regard, the region will continue to face the impact of climate change and sea level rise, which will have consequences for both straight and archipelagic baselines that have been drawn to and from islands, low-tide elevations and reefs that may become completely submerged. This will raise further tensions within the region regarding the status of baselines, the maritime claims upon which they are based, and concluded maritime boundaries. For Indonesia and the Philippines, there may even be a need to reassess their entitlements as archipelagic States. Regional solutions to this problem, within a LOSC framework, would be desirable.

### 15.3.2 Maritime security and the presence of non-State actors

The continued presence, and influence, of non-State actors in South East Asia is a source of concern that will require ongoing vigilance for the foreseeable future. Employment of a 'maritime militia' by China is destined to continue as a feature of responses to perceived threats to Chinese maritime interests in the region, and perhaps expanding to other areas in close proximity to the Chinese coastline.[39] The concept of 'hybridity' that accompanies the employment of the maritime militia obfuscates the ability of other States to classify militia vessels as being representatives of the State, and clouds the maritime picture with a degree of uncertainty. However, the presence of maritime militia is not the only way in which non-State actors are likely to influence the region in the future. The activities of a number of terrorist groups, most notably Abu Sayyaf in the southern Philippines, are likely to remain a factor that requires ongoing commitment in order to defeat threats to regional maritime security.[40] Although the Philippines government has taken decisive steps to neutralise the threat posed by Abu Sayyaf in the archipelagic mainland, there remains an ongoing threat of piracy[41] and other maritime crimes, especially in the Sulu and Celebes Seas. Elsewhere in the region, the actions of authorities in Indonesia have seen a drop in reported maritime security incidents with 'low level opportunistic thefts'[42] being the most common type of incident although both Indonesia and the eastern part of Malaysia have experienced hostage-taking or kidnapping.[43] The use of maritime routes for people smuggling and outflows of refugees both within

---

39 See the discussion by McLaughlin in Chapter 8.
40 See the discussion by Letts in Chapter 4.
41 The International Chamber of Commerce's International Maritime Bureau has stated that reports of piracy in the Philippines have decreased from 22 in 2017 to ten in 2018: International Maritime Bureau, 'IMB Piracy Report 2018: Attacks Multiply in the Gulf of Guinea', 16 January 2019, available online at www.icc-ccs.org/index.php/1259-imb-piracy-report-2018-attacks-multiply-in-the-gulf-of-guinea
42 Ibid.
43 Ibid.

## 252 David Letts and Donald R. Rothwell

South East Asia, and in an attempt to reach peripheral States such as Australia, will also likely continue as an important security concern.

### 15.3.3 Responding to maritime security threats: small-scale use of force and cooperative measures

Responding to maritime security threats will likely involve a combination of traditional 'on-water' maritime law enforcement response options as well as the increased use of intelligence gathering by regional States and organisations that support maritime security. The former has a well-established legal framework in which operations occur, involving a combination of international law and domestic implementing legislation, and jurisprudential principles governing the use of force in maritime law enforcement operations.[44] The latter is presently in an embryonic stage in South East Asia, although encouraging signs regarding regional cooperation between States are emerging. It has been noted that ASEAN's networks for the exchange of information are complex, comprising both informal and formal channels, and many of these are also built on 'long-term interpersonal and interagency relationships of trust'.[45] Measures such as the establishment of ReCAAP's Information Sharing Centre and the creation of Singapore's Information Fusion Centre provide an example of how intelligence can be collected and shared among regional States without undue concern, and the bolstering of the capacity of these existing bodies will be necessary to ensure that cooperation among regional States continues to grow.

### 15.3.4 Militarisation and military operations

In terms of the South China Sea littoral States, an ongoing upgrade of military capabilities has been underway for a number of years raising questions whether a regional 'arms race' is taking place, with suggestions that replacement of obsolete weapons systems, and those that are unable to be deployed at all, feature high on the upgrade agenda.[46] In terms of maritime capacity-building, there has reportedly been an increase in spending on '...maritime aviation, mobile anti-ship missile systems and maritime surveillance'.[47] It is expected that this

---

44 These principles have been derived from the often quoted cases of *The I'm Alone (Canada/United States of America) 3 RIAA 1609, The Red Crusader* (1962) 35 ILR 485, and *MV Saiga No. 2* (Saint Vincent and The Grenadines v Guinea) (1999) ITLOS case No. 2.

45 See J. Coyne and I. Kfir, 'Improving Maritime Security in the Asia-Pacific', *The Strategist*, 16 January 2019, available online at www.aspistrategist.org.au/improving-maritime-security-in-the-asia-pacific/?utm_medium=email&utm_campaign=Daily%20The%20Strategist&utm_content=Daily%20The%20Strategist+CID_b5165a9decc4a4ee978610cd299b107b&utm_source=CampaignMonitor&utm_term=Improving%20maritime%20security%20in%20the%20AsiaPacific

46 F. Heiduk, 'Is Southeast Asia Really in an Arms Race?', *East Asia Forum*, 21 February 2018, available online at www.eastasiaforum.org/2018/02/21/is-southeast-asia-really-in-an-arms-race/

47 Ibid.

*Challenges for the law of the sea* 253

trend of modernisation and spending on military capability will continue. It is questionable whether military spending in the region is a response to China's growing military capability.[48] Certainly, China's maritime capabilities have been enhanced in recent years with the shift in focus that is resulting in China's PLA-N becoming a 'blue-water' navy as evidenced through a number of naval task force deployments well beyond the immediate environs of the Chinese mainland. There are no signs that China's global maritime ambitions will diminish, and the vessel building programme that began in the early 2000s has been accelerated under the current Chinese leadership.[49] An increase in naval operations within the region, by both littoral States and extra-regional States, will inevitably heighten tensions and place a further strain on the law of the sea.

### 15.3.5 Impact of foreign aid and investment

Foreign aid and investment will continue to flow into South East Asia through a variety of mechanisms. Some of this aid and investment will be through vast infrastructure projects, such as the Chinese Belt and Road Initiative which will have implications for the development of new ports,[50] while other elements will comprise security assistance in the way of military equipment sales, training and support. Aid provided as a result of responses to natural disasters and tragic events, such as occurred when flight MH370 disappeared in 2014, will continue to be delivered as needed throughout the region. There are risks associated with any influx of foreign aid and investment which must be guarded against, both from the perspective of the donor and the recipient, with perhaps the most dangerous risk for recipient States being an inability to repay foreign loans that are tied to large infrastructure projects.[51]

### 15.3.6 Resource disputes

Disputes over harvesting the rich resources that exist in South East Asia's maritime spaces will remain a constant factor for the foreseeable future. There are ongoing challenges associated with exploiting the marine living and non-living resources in the region, in a highly charged environment where early resolution

---

48 S. Wu, 'What's Behind Southeast Asia's High Military Spending?', *East Asia Forum*, 25 May 2018, available online at www.eastasiaforum.org/2018/05/25/whats-behind-southeast-zasias-high-military-spending/

49 'With Ships and Missiles, China is Ready to Challenge US in the Pacific', *SBS News*, 29 August 2018, available online at www.sbs.com.au/news/with-ships-and-missiles-china-is-ready-to-challenge-us-in-the-pacific

50 See discussion regarding the Belt and Road Initiative by Tan in Chapter 12.

51 This has resulted in the so-called phenomena of 'debt trap diplomacy', which China has sought to respond to by way of a 2018 Measure for the Administration of Foreign Aid; see Laura Zhou, 'Debt-Trap Allegations Push China to Tighten Reins on Foreign Aid Programme' *South China Morning Post*, 14 November 2018, available online at www.scmp.com/news/china/diplomacy/article/2173235/debt-trap-allegations-push-china-tighten-reins-foreign-aid

of the region's maritime sovereignty disputes is not likely. Whilst there will be increased pressure for sustainable fishing practices to be widely adopted throughout the region, it is clear that this cannot occur to the detriment of other environmental concerns.[52] Regional oil and gas production and exploration will need to increase as current known reserves dwindle. It is in the interests of States to investigate the scope for cooperative resource exploration activities, especially in the resource-rich South China Sea, notwithstanding that these activities would likely take place in waters where sovereignty is contested. Lessons need to be learned from unilateral resource exploration and development such as that which occurred in May 2014 when the Chinese oil rig HYSY 981 started operating in Vietnamese-claimed waters.[53] The security and safety of submarine cables and pipelines is an often neglected aspect of resource management that will warrant close attention in the near future. Recognising this issue, the International Law Association has established a Committee to assess the adequacy of the existing international legal framework governing submarine cables and pipelines but this Committee is currently in its infancy with its first interim report not due until 2020.[54] As far as South East Asia is concerned, the security of submarine cables and pipelines is an issue that has fundamental importance for the region's resource exploitation and management due to the direct linkages between these assets and economic prosperity.

### 15.3.7 Marine scientific research

Undertaking relevant marine scientific research in the region will have increased importance as pressures on resource management continue to build. However, one of the complicating factors that accompanies marine scientific research is the difference in opinion among States regarding precisely which research activities fit within the authority of the coastal State through the application of the EEZ regime.[55] While on its face, it appears that the LOSC clearly provides that jurisdiction over marine scientific research in the EEZ rests with the coastal State, where the EEZ itself is contested or where States (such as the United States) claim that their research activities do not fit within the ambit of marine scientific research, the issue becomes problematic.[56] These differences in opinion have the

---

52 See, for example, the discussion by Warner in Chapter 5 in relation to the impact of mangrove clearance undertaken (in part) to support the establishment of prawn and fish farms and Tsirbas, Chapter 13, in relation to the parlous state of the South China Sea fishery.

53 M. Green et al., 'Counter-Coercion Series: China-Vietnam Oil Rig Standoff', *Asia Maritime Transparency Initiative*, 12 June 2017, available online at https://amti.csis.org/counter-co-oil-rig-standoff/

54 Proposal for establishment of a new ILA Committee on Submarine Cables and Pipelines under international law, available at www.ila-hq.org/index.php/committees.

55 See LOSC, Article 56.

56 The debate over the difference between marine scientific research and military marine scientific research or data collection has existed since the introduction of the EEZ regime in the LOSC; see for example, S. Bateman, 'Hydrographic Surveying in the EEZ: Differences and Overlaps

*Challenges for the law of the sea* 255

potential to increase tension in the region as States seek to assert what they see as their rights to undertake scientific research (however defined) in the region's maritime spaces.

### 15.3.8 Autonomous vessels

The potential use of autonomous vessels throughout South East Asia is on the horizon. The technology is being tested in a number of locations throughout the world, and China is among those States that is investing heavily in automated vessels.[57] The United States is also exploring the opportunities available from automated and unmanned vessels, with its main focus, at least initially, on military uses. For example, the United States Navy is developing the *Sea Hunter* Anti-Submarine Warfare (ASW) Continuous Trail Unmanned Vessel (ACTUV) which is reportedly able to travel for thousands of kilometres without any crew member onboard.[58] Opportunities to use autonomous vessels for commercial, military and law enforcement purposes will expand in the near future, and these developments will fundamentally alter the way in which maritime activity occurs in the region. The deployment and/or use of vessels that do not have a crew onboard, extending as far as being provided with berthing assistance by autonomous tug boats, represents a seismic shift in the way that maritime operations are undertaken. However, this potential also raises a number of important legal issues regarding how existing legal instruments, such as the LOSC, are able to cope with the change as none of the these instruments were agreed at a time when automation was a viable option.

### 15.3.9 United States presence/withdrawal from South East Asia

A vexed question arises over the future of the United States and its forward deployed military forces in South East Asia. At his inauguration, President Trump announced that 'America First' would be the 'new vision' for the United States. Subsequently, the Trump Administration initiated a 'Free and Open Indo-Pacific' (FOIP) policy which represents a difference in focus from the 'pivot' to South East Asia that was prompted by the Obama Administration.[59] However, what the practical effect of each of these policies has actually been

---

with Marine Scientific Research', (2005) 29 *Marine Policy* pp. 163–174; and R. Pedrozo, 'Military Activities in the Exclusive Economic Zone: East Asia Focus', (2014) 90 *International Law Studies* pp. 514–543.

57 See R. Jennings, 'China is Developing Ships to Cover the Globe Without Captains', *Forbes*, 14 March 2018, available online at www.forbes.com/sites/ralphjennings/2018/03/14/china-is-developing-a-fleet-of-high-tech-ships-with-no-captains/#f392cfd49be4

58 Defense Advanced Research Projects Agency, 'ACTUV "Sea Hunter" Prototype Transitions to Office of Naval Research for Further Development', 30 January 2018, available online at www.darpa.mil/news-events/2018-01-30a

59 Barack Obama, 'Remarks By President Obama to the Australian Parliament', 17 November 2011, available online at http://obamawhitehouse.archives.gov/the-press-office/2011/11/17/

## 256  *David Letts and Donald R. Rothwell*

remains a topic of debate. Some have stated that the Obama 'pivot' had little real consequence,[60] while others have opined that after two years of the Trump Administration, the FOIP was only just beginning to take shape.[61] The obvious difference between the 'pivot' and FOIP is the way in which the relationship between the United States and China is envisaged. Under the pivot, direct confrontation with China was to be avoided while under FOIP the opposite is true.[62] While political agendas regularly change, the impact of the United States implementing FOIP throughout the range of political, military and economic engagements that it has in South East Asia is yet to be fully assessed. One thing that does seem clear, however, is that regional States should prepare for a rollercoaster ride between China and the United States as both adjust their posture for future influence in the region. In that regard, whether the Trump Presidency extends beyond 2020 into a second term will be critical for implementation and the legacy of the FOIP.

### 15.3.10  Foreign naval engagement in South East Asia

Military presence in South East Asia is dominated by the United States and China and this situation is not likely to alter in the near future. Russia, India, Japan, South Korea and Australia all also play a prominent role in the region to varying degrees.[63] However, other States are also showing an increased level of regional interest, as evidenced by the announcement from the British Defence Secretary that the United Kingdom would seek to build a military base in South East Asia within the next few years.[64] Unsurprisingly, the announcement sparked mixed reactions. Chinese sources were reported as stating that the United Kingdom was acting at the behest of Washington and being 'provocative' by aligning with the hardened US approach towards Beijing.[65] However, it was also reported that the news of the planned UK base would be welcomed by key US allies in the region who '...have been concerned about Washington's reluctance to take a leadership role to challenge Beijing's assertiveness in the South China Sea dis-

---

remarks-president-obama-australian-parliament; in which it was stated, 'The United States is a Pacific power, and we are here to stay'.

60 M. Green, 'The Legacy of Obama's "Pivot" to Asia', *Foreign Policy*, 3 September 2016, available online at https://foreignpolicy.com/2016/09/03/the-legacy-of-obamas-pivot-to-asia/

61 I. Storey and M. Cook, 'The Trump Administration and Southeast Asia: America's Asia Policy Crystalizes', (2018) ISEAS – Yusof Ishak Institute *Perspective* Issue No. 77, available at www.iseas.edu.sg/images/pdf/ISEAS_Perspective_2018_77@50.pdf

62 Ibid.

63 All of these States are included among the 15 countries that have the largest military budgets (2017 data); see D. Brown, 'The 15 Countries with the Highest Military Budgets in 2017', *Business Insider Australia*, 3 May 2018, available online at www.businessinsider.com.au/highest-military-budgets-countries-2018-5?r=US&IR=T

64 'Britain's Planned Naval Base in Southeast Asia seen as 'Muscle-Flexing' Against China', *South China Morning Post*, 1 January 2019, available online at www.scmp.com/news/china/military/article/2180293/britains-planned-naval-base-southeast-asia-seen-muscle-flexing

65 Ibid.

putes'.[66] The United Kingdom also indicated on several occasions in 2017 and 2018 that it was prepared to send an aircraft carrier through the South China Sea, including with a regional partner such as Australia.[67]

Existing defence alliances involving ASEAN States and external States are not likely to diminish in the near future. While it could be considered that some of these alliances, such as the Five Power Defence Arrangements (FPDA) between Malaysia, Singapore, the United Kingdom, New Zealand and Australia have little contemporary relevance, they will nevertheless remain in force and may even expand in scope if perceived regional threats begin to materialise.[68] A further consideration arises from reports in May 2018 that President Trump sought options for United States troop reductions in South Korea, with both Japan and South Korea 'unnerved' at this prospect.[69] Whether any future United States military reduction in South East Asia would also include a reduced naval presence is yet to be seen, but the indicators that can be gleaned from the number of FONOPS conducted by the United States Navy since President Trump's inauguration would seem to point to at least maintaining the *status quo*.

## 15.4 Concluding remarks

South East Asia's maritime environs are a fascinating mix of threat and opportunity, risk and reward, playground and source of tension as well as being home to rich resources and a large and growing population. The region presents a complex geopolitical picture that is punctuated by competing maritime sovereignty claims and a variety of maritime security concerns. Terrorist threats in the region were recognised at the 2018 ASEAN/Australia meeting in Sydney, where a Memorandum of Understanding was signed to address a variety of actions that can be undertaken to counter international terrorism, including that which manifests itself in the region's maritime environs.[70] Other security threats, ranging from small-scale use of force to maritime crime and piracy, are also a constant source of concern. Yet, despite the challenges that exist, the vast majority of

---

66 Ibid. The report cited Australia, Japan and Vietnam as being examples of allies who would welcome the news of the future UK base.

67 S. Carrell, 'South China Sea: UK Could Send Aircraft Carrier to Back Australian Vessels', *The Guardian*, 21 July 2018, available online at www.theguardian.com/world/2018/jul/21/south-china-sea-uk-could-send-aircraft-carrier-to-back-australian-vessels

68 See P. Parameswaran, 'Joint Military Exercise Highlights Five Power Defense Agreements', *The Diplomat*, 17 October 2018, available online at https://thediplomat.com/2018/10/joint-military-exercise-highlights-five-power-defense-agreements/

69 C. Sang-Hun and M. Rich, 'Trump's Talk of U.S. Troop Cuts Unnerves South Korea and Japan', *New York Times*, 4 May 2018, available online at www.nytimes.com/2018/05/04/world/asia/south-korea-troop-withdrawal-united-states.html

70 *Memorandum of Understanding between the Association of Southeast Asian Nations and the Government of Australia to Counter International Terrorism*, 17 March 2018 available online at http://setnas-asean.id/vendor/webarq/admin-lte/plugins/elfinder/files/KS%20Eksternal/ASEAN-Australia%20MoU%20on%20International%20Terrorism.pdf

maritime activity that occurs in South East Asia does so in an environment that is relatively benign. Maritime trade flows through the region, commercial and military activity largely takes place without incident and the people of the region – for the most part – are able to live their lives in relative peace. But for this situation to continue the challenges and issues identified in this book will need to be seriously and comprehensively addressed by all States and other actors who possess an interest in the region's continued peace and prosperity, and to that end the law of the sea will be pivotal.

# Index

**Note: Bold** page numbers refer to tables; *italic* page numbers refer to figures and page numbers followed by "n" denote endnotes.

1996 London Protocol 105–6; amendment to 107–8

Abu Sayaff Group (ASG) 68, 69n21, 251; sinking of the *Superferry 14* 69
actor and act status 138
ADAPT strategy 87
adaptation to climate change 101, 110–16
*Agreement on Historic Waters of Vietnam and Kampuchea* (1982) 50
Agreement on the Basic Principles Guiding the Resolution of Maritime Issues 233
Air Defence Identification Zones 226–7
Ambalat offshore area 56, 91, 203–4
ambiguity of maritime militias 142–3
Amersinghe, Hamilton Shirley 3
Andaman Islands, archipelagic State claim 18
Andaman Sea 33; delimitation of maritime boundaries 35–8
Annex VII Arbitral Tribunal 8, 155, 220, 229–30, 243; *In the Matter of the Bay of Bengal Maritime Boundary Arbitration* 38; status of *South China Sea* arbitration 247–8; *see also South China Sea* arbitration
anthropogenic CO$_2$ 96
application of the natural state doctrine to features affected by artificial intervention: islands affected by climate change 126–30; islands transformed by artificial interventions 130–2
*ARA Libertad* case 143–4
Arafura Sea, maritime boundary delimitation 56–9

Arbitral Tribunal 133, 185–6, 220, 243; *South China Sea* arbitration 121–4; *South China Sea* case 46–8; *see also* natural state doctrine; *South China Sea* arbitration
archipelagic baseline 24
archipelagic sea lanes passage, legal issues 183
archipelagic states 17–20, 30–1; baseline adjustments 18–20; baselines 30–1; Indonesia 18–20; the Philippines 18–20; Taiwan as 26; *see also* straight baselines
archipelagic waters 18
arms proliferation 73–4
*Articles on the Responsibility of States for Internationally Wrongful Acts* (ASR) 145–8; Article 5 145, 146; Article 8 attribution of maritime militia conduct 146–7
artificial intervention 119–24; irrigation 131; islands transformed by 130–2; Itu Abu 123–4; natural state doctrine 124–6; technological innovations 125–6; *see also* application of the natural state doctrine to features affected by artificial intervention
artificial islands 211
Ascension Island 132
Asia Foundation 13
Asia Maritime Transparency Initiative (AMTI) 158, 217–18n43; 'Blueprint for Fisheries Management and Environmental Cooperation in the South China Sea' 219
Asia Pacific Adaptation Network (APAN) 112

## 260 *Index*

Asia Pacific Climate Change Adaptation Forum 112

Asia Pacific Economic Cooperation (APEC) Forum 9

Asia Pacific Fisheries Commission (APFIC) 88–9

Asia Pacific region: and climate change 95–101; fisheries 96–7; mangrove forest destruction 108–10; and natural disasters 94; and ocean acidification 98–100

Asia-Pacific Economic Cooperation (APEC) 153

Association of South East Asian Nations (ASEAN) 1, 2, 11, 12, 16, 64, 64n3, 116, 117, 150–2, 162, 234, 240, 257; Charter of 199–202; Climate Change Initiative 112; comparison with the European Union 199, 199n36; Declaration Against Trafficking in Persons, Particularly women and Children (2004) 76–7; Guidelines for hotline Communications 234; information sharing in 252; International Covenant on Civil and Political Rights 191; IUU fishing challenges 244; Marine Environment Protection for Southeast Asian Seas (MEPSEAS) 246; member states 1n1; member states' compliance with LOSC 158–61; Mutual Legal Assistance Treaty (2004) 90; regional agreements 230–3; Regional Forum 9; responses to maritime security threats 76–8; and rules-based governance 199–204; support for LOSC 157–8; *Treaty of Amity and Cooperation in Southeast Asia (TAC)* 231; Twelfth Ministerial Meeting on Transnational Crime 77

attack on the *MV Limburg* 68

Australia, Operation Sovereign Borders 72

Australia-Indonesia continental shelf agreement 57

Australia-Timor Leste maritime boundary agreement 59

autonomous navigation of vessels 190, 247, 255

Balakrishnan, Vivian 193

Bali Process 89–90

Bangladesh, *In the Matter of the Bay of Bengal Maritime Boundary Arbitration* 38

baselines 24–7, 30–1; for archipelagic states 18–20; fixed 114–17; Philippines, the 27–8; straight 24–5

Baselines of Maritime Zones Act (2006) 41

bay closing/straight baseline 24

Bay of Bengal, maritime boundary delimitation 38, *39*

Beibu Gulf, fishery cooperation in 92

Belt and Road Initiative (BRI) 136, 196, 253

Bergin, A. 217

Bethlehem, Daniel 178

*Black Sea Case* 35

Blue Carbon Initiative 110

Blue Forests 110

'Blueprint for Fisheries Management and Environmental Cooperation in the South China Sea' 219

boundaries 34; contiguous zone claims 27; fixed baselines 114–16; *see also* maritime boundary delimitation

Brooks, R. A. 129

Brunei, LOSC compliance 158

Bull, H. 193

Cabo Verde 131–2

Cambodia: LOSC compliance 158; *Memorandum of Understanding regarding the Area of their Overlapping Claims to the Continental Shelf* (2001) 50; Preah Vihear promontory dispute 202–3; protest of Malaysia-Thailand maritime boundary agreement in the Gulf of Thailand 49, 50

carbon dioxide ($CO_2$) 95–6; and exploitation of the ocean sink to mitigate climate change 105–10; and exploitation of the ocean's vegetated habitats 108–10; ocean acidification 98–100

*Case concerning Sovereignty over Pulau Ligitan and Pulau Sipadan* 8

*Case concerning Sovereignty over Pulau Sipadan and Pulau Ligitan (Indonesia/ Malaysia)* 56

cases: *ARA Libertad* 143–4; *Corfu Channel* 165; *Costa Rica v. Nicaragua* 239; *Golder* 166; *Libya/Malta* 58; *North Sea Continental Shelf* 57, 58; *Pedra Branca* 8, 43, 44; *Qatar v Bahrain* 25; The Schooner Exchange v. McFaddon and Others 142–3; *Sempra Energy International v Argentine Republic* 168;

*South China Sea* case 46–8; *Sovereignty over Pulau Ligitan and Pulau Sipadan* 19
Celebes Sea, maritime boundary delimitation 55–6
Centre for humanitarian Dialogue 78
certification of fisheries 216–17
Charter of the United Nations: Article 33 228; Chapter VIII 12
Cheung, W. L. 81
China: ad hoc employment of fishing vessels and fishers 139–42; Air Defence Identification Zones 226–7; Belt and Road Initiative (BRI) 136, 196, 253; diplomatic relations with the Phlippines 248; 'Five Dragons' 141; historic claims 31; maritime militias 147; maritme militias 138–42; 'Nine-Dash Line' 2, 16, 21–3, 47, 210, 211, 248; Peoples Armed Forces Maritime Militia (PAFMM) 139; People's Liberation Army-Navy (PLA-N) 140, 141, 253; relations with Singapore 194–7; and Singapore's rules-based governance 198–204; *South China Sea* case 46–8; state practice on naval activities in EEZs 171–2
Chinese Coast Guard (CCG) 139, 141; and state responsibility 145–6
Chinese Society of International Law 22
'choke points' 64
climate change 80, 91, 93, 94, 120, 245–6; ADAPT strategy 87; adaptation to 101; in Asia Pacific 95–101; and collaboration 111–12; and coral bleaching 81–2; coral reef adaptation 112–13; and depletion of fisheries 83; 'The Geopolitical Implications of Climate Change to 2030 for Southeast Asia' 83; human-induced 120; impact on food supplies 83; impact on marine biodiversity 81; impact on maritime disputes in South East Asia 85–6; impact on population movements in South East Asia 84–5; and mangrove forest destruction 108–10; and natural disasters 85, 120; and natural state doctrine 126–30; and ocean acidification 98–100; role of oceans in mitigating 96–7; and salinity changes 82; and sea level rise 82, 84, 97–8, 111; and severe weather events 82, 84, 100–1; *see also* climate-oceans regime complex; mitigating adverse impacts of climate change on maritime security

climate-oceans regime complex 101–2, 116; adaptation to climate change 110–16; exploitation of the ocean sink to mitigate climate change 105–10; reduction of greenhouse gas emissions 102–5
coastal erosion 120
coastal states 5–6; baselines 24–6; contiguous zone claims 27; and dispute resolution 224–5; maritime claims 7; Taiwan as 6–7; territorial seas 11–12, 187–8
Code for Unplanned Encounters at Sea (CUES) 224, 233–5
code of conduct in the South China Sea (COC) 11, 224, 231, 232, 249
collaboration 80; and climate change 111–12; and fisheries management 113–14; and fixed baselines 114–16; Global Ocean Acidification Observing Network (GOA-ON) 104
'collective security' 65
COLREGS 139, 233–4
commercial shipping 247; autonomous navigation of vessels 255; and technological innovation 190–1
Commission on the Limits of the Continental Shelf (CLCS) 2, 16, 243–4, 249; Continental Shelf claims 29; South East Asian states' participation in 155, 156; submissions for the Southern Kyushu-Palau Ridge Region 54
Common Fisheries Zone 92
conflict avoidance 233–5
contiguous zones 28–9
continental shelf rights 29; Australia-Indonesia continental shelf agreement 56, 57; in the East China Sea 51; in the South China Sea 44, 45; Taiwan 29–30
Convention for the Conservation of Antarctic Marine Living Resources (CCAMLR) 216, 218; Article IV 219; Article XII 218n45
Convention on the Continental Shelf (1958) 34
cooperative arrangements: for combating transnational crime 89–91; for environmental protection 87–8
Coordinating Bodies of the Seas of East Asia (COBSEA) 112
coral bleaching 81–2, 127
coral reef adaptation 112–13

262 *Index*

Coral Reef Triangle Initiative on Coral Reefs, Fisheries and Food Security (CTI-CFF) 112–13
Coral Triangle Initiative (CTI) 87–8
*Corfu Channel* case 165
*Costa Rica v. Nicaragua* 239
Council of Regional Organisations in the Pacific (CROP) 111–12
Crawford, J. 149
cyber-attacks 190

D'Amato, A. 176–7
Declaration Against Trafficking in Persons, Particularly women and Children (2004) 76–7
Declaration on the Conduct of Parties in the South China Sea (DOC) 11, 231–2
declarations, under the United Nations Convention on the Law of the Sea (LOSC) 4–5
delimitation of maritime boundaries 33–5; Andaman Sea 35–8; *Black Sea Case* 35; continental shelf 34; exclusive economic zone (EEZ) 34; Malacca Strait 39, 40–2; Singapore Straits 42–4; South China Sea 44–8
Deng, Xiaoping 193
depleting fish stocks, potential conflict over 213–14
depopulation 128
*détente* 194
development of security 65
Diaoyu 51
displaced populations 84–5
disproportionality test 35
*Dispute Concerning Delimitation of the Maritime Boundary between Bangladesh and Myanmar in the Bay of Bengal* 38
dispute resolution 1, 248–50; bilateral agreements and arrangements 233; LOSC, South East Asian states' participation in 154–5; LOSC framework for 229–30; regional agreements with ASEAN 230–3; in South East Asia 15
dispute settlement framework of LOSC 163–4
disputes: environmental 227; maritime boundary 225–6; navigation and overflight 226–7; resources 227–8; security 228; territorial sovereignty 224–5
dived transit 137n4
Duterte, Rodrigo 248

East China Sea 33; continental shelf delimitation 53; joint development zones (JDZs) 51, 53, 54; joint fishing arrangements 53, 54; maritime boundary delimitation 51, 53, 54
Eastern Sabah Security Zone 185
Eminent Persons Group (EPG) 200
environmental disputes 227
environmental impact assessment (EIA) 83
environmental protection/security: fisheries conservation and sustainable use arrangements 88–9; in South East Asia 14; transboundary initiatives 86–8
Erickson, A. 141
evolution of ocean boundary-making 34–5
exclusive economic zones (EEZs) 4, 12, 22, 23, 34, 41, 47, 92, 158, 179, 210, 242; boundaries 34; collaborative fisheries 114–16; naval activities in 171–2
exploitation of the ocean sink to mitigate climate change 105–10

*de facto* exercise of sovereign authority 188
ferries 7–8
fertilization of the oceans 106–8
fisheries 88–9; in Asia Pacific 96–7; in the Beibu Gulf 92; certification 216–17; collaborative 113–14; consequences of the *South China Sea* arbitration 219–20; depleting fish stocks, potential conflict over 213–14; impact of climate change on 83; managing to promote security 212–13; protecting through collective action 215–19; solutions to resource disputes 92; 'sovereignty neutral' management regime 211–12; subsidies 220–1
'fishing nationalism' 212, 214
fishing vessels 142; and sovereign immunity 143–4
'Five Dragons' 141
Five Power Defence Arrangements (FPDA) 257
fixed baselines 117
fixed maritime zones 134–5
flag states 5, 7–8
food supplies, climate change impact on 83
foreign naval engagement in South East Asia 256–7
Framework for a Pacific Oceanscape 111–12

## Index  263

Framework for Resilient Development in the Pacific (2017–2030) 111
'Free and Open Indo-Pacific' (FOIP) policy 255–6
freedom of navigation 11–12, 183–4; the Philippines' State practice of restricting navigational rights of warships 172–5; in South East Asia 242
Freedom of Navigation (FON) programme 175–7, 189
freshwater 131–2
freshwater lens 127

Gao, Z. 22
Geneva Conventions on the Law of the Sea (1958) 8
geoengineering 107–8
Global Environment Facility (GEF) 87
Global Ocean Acidification Observing Network (GOA-ON) 104
global warming 120
*Golder* case 166
government ships 142
Great Barrier Reef, coral bleaching in 81–2
Greater Sunrise fields 59
greenhouse gas emissions, reduction of 102–5
Grotius, H. 151
Gulf of Thailand 48–50; historic claims of 23–4; joint zones 50; maritime boundary agreement between Malaysia and Thailand 48–50
Gulf of Tonkin, historic claim of 23–4

He, Lei 198
high-tide features 123
historic claims 20, 31; Gulf of Thailand 23–4; 'Nine-Dash Line' 21–3
human rights 191–2
human security 63
human trafficking 71–2; Bali Process 89–90; combating 89–90

illegal, unreported and unregulated (IUU) fishing 74, 79, 215–16, 220–1, 220–1n57, 244
illicit goods, trafficking 71–2
India: boundary delimitation with Burma and Thailand 38; jurisdictiona dispute with Italy 184n32; maritime boundary delimitation in the Bay of Bengal 38, 39; *In the Matter of the Bay of Bengal Maritime Boundary Arbitration* 38;

state practice on naval activities in EEZs 171–2
Indonesia: Ambalat region dispute 203–4; archepelagic sea lanes 183; as archipelagic State 18–20; Australia-Indonesia continental shelf agreement 56, 57; Ligitan/Sipidan islands dispute 202; LOSC compliance 158–9; Malacca Strait 39, 40–2; maritime boundary agreement with the Philippines 55–6; Regulation No. 37 (2002) 159; Singapore Straits 42–4; straight baselines 40n30; threat of coastal flooding in 98
Indonesia and Malaysia boundary agreement of 1969 44
Information Fusion Centre 75–6
initiatives: for maritime security 78–9; for transboundary marine environmental protection 86–8
innocent passage 164–6, 165n8, 247; legal issues 181–2; and messaging 137, 138; the Philippines' State practice of restricting navigational rights of warships 172–5; and prior authorization/ notification 165–6; and state practice 168–70; *Tallinn Manual 2.0* 190; US Freedom of Navigation (FON) programme 175–7
insular features 46
Integrated Coastal Management (ICM) 87
Intergovernmental Oceanographic Commission of the United Nations Educational, Scientific, and Cultural Organization 110
Intergovernmental Panel on Climate Change (IPCC) 84–5
international armed conflict (IAC) 66, 189
International Committee of the Red Cross, 'LOAC at Sea' workshops 78
International Court of Justice 8, 11, 15; *Black Sea Case* 35; *Case concerning Sovereignty over Pulau Sipadan and Pulau Ligitan (Indonesia/Malaysia)* 56; *Corfu Channel* case 165; *Costa Rica v. Nicaragua* 239; legality of the use of nuclear weapons 65n7; *Libya/Malta* case 58; Ligitan/Sipidan islands dispute 202; maritime dispute settlement 155; *North Sea Continental Shelf* cases 57, 58; *Pedra Branca* case 8, 43, 43n45, 43n46, 44; Preah Vihear promontory dispute 202–3; *Qatar v Bahrain* 25; *Sovereignty over Pulau Ligitan and Pulau Sipadan* case 19

## 264 *Index*

International Energy Agency (IEA) 13
international humanitarian law (IHL)
177–9; and 'jurisdiction' 191
international law: and security 65–6;
sovereign immunity 142–3
International Law Commission 164, 168;
Articles Concerning the Law of the
Sea 125; interpretation of Article 31 of
VCLT 167
International Maritime Organization
(IMO) 8, 30, 159, 246
international order 193–4
International Seabed Authority 8
International Tribunal for the Law of the
Sea (ITLOS) 8, 35, 61, 154–5, 237;
*ARA Libertad* case 143–4; *Dispute
Concerning Delimitation of the Maritime
Boundary between Bangladesh and
Myanmar in the Bay of Bengal* 38
International Union for Conservation of
Nature (IUCN) 110
inter-state disputes, in the South China
Sea 11
irrigation 131
islands 210; archepelagos 17; artificial 211;
artificial intervention 121–4; impact of
climate change on 86; and natural state
doctrine 126–32; natural state doctrine
124–6; and rocks 129; sovereignty
disputes in the South China Sea 46; *see
also* rocks
Itu Aba 6; artificial intervention
123–4

Japan: Okinotorishima 54; Senkaku Islands
51
Japan-Korea JDZ agreement (1974) 54
Jia, B. B. 22
Johor Strait 42
joint development zones (JDZs), in the
East China Sea 51, 53, 54
joint fishery zones, in the East China Sea
53, 54
Joint National Action Plans 111
Joint Petroleum Development Area
(JPDA) 58, 59
*Joint Statement on the Uniform
Interpretation of Rules of International
Law Governing Innocent Passage* (1989)
169–70
joint zones 62; in the Gulf of Thailand 50;
Timor Gap Zone of Cooperation 58
*de jure* exercise of sovereign authority
185–6

jurisdiction, and sovereignty 215
jurisdictional immunity 143–4

Kausikan, Bilahari 206, 209
Kaye, S. B. 128, 130
Klein, N. 168, 169
Koh, Tommy T. B. 3, 152, 199, 200
Kraska, J. 171; *International Maritime
Security Law* 66
Kyoto Protocol, and reduction of
greenhouse gas emissions 103

land formations, natural state doctrine 124–6
land reclamation 122, 123, 245–6
Law on the Exclusive Economic Zone and
the Continental Shelf (1998) 30
Lee, Hsien Loong 196, 197, 205–8
Lee, Kuan Yew 194–7; on balance of
power 204–5
legal regimes of navigation 180; innocent
passage 181–2; transit passage 182–3
length constraints on straight
baselines 25
lessons learned from the *South China Sea*
arbitration: absence of a party 236–7;
remedies 238–9; scope of jurisdiction
235–6
*Libya/Malta* case 58
living resource management, in South East
Asia 12–13
'LOAC at Sea' workshops 78
London Protocol 105–6; amendment to
107–8
Lowe, A. V. 66
low-tide elevation (LTE) 44
low-water line 24

Ma, Ying-jeou 196
Macclesfield Bank 26
McLaughlin, R. 230
Malacca Strait, maritime boundary
delimitation 39–42
Malaysia: Ambalat region dispute 203–4;
archipelagic State claim 18; Baselines
of Maritime Zones Act (2006) 41;
Exclusive Economic Zone Act (1984)
159; Ligitan/Sipidan islands dispute
202; LOSC compliance 159; Malacca
Strait 39–42; *Petra Baru* 40–1n30;
straight baselines 41n34
Malaysia-Vietnam Memorandum of
Understanding 50
mangrove forest destruction 108–10
Mangroves for the Future (MFF) 110

*Index* 265

Marine Environment Protection for Southeast Asian Seas (MEPSEAS) 246
marine environmental protection/security 212n16
marine resources in South East Asia 244–5
marine scientific research 254–5
marine spatial planning (MSP) 83
maritime boundary agreements: in the Andaman Sea area 35–8; between Australia and Timor-Leste 59
maritime boundary delimitation: Andaman Sea 35–8; Bay of Bengal 38, *39*; *Black Sea Case* 35; in the Celebes Sea 55–6; in the East China Sea 51, 53, 54; fixed baselines 114–16; Gulf of Thailand 48–50; insular features 46; Malacca Strait 39–42; in the Philippine Sea 54, 55; Singapore Straits 42–4; in the South China Sea 44–8; Timor and Arafura Seas 56–9
maritime claims **32**, 225–6; Asia Maritime Transparency Initiative (AMTI) 158; of coastal states 7; contiguous zone claims 28–9; Continental Shelf claims 29; impact of climate change on 85–6; Philippines, the 27–8; regimes of navigation, uncertainty of 185–8; on resources, solutions to 91–3; in South East Asia 243–4; straight baselines 24–5; of Taiwan 29–30; territorial sea baselines 24–6; United Nations Convention on the Law of the Sea (LOSC) 26–30
maritime features 210; artificial intervention 121–4; legal classification of 186; natural state doctrine 123, 124–6; rocks 129
maritime militias: ambiguity of 142–3; China's ad hoc employment of fishing vessels and fishers 139–42; Chinese 138–42; 'hybridity' of 251; under LOSC 142–4; Peoples Armed Forces Maritime Militia (PAFMM) 139; private actors 147; responses to 147–8; and sovereign immunity 143–4; and state responsibility 145–7; status ambiguity 147–8
maritime security 63, 64, 66; arms proliferation 73–4; cooperative arrangements to combat transnational crime in the Asia Pacific 89–91; illegal fishing 74; maritime terrorism 68–9; and natural disasters 74; piracy 70–1; robbery at sea 70–1; in South East Asia 12; threats 67; trafficking of narcotics, people, and illicit goods 71–2; violence

at sea 70–1; *see also* mitigating adverse impacts of climate change on maritime security
maritime South East Asia 33
maritime terrorism 69n21
Marrakech Action Proclamation for our Climate and Sustainable Development (2016) 104
median lines 34
merchant ships 142; and sovereign immunity 144
messaging at sea 136, 137; actor and act status 138; ambiguity of 147–8; and location of the message 138; *see also* maritime militias
'migration by sea,' UN Secretary-General's Report on 71–2
mitigating adverse impacts of climate change on maritime security 86; exploitation of the ocean sink as means of 105–10; transboundary marine environmental protection initiatives 86–8; *see also* adaptation to climate change
MPAs 113
multilateral marine environmental protection initiatives 86–8; and protection of fisheries 215–19
Myanmar: boundary delimitation with Thailand and India 38; LOSC compliance 159; Territorial and Maritime Zones Act 159; Twelfth Ministerial Meeting on Transnational Crime 77

narcotics trafficking 71–2
Nasu, H. 230
National Adaptation Programmes of Action (NAPA) 111
national security 63, 63n1
nationally determined contributions (NDCs) 103, 105, 116; restoration of mangrove forests 109–10
natural disasters 85, 120; as threat to maritime security 74
natural gas 227–8, 254; development in South East Asia 13–14; Greater Sunrise fields 59; in the South China Sea 244–5
natural state doctrine 121, 122, 124–6; *see also* application of the natural state doctrine to features affected by artificial intervention
natural state of a feature 120–1
Nauru Agreement (1982) 113–14

## 266  Index

naval activities in EEZs 171–2

navigation and overflight disputes 226–7

navigational rights 181–4; in archipelagic
waters, the Philippines State practice on
172–5; regulation of 188–9; in South
East Asia 11–12, 246–7; US Freedom of
Navigation (FON) programme 175–7

Nicobar Islands, archipelagic State
claim 18

'Nine-Dash Line' 2, 16, 21–3, 47, 210,
211, 248

non-innocent activities in the territorial
sea 182

non-international armed conflict
(NIAC) 66

*North Sea Continental Shelf* cases 57, 58

Obama administration, Singapore-US
Strategic Partnership Dialogue (SPD)
205–6

ocean boundary-making, evolution
of 34–5

oceans: acidification 98–100; and $CO_2$
96; fertilization 106–8; mangrove
forest destruction 108–10; role in
mitigation of climate change 96–7; *see
also* exploitation of the ocean sink to
mitigate climate change

Oceans Pathway Partnership 104–5

Oegroseno, A. H. 234

oil and gas development 227–8, 244–5,
254; Ambalat region dispute 203–4; in
South East Asia 13–14

Okinotorishima 54

'one China' policy 6–7

Operation Sovereign Borders 72

outcomes of the *South China Sea*
arbitration 239–40

outer maritime limits 114–16

overfishing, living resource management in
South East Asia 12–13

overflight 183–4, 226–7

overlapping maritime claims 34, 47,
47n65, 53, 56, 60, 61

Pacific Adaptation to Climate Change
Project (PACC) 111

Pacific Community 153n22

Pacific Islands Forum 102

Pacific Islands Regional Ocean Policy
111–12

Pacific Resilience Partnership 111

Papua New Guinea, and sea level rise 98

Paris Agreement (2015) 105, 110;
nationally determined contributions
(NDCs) 105; and reduction of
greenhouse gas emissions 103

Parties to the Nauru Agreement (PNA)
113–14

Partnerships in Environmental
Management in East Asian Seas
(PEMSEA) 87, 89

Party Allowable Effort (PAE) 114

patrols 75, 76, 91

Pedra Branca 60

*Pedra Branca* case 8, 43, 43n45, 43n46

*Pedra Brance case* 44

Pedrozo, R. 171; *International Maritime
Security Law* 66

people smuggling, combating 89–90

Peoples Armed Forces Maritime Militia
(PAFMM) 139, 140, 142

People's Liberation Army-Navy (PLA-N)
140–2, 253; innocent passage through
US territorial seas 170

permanent baselines 114–17

*Petra Baru* 40–1n30

Philippine Sea, maritime boundary
delimitation 5, 54

Philippines, the: Abu Sayaff Group (ASG)
68, 69, 251; An Act to Define the
Maritime Zones of the Republic of the
Philippines (2014) 28; as archipelagic
State 18–20; baselines 27–8; diplomatic
relations with China 248; historic claims
31; LOSC compliance 160; maritime
boundary agreement with Indonesia
55–6; National Security Policy 174;
Republic Act No 3046 (1961) 27;
Republic Act No 9522 19–20; and sea
level rise 98; sinking of the *Superferry
14* 69; *South China Sea* case 46, 47, 48;
State practice on navigational rights in
archipelagic waters 172–5; territorial sea
claims 27

Piao, W. -J. 171

piracy 70–1, 70n27, 91, 144, 257

pollution 101

Pratas Reef 26

prior authorization/notification for
innocent passage 165–6; the Philippines'
State practice of restricting navigational
rights of warships 172–5; and state
practice 168–70

Pulau Ligitan 60

Pulau Sipadan 60

*Qatar v Bahrain* 25

reduction of greenhouse gas emissions 102–5

'regime complex' 101n64

regional fisheries management organisations (RFMOs) 83, 101, 111, 212, 213, 215, 217, 218, 221

Regional Plan of Action to Promote Responsible Fishing Practices (RPOA-IUU) 217

regulation of navigation in South East Asia 188–9

remedies derived from the *South China Sea* arbitration 238–9

resource disputes 227–8, 253–4; solutions to 91–3

responses to maritime security threats: by ASEAN 76–8; maritime militias 147–8; by the Red Cross 78; small-scale use of force and cooperative measures 252; state action 75–6

restoration of mangrove forests 109–10

Roach, J. A. 158, 168, 169

robbery at sea 70–1, 70n27, 91

rocks 118, 119, 129, 210; artificial intervention 121–4

Rothwell, D. R. 168

rules-based governance 197–204

Schofield, C. 25, 160

*Schooner Exchange, The v. McFaddon and Others* 142–3, 143–4n37

sea level rise 82, 84, 94, 97–8, 111

Secretariat of the Pacific Regional Environment Programme (SPREP) 102, 111

Secretary-General's annual reports 67

security 63; 'collective' 65; cyber 190; development of in the 20th century 65; from the individual perspective 65; from an international law perspective 65–6; national 63n1; promoting through fisheries management 212–13; threats 64–5; *see also* maritime security

*Sempra Energy International v Argentine Republic* 168

Senkaku Islands 51

Shangri-La dialogue 76

Singapore 27; alliance with the United States 204–5; *Arms Offences Act* 184; Information Fusion Centre 75–6, 252; LOSC compliance 160; relations with

China 194–7; rules-based governance 197–204; 'second wing' strategy 195; Shangri-La dialogue 76

Singapore Straits 42–4

Singapore-US Strategic Partnership Dialogue (SPD) 205–6

*Superferry 14* 69

small arms and light weapons (SALW), proliferation of 73–4

Smith, R. W. 158, 168, 169

smuggling *see* trafficking of narcotics, people, and illicit goods

South China Sea 60; artificial islands in 211; boundary disputes in 44–8; claimants to maritime features in 10–11; continental shelf boundaries 44, 45; critical law of the sea issues in 9–11; Declaration on the Conduct of Parties in the South China Sea (DOC) 11; depleting fish stocks, potential conflict over 213–14; fisheries management 212–13; insular features 46; inter-state disputes 11; maritime boundary delimitation 44–8; maritime zones 185–6; military operations in 252–3; natural gas development in 244–5; navigational rights and freedoms 246–7; semi-enclosed status of 64; strategic significance of 10–11; territorial disputes 184–5; trade in 10; water column boundaries 44, 45

*South China Sea* arbitration 21–3, 25–6, 30, 31, 46–8, 118–19, 150, 155, 162, 186–7, 196, 198, 209, 223, 226, 227, 230, 243, 246, 249, 250; and artificial intervention 121–4; awards 47n61; consequences for fisheries 219–20; outcomes 239–40; status of 247–8; *see also* lessons learned from the *South China Sea* arbitration

South East Asia: baselines 24–5; challenges presented by LOSC for 242; coastal states 5–6; contested maritime areas 150; contiguous zone claims 28–9; Continental Shelf claims 29; dispute settlement 15, 248–50; and the evolution of ocean boundary-making 34–5; ferries 7–8; flag states 7–8; foreign naval engagement in 256–7; freedoms of navigation in 242; historic claims 20, 21; impact of foreign aid and investment 253; land boundaries 33; living resource management 12–13; and the LOSC 3–5;

LOSC member states 152, 153; marine environmental protection/security 14, 245–6; marine resources 244–5; maritime boundary agreements 153; maritime claims in 1–2, 26–30, **32**, 34; maritime security in 12, 251–2; navigational rights and freedoms 11–12, 246–7; oil and gas development 13–14; participation in CLCS 155, 156; participation in law of the sea dispute settlement 154–5; resource disputes 253–4; and rules-based governance 199–204; straits 150; support for LOSC 156, 157; territorial and maritime claims 243–4; trade routes 64; United States' presence in 255–6; *see also* maritime security
South East Asian Fisheries Development Centre (SEAFDEC) 88–9
South East Asian maritime domain 2, 3, *3*
Southern Kyushu-Palau Ridge Region 54, 55
sovereign immunity 142–3
sovereignty disputes 224–5; and jurisdiction 215; between Malaysia and Singapore 43, 44; Middle Rocks 43; Pedra Branca 43–4; regimes of navigation, uncertainty of 185–8; in the South China Sea 186–7; *see also* maritime boundary delimitation
*Sovereignty over Pulau Ligitan and Pulau Sipadan* case 19
Spratly Islands 25–6; and climate change 86; *see also South China Sea* arbitration
State Parties to the Law of the Sea (SPLOS) 8
State practice 166–8; and exercise of innocent passage 168–70; of international humanitarian law (IHL) 177–9; naval activities in EEZs 171–2; of the Philippines on navigational rights in archipelagic waters 172–5; responses to maritime security issues 75–6; US Freedom of Navigation (FON) programme 175–7
straight baselines 24–6; disputed status of 187–8; Malaysia 40
straits 150n6
*Straits of Johor* arbitration 155
strategic significance of the South China Sea 10–11
sustainable development 246
Sustainable Development Strategy for the Seas of East Asia (SDS-SEA) 87
sustainable use arrangements 88–9

Taiwan: as archipelagic State 26; as coastal state 6–7; maritime claims 29–30; status as 'Fishing Entity' 225
*Tallinn Manual 2.0* 190
Tan-Mullins, M. 160
Taputapuātea Declaration on Climate Change 114–15
technological innovations, and artificial intervention 125–6
temperature increases in the oceans 96–7
temporary uninhabitability 128
territorial disputes 224–5; *Case concerning Sovereignty over Pulau Ligitan and Pulau Sipadan* 8; impact of climate change on 85–6; regimes of navigation, uncertainty of 185–8; Senkaku Islands 51; in the South China Sea 184–5; in South East Asia 243–4
territorial seas 27, 34; baselines 24–6; boundaries 34; contiguous zone claims 28–9; freedom of navigation in 11–12; innocent passage 164, 165; non-innocent activities 182; outer reach of 187–8; Singapore Straits 43, 44; state practice and exercise of innocent passage 168–70; *see also* innocent passage
terrorism 68–9; attack on the *MV Limburg* 68; sinking of the *Superferry 14* 69; *see also* maritime terrorism
Thailand: boundary delimitation with Burma and India 37, 38; LOSC compliance 160; *Memorandum of Understanding regarding the Area of their Overlapping Claims to the Continental Shelf* (2001) 50; Preah Vihear promontory dispute 202–3
Thai-Malaysian Memorandum of Understanding 50
'The Geopolitical Implications of Climate Change to 2030 for Southeast Asia' 83
Third United Nations Conference on the Law of the Sea 3
Third United Nations Conference on the Law of the Sea (UNCLOS III) 163
threats to maritime security 67; arms proliferation 73–4; ASEAN response to 76–8; illegal fishing 74; natural disasters 74; piracy 70–1; robbery at sea 70–1; state responses to 75–6; terrorism 68–9; trafficking of narcotics, people, and illicit goods 71–2; UN initiatives in response to 78–9; violence at sea 70–1; *see also* responses to maritime security threats

## Index 269

Tiao Yu T'ai 51
Timor Gap 57, 58
Timor Gap Zone of Cooperation 58, 58n109
Timor Sea, maritime boundary delimitation 56–9
Timor Sea Treaty (2002) 58, 91
Timor-Leste: application for ASEAN membership 151; LOSC compliance 160–1
Total Allowable Effort (TAE) 114
trade, in the South China Sea 10
trade routes 64; attacks on shipping 69; 'choke points' 64
traditional legal issues of navigation 181–4
trafficking of narcotics, people, and illicit goods 71–2
transboundary marine environmental protection initiatives 86–8
transit passage 242; legal issues 182–3
transnational crime, cooperative arrangements for combating 89–91
Trans-Pacific Partnership, US withdrawal from 206
treaties, role of State practice 166–8
*Treaty of Amity and Cooperation in Southeast Asia (TAC)* 231
*Treaty of Paris* (1898) 27, 28, 31
*Treaty of Peace* (1898) 27
*Treaty of Washington* (1900) 27
*Treaty on Certain Maritime Arrangements in the Timor Sea* (CMATS (2006)) 58, 59
trilateral agreements, on location of tripoints 38
Trump Administration: 'Free and Open Indo-Pacific' (FOIP) policy 255–6; military reduction in South East Asia 257; withdrawal from TPP 206
Twelfth Ministerial Meeting on Transnational Crime 77

UN General Assembly (UNGA): Development Goal 14 102; Resolution 66/288 *The Future We Want* (2012) 102
UN High Commissioner for Refugees (UNHCR) 90
uninhabitability: and artificial intervention 130–2; climate change as cause of 126–30
United Kingdom: Ascension Island 132; "islands" 124–5; planned military base in South East Asia 256–7

United Nations 8; initiatives in response to maritime security threats 78–9; Secretary-General's annual Report on *Oceans and the law of the sea* 13; Secretary-General's annual reports 67; treaties 73
United Nations Conference on the Law of the Sea (UNCLOS I) 165
United Nations Conference on Trade and Development (UNCTAD) 10
United Nations Convention on the Law of the Sea (LOSC) 1, 2, 3–5, 8, 10, 16, 34, 47, 75, 94–5, 138, 149–50, 161–3, 175, 176, 179, 180, 184, 191, 197, 223, 224, 235–6, 240, 242, 246, 247, 249, 255; addressing excessive maritime claims 250–1; Annex V 59; Annex VII Arbitral Tribunal 8, 38, 61, 155, 185–6, 220, 229–30, 243, 247–8; archipelagic states 17–20, 18n8; Article 5 24; Article 7 24–6; Article 13(2) 137n5; Article 15 34; Article 19 165–7, 165n8, 170; Article 24 166; Article 46 17, 18; Article 47 18–20, 24, 26; Article 48 20; Article 53 173; Article 58 171; Article 74 34, 50; Article 83 34, 50, 244; Article 121 18, 20, 54, 118, 120, 121, 123, 125, 129; Article 121(3) 133, 134; Article 192 227; Article 298 59, 164; Article 310 4; ASEAN state compliance 158–61; baselines 24–6; challenges of for South East Asian states 242; coastal states 5–6; compulsory dispute settlement 163–4; declarations 4–5; dispute resolution framework 229–30; dispute resolution, South East Asian states' participation in 154–5; dispute settlement regime 15; exclusive economic zones (EEZs) 211; Fish Stocks Agreement (1995) 152, 153; flag states 7–8; and historic claims 20–4; Implementing Agreement (1994) 152, 153; innocent passage by warships and rights under 165–6; legal classification of maritime features 186; maritime claims 26–30; maritime militias under 142–4; navigational rights and freedoms in South East Asia 11–12; Part IV 31; Part XII 108; Part XV 15, 20, 154, 161, 229; port states 5n13; Preamble 20; prior authorization/notification for innocent passage 165–6; reduction of greenhouse gas emissions 103–4; South East Asian state membership 152,

270 *Index*

153; and State practice 166–8; Taiwan as coastal state 6–7; *see also* Annex VII Arbitral Tribunal; coastal states; flag states; historic claims

United Nations Framework Convention on Climate Change (UNFCCC) 94, 106; 21st Conference of the Parties (COP) 104; Article 4(1)(e) 110; reduction of greenhouse gas emissions 102–3

United Nations Regional Centre for Peace and Disarmament in Asia and the Pacific (UNRCPD) 73–4

United Nations Security Council 12, 12n48, 67; Resolution 1816 70n30

United Nations (UN), 'collective security' 65

United States: alliance with Singapore 204–5; Freedom of Navigation (FON) programme 174–7, 189, 247; presence in South East Asia 255–6; *Sea Hunter* 255; *USNS Bowditch* 190; withdrawal from TPP 206

*US Manual on Maritime Claims* 175

US National Intelligence Council, 'The Geopolitical Implications of Climate Change to 2030 for Southeast Asia' 83

US Supreme Court cases, *The Schooner Exchange v. McFaddon and Others* 142–3

Valencia, M. J. 232
Van Dyke, J. M. 129
Vessel Day Scheme (VDS) 113–14

Vienna Convention on the Law of Treaties (VCLT) 179; Article 31 166; Article 31(1) 170; Article 31(3)(b) 167

Vietnam: Gulf of Tonkin 23–4; LOSC compliance 161; and sea level rise 98; straight baselines 25

violence at sea 70–1

warships 142; disputed regimes of navigation 185–8; innocent passage 164–6; the Philippines' State practice of restricting navigational rights of 172–5; prior authorization/notification for innocent passage 165–6; and sovereign immunity 143–4; state practice and exercise of innocent passage 168–70; US Freedom of Navigation (FON) programme 175–7

water column boundaries, in the South China Sea 44, 45

Watts, S. 177–8

weapons of mass destruction (WMD), proliferation of 73–4

weapons proliferation 73–4

Western and Central Pacific Fisheries Commission (WCPFC) 114, 216, 218; member states 216n35

World Energy Council 14

World Trade Organisation (WTO) 220–1

Xi, Jinping 193, 194, 196, 248

Yo, Y. -D. 171